Creative Power
The Nature and Nurture of Children's Writing

Ronald L. Cramer

Oakland University

Longman

New York   San Francisco   Boston
London   Toronto   Sydney   Singapore   Madrid
Mexico City   Munich   Paris   Cape Town   Hong Kong   Montreal

Publisher: Priscilla McGeehon
Senior Acquisitions Editor: Virginia L. Blanford
Marketing Manager: Marilyn Borysek
Production Manager: Joseph Vella
Project Coordination, Text Design, and Electronic Page Makeup: Shepherd, Inc.
Cover Design Manager: John Callahan
Cover Designer: Maria Ilardi
Cover Photo: Copyright © PhotoDisc, Inc.
Manufacturing Buyer: Al Dorsey
Printer and Binder: Courier–Stoughton
Cover Printer: The Lehigh Press, Inc.
Photography: Amy Ronelle Cramer

For permission to use copyrighted material, grateful acknowledgment is made to the copyright holders on p. 421, which are hereby made part of this copyright page.

Library of Congress Cataloging-in-Publication Data

Cramer, Ronald L.
    Creative power : the nature and nurture of children's writing / by Ronald L. Cramer.
        p. cm.
    Includes bibliographical references and index.
    ISBN 0-321-04913-6
    1. English language--Composition and exercises--Study and teaching. 2.
Children--Language. I. Title.

LB1576. C758 2001
372.62'3--dc21

00-020966

Please visit our website at http://www.awl.com/cramer

ISBN 0-321-04913-6

12345678910—CRS—03020100

Dedication

Dedicated, with love,
to my children,
Amy, Jen, and Ben
whose journey to literacy
has informed my thinking
and delighted my soul.

Contents

Chapter 3

PREWRITING: CREATING A PLAN 57

Chapter 4

DRAFTING: FIRST THOUGHTS 81

Chapter 5   REVISING: MAKING WRITING BETTER   97

Chapter 6   POST WRITING: SHARING AND PUBLISHING   139

Chapter 7

LITERATURE AND WRITING   155

Chapter 8

EVALUATING WRITING   195

Chapter **11**   WRITING POETRY WITH CHILDREN   271

APPENDICES 395

Preface

Atornado whisked Dorothy from Kansas and landed her in Munchkin Land where Glinda, the Good Witch of the North, told Dorothy, "It's always best to start at the beginning, and follow the Yellow Brick Road." Dorothy needed to get to the Land of Oz to see the Wizard. All she knew was that the Land of Oz was down the Yellow Brick Road—somewhere over the rainbow. Dorothy wanted to return to Kansas. She understood that the Wizard of Oz could help. Four friends accompanied Dorothy on her quest: Scarecrow, Tin Man, Cowardly Lion, and Toto, her little dog. She had an enemy to overcome—the Wicked Witch of the West. The Wizard, who turned out to be a good hearted fraud, was no help. His balloon lifted off for Kansas without her: "Now, I'll never get back to Kansas," Dorothy lamented. But the Good Witch of the North reminded Dorothy that she only needed to click her heels three times and she would be returned to Kansas. Dorothy clicked her heels and returned to Kansas, saying fervently, "There's no place like home." What a great story!

Every teacher has a story; so does every child. This book has a story, too. The story begins with language and thinking; it ends with "the impossible flight of the bumblebee"—a metaphor for the creative power children possess. All children possess creative potential; it is resident in them from the beginning, but too often it is creative power unrealized. Someone has to tell them; someone has to apprise them of their "wonderful ideas." Someone has to entice talent out of the closets of children's minds. And who might that someone be? Teachers, parents, peers, but especially teachers. It is our mission; it is our sacred duty. We have the same power as Glinda, the Good Witch of the North. Dorothy carried her own magic with her, but someone had to inform her of that power, or she might never have exercised it—stuck in the Land of Oz forever when she wanted to be in Kansas. Teachers must show and tell their children that they have within them the power to "click their heels," the power to realize the dreams they dream. Not somewhere over the rainbow, but here and now, in this classroom you can exercise the talent you possess. The "magic" teachers have to offer is to help children actualize the gifts they possess, gifts they often are unaware of possessing.

Writing is an outlet for creative expression, a way of transmitting the scenes inside our heads to the world at large—which may or may not be interested in the scenes inside our heads. Nevertheless, we write. Some write for therapeutic reasons. Sarah McHugh said, "I began to write because I was too shy to talk, and too lonely not to send messages." Others write to experience and reexperience life. Anais Nin said, "We write to taste life twice, in the moment, and in retrospection." We write to learn, to teach ourselves, to justify our existence, to recall, to discover our mind, to empty our mind, to know, to think. Whatever the reasons for writing, it is important for children to learn how to write well. And, as they mature as writers, they will discover their own reasons for writing.

Donald Murray (1990)* said, "The content of the text is important, and no writer can produce a worthwhile text from nothing, although many try. But we rarely read to the end of a text because of content, rarely provoked to thought or action, moved to feel, by content. It is the writer's vision of that content that attracts us, holds us, influences us" (p. 127). As you peruse this book, I hope you will agree that I have covered the essential content associated with teaching children to write. But, that is likely to be true of any good text dealing with this topic. Appropriate content is necessary, but it is not sufficient. The voice of the writer, the writer's vision of the content is what interests readers, what makes readers want to read on in a text. If there is no voice, there is no text worth attending to. If, as you read this book, you are unable to "hear" my voice I expect you to lay this text aside and pursue a more enlightening activity.

Great accomplishments are born out of faith in one's ideals. Father Flanagan founded Boys Town on the ideal that "There is no such thing as a bad boy." One may disagree with his ideal, may cite chapter and verse to refute it, may know from personal experience that bad boys abound. All this is irrelevant to an act of faith. I, too, have an ideal. I do not appeal to empirical data to verify it. *I believe that every child possesses creative power, and teachers possess the capability of releasing that creative power through writing.* Some will say that this is an impossibly romantic ideal, an ideal not borne out by experience, not supported by research. Undoubtedly true. Nevertheless, I have based my teaching and writing life on this ideal. It is irrelevant to me if others choose to live in a more realistic universe, deride my ideal as a fairy tale, write off my ideal as a worn-out remnant of a hopelessly outdated philosophy.

I believe children are creative; I believe that creativity is as natural to children as breathing. I also believe that its manifestations are often kept under lock and key, that children are reluctant to exhibit their creative instincts if they suspect their gifts will not be well received, if they sense hostility, if they sense indifference. Good teachers strive to unlock children's creative potential; they understand that the mind and spirit within a child is as tangible as blood and bone; they understand that the mind and spirit of a child is as fragile as it is malleable. Children are artists of language, not language scholars. They use language not to impress but to express. Given a little fall of rain from a fine teacher, children can make the flowers grow.

I revere and respect dedicated teachers. I know there are many more dedicated teachers than the general public imagines. Most teachers are idealists. They entered the profession because they love children, wanted to make a difference, suspected that their efforts would be unappreciated, knew that whatever rewards awaited them would be psychic not monetary. Nevertheless, they embarked on the journey, and most of the good ones have reenlisted for life. These idealists, these dedicated teachers, respect and revere the creative potential that children possess; they believe they can, through acts of faith, will, and knowledge, kindle

---

Murray, D. K. (1990). Shoptalk: Learning to write with writers. Portsmouth, NH: Boynton/Cook Heinemann.

the flame of creativity in the hearts and minds of the children they teach. This book is intended for all such heroic teachers.

HOW THIS BOOK IS ORGANIZED

Creative Power: The Nature and Nurture of Children's Writing has 14 chapters:

Chapter 1 concentrates on language, thinking, and patterns of early writing. Discussions revolve around writing and thinking, theories and applications of Piaget, Vygotsky, and Bruner, stages of early writing, Clay's principles of beginning writing, and strategies for beginning writing instruction.

Chapter 2 is an overview of the writing process. It includes definitions of writing process terms and outlines the traditional approach to writing instruction, Graves' writing principles, and Cambourne's conditions for acquiring literacy.

Chapter 3 focuses on prewriting. Discussion revolves around rehearsal, research, time for writing, choosing writing topics, audience considerations, forms of writing, and prewriting strategies.

Chapter 4 is on drafting. Strategies for successful drafting and the teacher's role in drafting are discussed in detail.

Chapter 5 focuses on revision. It discusses revision terminology, defines revision, and presents a revision taxonomy. Principles of revision are reviewed and instruction and strategies are suggested.

Chapter 6 outlines reasons for sharing and publishing children's writing and suggests instructional strategies for sharing and publishing.

Chapter 7 deals with literature and writing. It includes discussions of what literature does for writing, reading literature to children, modeling literature with children, and using literature in writing fiction.

Chapter 8 examines issues and procedures for evaluating writing. It examines purposes and premises for evaluating writing, student evaluation of writing, evaluation methods and procedures for teachers, and issues in grading children's writing.

Chapter 9 deals with writing as therapy. It emphasizes the need and value of expressing feelings through writing and considers ways in which teachers can create a therapeutic writing environment.

Chapter 10 is about teachers as writers. It identifies issues that impede or promote the possibilities for writing and presents ways in which teachers can be writing models for their children.

Chapter 11 focuses on writing poetry with children. It presents ideas and principles for developing children's poetic instincts and discusses the language and forms of poetic expression.

Chapter 12 emphasizes integrating reading, writing, and spelling. It describes stages of growth, approaches to instruction, influences on spelling knowledge, teaching and learning strategies, criteria for choosing words, invented spelling, and assessment.

Chapter 13 discusses the role of grammar and punctuation in learning to write. Grammar and punctuation research are reviewed and reasons given for teaching grammar and punctuation within the context of writing.

Chapter 14 discusses managing classroom writing environments and nurturing creative potential. Crucial environments for learning are identified and discussed and issues involved in enhancing creative potential are identified.

Supplements

There is an Instructor's *Manual with Test Bank* to accompany *Creative Power: The Nature and Nuture of Children's Writing* available to all qualified adopters. Written by Susan Gilbert of Appalachian State University, this manual will provide users with a variety of instructional tools, including chapter summaries, student objectives, activities and discussion questions, vocabulary, test questions, and reflections inspired by the text.

Companion Website

This online course companion (www.awl.com/cramer) provides a wealth of resources for both students and instructors using *Creative Power*. Students will find chapter summaries, test questions with page references and answer explanations, annotated web links, a complete guide to conducting research on the Internet, and more! Instructors will have access to the instructor's manual and teaching links, and can also take advantage of Syllabus Builder, our comprehensive course management system.

ACKNOWLEDGMENTS

As I wrote this book, I sought the advice and help of my students and colleagues. I especially wish to acknowledge those teachers who contributed pieces to the "Voices from the Classroom" feature that appear throughout this book: Debbie Clark, Nancy Cohen, Janice Conroy, Melissa DeClerck, Jennifer DeWard, Sheri Dudzinski, Barbara Head, Gail Marinelli, Susan Martin, Christie McVean, Jonella Mongo, Teri Pangori, Carol Sievert, Elizabeth Williamson, Chris Wilson. Special thanks goes to Jennifer DeWard who wrote the "Teacher's Diary" feature. Ms. DeWard maintained a diary throughout the 1998–1999 school year and excerpts from that diary appear in most chapters of this book.

My colleagues and good friends, George and Geraldine Coon, read every word in this book—this paragraph excepted. To paraphrase Sherwood Anderson, I can hear them now laughing at some delicious grammar, punctuation, or spelling error they have excavated. But they were more than excavators of trivial errors; they contributed ideas and materials that enriched this book; they offered words of praise and pointed out flaws in my thinking and my writing. They are dear friends whose faith in this work kept me at the task.

My colleagues in the Reading and Language Arts Department at Oakland University also helped in various ways, and I thank them: Richard Barron, Jane Bingham, Gloria Blatt, Robert Christina, Jim Cipielewski, Jim Gavelek, Dorsey Hammond, Joan Kaye, Laurie Kaufman, John McEneaney, Linda Pavonetti, Anne Porter, Taffy Raphael, Robert Schwartz, Sigrid Touhy, Tony Walters, Joyce Wiencek.

Writing friends tell me I'm weird, but I like editors. Editors and writers are natural enemies and unnatural allies. Good editors spin gold out of straw; bad ones reverse the process. Good editors find boo-boos and soothe egos. I've worked with lots of editors over the years. Most I remember with great fondness; one I revisit only in nightmares; two became good friends—Roxy McLean and Mary Ann Hiland, editors I worked with at Scott Foresman Addison Wesley. I've had two good editors on this project. Virginia Blanford, acquisitions editor, soothed my ego throughout the long review process. Without her patience, no book at all. Andrea Bednar, production editor, along with the entire book team at Shepherd, found enough boo-boos in my manuscript to embarrass a clown. I thank them profoundly.

I thank the reviewers whose comments sometimes made me smile and sometimes hurt, but always made this a better book: James Beers, the College of William and Mary; Lisa Beck, Middlebury University; Anna Bolling, California State University/Stanislaus; Jenny Denyer, Michigan State University; Stephen Hancock, Brigham Young University; Karen Hicks, Southwestern Louisiana University; Mary Quinn, Hofstra University; Tonja Root, Valdosta University; and Sara Simmons, Western Illinois University.

Finally, I thank the children whose works appear throughout this book. What I know about children's writing comes from my association with children across the decades of my work as a public school teacher and a university professor. Teaching children and teachers has enriched my understanding of writing and has been one of the great pleasures of my life. The writing of children demonstrates that there is nothing quite so marvelous as the native language of childhood.

CHAPTER 1

Language, Thinking, and Patterns of Early Writing

> In many ways writing is the act of saying I, of imposing oneself upon
> other people, of saying *listen to me, see it my way, change your mind.*
> Joan Didion

A WRITER'S STORY

Alisha wrote her first story in February of her first grade year. She had dictated stories to her teacher, Ms. Motrik, but she never attempted independent writing. Ms. Motrik considered Alisha her best reader, but still no independent writing. Seems curious, doesn't it? But there was a reason. Ms. Motrik had reservations about encouraging writing with invented spelling. I asked Ms. Motrik to pick out her best reader, introduce invented spelling, and see what might happen. Ms. Motrik took up the challenge. Alisha wrote four pages on her own. She decided to dictate the last page of her story because, she said, "My hand's tired." The four pages of the story she wrote on her own, One Lonely Bear, went like this:

> One night thar was a sad bear he was so sad that he cad cri. one day he wat away to fid hany But he sdred to cri so he datat no wat to do so he sayd "yi am I so an happy?" sa din Lee he hrd a vos he lotd a rad he dete see anee thg. But than he sa samthen in has shado he lact and he sa a snail tacen to haim the snail "sayd you r so sad b cas no bdey lics you y no't "sayd the Bear. Bet the snail cate halp the bear so the snail wat away Bet sapthen als was in has shado at was a racoon the racoon sayd "nan av the anam can halp you"

We know three things about Alisha from this story. She's a good writer. *She's written a lively story, and she has made some good guesses about punctuation. For instance, she uses quotation marks twice—once correctly, once incorrectly. Both times her quotation marks are used in conjunction with* said. She's a good speller. *She has a small set of known words. Words she misspells are usually close enough for an experienced teacher to figure out.* She's a good reader. *Alisha knows a lot about print. She uses periods, quota-*

1

tions marks, and a contraction. Punctuation marks are not always correctly placed, but she knows they belong in written language.

Ms. Motrik, a very special person, had the courage to try something she wasn't sure would work. She took a risk that paid off for her and for Alisha. Try it. You may be pleasantly surprised. No harm done if you're not.

INTRODUCTION

A four- and a six-year-old are having a heated conversation, perhaps we might even call it a philosophical debate:

> Six-year-old asks, "Jessie what are you doing?"
> Four-year-old replies, "I'm writing."
> Six-year-old says, "No you're not."
> Four-year-old answers, "Yes, I am."
> Six-year-old: "You can't be. I don't see any letters." (Temple, Nathan, and Burris, 1982, p. 18)

End of debate, right? Wrong. Six-year-old represents the adult view, the traditional view of writing. Put in street vernacular the traditional view says, "You don't got no letters, you don't got no writin'." In this chapter, we consider a different perspective: *writing emerges from the crib with the first thought, the first sound uttered, the first mark scribbled.*

Themes we will pursue include writing and thinking, language, learning, and thought, focus on meaning, prerequisite skills for beginning writing, early writing stages, Clay's principles of beginning writing, and strategies for beginning writing.

WRITING AND THINKING

My colleagues, Jim Cipielewski and Joyce Wiencek, asked first graders questions about reading and writing. When they asked Billy, "Why do you like to write?" he answered: "Because writing lets you think about *awesome* things." Billy is right. Writing facilitates thinking. Of course we don't always think "awesome" thoughts, but it's possible. And it happens with young writers as well as experienced ones. Writing is the supreme intellectual achievement of humankind. The invention of writing made possible the promulgation of scientific and philosophic thought. Writing has influenced every significant cultural development of the human race. Recorded history, schooling, literature, science, and philosophy would all be impossible or impoverished without the invention of writing. Writing is ideally suited to influence thinking and learning. Writing allows time to think again, choosing thoughts and words carefully. Furthermore, the writer has access to strategies which can lift the quality of thinking to higher levels due to the potential for long preparation, the limitless potential for pondering, cutting, extending, putting aside, returning, and so on until the piece is right. So, writing can create a deeper kind of thinking than other means allow.

Five characteristics of writing influence thinking. Writing is visible, permanent, active, precise, and focusing.

FIVE CHARACTERISTICS OF WRITING THAT INFLUENCE THINKING

1. **Writing is visible:** E. M. Forster said, "How can I know what I think until I see what I say?" Sartre, the French existentialist, is said to have quit writing when his eyesight deteriorated because he could no longer see the words. Apparently, Sartre, like most writers, needed to manipulate the visible symbols of thought in order to generate the meaning he wished to convey. No longer able to visualize his thoughts, Sartre found writing impossible. Writing makes visible what is ordinarily invisible—thought. Once thought is made visible through written symbols, it can be manipulated. The visibility of written thought enables writers to discover relationships among ideas they might have missed if thought depended entirely on verbal manipulations.

2. **Writing is permanent:** Oral language is forgettable, a funeral. Once words are spoken they cannot be recaptured or even remembered for very long. Not so with writing. Writing leaps the bonds of time and space, and gives eternal life to our words and ideas. Writing is the repository of humanity's accumulated knowledge.

3. **Writing is active:** Writing is active, a search for meaning enlisting the resources of mind and body. Writing requires the fullest possible use of mental capacity. No other mental process enables us to develop our ideas so thoroughly. Writing involves the physical task of depicting writing: handwriting, spelling, punctuation, depressing the keys on the typewriter or computer, erasing, crossing out, rereading, rewriting.

4. **Writing is precise:** Writing disciplines the mind into precise formulation of its thoughts. This is what Francis Bacon had in mind when he said, "Reading maketh a full man, conference a ready man, and writing an exact man" (Ehrlich and DeBruhl, 1996, p. 766). Of course, written language is not inherently precise. Like oral language, it is subject to the vagaries of the sender and the receiver. Nevertheless, as a form of communication, writing holds the greater promise of precision.

5. **Writing focuses thinking:** Few activities focus the mind as keenly as writing. Revision is especially effective in refocusing thinking, since it enables us to rethink our first draft thoughts. Writing enables us to summon thoughts out of darkness and into the light.

LANGUAGE, LEARNING, AND THOUGHT

William Makepeace Thackeray said, "There are a thousand thoughts lying within a man that he does not know till he takes up the pen to write." For thousands of years, writers have struggled to understand themselves and their universe, to establish their place in the cosmos. They have used language, particularly written

Writing influences thinking. Matt is writing a second draft of a story he's been working on for the past week.

language, to uncover their thoughts, to fathom good and evil, to learn their own truths. Why writers write is the quintessential question. Writers have different answers, but I like the answer Jean Malaquais gave to his friend and fellow writer, Norman Mailer (1989). Malaquais said, "The only time I know the truth is when it reveals itself at the point of my pen" (p. 4).

Language and thought are seemingly inseparable, bound together in ways we do not fully comprehend. Perhaps language is the tool of thought, and thought the consequence of language. The two, working in harmony, make learning possible. What we do know for certain about language, learning, and thought is best summed in the words of St. Paul, "Now we see as through a glass darkly." Perhaps, down the road a piece, we shall understand more fully.

Language and Learning

Language enables children to organize and classify their experiences into increasingly sophisticated thought structures. As children learn language, they acquire more than a set of words and sentences; they also acquire strategies for thinking about language and thinking about the ideas that language describes (Bruner, 1966).

The acquisition of language is the pivotal event in a child's life. Language is a miracle, and an intellectually curious individual cannot help wondering how it comes about. Children probe and prod, push and pull, pummel and play with their language until it yields up its mysteries.

Children use language as it was meant to be used: probing it for meaning, pushing it to its logical limits, creating unforgettable images. First grader, Jessica, explains why the story she had so laboriously written isn't as pretty as the smooth, cursive hand of her teacher, "I didn't write in grown-up because my hands can't move as fast as my brain." Children understand the essential elements of their language, even before they have mastered all of its nuances. Notice how Ben, age four, uses language to resist a small chore his father has urged upon him:

DAD: Son, step outside and get the paper.

BEN: Dad! It's raining outside and I'm sock-footed.

The image, *sock-footed*, plays off of the well known term, *bare footed*. But sock-footed is a description unavailable to grown-ups, perhaps because adults use language less flexibly than children. Adults are chained to language norms which diminish our capacity to create fresh images, such as *sock-footed*. Fortunately, young children are not chained to language norms. For them, every encounter with language is an adventure.

Bedtime brings out children's fears and strategies for putting it off. Night lights, kisses, questions, checking under the bed for night creatures were all part of five-year-old Jennifer's procrastination routine at bedtime.

JEN: Daddy, who got the word *bogeyman* in the first part of life?

DAD: That's a good question Honey. I'm afraid I don't know. Why do you ask?

JEN: I just wanted to know if there *really* is a bogeyman.

DAD: No, I don't think so, Jen.

JEN: Well then! Where did the word bogeyman come from in the first part of life?

What accounts for this interesting language question? I think it is more than idle curiosity. It is Jennifer's attempt to make language conform to her reality. God, ghosts, and goblins were well-known words to Jennifer, but where, she asks, is the corporeal substance that gives reality to these familiar words? Jennifer is doing what all children do—pushing language to its logical limits in order to understand its functions and meaning. Her reasoning may go something like this: "There is a word, *bogeyman*, so there must be some reality to go with it. Where did it come from in the first place? Where is the real life counterpart for the word *bogeyman*?" Children demand more of language than adults. Would that I demanded as much of language as the typical five-year-old. How much fresher my language would be.

Piaget, Vygotsky, and Bruner: Theories and Their Application

As children acquire language, they acquire more than a set of words and sentences. They also acquire thought structures and learning strategies that can be applied in learning to read and write. As children develop, language becomes instrumental in directing thinking and learning. The richer the language, the more bountiful thinking and learning can be. Language profoundly influences children's intellectual development. Jean Piaget, Lev Vygotsky, and Jerome Bruner, who rank among last century's most influential developmental psychologists, proposed related but somewhat different theories of language and thought.

Piaget: Piaget (1955) maintained that thinking stimulated language learning. Language acquisition is dependent, in Piaget's theory, on the presence of sensorimotor schemas. He believed that children's thinking stems from their actions upon the concrete world. For example, children understand the uses of a rattle before they give it a name; they know a needle is sharp before they have language to describe the property of sharpness. Language, for Piaget, is a way of labeling stored cognitive schema. Seeing, hearing, touching, smelling, and tasting objects in the concrete world enables children to understand the functions and properties of objects before they have language to describe them. Piaget argued, therefore, that language does not organize thinking, it transmits it. He recognized, however, that language refines and elaborates thinking. Language and thought are interactive; they influence one another.

Vygotsky: Vygotsky (1962) assigned language a major role in the development of thinking and learning. Language accompanies nearly all of the experiences children have in their world. Consequently, language is a major part of children's experience with the world. Vygotsky believed that children gain understanding and meaning through their exposure to adult language models. Concrete experiences with the world, accompanied by simultaneous experiences with language, provide the milieu through which children's thinking develops. Vygotsky also emphasized a concept known as the zone of proximal development. He believed children learn best when they are "in the zone" where they need interaction and guidance from an adult. Vygotsky's "zone" is conceptually similar to what Emmet Betts (1957) called the "instructional level" in reading.

Bruner: Bruner's (1966) conclusions about language and thought closely parallel Vygotsky's. Bruner believed that it is only through the use of language that children learn to think abstractly. Thinking competence grows through the use of language. Bruner also recognized the importance of adult language models. Through talk with adults, children learn to examine, structure, and reflect on their experiences. He stressed that, while language stimulates thought, the strategies learned during language learning are useful for other types of thought maturation. Bruner's theories suggest the importance of discovery learning and problem solving.

APPLYING PIAGET, VYGOTSKY, AND BRUNER'S CONCEPTS TO CLASSROOM INSTRUCTION

Piaget

1. Provide activities and experiences which emphasize experimentation within the physical and social environment.
2. Use art, dance, music, drama, and play in group and individual settings to motivate language and provide experiences that give language concrete and direct referents in the physical and social environment.
3. Encourage children to actively participate in real world events so that language and experience fit together naturally.
4. Activate prior knowledge, since only concepts for which the child is ready will be understood.

Vygotsky

1. Model language by interacting with children as listener, speaker, questioner, and friend.
2. Extend and expand children's thinking beyond the limits they may have constructed for themselves.
3. Stress social interaction with adults and peers, since it focuses children's attention on elements of their experience that might otherwise elude them.
4. Social interaction and the need to communicate are essential components in the development of language.
5. Create learning communities where the teacher and children work cooperatively and collaboratively through sharing, think-aloud modeling, and teacher-student conferences.
6. Emphasize imaginative play, role playing, experimentation, and manipulation.

Bruner

1. Stress active experimentation and interaction with the physical and intellectual world on children's own terms.
2. Apply children's oral language knowledge to literacy instruction.
3. Exploit the natural relationship that exists between oral and written language in teaching of reading and writing.
4. All present learning is intended to serve the learner in the future; therefore, create activities that serve both pleasurable and practical purposes.
5. Make extensive use of independent reading, process writing, display centers, learning stations, cooperative study, computers, and educational games.

The diary entry marks the first appearance of a feature that will appear throughout this book: "A Teacher's Diary." Ms. Jennifer DeWard teachers fourth grade and is in her fourth year of teaching. She has a Bachelor of Arts from the University of Michigan and a Master of Arts in Teaching Reading and Language Arts from Oakland University. Ms. DeWard teaches in a "full inclusion" classroom. Consequently, students are not pulled out of her classroom for special instruction. Rather, resource teachers come into her classroom to provide instruction for students who require special services. Ms. DeWard has, for the past year, kept a journal of her experiences teaching writing, The intent of this feature is to give readers a sense of the daily challenges, problems, and pleasures of teaching writing from the perspective of one teacher who is on the firing line every day. In her first entry, Ms. DeWard describes how reading poetry aloud influences writing.

A TEACHER'S DIARY: Jennifer DeWard

Today my students received letters from a second grade class in North Carolina. Earlier, my students had written to them as part of a project with the book *Flat Stanley*. The second graders wrote to us about their community and asked us to write back to them about our community.

After we read the letters, we brainstormed for ideas about our community. We came up with many terrific ideas and webbed them on the board. Since we were writing to second graders, it gave me an opportunity to discuss the concept of audience. My fourth graders decided that they would use words that second graders could understand *without treating them like babies.* Each student then started a draft, using our web. As I walked around the classroom, I was pleased about the content and quality of their letters. The next day we formed peer revision groups and revised our letters. After we had completed final proofreading, we sent out the letters. This turned out to be a great project.

WHAT BEGINNING WRITING REQUIRES

Writing requires the presence of a few prerequisite skills: writing the letters of the alphabet, phonemic awareness, and associating letters with sounds. *None of these prerequisites need be fully mastered. It is sufficient to have a moderate level of capability in each.*

Writing the Alphabet

Writing the letters of the alphabet is prerequisite to independent writing. Even Joe, the unlettered blacksmith in Dickens' *Great Expectations* understood this concept. Joe tells Pip, "The king upon his throne, with his crown upon his ed, can't sit and write his acts of Parliament in print, without having begun, when he were an unpromoted Prince, with the alphabet . . . and begun at A too, and worked his way to Z. And I know what that is to do, though I can't say I've exactly done it" (p. 71, Dickens). Alphabet knowledge, along with phonemic awareness, makes it possible for children to connect letters to sounds. When knowledge of sounds and letters is present, children can begin to invent the spelling of many words. Of course, children can copy words and names without a knowledge of sounds and letters, but this is not the same as consciously making connections between letters and sounds. Fortunately, with patient instruction, most children can learn to write the letters well enough to begin writing within a few weeks of entering first grade, and many children bring this knowledge from home or kindergarten.

Handwriting practice can accompany learning to write. Independent writing provides opportunities for meaningful handwriting instruction. Practice works best when meaningful language experiences are part of the practice routine. Individual handwriting tips can be given during on-the-spot conferences as children write. For example, as children are writing stop at Benny's desk and say: "Your story is coming nicely, Benny. I like the way you started your story. Let me show you how to make the letter *d*. The ball comes before the stick." Some teachers worry that handwriting instruction will interfere with the content of writing. Such worry is justified if content is ignored or seldom considered. Without question, communicating ideas is the first concern of writing instruction. But handwriting is best taught within the context of meaningful writing.

Phonemic Awareness

Phonemic awareness is the ability to distinguish one speech sound from another and segment sounds within words. Most children learn to do this on their own, but those who do not can be taught to distinguish and segment sounds within words. Once children can segment or isolate one sound from another within words, they can begin to associate speech sounds with the letters that represent them. This capability is prerequisite to learning to read and write (Adams, 1990; Ayres, 1993).

Associating Letters with Sounds

Children's knowledge of the phonology of their language can be put to use in writing sooner than has been generally understood. Children who can talk have learned the phonetics of their language. Before starting school, they can recognize nuances of sounds that surround them. They easily recognize friendliness, anger, sadness in the voices around them. Young children are extraordinarily sensitive to the phonology of language. Linguists have found, for example, that by age six months, infants have eliminated from their utterances all sounds that are irrelevant to the language they will shortly speak.

The feature piece, "Voices from the Classroom," is written by classroom teachers and will appear from time to time throughout this book. I've included this feature because it represents the authentic "voices" of classroom teachers. Throughout this book teachers describe the experiences they encounter in their day-to-day writing with children. Their experiences represent the realities, not necessarily the theories, that motivate their instructional practices. In the "Voices" piece, Nancy Cohen, a first grade teacher from Detroit, Michigan, tells how she introduces writing to her first graders who are at all stages of preparation to write.

VOICES FROM THE CLASSROOM: Nancy Cohen

Getting Started in First Grade

I have taught this grade for four years. My students enter first grade with varied writing skills and knowledge. Some struggle with letter recognition, others can connect letters with sounds. I try to organize a writing program that meets my students' needs and entices them to write.

We start writing immediately. So, on the first day of school, I distribute journals and explain their purpose. My first graders are always delighted when they first see their journals. Although it can be difficult, I have journal writing daily. Usually, I encourage my students to select their own topic, but at times my guidance is needed. I often plan writing lessons which correlate with the themes of our literature program. For example, we recently read the story, *When This Box Is Full* by Patricia Lillie. We used the themes of seasons and hobbies to get started.

I stress the importance of thinking before diving into writing. Frequently, I create webs with my children's own ideas. For example, my students brainstormed ideas of objects that they would like to collect. After our web was complete, they had an organized way to begin writing. My students understand the value of graphic organizers. Soon they are able create their own webs independently.

Another way I encourage my children to write is to encourage the use of invented spelling and dictation. At the beginning of the school year, I model how invented spelling works. It is amazing to see the progress they make. Some of my kids need extra help. They draw pictures and I take dictation from them. Afterwards, they read their dictated accounts. My students enjoy reading their writings to their classmates. I want every child to feel they belong to our learning community.

FOUR EARLY WRITING STAGES

Four stages of writing growth can be observed among emerging writers: scribbling, drawing, letter-strings, and developmental. The first three stages are prephonetic, the last phonetic. The developmental stage marks the first appearance of invented spelling, and the first appearance of systematic connections between letters and sounds. Phonetic writers use invented spelling to approximate the correct spelling of words. Prephonetic writers may write cursive-like lines, letters, and copied words, but they do not make systematic connections between letters and sounds.

Stages are merely a convenient way of discussing a continuous process in discrete terms. However, children do not move in a strictly linear fashion from one stage of writing growth to another. For example, letter-strings are most characteristic of the third stage of emerging writing, but that does not mean that scribbling, characteristic of the first stage, has been entirely abandoned.

Scribbling Stage

Writing begins as play. Children begin writing the moment they reach out and grasp a pencil or crayon. Imagine Toni the Toddler, age 18 months. She seizes a stray crayon, tastes it, finds it unsatisfactory. Not content to discard the crayon, she reaches out and draws a black mark on a nearby wall. Toni's first experiment with writing is delightful. She senses she has caused this mark to magically appear, so she reaches out and swipes the wall again and again. Making random black marks on walls pleases her. This is the beginnings of writing for Toni. The seeds of writing are sown, but whether or not a harvest will follow depends on Toni's parents and teachers.

Between ages two and five, many children believe that the marks they make on paper have meaning. The marks are called *scribbling*, but it is scribbling with a purpose. For very young children, such as Toni, scribbling is probably a pleasurable physical activity, but for children two to five years old, scribbling often conveys meaning. Scribbling has features similar to conventional writing. For example, there is evidence of left-to-right and top-to-bottom orientation—a kind of mock writing resembling print or cursive writing. Letters and cursive-like lines may appear within a drawing. Often these drawings and "mock" writing convey a message.

At age three, if Toni brings a paper covered with cursive and print-like forms to her Mom she is apt to ask, "Mom, what does this say?" Toni's parents should encourage scribbling, but redirect it from wall to paper. They can provide the appropriate experiences: read books, play letter blocks, talk about letters, write Toni's name on paper, hang Toni's "writing" on the refrigerator. Anything that tells Toni that her "writing" is valued makes a contribution to her future as a writer. Toni's teachers should do likewise. If Toni's scribblings, drawings, and strings of letters are valued, Toni will emerge from these early stages of emergent literacy into alphabetic writing where there are systematic connections between letters and sounds—the developmental stage. It won't take long for this stage to emerge. What began as play, scribbling on walls, evolves into the beginnings of writing.

Figure 1.1 is an example of scribble writing. Katie writes a letter to her Grandma thanking her for a present. Katie is three years old and uses mock-cursive writing. Katie's mother wrote a note at the bottom in "big people" writing.

Drawing Stage

Picture writing is thousands of years older than alphabetic writing. Drawings on ancient cave walls tell of the cultural life of the cave's former inhabitants. The earliest known humans drew animals, people, and objects that illustrated important events in their lives. Recent evidence suggests they may also have drawn simply as a means of expressing their creative interests. Children do something similar. Their drawings illustrate their daily experiences as well as express their creative interests. Drawing plays a supporting role in writing long after children have learned the conventional forms of writing. For young children, drawing and writing are ways of communicating meaning (Dyson, 1988). This is true whether or not their drawings are accompanied by scribbles, letter-like forms, or invented spelling.

Figure 1.1 **Scribble Stage** Katie, Age 3

There are reasons why young children write with drawings. First, they may not have mastered the alphabetic system for representing meaning, so an alternative is necessary. Second, since they can represent meaning through pictures there is no pressing need for alphabetic writing. Third, drawing does not require the same fine motor control as writing. Fourth, drawing is itself a form of writing suitable for conveying meaning, as Dyson (1997) has documented. Fifth, drawing helps children recall the message they may have written or that may have been recorded for them by an adult.

Kate, age 4, drew a picture (Figure 1.2). At age four, Kate can write her name. Letters of the alphabet are often included in her drawings. She usually tells Mom, "what her picture says," and often it "says" a story.

Letter-String Stage

Children begin stringing letters and numbers together soon after they have learned to write them. Writing is produced by combining and recombining a limited set of letters and numbers. Once children discover that words can be generated using only a few letters in varying combinations, they may string letters together which, they believe, convey a message.

Figure 1.2 **Drawing Stage** Kate, Age 4

The letter-string stage is prephonetic writing because there is no systematic connection between letters and sounds. As in earlier patterns of writing, features of conventional writing appear in the letter-strings children produce. Features include letters, names, punctuation, words they can spell or copy, and evidence of directional orientation. Children explore the world of letters and words long before they have figured out the principles needed to generate phonetic writing. Marie Clay (1975) describes how a child might view writing at this stage: "The child seems to say, 'I hope I've said something important. You must be able to understand what I've said. What did I write?' " (p. 24). Figure 1.3 illustrates one aspect of the letter-string stage. Brett embedded a string of letters in a picture she drew in kindergarten.

Developmental Stage

As I watched Angie, a first grader, invent the spelling of *sand,* I saw an amateur linguist at work. She hissed the /s/ several times, turned to her paper and wrote a big curvy *S.* She looked pleased with herself. Then she continued. She exploded a "duh" a couple of times, turned to her paper and drew a big fat *D.* I said, "*SD* for *sand* is very good, Angie." She looked at me with a satisfied smile and said, "Thanks. I'm pretty good at it." Invented spelling is a boon to early writing. It

Figure 1.3   Letter-String Stage   Brett

teaches children much of what they need to know about written language and contributes to learning to read and write (Chomsky, 1971).

At the developmental stage of writing, a significant shift occurs. Children begin to make *systematic* connections between letters and sounds. It is a big step. Writing now is alphabetic. Letters and sounds are connected. Scribbling, drawing, and letter-string writing are prephonetic, but the developmental stage is phonetic. Once children understand that letters can represent sounds, show them how to make educated guesses about spelling words. The three questions I ask children are:

1. What do you hear first in **el**ephant? Good, write it.
2. What do you hear next in ele**ph**ant? That's good, write it.
3. Now, what's the last sound you hear in elephan**t**? Fine, write it.

Each time I say the target word I emphasize slightly the sound I want them to attend to. These questions may elicit such spellings as: *lt, lft, elfnt.* It doesn't matter whether they get one, two, three or more letters in the early going. The point is to get children to use what they know to invent the unknown. Children who can talk have acquired knowledge of phonetics, the speech sounds of language. When this knowledge is joined with the understanding that letters stand for speech sounds, children are ready to approximate the spelling of unknown words. Research shows they can do this remarkably well at an early age (Cramer, 1968, 1970;

Chomsky, 1971; Read, 1971). While most children have little difficulty listening to the sounds they hear in words and matching letters to sounds, they do not automatically understand the uses to which this knowledge can be put. Show children how to use invented spelling, and they will often surprise you with their facility.

Billy writes in his journal every day, and his teacher responds. He wrote the piece shown in Figure 1.4 during the fourth week of his first grade year. Compare Figure 1.4 with Figure 1.11. Figure 1.11 was written during the first week of school. There is growth over this short span of time in Billy's knowledge of spelling and writing conventions. What changes can you identify?

Translation

Line 1: Once I took a walk
Line 2: When I was up
Line 3: North. And it was raining.
Line 4: And I went with some
Line 5: of my family.

Figure 1.4   Developmental Stage   Billy, Age 6

ENCOURAGING EARLY WRITING

Scribbling Stage

1. Encourage early attempts to write (scribble).
2. Provide crayons, paper, and other writing devices.
3. Read books, play letter blocks, talk about letters and words.
4. Write children's names on their writing.
5. Display writing in conspicuous places.

Drawing Stage

1. Comment positively on the details within a drawing.
2. Comment on letters, names, or words incorporated into drawings.
3. Read writing back to the author if asked, "What did I write?"
4. Praise and make specific observations about the piece.
5. Display drawings and writing prominently.

Letter-String Stage

1. Encourage the incorporation of environmental print into writing.
2. Suggest ideas for inventorying letter and word knowledge.
3. Answer questions and make observations about words and letters.
4. Ask children to tell you about their writing and drawing.
5. Share writing within the learning community.

Developmental Stage

1. Encourage spelling inventions and provide help as needed.
2. Encourage detailed illustrations.
3. Have children read their writing aloud.
4. Read good literature and talk about the authors.
5. Share writing from the author's chair.

CLAY'S PRINCIPLES OF BEGINNING WRITING

In every era, educators arise who see farther and understand more deeply than their colleagues. There is no shortage of such seers in our profession. Marie Clay ranks among the most farsighted and influential educators of our time. Her work in reading led to Reading Recovery, a highly successful tutorial reading program for the lowest achieving first grade children. Perhaps less well known is the work Marie Clay has done in writing. Her book, *What Did I Write?*, has made an important contribution to our understanding of early writing.

Clay (1975) identified principles which describe children's early writing exploration. These principles describe the nature of children's early writing and provide clues for nurturing it. Some of her principles are obvious to the casual observer, others more subtle. I have reviewed a number of Clay's principles while adding my own understanding of what her principles suggest for teaching children to write.

Meaning Principle

Amy learned the meaningfulness of words early. Her first written word was *Pepsi*, her favorite drink. She knew where Dad could buy it. At stores, she easily distinguished her favorite from the lesser brands. Since she could not yet match letters to sounds, how could she read this word? Context. The red, white, and blue logo, with *Pepsi* embedded in the center, cued the response. *Pepsi* became her first known word outside of its context. *Pepsi* meant pleasure, enjoyment, fulfillment. Meaning drove this minor learning episode.

Long before children command the written language, it commands them. Written language shouts its meaning from every crevice of society. Meaning is the most pervasive characteristic of emerging literacy. Children expect language to be meaningful (Dyson, 1983; Harste, Woodward, and Burke, 1984; Sultzby and Teale, 1985; Smith and Warwick, 1997; Spandel and Stiggins, 1997). The expectation that language will be meaningful is deeply embedded in our culture. Kids see written language on television, in books, on signs. Few children fail to recognize two golden arches and the embedded word, *McDonald's.* Kids know this means hamburgers, French fries, and toys. Preschoolers recognize their favorite cereal or toy while traversing the aisles of a supermarket. Even the clothes they wear convey messages.

Children's early writing quickly turns purposeful. Wavy lines left to right across a page imitate adult cursive writing. Letters appear in preschoolers' drawings. Often the drawings are labeled with letters. Names or initials may appear on their papers. These meaningful experiences with written language prepare children to read and write at an early age.

Teri's drawing (Figure 1.5) illustrates the meaning principle. There are six objects depicted in this picture, and five of them are labeled with a letter of the alphabet. The letters Teri uses may be best-guesses at letter-sound connections: *C* stands for Teri's brother, *n* for Ninja, *e* for Brennan, *F* (reversed) for friend, and *Mom,* spelled out correctly. *House* is not labeled.

Figure 1.5   Meaning Principle   Teri's Drawing and labeling

Exploration Principle

Risk taking and discovery are central to learning to write, according to Clay (1975). Children must explore the conventions of writing through risk taking and discovery, just as they do when learning their oral language. I once heard four-year-old Ben say to his father, who had returned sooner than expected, "What took you so short?" Ben could not have heard this sentence spoken in adult speech. It does not occur. Where did his idea come from? The exploration principle. Ben, like all four-year-olds, constantly explores possible constructions of language. Later, he will discover that "What took you so short" is not used in mature speech. At the time, however, it worked quite well as an expression of his surprise at Dad's unexpected return.

Gradually children sort out the conventions that govern oral and written language, but first they explore possibilities. The more they explore, the more readily they will learn the conventions of oral and written language. Oral language learning allows for errors; we expect them; we do not punish them. Where risk taking and discovery bring censure, writing will be timid. Where mistakes earn only scorn, avoidance and reluctance are the consequence. Beginning writers need support as they explore written language. They need to feel comfortable as they tackle the complex tasks of using pencil and paper, hand-eye coordination, distinguishing one letter from another, associating sounds with letters, conveying a meaningful message. Kids can do it, but they need someone to patiently guide them and serve as an appreciative audience.

Nick drew pictures but they aren't easily identifiable (Figure 1.6). Letters are scattered throughout the drawing, some of which seem to explore formation, direction, and placement within a context of objects. There is also the curious *t-reX* which appears twice. Why the dash and the super large *X?* Nick is exploring written language.

Sign Principle

Jenny bursts into the living room waving a piece of paper, "Dad, what does this say?" Jenny thinks her string of letters is just like the writing she has seen in books. Dad accepts Jenny's piece of writing and solemnly reads it to her. Soon Jenny is back with another written piece. This time she doesn't ask what it says, she knows: "Dad, this says, 'I love you very much.' " Jenny has discovered that writing stands for something besides itself; she knows it says important things.

Once children make the crucial discovery that letters (signs) are carrying the message, they have understood the sign principle: writing stands for something besides itself, and it conveys meaning. Learning the signs of written language is a challenging task. Letters appear in many different disguises, and children must learn the many forms that written language can take. There are 26 small letters, 26 capital letters. Printers' *a* and *g* are formed differently than the handwritten forms of *a* and *g*. Cursive writing is different from printed forms. In addition to letters, there are numbers, punctuation marks, and other conventions of written language. These many *signs* are used in an almost infinite number of combinations.

As learning proceeds, kids invent new shapes, reverse letters and numbers, and elaborate on traditional shapes. They invent and explore in order to discover what the signs are and how they work. Clay (1975) explains the purpose of this ex-

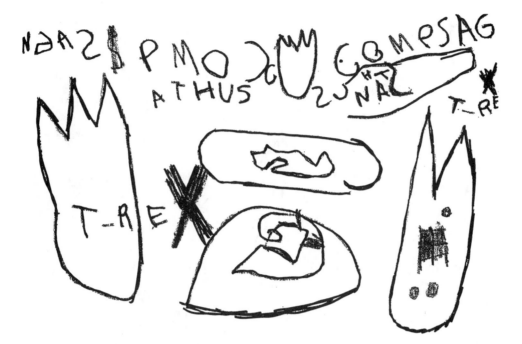

Figure 1.6 **Exploration Principle** Nick's Letters and Drawing

ploration with the signs of the written language: "Left to experiment with letter forms children will create a variety of new symbols by repositioning or decorating the standard forms. In this way they explore the limits within which each letter may vary and still retain its identity" (p. 43). Children learn the sign principle readily when their environment provides meaningful exposure to print (Figure 1.7).

Generative Principle

Emerging writers soon discover that a few letters, used in varying combinations, can generate many words. This is the generative principle. Katie wrote a page of letter-like forms (Figure 1.8). At the top-right she "addresses" her letter to Grandma and at the top-left she places the date. She knows this is what's done with letters; she has seen her mother write them this way. She can point to the precise place where she has addressed her letter and placed the date. She tells her mother what she's written to Grandma, and a long newsy letter it is. Katie does not yet make traditional letters, but letter-like forms. She cannot spell and it doesn't matter. She cannot make traditional letters and that doesn't matter either. She knows that the "letters" she writes carry messages, though she doesn't yet know the orderly principles of alphabetic writing. Once she learns to form the letters of the alphabet and can make letter-sound connections, she will move rapidly into invented spelling and traditional writing. For now, strings of letter-like forms represent real writing for Katie. She believes she has discovered how to write real

Figure 1.7 Sign Principle

messages, and she is partly right. She has discovered a principle by which writing is generated, and this is an important beginning: Katie has discovered the generative principle.

Directional Principle

B. W. entered the Oakland University Reading Clinic writing many words backwards. To many folks, including mom and dad, this looked like a case of dyslexia. B. W's clinic teacher worked for a few sessions, showing him that letters are written from left to right, not right to left. *Good-by dyslexia!* Is this a good clinic or what? Well, yes, but B. W. didn't have dyslexia. He had garden variety directional confusion, a symptom common among developing readers. Fortunately, directional confusion is seldom a sign, and probably never a cause, of dyslexia. Directional confusion is a symptom of the predictable confusion that accompanies complex learning. It rarely signals dyslexia or learning disability. The popular press, and some of the professional literature, have given the impression that directional confusion is a sign of serious perceptual deficits. This is seldom the case.

English is written from left-to-right and top-to-bottom. This arrangement is arbitrary. Hebrew is written from right-to-left, traditional Chinese right-to-left and vertically. Culture determines directional orientation in writing. While learning to

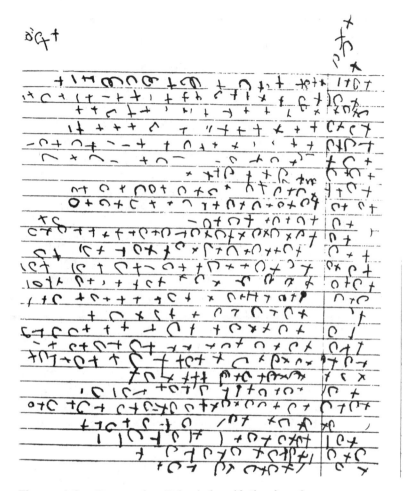

Figure 1.8   **Generative Principle**   Katie, Age 3

orient writing according to the directional principles of English, children have periods of confusion. Sensibly, they experiment with print; they try different arrangements and orientations of print. It is important to understand that directional confusion is often an experiment, children exploring their way to understanding how English is written. Thus, most directional confusion is normal, temporary, and developmental. Usually, it disappears as reading and writing knowledge increases.

Sometimes reversal tendencies persist for years. Janet, a third grader, reverses the *J* in her name quite often and a few other letters as well. Since she is an above-average reader and writer, patience and an occasional gentle reminder will suffice as correction. Jeffrey, a second grader making slow progress in reading, also exhibits reversals—more often and more persistently than Janet. The following instructional prescription is adequate for Jeffrey and many others like him.

UNDERSTANDING REVERSAL TENDENCIES

1. Do not assume Jeffrey has a learning disability. Treat him as a normal child who may need extra help in learning to read and write.
2. Recognize that reversal tendencies are developmental; they usually disappear as progress is made in reading and writing.
3. Integrate reading and writing instruction for Jeffrey. Make sure he has plenty of time to read and write every day. Give him any extra instructional attention you can.
4. Pay only minor attention to Jeffrey's reversals. They are far more likely to be symptoms of a reading deficiency than a perceptual deficit.
5. Occasional verbal reminders about letter orientation (*b, d, p, q*) can be given: "Let me show you, Jeffrey. When making the letter *b*, the ball comes after the stick." Then demonstrate what you're explaining.
6. Trace reversed letters or words in sand or trace them with a large crayon if reversals persist past the developmental stage of reading and writing.

Figure 1.9 pictures a dinosaur and a two lines of print. Jay writes, *This is a dinosaur of long ago.* There are two kinds of directional confusions in Jay's piece: (1) reversed words: is and of, and (2) reversed letters: *d, g, j, s.* These are minor developmental problems, and they often accompany learning to read and write. As Jay's reading and writing skills develop, these minor directional confusions will disappear. They are not a sign or symptom of learning or perceptual problems.

Inventory Principle

Children enjoy assessing their letter and word knowledge. So, they often write "inventories" of what they know. Inventories may include upper and lower case letters, known words, words beginning with a certain letter, and members of a category such as friends, family, and animals. The common characteristic of inventories is that they take stock of what is known. Checking on what you know is a metacognitive activity. It is a way of assuring yourself that you know it. Inventories help children evaluate their progress. When children take stock of what they know, they can set new goals and recognize past achievements.

Inventories give teachers information about children's progress. Occasionally ask children to write all the letters or words they know. When a child gets stuck say, "Some children can write the word *dog*. Can you?" Or say something similar to encourage children to search the store of knowledge which they may have but cannot access on short notice. Encourage children to include a drawing along with their word or letter inventories. When children inventory some aspect of their writing knowledge, praise their effort and share it with the class.

Ben, age 4, drew a picture and inventoried his knowledge of the alphabet (Figure 1.10). Ben knows some words but he chose not to include words in this inventory. He handed this picture to Dad and said, "Here's the alphabet."

Figure 1.9   **Directional Principle**   Jay, Age 6

Spacing Principle

We are accustomed to spacing between words. It seems so sensible that it is difficult to imagine any other arrangement. However, some ancient languages didn't require spacing between words. For example, some ancient Greek manuscripts of the Bible did not have spaces between words. Try reading the string of unspaced words below. Surprisingly, it is not as hard as you might think.

Forexampleyoucanprobablyreadthissentencequiteeasilywithoutspaces.

Some beginning writers leave little or no space between words. Others invent special devices—stars, periods, and drawings—to mark the boundaries between words. Difficulty with spacing does not necessarily mean children are unable to distinguish word boundaries. If children have difficulty spacing between words, suggest that they leave a space between words the width of their finger, pencil, or strip of cardboard. These devices provide a helpful physical solution to the

Figure 1.10   Inventory Principle   Ben, Age 4

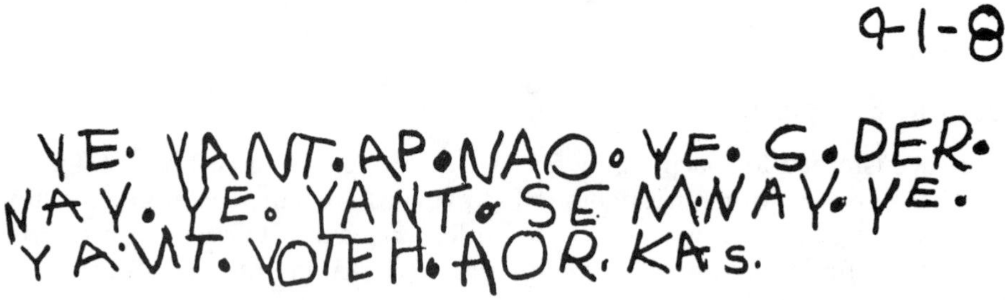

Translation

Line 1: We went up north. We saw deer.

Line 2: Then we went swimming. Then we

Line 3: went over to our cousins.

Figure 1.11   **Spacing Principle**   Billy, Age 6

problem of word spacing. This temporary aid is usually abandoned once children have the hang of word spacing. Fingers and pencils for spacing are a temporary crutch, of course, but crutches are necessary on certain occasions. I suppose that's why Baron Wilhelm Von Crutchenfelt invented them.

Billy wrote a story in his response journal in the first week of school (Figure 1.11). He drew round dots to indicate boundaries between words. His boundaries are correct with one exception. He decided that *over to* (yoteh) was one not two words. Compare this story with Figure 1.4 which Billy wrote during the fourth week of school. The spacing devices used during the first week of school have disappeared by the fourth, and they disappeared spontaneously.

CLAY'S PRINCIPLES SUMMARIZED

1. Meaning principle: Children's early writings are intended to convey meaning, and meaning is the most pervasive characteristic of emerging literacy.
2. Exploration principle: Children's early writings are explorations in how to represent letters, words, and ideas on paper.
3. Sign principle: Writing stands for something besides itself.
4. Generative principle: A few letters, used in varying combinations, can generate many words and messages.
5. Directional principle: Directional confusion is normal and developmental; children acquire the understandings needed to orient and arrange print as they make progress in reading and writing.
6. Inventory principle: Children assess their knowledge of letters and words by writing "inventories" of letters and words.
7. Spacing principle: Initially, children may ignore word boundaries or they may use periods or stars to represent spaces between words.

STRATEGIES FOR BEGINNING WRITING

Any instructional strategy must be adapted to circumstances, personality, and teaching style. Persistence is a virtue when trying out a new instructional strategy. When a strategy seems not to work, consider the possible causes. Often it is a matter of adjusting the strategy to suit your circumstances, personality, or teaching style. Other times it is a matter of giving the strategy time to work. After a fair trial, of course, a strategy that does not work should be abandoned.

Consider the five strategies described below: language experience, reading aloud, modeling, connecting drawing and writing, and using predictable books. They may not all work equally well for you, but try them. See if you can adapt them to your circumstances, personality, and teaching style.

Recording Dictated Language Experience Accounts

Recording children's language through dictated accounts prepares children for writing. It has several advantages. First, it models the writing process. The conventions of written language are modeled through dictation. Recording oral language enables children to observe the connections between speech and written language. They can watch as you manipulate print, punctuation, spelling. They see how their words are organized and sequenced and the changes that result from student initiated revisions. Most importantly, they see their words turned into written language.

Second, recorded accounts illustrate the connection between reading and writing. Rereading dictated accounts closes the circle between talking, writing, and reading: What I say can be written. What I write can be read.

Third, dictation models the stages of the writing process. Prior to dictation, children choose a topic and brainstorm ideas. When ready, they dictate a draft. Sometimes the draft is the only draft, but children sometimes add, delete, or rearrange information in their draft account. Dictated accounts are illustrated and shared with classmates. Dictation paves the way for independent writing and gives experience in planning, drafting, revising, and presenting writing.

Fourth, dictation increases reading and writing fluency. Fluency is a crucial objective in reading and writing. Having practiced composing through dictation, children come to writing with experience in composing, topic selection, drafting, revising, and presenting.

If you want to use dictated language experience accounts as part of your reading and writing program, the following procedures can be followed for group stories as well as for individually dictated accounts.

TAKING AND REREADING DICTATED STORIES

Taking a Dictated Story

1. Initially, it helps to provide a stimulus—read a book, take a walk, conduct a science experiment. Later, a stimulus may not be necessary.
2. Write the story exactly as the child dictates it and supply appropriate punctuation. Say, "I'm going to write your story as you tell it. Watch me as I write."
3. Position the paper so that the child can observe as you print the dictated story. Comment casually on punctuation now and then: "I'm putting these words in quotation marks because this is what your friend said to you."

Rereading a Dictated Story

1. After taking the story, read it back to the child. Point to the words as you go, including the sweep to a new line. Read fluently and naturally.
2. Read the story together. Stay slightly in front of the child so that the reader will not falter. The objective is to achieve immediate success in reading.

3. Ask the child to read the story independently. Supply any words the child does not know.

4. Have the child underline known words. After a second day of rereading, known words can be put on cards and kept in a word bank. Word sort activities can follow as independent work.

5. After rereading, spend a few minutes on word recognition. For example, find a word that appears two or more times in a story. Point to its first occurrence and say, "Can you find this word somewhere else in your story?"

6. Have the child illustrate the story. Encourage as much detail as possible, as this aids recall on the second or third day of rereading.

Reading Aloud

Reading enriches language, builds background knowledge, sparks imagination, gives pleasure. Reading aloud lays the foundation on which the superstructure of writing can be erected. Read to children every day. Consider your own likes and dislikes, as well as those of your children, when selecting read-aloud literature. Your choices are your legacy. Show enthusiasm for what you are reading. Make your classroom conducive to listening. Ensure children's comfort and freedom from distractions. Suggest mood and tone by the inflection or volume of your voice. For instance, if you are reading the words of a Troll, bodily posture and voice can add interest to the reading. Connect reading and writing by having children write their reactions to books you've read. Let them choose their own topics to react to: characters, places, story line, events.

Modeling Writing

We learn much of what we know, good and bad, from the example of others. I taught fifth grade in Maine-Endwell Elementary School in upstate New York. It was my first teaching job. Ed Ferencik, a sixth grade teacher, gave me my first graduate course in teaching. He loved teaching, whether sixth graders or colleagues. I learned much of what this good man knew about teaching. We never used the words role model or mentor, but I see now that Ed was my mentor and role model.

Model reading and writing for your children. Children learn by observing the behavior of their teachers. For example, as you read explain what you do, show how you do it, and tell why you enjoy it. As you write, show how words and sentences fit together, how you make writing decisions, what you are thinking about, how punctuation works. If you make mistakes, explain how you fix them. As you write, comment casually on the substance of what you want your children to understand about writing.

Connecting Drawing and Writing

Children compose with pictures as well as words. Crayons and paper, paint and brush are tools for composing that enable children to create their own world of thought and imagination (Dyson, 1997). Help children connect their drawings to spoken or written language. Talk with them about their drawings. Label their drawings. Encourage them to make their drawings as complete as possible so that their ideas are fully expressed. Elaboration is important. Dyson (1988) found that elaborating drawings helps children elaborate their written texts. The additional detail they include in their drawings also helps them recall their written words.

In the "Voices" piece, Biz Smith Williamson describes how she connects drawing and writing in her kindergarten class.

VOICES FROM THE CLASSROOM: Biz Smith Williamson

Connecting Drawing and Writing

I have been teaching elementary school for nine years. Currently, I am teaching Kindergarten. Writing is an important part of a kindergartner's day. Every student in my class has a writing journal. The writing journals are sketchpads that I purchased at an art supply store. I chose sketchpads because the pages are bound together and they are unlined. My students are not ready to write on lines just yet. The unlined pages also give the students plenty of room to draw pictures.

My students draw pictures in their journals regularly. By the beginning of October, many of my students are ready to label their own pictures. Some of my children prefer to dictate a sentence to me, and I write their sentence on a piece of paper. The students then copy what I have written into their journals. After they have finished writing, they read their sentence back to me. Once a week we review their journals and they reread two or three of their pieces to me.

The drawing and writing connection is crucial in the emerging stages of writing. My students write about things that are meaningful to them. They are forming the habit of using picture clues when reading. Finally, they have the opportunity to read something they know. Connecting drawing and writing allows for early writing and reading success.

Using Predictable Books

Predictable books add a valuable dimension to a writing program. Modeling helps writers use literary patterns to guide their writing. Predictable books provide models for writing that are easy to follow. For example, *The Three Little Pigs* illustrates how recurring language themes can create a pattern that is easy to remember: "I'll huff and I'll puff till I blow your house down." Predictable books provide easily accessible models for writing. The value of such models is that they are easily remembered, so story elements, particularly the recurring theme, can be adapted for use in children's own writing.

Drawing helps young writers eleborate their texts. Victor is writing a chapter book. After completing each chapter, Victor drew illustrations of key ideas. Victor is shown here getting ready to illustrate a just completed chapter.

A fine book for initiating patterned writing is *The Important Book,* by Margaret Wise Brown (1949). The rhythm and structure of her book makes it an instant hit with children. The book can be easily adapted to content writing, as the example below illustrates. The piece entitled, "The Most Important Thing About the Civil War," shows how main idea and supporting detail can be adapted to a writing format.

The Most Important Thing About the Civil War

The most important thing about the Civil War
Is that it ended slavery.
It was fought between the North and South.
Both sides had famous generals.
The North, had Grant and Burnside
The South, had Lee and Jackson.
(Several paragraphs not included here)
But the most important thing about the Civil War
Is that it ended slavery.

Ms. Elson's Fifth Grade Class

Predictable books can make good writing models, but they can be overdone. Bill Martin Jr.'s *Brown Bear, Brown Bear: What Do You See?* is a classic in the predictable book genre, but it has been followed by many similar books whose quality is questionable. Suggested steps for using predictable books to aid writing are listed below.

USING PREDICTABLE BOOKS AS MODELS FOR WRITING

1. Read the book or poem aloud once or twice.
2. Provide children with a copy of the words, and choral read or chant the story or poem together.
3. Discuss the story or poem by asking questions and inviting comments. Here are five questions that are useful to ask:
   a. What did you like best about this book?
   b. Did anything surprise you?
   c. Did anything make you laugh, feel happy, feel sad?
   d. What part is repeated more than once?
   e. How would you change it if you wrote a book like this?
4. Write a group story or poem using the predictable book as a model. Write the first lines yourself, then ask volunteers to add their lines.
5. Next day, read the story together. Then add new lines or revise old ones.
6. Have children write their own story or poem following the pattern of the book or poem.

IDEAS FOR WRITING

1. Make a collage. Cut out pictures from magazines and make a collage with a theme such as: happy, angry, lazy, brave, sleepy, cold, hungry. Label your collage with a word or words that best describes it.

2. Using your senses. Make a list of items that fit one of the senses. For example, make a list of things that have to do with touch: rough, smooth, hard, soft, bumpy. Choose one to write about.

3. Word mobile. Make a word mobile using color words, foods, wild animals, tame animals, desserts, names of cars, football players, movie stars, singers, presidents, friends, birds.

4. Show and tell. Write two or three sentences about what they are going to share during show and tell.

5. Make a spelling dictionary. Staple thirteen pages of paper together with a cover. Label each page with a letter of the alphabet in order. Use this booklet as a dictionary of words you can spell and read.

6. Write about a picture. Choose an interesting photograph or picture. Write a sentence or two to answer each of the following questions:
   a. What do you see?
   b. Describe something about what you see.
   c. What may have happened just before this picture was taken?
   d. What may have happened just after the picture was taken?

7. Listen. Listen for the next five sounds you hear and list them. Then choose one sound and describe it more fully. Think about these questions: What made the sound? Is it a good or bad sound? Does this sound remind you of something or someone else?

8. Choose a color. Cut out pictures from magazines which illustrate the color. Make a collage with the pictures. List other objects that are usually the same color.

9. Make a dictionary. Work in teams to make a rhyming dictionary. Each team should choose several phonograms to work with such as: -ick, -og, -and, -ed, -ug, -ent, -ay, -ame, -ight. Put your work together with the work of other teams. Mimeograph the lists and make booklets for everyone. Rhyming dictionaries can also be purchased, and they are a useful classroom reference book.

10. Write a cartoon. Cut a cartoon from the newspaper leaving out the captions. Write your own funny lines for the cartoon. Display your cartoon on the bulletin board along with the original cartoon captions.

REFLECTION AND SUMMARY

Reflection

Bernard Malamud said, "I work with language. I love the flowers of afterthought." Children love language too, they use it beautifully. Sometimes their language is crude and unsophisticated, but if you have an ear to hear its nuances, you will detect its power, recognize its creativity, and appreciate its freshness. Children's oral language ebbs and flows from a wellspring of pulsating thought and feeling. Oral language can be channeled into written language. Written language, with its conventions and complexities, takes years to master. Yet, all things must have a beginning, and when children are given a good beginning, it is amazing how quickly they learn to write.

Children can write; oh, how they can write. Even so, much of what they write is trite, uninteresting. I hope I haven't shocked you. You see, this is so for all writers—even the best. If you could look into the wastebaskets of the best writers, you would discover the trite and uninteresting stuff that never, of course, gets published. Writers avoid the trite and uninteresting most of the time by revising themselves into "something resembling intelligence," as Kurt Vonnegut put it.

We should not judge children's writing by their beginnings but by their endings. Neither should we judge young children's writing by impossible standards. If we are patient, children will produce those fine pieces that we long to see. But just as in mining diamonds, we have to crush tons of low-grade ore before we are rewarded with that piece of writing that sparkles.

Summary

This chapter has presented the following main ideas:

1. Writing enhances thinking because it is visible, permanent, active, precise, and focuses thought.

2. As children acquire language, they acquire thought structures and learning strategies that can be applied to learning to read and write according to Piaget, Vygotsky, and Bruner.

3. Focusing on children's meaning strengthens oral language and improves prospects for learning to read and write.

4. There are three prerequisites for writing: forming the letters of the alphabet, developing phonemic awareness, and associating letters with sounds.

5. Emergent writers move through four stages of writing growth: scribbling, drawing, letter-string, and developmental spelling.

6. Clay's seven principles describe what children discover about writing as literacy emerges. These principles include meaning, exploration, sign, generative, directional, inventory, and spacing.

7. Five strategies for writing were presented: language experience accounts, reading aloud, modeling writing, connecting drawing and writing, and using predictable books.

QUESTIONS FOR REFLECTIVE THINKING

1. Assume that writing influences thinking. What application might this idea have for teaching social studies or science?

2. What writing activities might you use in applying Vygotsky's philosophy of instruction with primary grade children? Explain your choices.

3. Why should parents and teachers focus on meaning in conversations they might have with their children?

4. What must a child know in order to begin independent writing? Why?

5. In what singular way does the developmental stage of writing differ from the preceding three?

6. Which of Clay's principles of early writing do you find most interesting? Why?

7. *The Three Little Pigs* and *The Three Billy Goats Gruff* are examples of predictable books. Chose a predictable book and plan a writing lesson based on your predictable book.

8. What have you learned that you didn't know or fully appreciate before you read this chapter?

9. Mini case study: You teach a group of 25 fifth grade children in a rural community. The staff of your school has concluded that content learning in social studies and science needs to be strengthened. In the past, rote memorization of social studies and science facts has been emphasized. What suggestions might you make at the next staff meeting that might strengthen content learning?

REFERENCES

Adams, M. J. (1990). *Beginning to read: Thinking and learning about print.* Cambridge, MA: MIT Press.

Ayres, L. (1993). *The efficacy of three training conditions on phonological awareness of kindergarten children and the longitudinal effect of each on later reading acquisition.* Unpublished Dissertation, Oakland University, Rochester, MI.

Betts, E. (1975). *Foundations of reading instruction.* New York: American Book Company.

Brown, M. W. (1949). *The important book.* New York: Harper.

Bruner, J. (1966). *The process of education.* Cambridge, MA: Harvard University Press.

Chomsky, C. (1971). "Reading, writing, and phonology." *Harvard Educational Review,* 40, 287–309.

Clay, M. (1975). *What did I write?* Auckland, New Zealand: Heinemann Educational Books.

Cramer, R. L. (1968). *An investigation of the spelling achievement of two groups of first-grade classes on phonologically regular and irregular words and in written composition.* Unpublished Doctoral Dissertation, Newark, Delaware, Reading Study Center, University of Delaware, Newark, DE.

Cramer, R. L. (1970). "An investigation of first grade spelling achievement." *Elementary English,* February, 230–237.

Dickens, C. (1992). *Great expectations.* Denmark by Norhaven: Wordsworth Editions Limited.

Dyson, A. H. (1983). "Research currents: Young children as composers." *Language Arts,* 60, 884–891.

Dyson, A. H. (1988). "Appreciate the drawing and dictating of young children." *Young Children,* 43, 25–32.

Dyson, A. H. (1997). *Writing superheroes: Contemporary childhood, popular culture, and classroom literacy.* New York: Teachers College Press.

Ehrlich, E. and DeBruhl, M. (1996). *The international thesaurus of quotations.* New York: HarperCollins Publishers, Inc.

Halliday, M. A. K. (1975). *Learning how to mean.* London: Edward Arnold.

Harste, J. C., Woodward, V. A., and Burke, C. L. (1984). *Language stories and literacy lessons.* Portsmouth, NH: Heinemann.

Mailer, N. (1989). "At the point of my pen." In *Why I write: Thoughts on the craft of fiction,* Will Blythe, Ed. New York: Little, Brown, and Co.

Piaget, J. (1955). *The language and thought of the child.* NY: Meridian Books.

Read, C. (1971). "Pre-school children's knowledge of English phonology." *Harvard Educational Review,* 41, 1–34.

Smith, J. and Warwick, E. (1997). *How children learn to write.* New York: Owen Publishers, Inc.

Spandel, V. and Stiggins, R. (1997). *Creating writers: Linking writing assessment and instruction,* 2nd ed. New York: Longman.

Sultzby, E. and Teale, W. H. (1985). "Writing development in early childhood." *Educational Horizons,* Fall, 8–12.

Temple, C., Nathan, R., and Burris, N. (1982). *The beginnings of writing: Second edition.* Boston: Allyn and Bacon, Inc.

Tough, J. (1973). *Focus on meaning.* London: George Allen & Unwin Ltd.

Vygotsky, L. (1962). *Thought and language.* Cambridge, MA: M. I. T. Press

CHAPTER 2
The Writing Process

Writing in its broad sense—as distinct from simply putting words on paper—
has three steps: thinking about it, doing it, and doing it again (and again
and again, as often as time will allow and patience will endure).

Thomas S. Kane

A WRITER'S STORY

First encouragements sink deeper and last longer than any that come later. While I had not done well in high school, a two-year hitch in the Army had convinced me of the value of a college education. So, I enrolled in college but with little confidence in my academic potential. When Professor Anderson gave us our first writing assignment she said, "Write a short story." I had never written a short story, but I knew that the Saturday Evening Post published short stories. I went straight from that class to the library where I came across a good story. It was set in a steel mill and featured a character who reminded me of my father, a coal miner. It seemed a good model for my story. I was struck by a description of a blast furnace as, ". . . a scarlet-mawed monster." Perhaps, I thought, there will be an occasion to use that phrase in my story. I made note of that phrase, and I used it in my story, though I've no recollection of how or why.

I knew I needed models of short stories if I were to write one. I had read short stories before, but without a specific purpose. Now I had a purpose. I wrote my story and turned it in, not expecting much. When Professor Anderson returned my story, I read these encouraging words, "Ron, you have wonderful ideas!" Those five words fell like rain on a summer savanna. I did not know what ideas she thought were wonderful, and I was wise enough not to ask. I could make her words mean whatever I wanted them to mean, and I have been doing so ever since. I trace my love of writing to Professor Anderson's generous first encouragement. Those of us who teach are fortunate. We can give early encouragement to our students. Early encouragements sink deepest and last longest.

INTRODUCTION

Writing is a process of moving a composition through stages or steps, but not in a straight line linear fashion. Writers go back and forth. Kane (1988) puts it like this: "As you work on a composition you will be, at any given point, concentrating on one phase of writing. But always you are engaged with the process in its entirety" p. 15.

Writing arises out of a complex of theory, procedure, and activity. One name for this complex is *the* writing process. It has been adapted and adopted by teachers throughout this country and, indeed, throughout the world. But is there such a thing as *the* writing process? Or, is *the* writing process merely a convenient fiction, little more than an abstraction around which we organize our uncertainties? Is writing too idiosyncratic, too complex to fit into the box we have constructed? This chapter discusses such questions and provides an overview of the writing process. In addition, this chapter discusses the traditional approach to writing instruction and gives a summary of the major instructional concepts popularized by Donald Graves and Brian Cambourne.

DEFINING THE WRITING PROCESS

You seldom find a definition of the writing process, perhaps because, like Whole Language, it is so diffuse that definitions are inevitably inadequate. So, with inadequacy a near certainty, I'll attempt a definition. Process has a number of meanings, but in a writing context process suggests three things: a particular method of doing writing; a number of operations involved in doing writing; and a continuing development of writing that involves many changes. The writing process includes theories, procedures, and activities which emphasize the operations by which writing is accomplished, as opposed to emphasizing the product itself. The writing process is organized around stages through which writing usually, though certainly not always, progresses. These stages are called prewriting, drafting, revising, and publishing. The writing process is said to be *recursive*.

Recursive Nature of the Writing Process

The writing process is recursive. Recursive means to occur again or to return. Writers move back and forth from one stage or operation of writing to another in a nonlinear fashion. The sequence of reoccurring activity varies with the writer's purpose, audience, and personal writing habits. For example, a writer might plunge into drafting without planning, and soon discover the need for more information. So, the writer stops drafting and collects the needed information—a prewriting activity. Such a scenario, not at all uncommon among writers, not only demonstrates that the writing process is not linear, but also reveals a not very well kept secret: every writer blazes his or her own trail; every writer has his or her personal writing process. Does this mean that *the* writing process is a convenient fiction, a way in which we organize our uncertainties about how writing is produced? Not at all. But it does remind us that writing interacts with and is influenced by purpose, audience, and personal writing habits. It should also remind us that the box we have constructed, the writing process, may house more complexities than we have imagined.

The Importance of Process

Every era elevates a favored theory of how writing competence is acquired—our era is no exception. The current favorite among educators, though not necessarily writers, is called writing process, or process writing, or *the* writing process. The word *process* is common to all three descriptions, and stands in contrast to *product*. The traditional approach to writing instruction emphasizes product, and pays less attention to process. The writing process approach emphasizes the operations by which writing is accomplished. It would be a mistake, however, to assume that process writing is unconcerned about the final product, just as it would be mistaken to assume that the traditional approach is unconcerned about process. While there are fundamental philosophical distinctions between the two approaches, it serves no purpose to make a straw man argument for either approach. I have tried, I hope successfully, to describe each approach fairly.

The Importance of Product

Product is the *ultimate* goal of writing, not process. When we read a book, we expect a good product. We want poetry and fiction well written, absorbing, thought provoking. We want exposition that is accurate, complete, well organized. Readers couldn't care less about the process a writer went through to produce a novel, poem, or essay. This is as it should be. Process is the business of the writer, not the reader. Process should lead to a better product, and if it does not then it has failed. A sound theory of instruction should promote procedures and activities that lead to the best possible product.

Overemphasis on product is destructive to good writing; so is overemphasis on process. The traditional approach focuses on correctness to the detriment of content. The process approach sometimes undervalues correctness to the detriment of the product. Neither condition is healthy, though it is quite clear that valuing good ideas is more important than correctly expressing mundane ones.

Critiquing the Writing Process

Some critics of the writing process offer an alternative that has no credibility. For example, Tremmel (1986), in a long critique of the writing process, offers a one-paragraph alternative:

> As with the applications of deconstructive processes to literary texts, it may be necessary to sacrifice attractive generalizable conclusions for more chaotic and conflicting sets of possibilities. However, we stand to gain a great deal in return, not the least of which is a sharpened awareness of how to pay closer attention to the practices of individual writers and the problem of teaching students how to respond to the complexities of particular rhetorical situations. I would like to suggest that this "close attention" or as Richard Lloyd-Jones calls it, "careful looking" is a much more useful focus for both teaching and research than any theory or hope-for-salvation-through-paradigm shift, and that in the long run it will be a much firmer foundation for the teaching of writing and the growth of writing teachers. (p. 82)

According to Tremmel, we are to find salvation by imitating the methods the deconstructionists inflicted upon literary texts. Heaven forfend! For complexity you can't beat deconstruction theory. But what, if any, is its potential contribution to teaching children to write? Tremmel doesn't say.

George Steiner (1995), literary critic and Lord Weidenfeld Professor of Comparative Literature at Oxford University, made the following comment about the influence of deconstructionist theory of literary criticism:

> Today we're told there is critical theory, that criticism dominates—deconstruction, semiotics, post-structuralism, post-modernism. It is a very peculiar climate, summed up by that man of undoubted genius, Monsieur Derrida, when he says that every text is a "pretext." This is one of the most formidably erroneous, destructive, brilliantly trivial word plays ever launched. Meaning what? That whatever the stature of the poem, it waits for the deconstructive commentator; it is the mere occasion of the exercise. This is to me ridiculous beyond words. (p. 51)

I couldn't agree more. And, it is ridiculous beyond words to recommend applying deconstruction theory to teaching writing. Writing is complex and implementing writing instruction even more complex. Who needs more? While the writing process is not a precursor to the arrival of the millennium, it is a more hopeful paradigm for writing instruction than its predecessors or any approach recently proposed, including deconstruction.

On the other hand, thoughtful criticism of the writing process is most welcome. For instance, Applebee's (1986) critique of the writing process is constructive. Evidently, he sees no point in throwing the baby out with the bath water. Applebee believes the research base for writing process is weak and needs to be augmented. He says that implementation of writing instruction is weak and needs strengthening. These are reasonable criticisms, and he is right on both counts. Applebee proposes three ways in which writing process instruction can be improved.

1. Writing process must be reconstrued as strategies that writers employ for particular purposes.
2. For difficult tasks, writers will use different strategies, and for some tasks these strategies may involve no more than the routine production of a first and final draft.
3. More extensive writing routines must be recognized as problem-solving heuristics appropriate to work-in-progress; they are unlikely to be useful in writing about things (or in ways) the writer already knows well. (p. 106)

Items 1 and 2, while not new, are constructive ideas. They identify weaknesses in implementation that require additional consideration. Proponents of the writing process have had some success in conveying these two ideas to teachers, but clearly not enough. Item 3 presents something of a mystery. Applebee seems to be suggesting that longer pieces of writing may require different or at least additional procedures of discovery and learning. This seems a reasonable suggestion, though Applebee leaves unsaid what these procedures might be.

Conclusion

Critics of the writing process have pointed out its weaknesses: an inadequate research base, uneven implementation, overemphasis on process, a corresponding underemphasis on product, overdependence on stage theory as an organizing principle, and failure to stress the uniqueness of each individual's writing process. Each of these criticisms has merit, most criticisms do. But are these criticisms of sufficient weight that we must abandon process writing? Is there a better alternative? No and No. Saul Bellow explains why, "Alternatives, and particularly desirable alternatives, grow only on imaginary trees."

It is best to face this truth: the writing process has its weaknesses; it is poorly implemented in many instances; it is not a panacea. But it is a better candidate for improving writing performance than the traditional approach. Few educational reforms have lasting impact—writing process is a notable exception. The writing process movement has crossed that difficult barrier from academic theory into classroom practice. The writing process is widely known and practiced among classroom teachers. While it cannot be said that it has been implemented in even a majority of classrooms, it is widely used in elementary schools, and has adherents in secondary levels as well.

Progress has been made, but problems remain. For example, many teachers, particularly high school English teachers, remain unconvinced of the merits of the writing process. Furthermore, most subject matter teachers, who control as much as half the writing that takes place in schools, know little or nothing of the writing process (Applebee, 1986). Yet, this is hardly a criticism of the writing process itself. It simply tells us that much remains to be done. Weaknesses can be strengthened, procedures modified, implementation improved. Such improvements will require modification of theory, procedure, and practice. A return to traditional writing instruction, however, is not the answer. We must listen to the critics; we must be willing to rethink and adjust our theories, procedures, and practices. But there is not sufficient evidence to cause us to abandon the writing process.

THE TRADITIONAL APPROACH

The philosophy and approach to writing instruction proposed in this book takes the view that the writing process, when effectively implemented, is more likely to lead to good writing than the traditional writing approach. The traditional approach is dominant in many school venues. It is particularly prevalent in high schools. It has prevailed for a century or more, and it is not going away any time soon. I have compared and contrasted the role of teachers and students as a way of understanding the salient features of the traditional approach.

Teachers' Role

Teachers provide models of good form and explore them with students. The models include narration, exposition, description, persuasion, and poetry (Applebee, 1986). The rules of grammar, usage, mechanics, and spelling are stressed. Generally, rules are taught in isolation, seldom within the context of writing itself. Writing topics and genres are assigned by the teacher. The teacher evaluates writing, often analytically, highlighting errors. Mastery of the rules and exposure to models, it is presumed, will result in good writing or at least correct writing.

Students' Role

Students examine the models presented and conform as closely as possible to them. They are to learn the rules of good writing: grammar, usage, mechanics, and spelling. Students are assigned topics within the genre specified. The teacher is the audience for writing. Students are expected to correct the errors their teachers have identified. This is often called revision, though it falls far short of that goal. Students are often passive recipients of whatever expert knowledge is delivered to them by their teachers.

The Result

The traditional approach has many problems: it takes ownership out of the hands of students; it limits the audience for writing; it focuses on error as a measure of achievement; it fosters a negative attitude toward writing; it reduces writing to a dull routine; it places students in a passive role; it avoids risk; and it concedes serious writing to the "more gifted" students—a fictional aristocracy.

Why have teachers stuck with the traditional approach? First, a viable alternative has only existed for a score of years. The writing process has just begun to take root in American schools. Even so, the traditional approach has lost considerable ground. Second, change is difficult and support scarce. I believe teachers are willing to change, but they need a support system. They need workshops, like-minded colleagues, university courses, administrative encouragement. Very often they do not get the support they need.

Some critics think the major weakness of the traditional approach is that it elevates form over substance. I disagree, though this is a serious deficiency indeed. I believe the most devastating outcome of the traditional approach is that it teaches children to hate writing. A negative attitude toward writing smothers talent in the crib. Few experiences in life are as melancholy as talent thwarted, dreams unrealized, potential ignored.

Teachers are creative problem solvers. They are used to overcoming limitations imposed upon them. Many teachers rise above the limitations of the traditional approach. They infuse their own higher standards into writing instruction; they integrate elements of process writing with traditional writing; they care so strongly about their students that approach matters less; they teach from the heart. I salute those teachers who have found ways to teach writing effectively, in spite of the limitations that the traditional approach imposes.

The following piece was written by a ten-year-old English lad. His teacher knew that Paul's piece was exceptional because of its powerful use of metaphor. She displayed it, commented thoughtfully on it, and shared it with a visitor. Though a follower of the traditional approach to writing, this excellent teacher knew good writing when she saw it, and she had the wisdom to recognize its substantive merit while tolerating, for the time being, its minor mechanical deficiencies.

Bird

You glide and swoop through the air performing endless feats of acrobatics. You are a graceful creature who has the whole world at your feet. Out of the forest you fly your feathers, some smooth some fluffy hold your body in the air. You are the earths eye witness to the everyday events. You perch on the wires like a human would wait at a railway station, waiting for the right time to take off for the south and the warmth.

Ten, nine, eight, seven, six, five, four, three, two, one and a cloud of feathered creatures lifts into the sky like a cloud of locusts swarming to the crop of warmth. Over the sea, over the ocean your body flys. A ship sounds a warning as the cotton wool fog closes in. You see an ice berg the ship does not and the sea is the scene of death again. The fog clears and you see land a magnetic impulse tells you that this is your destination. You can feel the warmth of the friendliness of your new home.

Paul, Age 10

GRAVES' WRITING PRINCIPLES

Donald Graves is largely responsible for spreading the gospel of the writing process. He has done more than anyone to popularize process writing throughout America, Canada, Australia, New Zealand, and England. His students, associates, and followers have also played an important role. Murray (1985), Calkins (1994), and Atwell (1998) have been especially influential. Graves is a modest, generous, and thoughtful man, and I've no doubt he is more than willing to share the honors. Still, the major credit belongs to Graves.

Key principles of process writing were first articulated as a coherent system in Graves' (1983) classic book, *Writing: Teachers and Children at Work.* I have outlined six principles of process writing that Graves describes in his books and other writings.

Writing Time

Over a decade ago, I heard Graves say that if you don't schedule writing four days a week for 40 minutes, you might as well not write at all. He still holds to the substance of that remark: "If students are not engaged in writing at least four days out of five, and for a period of thirty-five to forty minutes, beginning in first grade, they will have little opportunity to learn to think through the medium of writing. Three days a week are not sufficient" (Graves, 1994, p. 104). This is sound advice, and there is good reason for it. Children who do not write daily cannot get into the rhythm of writing. They cannot rehearse their ideas for writing because they cannot depend on writing regularly. Oh, a few students might survive on an irregular schedule of writing, but the majority of students will suffer.

Modeling

Graves (1983) gives this advice about modeling: "Children need to hear the teacher speak aloud about the thinking that accompanies the process: topic choice, how to start the piece, lining out, looking for a better word, etc. Children merely select those elements from the teacher's composing that are relevant to their own writing" (p. 43). Teachers must write with their children, for they are the models. The teacher who can say, "I write, and this is how I do it" has credibility. Such teachers can also say to students who complain that writing is hard, "You're right, writing *is* hard, but it has many pleasures."

Model writing in a variety of ways. Write at your desk for ten minutes during journal time, and occasionally share your writing. Write on chart paper, transparencies, or the chalkboard to illustrate writing skills. A writing teacher can say, for example, "Here are three leads to a story I'm working on. Which one do you like best?" Or, bring in a poem you have written at home and share it. It's good for students to know that the classroom is not the only place where writing takes place. Writing enhances teachers' credibility because it shows they are players not just arrangers.

There are many ways to model writing. Andrew's teacher, Ms. Amy Doty, writes poems and stories and shares them with her students.

Ownership

Graves (1983, 1994) believes children must own their writing. This is why children need to choose their own writing topics. One reason for choosing their own topics is that it places ownership in their hands rather than in the hands of assigners of writing. Graves (1994) says, "When children write every day they don't find it as difficult to choose topics. If a child knows she will write again tomorrow, her mind can go to work pondering her writing topics. Choosing a topic once a week is difficult. The moment for writing suddenly arrives and the mind is caught unprepared" (p. 106).

Graves (1994) has modified his earlier views on topic choice, allowing for more assigned writing than he had earlier recommended. He now believes that "Sometimes topic assignments are helpful and even necessary. Students do make bad choices and experience writer's block, or they need to shift to new topics after exhausting their usual few" (p. 108). While it is important to allow as much topic choice as possible, it is desirable for teachers to retain some control as well. Many teachers solve this dilemma by allowing topic choice within the parameters of specified genres, goals, and subject matter.

Janice Conroy, a first grade teacher, starts with assigned topics, provides scaffolding in the initial phases of writing, and gradually moves into student chosen writing topics. She describes her first steps in the "Voices" piece.

VOICES FROM THE CLASSROOM: Janice Conroy

Assigned Topics Versus Choice

Each year, I start the first day of school with a journal entry. Many of my students have had no experience with writing. So when preparing my first graders to write, I start by modeling how to use pencil and paper. I model by drawing lines on the chalkboard and demonstrating where to put the date and where to begin the first sentence.

I have heard the argument that assigning writing topics is bad. I have found, however, that it is not only good but necessary for beginning writers. I choose a topic and give my students most of the words to put in their first journal entry. Otherwise, they get frustrated.

I teach them how to invent the spelling of the words they need by modeling. I model how to say the word they want to spell and how to write the letter-sounds they hear. True, this is a controlled writing exercise, but it helps the students begin writing during their first days in school. As children gain experience in writing, I encourage them to choose their own writing topics.

Conferencing

Conferences are a crucial component of Graves' approach to writing instruction: "The purpose of the writing conference is to help children teach you about what they know so that you can help them more effectively with their writing" (Graves, 1994, p. 59). Graves' perspective is that children know things about their writing that the teacher does not know. Since conducting an effective conference requires understanding children's perspective, questions and conversation must reflect their perspective: *What are you writing about? What have you written so far? What will you write next?* Teaching works best when we observe learning from the child's perspective.

Conferences are dynamic in Graves' model. Some are formally scheduled and pertain to predetermined objectives. Others are roving and spontaneous, intended to provide on-the-spot encouragement and guidance. Some conferences are peer directed. Conferences, whether teacher or peer directed, provide an outside audience for writing. The writer gets an opportunity to see how an audience reacts to what is written. "Remember, the main purpose of the conference is to encourage the student to show you what he knows and gain a clear picture of what he will write next. I concentrate on *flow* for the student and *learning* for me" (Graves, 1994, p. 62).

Revising

Graves (1994) believes revision is central to writing. Writing evolves through revision; writers establish content through revision. Few writers, including profes-

Skill in revising is achieved through practice and instruction. Danny is in the early stages of learning to revise. Ms. Retell asked Danny a few questions about his piece. She listened carefully to his replies and suggested he might want to add a few details. Adding is the easiest step in revision. Later, he can move on to the more difficult revision skills of deleting and rearranging.

sional writers, are able to produce finished writing without going through successive drafts. Successive drafts help writers discover what they have to say and how to say it. As they revise successive drafts, writers polish their writing and correct faults in grammar, punctuation, and spelling, though this is seldom in any specific order, nor need it be.

Skill in revising is achieved through practice and instruction. Graves (1994) points out that, "Children don't suddenly begin to revise during writing time. They need guidance" (p. 226). Teachers need to instruct children about the operations of revision—adding, deleting, rearranging, substituting. Mini-lessons, conferences, and teacher modeling are three instructional options.

Sharing and Publishing

Sharing and publishing writing is central to Graves' philosophy of writing. Graves (1994) says, "What authors of any age need most is attentive listeners" (p. 133). Sharing and publishing can take many forms in addition to the Author's Chair. Sharing can occur in small groups or whole class sessions; it can be posting writing on a bulletin board; it can be the publication of books, newsletters, or magazines; it can be communication on the Internet. There are many alternatives for sharing and publishing, and teachers can decide for themselves what types of sharing and publishing work best.

Graves cautions that much of what passes for sharing in classrooms lacks vitality. Graves (1994) recommends rethinking the goals and procedures of the Author's Chair, though he retains his belief in its importance. Praise is vital, but routine, insincere, or unearned praise diminishes its value. Careful listening and thoughtful response to writing can be modeled by the teacher because the teacher's example is crucial.

Publishing writing in the classroom often creates minor problems which teachers have to solve. In her diary piece, Ms. DeWard discusses a publishing problem that arose in her fourth grade classroom and describes her attempts to solve it.

A TEACHER'S DIARY: Jennifer DeWard

A few weeks ago I was stressed out about how long it takes to help some students revise their writing in preparation for publishing. An experienced colleague told me that not everything that is written has to be published. I talked with my students today about not publishing all of their writing. Then I asked, "What do you think about this idea?" Some students said they like drawing illustrations too much to give up publishing. Others said they still wanted to publish their writing in book form so that it could become part of our classroom library. Only a few students seemed interested in this option. One student said his writing is so sloppy that it takes too long to recopy for publication. I suspect that others will choose not to publish a piece in the next few months.

Next year I plan on giving students the option of publishing or not publishing right from the start. However, I can already envision a problem. What happens if some students never want to publish their work. I have time to think about it, so there is no need to get stressed out now.

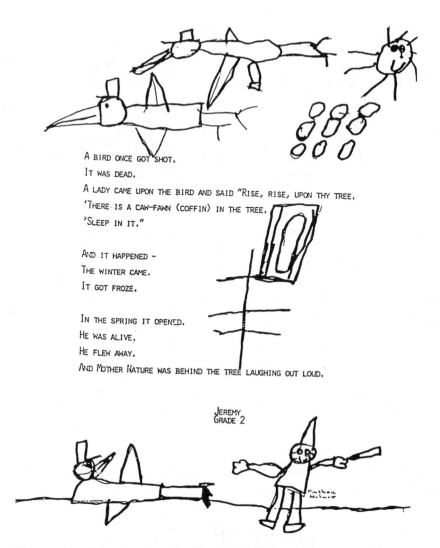

A BIRD ONCE GOT SHOT.

IT WAS DEAD.

A LADY CAME UPON THE BIRD AND SAID "RISE, RISE, UPON THY TREE.

'THERE IS A CAW-FAWN (COFFIN) IN THE TREE.

'SLEEP IN IT."

AND IT HAPPENED –

THE WINTER CAME.

IT GOT FROZE.

IN THE SPRING IT OPENED.

HE WAS ALIVE.

HE FLEW AWAY.

AND MOTHER NATURE WAS BEHIND THE TREE LAUGHING OUT LOUD.

JEREMY
GRADE 2

Figure 2.1 Poem by Jeremy Simmons, Grade 2 with drawing.

Jeremy wrote the poem in Figure 2.1, illustrated it, and shared it with his classmates. I think you'll agree that it is rather a remarkable piece of writing for a second grader.

SUMMARY OF GRAVES' WRITING PROCESS PRINCIPLES

1. Writing time: Frequent writing practice is essential. Graves recommends a minimum of 40 minutes a day four times a week

2. Modeling: Writers must have models. Teachers can provide models of writing through texts and personal example.

3. Ownership: Children should choose their own topics, and teachers should avoid substituting their ideas in place of children's ideas.

4. Conferencing: Children need to talk about their writing with their teacher and other members of the writing community.

5. Revising: Through revision, writers discover what they have to say and learn the skills needed for effective writing.

6. Sharing and publishing: Writers need an audience to hear or read what they have to say.

CAMBOURNE'S CONDITIONS FOR ACQUIRING LITERACY

Brian Cambourne (1988), an Australian educator, describes a "natural" theory of how children learn literacy in his book, *The Whole Story: Natural Learning and the Acquisition of Literacy in the Classroom.* As a young teacher, Cambourne puzzled over his observation that students who had difficulty learning concepts associated with reading and writing learned complex knowledge in their everyday world. Traditional models of learning tended to explain failure as a neurological impairment, learning disability, or cultural deficiency or some combination of these three. Cambourne rejected these "deficit" theories of learning because they did not explain why children who failed in school, nevertheless, learned complex knowledge in the more natural settings of the everyday world.

Having rejected traditional explanations for school failure, Cambourne looked for a better explanation. He noted that virtually all children learn their native language without difficulty. Language learning, it is generally thought, is facilitated by two interacting factors—biological inheritance and environmental conditions. Cambourne (1995) asked two questions: (1) If oral language is acquired in a natural setting so successfully, what are the conditions that make it so successful? (2) Can these conditions be translated into classroom pedagogy for learning to read and write? Cambourne believes they can.

Cambourne (1995) derived eight principles of learning by observing children in natural settings. He defines *conditions* as: ". . . particular states of being (doing, behaving, creating), as well as being a set of indispensable circumstances that co-occur and are synergistic in the sense that they both affect and are affected by each other" (p. 184). The eight conditions Cambourne identified are: immersion, demonstration, engagement, expectations, responsibility, employment, approximation, and response. Cambourne's eight conditions are described below.

Immersion

Children are immersed in their native language. They are plunged into the world of speech. Immersion in one's native language is a constant condition of normal living, and unless some unusual circumstance intervenes, such as deafness, success is inevitable. Cambourne believes that learning to read and write ought to occur in a similar way. Children should be surrounded by and saturated with written language. When immersion occurs in a "natural" setting, the presumption is that this will have the same beneficial influence on learning to read and write that it has on learning oral language.

Demonstration

Children are constantly surrounded by thousands of demonstrations of oral language. The baby points to its bottle and father says, "You want your bottle, do you? Here it is, Amy." From this and countless other demonstrations, children learn the meanings and functions of language. Children learn how language works and how to work language to fulfill their needs. Constant interactions and demonstrations with parents, peers, and siblings provide the raw data from which extrapolations about language emerge. Learning to read and write can proceed on a similar strategy. Shared writing, modeled writing, and language experiences are examples of how demonstrations can aid learning to read and write. From these shared experiences, children see how written language works, how problems are solved, how meaning is expressed, and how conventions support the written message.

Biz Smith Williamson explains, in the "Voices" piece, how she demonstrates writing concepts that she wants her kindergarten children to learn through mini-lessons.

VOICES FROM THE CLASSROOM: Biz Smith Williamson

Mini-Lessons

My students write every day for at least ten minutes. Three to four days a week they spend about 30–40 minutes writing during writing workshop.

I usually begin with a mini-lesson. Most often my mini-lessons are presented to the entire class. However, if some of my students have already mastered the skill I'm teaching, I encourage them to work on a piece of their writing. As I listen to the students read their stories, I note areas where they need help, and I plan mini-lessons from observations I have made.

One mini-lesson I recently taught was entitled, "Andthenitis." My students were writing interesting stories, but many of them were beginning sentences with, *And then.* I told them that there was a bug flying around our room and it was causing an epidemic among authors. The authors were coming down with, *"Andthenitis."* I displayed several anonymous pieces of work on the overhead that illustrated the overuse of *And then.* I had already received permission from the authors whose work I shared. I explained that in order to make writing more interesting and varied, they needed other alternatives. I gave them a list of alternatives and asked them to glue the list into their writing journals. I taught them to refer to the list when they needed an alternative to *"Andthenitis."*

Engagement

Cambourne (1995) says, "Immersions and demonstrations are necessary conditions for learning to occur, but they are not sufficient" (p. 185). Students must be involved in their learning, attracted to it, occupied with it. Children learn to speak because they see its relevance. Learning to talk enables children to acquire and do the things they want or need. Engagement requires attention and purpose. We see how naturally this occurs in play and other informal settings. For example, in a natural setting, such as a playground, no one needs to set a purpose or urge children to attend; children do it for themselves.

Classrooms, however, do not have the "natural" ambience of playgrounds, nor do they have the same freedom. Literacy instruction takes place in classrooms where a modicum of structure is required. The ambience of a playground setting, "natural" thought it may be, might work against literacy instruction. On the other hand, it is possible to make reading and writing engaging and informal. The British Infant School Movement of the 1970s and the more recent Whole Language Movement were laudable, and often successful, attempts to move toward more "natural" instructional environments.

Expectations

At six months, Andy said *Duh,* or some such sound, and Dad pounced on this utterance like it was a golden nugget: "Hear that. Andy said *Dad*—clear as a bell." Mom and Dad expect Andy to learn to talk "Just like them." No Las Vegas odds maker would bet against it because Andy undoubtedly will do just that. It is close to a 100 percent certainty that whether Mom and Dad are from Austin or Boston, Andy will soon utter sounds, words, and sentences like those in which he is immersed. Mom and Dad not only expect this to happen, they believe it is inevitable. Parents, siblings, playmates, everyone in Andy's speech community, conveys the expectation that he will learn to speak his native language. And, so he will.

Good teachers convey similar expectations to their students: "You will learn to read and write in this classroom." The message may be subtle; it may be conveyed through personality, manner, tone, word, and deed. Good teachers convey their expectations without discrimination. The message is not just for bright students, white students, suburban students, rich students. It must be for all students. Expectation is a necessary but insufficient condition for learning. Nevertheless, it is a powerful and necessary condition.

Responsibility

Learners need to make their own choices, control their own learning, and take responsibility for them. Cambourne (1995) believes that everyday discourse provides consistent language demonstrations that: "(a) are always in a context that supports the meaning being transacted; (b) always serve a relevant purpose; (c) are usually wholes of language; and (d) are rarely (if ever) arranged according to some predetermined sequence" (p. 185). From these premises, Cambourne advances the theory that literacy learning should operate on similar premises. In his view, literacy instruction should be natural, whole, relevant, and meaningful. Instruction cannot be sequenced in predetermined partial bites, but must occur in "natural" wholes that are relevant and meaningful to the learner. From Cambourne's premises, one can deduce that a Whole Language or a Language Experience Approach best describes Cambourne's sense of appropriate literacy instruction.

Employment

Learning requires practice. Practice, or employment as Cambourne prefers, must include social interaction with other language users and independent practice. These two types of practice help children gain control of the conventional forms of language. Cambourne argues that purpose, relevance, and appropriate contexts occur naturally and inevitably in oral language learning. Readers and writers need similar kinds of practice. Emphasis should be on purpose and meaning rather than form. It is assumed that conventions will be learned with sufficient practice of the right sort. Just as oral language practice occurs naturally, constantly, and regularly, so reading and writing must be similarly practiced.

Approximation

Children use oral language from birth and do so in meaningful and purposeful ways before they are in full control of all language conventions. Indeed, children use language before they know any conventions at all. First utterances are probably random and definitely uncertain. First utterances are always approximations of wholes. Partial sounds stand for full words; single words stand for full sentences. No one censors this use of language because it is incomplete. Indeed, attempts are nearly always rewarded. Early language use is treated as meaningful and relevant. Often it is considered wondrous and lovely. This encouraging environment makes risk taking safe. Gradually, incomplete language is replaced, gaps are filled, conventions mastered. Immature language is left behind. It takes only six to nine years to acquire the complete oral language of the dominant speech community.

Accepting approximation as an instructional philosophy can benefit learning to read and write. For example, first graders have a large oral vocabulary but a minuscule spelling vocabulary. Invented spelling, approximations of correct spelling, enables young writers to use their wealth of oral language to leverage early reading and writing. Immature use of the conventions of written language should be accepted for the same reason. Meaningful writing during the primary years is hindered unless approximations are accepted. Waiting until a full repertoire of written language conventions are complete hinders and delays reading and writing, and much that is beneficial about early reading and writing is irrevocably lost.

Response

Feedback is essential in early language learning. If feedback is not given, language learning may be delayed or damaged. Children need human models to complete the incomplete, expand one- and two-word utterances, interpret approximation of words. When response is information laden and nonthreatening, language learning proceeds well. Effective response fosters growth and a healthy attitude toward language. Effective response is also essential in learning to read and write. Response includes supportive instruction, scaffolding as it is sometimes called, as well as corrective, informative, and appreciative commentary. Children need an answer to the unarticulated question, "How am I doing?"

SUMMARY OF CAMBOURNE'S EIGHT PRINCIPLES OF LEARNING

1. Immersion: Saturate children with written language much as they are saturated and surrounded by oral language.
2. Demonstration: Provide demonstrations of reading and writing through shared writing, modeled writing, and language experiences.
3. Engagement: Children must be involved in their learning, attracted to it, and occupied with it.
4. Expectations: Through personality, manner, word, and deed convey to children the idea that success is inevitable.
5. Responsibility: Encourage children to make their own choices, control their own learning, and take responsibility for them.
6. Employment: Learning requires practice that includes social interaction with other language users as well as independent practice.
7. Approximation: Learning occurs gradually. Through approximations incomplete language is replaced, gaps filled, and conventions mastered.
8. Response: Feedback through response is essential. Provide supportive instruction, scaffolding, corrective, informative, and appreciative commentary.

Conclusion

Cambourne's ideal classroom would have these characteristics. Teachers would create a "natural" environment similar to the "natural" environment in which oral language is learned. While the classroom might appear chaotic, it would have structure. Children would write regularly, work cooperatively with one another, respond responsibly to their own and others' writing. Reading, writing, spelling, listening, talking would be integrated. Teachers as well as students would model writing. Children would be immersed in written language from every sensible perspective. Children would know what's expected of them as they engage responsibly in their work. Written language would be learned through approximation. The conventions of written language would be learned and applied over the course of time.

IDEAS FOR WRITING

1. Writing leads. A lead is the opening sentence of a piece of writing. Leads are especially important in newspaper writing and stories. A lead is intended to "hook" the interest of the reader and keep the reader reading. Choose three stories or books and read the opening sentence. Which opening sentence did you like best? Why? Then write three or four leads to a story you want to write, or rewrite the lead sentence in a story you have already written.

2. Giving advice. Parents and teachers love to give advice, and there are newspaper columnists who make big bucks giving advice to readers. Below is a letter written to an advice-giving columnist. Answer Confused's letter:

Dear Gabby:

   I can't seem to get interested in doing my homework. I suppose it's important, but I have so many other things to do. I have favorite TV shows to watch, two dogs to feed, and I must read my magazines and catalogs. What would you advise me to do?

   Confused in Connecticut

3. Writing song lyrics. Lyrics are the words to a song, and they often tell a story. Rap, popular, folk, and country music are examples of types of songs that usually have lyrics to go with the music. Sometimes a song lyric will rhyme, like rhyming poetry. But a song lyric need not rhyme. Write the lyrics for a song based on your favorite type of music.

4. Imaginative writing. "It has been reported that Bill Bugle, Principal of Madison High School, was seen early this morning walking his pet cheetah in the school parking lot." Imagine you had read this sentence in the newspaper. Write the rest of the story.

5. Collaborative writing. It's a challenge to write with another person. Sometimes it makes things easier, sometimes harder. But it is an interesting experience in any case. Choose a partner and write a collaborative story, poem, or essay.

6. Fast write. Sometimes you just can't think of an idea to write about. In such cases, sit down and write for ten minutes about whatever thoughts are running through your mind, whether or not they seem suitable for writing. You can even write about not having anything to write about.

7. Stories do not have to be told in words. Cave dwellers wrote with pictures. Cave writings are stories about hunting, seeking food, daily living. Draw a series of pictures that tell a story. This could be a picture story you made up, or you can retell a story you already know, for example: *Frankenstein's Monster, The Bride of Frankenstein, Star Wars, E. T. Come Home, Home Alone, Cinderella, The Three Little Pigs*. After you have drawn your pictures, tell your picture story to your classmates.

REFLECTION AND SUMMARY

Reflection

Graves (1994) found that, ". . . if students had *one* good teacher of writing in their entire career, irrespective of grade level, they could be successful writers" (p. 15). I believe that one teacher can make a difference. I believe that teachers can establish expectations that children will live up to. Children have potential of which they may be unaware. Apprise them of their potential, and they may exceed your highest expectations.

Are you inclined to look too closely at grammar, spelling, and punctuation as a measure of writing achievement? This is like looking at the ground when the sky is filled with stars. As there is no shortage of stars in the sky, so there is no shortage of children with wonderful ideas. But if you do not look, you will not see. Seek out wonderful ideas in your children. When a child surprises you with a thoughtful remark or piece of writing, say something like this: "What wonderful ideas you have, Angie." Such a remark, sincere and deserved, may do more to nourish Angie's writing than identifying a thousand errors. My own experience tells me this is so. Mrs. Anderson was that *one* teacher for me. I want to be that *one* teacher for my students. Don't you?

Summary

1. The writing process includes a set of theories, procedures, and activities which emphasize the operations, changes, and procedures by which writing is accomplished.

   - Writing is recursive. The operations of writing occur and reoccur in a nonlinear fashion.
   - Process writing implies three concepts: (1) a particular method of doing writing, (2) a number of operations involved in doing writing, and (3) a continuing development of writing that involves many changes.
   - Product is the ultimate goal of writing, and effective writing process can lead to a better written product.
   - Critiques of the writing process reveal weaknesses as well as strengths. No viable alternative to the writing process has appeared on the horizon.

2. The traditional approach to writing is product oriented. It is based on a correctness model. The traditional approach emphasizes models and mastery of the rules of grammar, usage, mechanics, and spelling.

   - The teacher's responsibility is to provide models of good writing, evaluate writing, and teach the rules of grammar, usage, mechanics, and spelling.
   - Students are expected to study models of good writing, learn the rules, and correct errors identified by the teacher.
   - Traditional writing has resulted in some students learning to write well, but most do not.

3. Graves is responsible for popularizing the writing process. He was the first to articulate a coherent system describing the writing process. He proposed six principles of effective writing instruction:

   - Children must write regularly—four times a week for 40 minutes.
   - The teacher writes and models writing.
   - Children own their writing, primarily through topic choice.
   - Teacher and peer conferences help nurture writing growth.

- Revision is the key to successful writing.
- Publishing and sharing are crucial to motivating writing.

4. Cambourne likens learning to read and write to learning oral language—it is a natural process. He identified eight conditions of natural learning: immersion, demonstration, engagement, expectations, responsibility, employment, approximation, and response.

QUESTIONS FOR REFLECTIVE THINKING

1. How can an overemphasis on the written product be destructive to good writing?

2. How is the traditional approach to writing different from the writing process approach?

3. What is meant by "owning" one's writing? Why is it a central concept in Graves' work?

4. Many writers, including Graves, argue that revision is the key to effective writing. Why might this be so?

5. What is the "deficit" theory of learning? Why did Cambourne reject it? What did he propose in its place?

6. Choose one of Camborne's eight principles that interest you. Describe its characteristics and give an example of this principle as it applies to learning.

7. Research tells us that many children do not learn to write effectively. Why do you think this is so? What do you think can be done about it?

8. What did you learn about the writing process that you didn't know before you read this chapter?

9. What aspect of the writing process do you want to know more about? Where might you find the additional information you require?

10. What question(s) might you ask your teacher that will help clarify writing process issues you didn't fully understand?

11. Mini case study: You are teaching in a school equally divided between teachers who emphasize writing process and teachers who prefer the more traditional approach. How might you persuade your more traditional colleagues to adopt a more process oriented approach to writing?

REFERENCES

Applebee, A. N. (1986). "Problems in process approaches: Toward a reconceptualization of process instruction." In A. R. Petrosky and D. Bartholomae (Eds.), *The teaching of writing: Eighty-fifth yearbook of the National Society for the Study of Education*, Chicago: University of Chicago Press.

Atwell, N. (1998). *In the middle: New understandings about writing, reading, and learning*, 2nd ed. Portsmouth, NH: Boynton/Cook.

Calkins, L. (1994). *The art of teaching writing,* 2nd ed. Portsmouth, NH: Heinemann.

Cambourne, B. (1988). *The whole story: Natural learning and the acquisition of literacy in the classroom.* New South Wales: Ashton Scholastic, Gosford.

Cambourne B. (1995). "Toward an educationally relevant theory of literacy learning: Twenty years of inquiry." *The Reading Teacher,* Vol. 49, No. 3, 182–190.

Graves, D. (1983). *Writing: Teachers and children at work.* Portsmouth, NH: Heinemann.

Graves, D. (1994). *A fresh look at writing.* Portsmouth, NH: Heinemann.

Kane, T. S. (1988). *The new Oxford guide to writing.* Oxford: Oxford University Press.

Murray, D. (1985). *A writer teaches writing,* 2nd ed. Boston, MA: Houghton Mifflin Co.

Steiner, G. (1995). "The art of criticism II." *The Paris Review,* Winter, 1995, 43–102.

Tremmel, R. (1986). "Going back and paying attention: Solving the problem of the writing process." *Journal of Teaching Writing,* Spring, Vol. 5, No. 1.

CHAPTER 3
Prewriting: Creating a Plan

For all the planning, writers are surprised by what they write. At least
when the writing goes well. We expect and hope for the unexpected.

Donald Murray

A WRITER'S STORY

*Larry is five years old and in kindergarten. He draws and writes and these two pleasures
are as one to Larry. Ms. O'Brien is Larry's teacher. She believes that kindergarten kids can
write. She has a writing philosophy, the simplified version of which is: connect drawing to
writing; label children's drawings with words and sentences dictated by the children; encourage invented spelling for those who can make letter-sound connections; share writing
with parents, classmates, schoolmates, and community.*

*Larry loves to draw and he often writes a personal message on the drawings he pre-
sents to Ms. O'Brien. A while back he brought a lovely drawing to her. He explained the
story behind his drawing in these words: "This is a story about me and my sister. We're
riding horses. This is the trail we rode on." Larry's explanation included more detail than
he managed in his actual writing, which simply said, ye redg hrs—we're riding horses.
The drawing showed two children riding horses, trees, bushes, sky, and animals. Larry
brings a piece of writing to Ms. O'Brien just about every day. It is always a drawing and
often has a personally written message.*

*Larry doesn't think it's unusual that he can write. He came to school believing he
could, even though he knew perfectly well that he could not read. Ms. O'Brien can say
at any time, "Larry, why don't you go write me a story," and Larry will do so without
hesitation. But Ms. O'Brien doesn't say, "Larry, why don't you go get a book and
read." Larry doesn't yet communicate in that medium. But he can communicate in the
complex medium of drawn and written ideas and words. Larry wouldn't think of it this
way, but Ms. O'Brien does: "Larry is on his way to becoming a writer and a reader,"
she said.*

INTRODUCTION

Writing must be planned, as Murray says, still you hope for surprise, you hope for the unexpected. James Baldwin says something of this sort, as well: "You go into a book and you're in the dark, really. You go in with a certain fear and trembling. You know one thing. You know you will not be the same person when this voyage is over. But you don't know what is going to happen to you between getting on the boat and stepping off. And you have to trust that" (p. 94, Murray, 1990). Still we must plan our writing. Writers have given us much of what we treasure in our culture. Without writers, how would we experience the delicious fright as Long John Silver thumped behind us as our trembling fingers fumbled for the light switch? How would we travel with Gulliver in Lilliput or chase buffalo across the great plains on Appaloosa ponies? How would we imagine the knights and ladies of the round table or slay the fire-breathing dragon that had imprisoned our loved ones? Writers arouse imagination, raise goose-bumps on our arms. How do they do it? I can't answer that complex question, but I know that it starts with preparation, planning, collecting, organizing, journal notes, rehearsing—the hard work that precedes the actual drafting.

I have debated whether to call this chapter *prewriting* or *planning.* I ended up using both terms in the chapter heading. Planning may be the more inclusive term, but prewriting has a ring of familiarity among teachers that I wish to retain. The term *prewriting* gives the misleading impression that it deals only with what occurs prior to writing—that is its limitation. Actually, prewriting or planning occurs throughout the composing process. So, I have generally used the term prewriting, but it is important to understand that it stretches from the first thought one has about a piece of writing to the last act of producing a piece of writing.

REHEARSAL AND RESEARCH

Prewriting is planning, collecting, and organizing ideas and information prior to and throughout writing. There are two dimensions to prewriting. The first is rehearsal. It is largely invisible since it involves thinking, considering, and reflecting upon a topic. The second is research. It is visible and involves physical activities such as reading, making notes, and organizing information.

Rehearsal, Mental Preparation for Writing

Sean shed his backpack hastily, and hurried to Ms. DeClerck's desk. Holding aloft a piece of paper he announced, "I thought of a poem in bed last night. This morning I wrote it down. Would you like to read it?" Sean's writing rehearsal is no surprise because Sean and his classmates write poetry regularly in Ms. DeClerck's third grade classroom. This is Sean's poem:

> Nap
> Closed eyes
> Day or night
> Rest.

Rehearsal is mental preparation for a performance. Writing rehearsal is the mental preparation for writing that occurs prior to writing, getting ready to perform as a writer. Rehearsal may occur at any time prior to actually writing and, of course, it occurs in the spaces and pauses between one sentence or paragraph and another. Rehearsal takes place moments or months, hours or even years before writers put a single word on paper. They refine and reject, nurse and nudge their topics about until they are ready to write. Rehearsal sometimes involves broad issues such as choosing a topic or plot. More often it deals with narrower issues such as rehearsing a lead or planning a story event. Once writing has commenced, rehearsal of characters, conversation, words, continues throughout the construction of a piece.

How do you get rehearsal started among children who have little experience in rehearsing for their writing? Rehearsal is a habit that evolves as one gains experience in writing. It develops in conjunction with writing frequency. When writing is infrequent, rehearsal habits have little opportunity to evolve. Consequently, writing must be a dependable part of the daily routine. Only then are children able to develop dependable rehearsal habits. Rehearsal can be modeled, described, and encouraged. Teachers can share their rehearsal techniques, and once established, children can share their rehearsal habits with one another.

Sean's poem evolved within a context of excellent writing instruction provided by Ms. DeClerck. She has created a writing community where rehearsal for writing is a natural outcome of the writing context her children experience every day. In her diary comments Ms. Jennifer DeWard talks about a discussion she had with her fourth graders about mentally rehearsing for a writing topic she had assigned for the coming week—Thanksgiving week.

A TEACHER'S DIARY: Jennifer DeWard

Next week my students will be writing a funny piece from a turkey's point of view. They will write a letter to a family explaining why he or she should not be eaten for Thanksgiving dinner. Today I mentioned the assignment to my class, and explained that I wanted them to "rehearse" in their heads what they might say next week when they actually write the letter. I told the students that good writers often spend time planning ideas and thoughts in their heads before they begin to write. Many students seemed receptive to the idea, while many others seemed totally confused by the notion. That's OK. If I can get just a few students to mentally rehearse their writing, then I will be successful in my endeavor. One student asked me if she could jot down some ideas for her writing over the weekend, and I praised her for the wonderful idea. I am anxious to see how my students' writing will turn out next week.

Research, Physical Preparation for Writing

Research is as crucial to effective planning as mental rehearsal. Writers conduct research in libraries or the Internet, searching through books and files, journals and magazines until they have located useful sources. They may make notes and organize them into maps or outlines to guide their writing. Prewriting is guided by physical and mental preparation. There is constant interaction between mental rehearsal for writing and physical preparation for writing. Angus Wilson, a British writer, was asked if he took notes: "Books of them," he said. "The gestatory period before I start to write is very important to me. That's when I'm persuading myself of the truth of what I want to say, and I don't think I could persuade my readers unless I'd persuaded myself first" (Cowley, 1958, p. 256).

The Mecca of the intellectual life is the library, although the Internet is rapidly becoming, for many has already become, the electronic alternative to the library. Nevertheless, for many the library remains the intellectual center on which research ultimately depends. Libraries can arouse in children a sense of wonder and joy. Once the library is established as central in the intellectual life of a child, its influence will never disappear. The writer, Sherwood Anderson, describes how he remembered the library of the schoolmaster who first encouraged Anderson's interest in books: "My imagination has built the little study of the small-town schoolmaster into a kind of palace. Now, in my fancy, the room becomes huge. Once, many years later, I was in the library of the Emperor Napoleon, in his palace at Fontainebleau. Now, in my fancy, the schoolmaster's study seems rather like that" (Gilbar, 1989, p. 44). Teachers can help make the library central in the intellectual lives of children. The first task is to awaken imagination. Reading to children is nearly always a good place to start.

An adequate library will have general books, special references books, magazines, journals, computers, and other resources. Children should become familiar with dictionaries that deal with one specific subject such as musicians, writers, and athletes. They should learn that libraries have almanacs where general information on weather, history, and hobbies can be obtained. They should be taught how to pursue topics in multi-volume encyclopedias. Children should learn to manipulate card catalogs or computers to locate books by author, subject, or title. These are a few of the technical skills children must learn about libraries or libraries will forever remain alien space. But there are even more important things to be learned about libraries. Libraries are palaces in which children can seek their destinies and pursue their dreams. As a young boy, Isaac Bashevis Singer, the Nobel prize winning author, walked into a library in Poland and said to the librarian, "I want to know the secret of life." The kindly librarian found two books, one in Hebrew and the other in Yiddish, and said encouragingly to young Isaac, "If a boy wants to learn the secret of life, you have to accommodate him." So began a life devoted to the written word. It started as the dream of a shy boy seeking knowledge in a palace for books, a library.

Professional writers may spend more time collecting information and planning their writing than they do actually writing. John Grisham, one of America's most popular writers, writes his books from a 40 to 50 page outline, which can take years to develop. Writing the book itself can take as few as 90 days (N.Y. Times, April 17, p. B2). Murray (1985) discovered that he spent three-fifths of his time collecting information and planning his writing. While this pattern is not necessarily appropriate for young writers, they should learn early that libraries are wonderful places to spend time.

Mental and physical preparation for writing is undoubtedly more sophisticated for experienced writers than for inexperienced. Children need time to grow into the skills needed to perform mental and physical preparation for writing. But it is never too early for writers to learn about these two dimensions of prewriting.

TIME FOR PLANNING AND COMPLETING WRITING

Just as a field produces better crops when it lies fallow for a season, so writing may be enriched by allowing time for an idea to lie fallow before it is developed into a story, poem, or essay. Of course, delay can sometimes be merely an excuse for not writing at all, but good writing is seldom produced on command. There are forces of resistance to writing. They are powerful but not necessarily destructive, as Murray (1982) points out: "When I get an idea for a poem or an article or a talk or a short story, I feel myself consciously draw away from it. I seek procrastination and delay. There must be time for the seed of an idea to be nurtured in the mind" (p. 33). But just as there are forces of resistance to writing, so there are forces of attraction that draw children toward writing. Three forces which attract are information, interest, and deadlines (Murray, 1985). These forces can be marshaled to get writers prepared to write.

Information

Information is the straw that binds the mortar of writing. Whether writing topics are chosen or assigned, children must have access to information. As writers prepare their minds with information, interest in the topic accelerates. As the mind is saturated with information on a topic, drafting begins to flow. We want children to respect accurate information and to appreciate the quality it adds to their writing. Information is as necessary for fiction as it is for expository writing, though there is a tendency to think that information gathering is only relevant for expository writing.

Interest

Just as gas fuels an engine, so interest fuels the writer. Children are curious, but curiosity must be ignited, just as a spark plug ignites the fuel in an engine. Teachers can be that spark plug. Interest feeds a desire to get ideas on paper. But interest seldom arises spontaneously. Interest results from an interaction between curiosity and growing knowledge. Interest may lay dormant, like a smoldering fire, then suddenly leap into flame—the air of curiosity added to the fuel of information. Teachers can feed children's curiosity by providing information through discussion, reading aloud, independent reading, films, plays, music, and art.

Deadlines

Nothing concentrates the mind so readily as an approaching deadline. Without deadlines, little would ever get written. This is as true in the classroom as it is in the world of professional writers. Truman Capote seemed to appreciate the usefulness of deadlines. He said, "But I must say an iota of stress, striving toward deadlines, does me good" (Cowley, 1958, p. 292). Deadlines are useful external motivators. Deadlines can be set for completing certain pieces of writing or for moving writing from one stage of completion to another. One must be flexible in setting deadlines for children's writing. Some pieces can be worked on at leisure, no deadlines needed. Others may require deadlines so that objectives can be achieved. Deadlines serve a useful purpose when judiciously applied.

WHAT TO WRITE ABOUT: CHOOSING TOPICS

Pesaldena, a fifth grader, approached her teacher with the all too common question, "What can I write about, Ms. Elson?" Ms. Elson had heard this question before. She knew how to help Pesaldena, and she did, using some of the ideas discussed later in this section. There are many issues involved when asked, "What can I write about?" The question itself is controversial. Should children choose their own writing topics? Do children write better when they choose their own topics? Are assigned topics ever appropriate? Research has suggested some answers, but not definitively. There is reason to believe that self-selection results in more and better writing, but a conditional case can be made for assigning topics. This section examines the issues involved in assigned and self-selected writing topics.

Self-Selected Topics

Powerful writing does not stem from a teacher's bag of motivating topics, even if the topics are innovative and interesting. Powerful writing stems from a desire to make a personal statement. Children's best writing deals with what they know and what they care about. Calkins (1986) concurs, "Beneath layers of resistance, we have a primal need to write. We need to make our truths beautiful, and we need to say to others, 'This is me. This is my story, my life, my truth.' We need to be heard" (p. 5).

Encouraging children to make their own choices and statements will often result in more and better writing. Forcing topics on children without considering interest, knowledge, or personal commitment is unlikely to draw the best children have to offer (Graves, 1983, 1994; Clark, 1987). Having children select their own topics requires planning. You cannot say, "Write about what you want." Children are willing to choose their own topics, but they need preparation. Three ways of preparing children for choosing their own topics are topic lists, writer's journal, and content discussions.

Topic list: Fortunately, as children come into their own in writing, they generate their own topics. But at early stages of writing, measures for helping children choose topics are useful. Conduct a topic brainstorming session the first week of school or whenever necessary. Write the resulting list of topics on the board. Have children choose topics from the list to add to their own lists. Good writing topics often arise spontaneously during class discussions and writing conferences. When this happens, remind children to add topics that interest them to their lists. Early attention to topic selection will result in an abundance of potential writing topics.

Writer's journal: A writer's journal is a notebook for recording ideas, observations, and information. Some writers keep a journal in which they jot ideas for future reference. A journal can be a gold mine. One can enter the mine looking for nuggets: topics, scraps of conversation, ideas for stories. A journal can be informal, simply a place where dated notes are kept. It can also be made more elaborate by rewriting and organizing the notes in more complete form. How regularly children write in them, organize them, and use them is a matter of individual choice. Teachers can also keep journals and use them for writing as well as for modeling.

Content discussions: A third way to help children identify tropics is to connect writing to content subjects. Following a social studies lesson, for example, have children suggest a half-dozen possible writing topics. After reading a book aloud or following a science project, suggest two or three writing topics, and have children add a few of their own. As writing topics are suggested, list them on a chart. Encourage children to add topics from class-generated lists to their personal lists.

Assigned Topics

When children choose their topics, they usually already possess a spark of interest and some prior knowledge about the topic. This is the advantage of self-selected topics. Since assigned topics may not meet these two conditions, weak writing may result. This is why advocates of self-selection question assigned topics (Newkirk and Atwell, 1986; Calkins, 1994). Nevertheless, there are sound reasons why assigning topics may be useful, or even necessary.

First, writing helps children learn (Langer and Applebee, 1987). Rather than simply reading and memorizing science information, children can expand their scientific knowledge and retain more of it if they write about it. George Will, a political commentator, wrote a book about baseball. Will explained his curious choice of topic, saying, "I don't write to say what I know, I write to get to know things." Of course, Will selected his topic, but did so in order to learn more about baseball. Assigned writing expands knowledge, especially when teachers generate interest in the topic. Writing to learn is a sound reason for assigning writing in content subjects.

Second, when writing is assigned, there is nearly always room for student participation. Suppose you are studying Inca, Aztec, and Mayan civilizations. There is no shortage of topics from which children can choose: architecture, customs, religious rituals, dress, schooling, family life, roads, leaders, agriculture. For example, you might say, "I'm going to write four topics on the board. Choose one of these topics, but if none of them interests you, choose your own topic. Your topic must be related to our work on the Aztec, Mayan, and Inca civilizations. If you choose your own topic, let's talk about it before you start." Giving choice within a range of curricular goals increases the likelihood that both interest and prior knowledge will enter into children's topic selection.

Third, assigned writing prepares children for real-world academics. Writing is commonly assigned in high schools and colleges. Students are expected to research the assigned topic, but preparation is needed. When writing is assigned, the skills needed to gather and organize information should be taught. When this is not done, children's writing echoes the voice of the encyclopedia. Children copy from reference sources because they have no realistic alternative. Give them an alternative by teaching the skills needed to transform information into their own words and ideas.

AUDIENCE FOR WRITING

Some writers write to please themselves. William Faulkner is an example. Others imagine a broader audience. Children develop a sense of audience as they learn to write. Audience sensitivity is dulled when the teacher is the only audience.

Children can learn to please their teacher, but their sense of audience may not expand unless they have additional audiences for their writing.

Young children have difficulty with audience because their thinking centers around their own point of view (Piaget, 1955; Moffett, 1968). Children up to the age of seven or eight often act as though their readers think and feel as they do. So, part of the solution is cognitive and social maturation. Kroll (1978) suggests that, "We need to help children 'decenter'—to take the perspective of a reader—by structuring experiences that systematically challenge the children's assumptions that they are taking the reader's view into account (p. 830)."

Writing can be organized so that audience sensitivity is incorporated into the fabric of the writing program. Children learn to write for their readers when writing is shared within a school community and when writing is published. Peer conferences, where children listen to each other's writing, help writers learn how others perceive their work. The following exchange between Billy and his teacher illustrates the value of classmates as an audience:

Ms. Elson: When you write, who do you write for? Who do you think your audience is going to be? Do you think about that?

Billy: Yes, mostly I write for my teacher and some of the kids in school.

Ms. Elson: What kids do you keep in mind or think might read your writing?

Billy: Umm, Robbie, Ryan, Matt, Alexandro, and I think Peter or Andy. Mark likes to read 'em.

Ms. Elson: Mark J.?

Billy: Mark J. and Mark K. And Peter likes to read them and Frank. (Elson, 1990, p. 73)

Billy has access to an interested audience, and this leads to improved writing. Repetition, irrelevant detail, omission of essential information are often traceable to lack of audience sensitivity. Some ideas for developing audience sensitivity are suggested below.

DEVELOPING AUDIENCE SENSITIVITY

1. Through modeling, teach children to ask audience-centered questions: Who is going to read my story? What will they find interesting? How much detail do they need to know? Are my ideas clear? Have I chosen the right words?

2. Have children work together in groups to listen to each other's writing. These sessions can be informal or organized. Recall that Billy wrote in a classroom where he was free to consult his peers as and when necessary.

3. Have children write the same story for two different audiences. Fifth graders might, for example, write a story for their classmates, and then rewrite it to be read aloud to kindergarten children.

4. Have children imagine they are writing a description of the fall colors for a sighted and unsighted audience. Other exercises of this sort can be devised.

5. Have children write separate persuasive letters to Mom and Dad or Grandmother and Grandfather. Children know well that what appeals to one parent or grandparent does not work with another.

Writers, even those who profess to disregard audience, exhibit some degree of audience awareness, if nothing more than dreams of a huge royalty check awaiting them at the end of the rainbow. Children are not so crass as to dream of royalty checks, but they may well dream of becoming a writer. Truman Capote said that he knew by age ten that he wanted to be a writer. When children have access to appreciative audiences early, they are more likely to realize their dream of actually becoming a writer, whether professional or not.

CHOOSING A WRITING FORM

Writing takes many forms. An early prewriting task is to consider what writing form best serves the writer's purpose and audience. Unfortunately, choice of a writing form is often limited to a few traditional forms such as reports, letters, poems, and stories. Children are seldom encouraged, for example, to present a social studies report in the form of a rap or a song lyric. Yet, such an approach might prove motivating to a generation brought up on rap and rock and roll lyrics, forms with which children are more familiar than most adults. Children encounter many writing forms through reading, but have fewer opportunities to use diverse forms when writing.

Form influences content and organization. Third grade children include different kinds of information and present it differently when asked to write about the same topic in a story versus a report (Langer, 1985). Exposure to different writing forms adds variety and gives children opportunities to see how purpose and audience are related to form. For example, if a rap is used to present a message about peace, writers will have to consider that this form may appeal differently to teenagers than to adults. Writers might debate the question as to whether their message would work better as a play for one audience or as a rap for a different audience.

Two lists of writing forms are shown on page 66, traditional and nontradition.

TRADITIONAL WRITING FORMS

autobiographies	invitations	plays
biographies	journals	poems
book reports	letters	reports
books	mysteries	reviews
essays	myths	speeches
fables	news stories	skits
fairy tales	outlines	stories
folk tales	personal narratives	tall tales
interviews		

NONTRADITIONAL WRITING FORMS

advertisements	greeting cards	proverbs
book blurbs	jokes	raps
bumper stickers	maps	recipes
cartoons	menus	riddles
comics	obituaries	song lyrics
editorials	posters	telegrams

PREWRITING STRATEGIES

Prewriting strategies should stimulate ideas and motivate students to write. They should expand knowledge and develop thinking skills. They should give access to knowledge stored in memory and add new knowledge. Strategies should differ with children's age, writing experience, purpose, and the demands of the form. The strategies discussed include: drawing, talking, reading, observing, mapping, interviewing, brainstorming, and factstorming.

Drawing

Drawing has a beneficial influence on young children's writing (Dyson, 1986; Heimlich and Pittelman, 1986). Drawing is a particularly valuable prewriting activity for children in primary grades, and it can also be helpful for older children. Drawing increases writing fluency and stimulates ideas for writing. Young children often regard their drawings as a pictorial way of expressing narrative meanings, as interviews with young children show (Dyson, 1982, 1993).

As children draw, encourage talking aloud about the drawing. Record words and sentences on the drawings of children who are unable to write independently. As children master invented spellings, they can write their own messages to accompany their drawings. Drawing helps children recall written messages they might otherwise have forgotten and also helps dramatize the meaning the writer intends to convey. Jeni's drawing (Figure 3.1) dramatically illustrates her message that as the middle child she is "squshed in here." The drawing also reveals a tight connection between the written message and the drawing itself.

Talking

Talk is cheap, some say, but it is a valuable tool for writing. Three kinds of talk can be encouraged. First, encourage children to talk to themselves as they plan their writing, a barely audible whispering about their writing plans. Some writers talk to themselves as they write, a sort of inner speech that rises to the surface. Such speech is a form of monitoring thinking.

Second, organize opportunities for peer talk. Encourage children to talk informally to their classmates about drawings done in preparation for writing. Model how this may be done. Peer talk can be informal, but it can also be planned. Set aside short periods of time for small groups to discuss their writing plans.

Third, teacher-student talk helps children prepare for writing. Prewriting conferences help children confront the issues involved in selecting, narrowing, and developing a topic. The teacher's guidance is often crucial in getting children off to a proper start. Conferences can be conducted with the whole class, groups, or one-to-one.

Reading

When I think of loving to read, I often think of Francie, the young girl in Betty Smith's classic book, *A Tree Grows in Brooklyn.* Francie loved to write, and her passion for reading fed her passion for writing. Francie read everything. She planned to read all the books in the library, and so she started with the A's. She even planned to start over again when she had finished with the Z's. Francie loved the library, a shabby place, but to Francie it was a cathedral. Home with her books, she retreated to the fire escape to read, ". . . at peace with the world and happy as only a little girl could be with a fine book and a little bowl of candy, and all alone in the house, the leaf shadows shifted as the afternoon passed" (p. 21).

The following conversation between Ms. Elson and Mercedes, a fifth grade student, illustrates how reading can help writers make decisions about their writing.

MS. ELSON: Is "Boblo" your third draft? (Refers to published book)

MERCEDES: Um huh.

MS. ELSON: Okay, now I notice you did some cutting there.

MERCEDES: I decided to put it in a book with no chapters.

MS. ELSON: But you were experimenting at that point. Did that help?

MERCEDES: Yeah, it helped a lot and I looked in the other books like you told me to and looking through the books really helped me. And then I decided to put it into a book with no chapters.

you know I'm the
Middle child and
im Sqashed in here

Figure 3.1 Drawing and Writing Jeni, Age 6

Ms. Elson: Did you use books that former student authors had made or other
books by other authors?

Mercedes: By other writers and kid writers. Both.

Ms. Elson: And that helped?

Mercedes: Yes, a lot. Because it got me ideas and I decided my story wasn't
long enough for chapters.

Ms. Elson: And so what did you end up doing?

Mercedes: I decided to put it into a book with no chapters. (Elson, 1990, p. 71)

Reading to prepare for writing takes two forms: reading aloud and reading independently. Each has a powerful influence on writing. Reading aloud about sharks or dinosaurs, for example, will stimulate interest and provide the factual information needed to authenticate writing. Reading aloud often leads to independent reading. Children often read books that have recently been read aloud in class.

Encourage children to prepare for writing by reading. Show them how reading can provide the information they need to make their writing accurate and interesting. Show them how reading provides models for the poems, stories, and essays they choose to write. If children are having difficulty with story beginnings, have them read the first page or two of several books from the school or classroom library. Have them read and consider, for example, how the authors of the following books started their narratives: *Wind in the Willows* by Kenneth Grahame, *Johnny Tremain* by Esther Forbes, or *The Lion, the Witch, and the Wardrobe*, by C. S. Lewis. Then encourage them to try something similar.

Observing

Imagine yourself an observer in the sitting room of Sherlock Holmes' lodgings on 221B Baker Street, London. Holmes has just handed a worn billycock to Dr. Watson and asks him to examine it. Watson accepts the challenge and notes the following facts about the hat: it is a very large black derby much the worse for wear, worn felt, tallow stains, exceedingly dusty exterior, red silk lining, the smell of lime-cream, freshly cut hairs in the hat band, exterior cracked and discolored. Upon finishing his examination, Watson hands the hat back to Holmes, saying, "I can see nothing." Holmes chides Watson, "On the contrary, Watson, you can see everything. You fail, however, to reason from what you see. You are too timid in drawing your inferences."

The scene you have, in your imagination, observed is described in Sir Arthur Conan Doyle's, *The Adventure of the Blue Carbuncle.* The exchange between Holmes and Watson hints at an important lesson for writers. The good writer, like the good detective, must cultivate the skill of observation. Observation is the product of what the senses detect and what the brain deduces. The senses and the brain are partners in the enterprise of writing. The observant writer pays keen attention to detail, accurately perceives what is available to the senses, and makes bold inferences about what has been observed. What made Sherlock Holmes a great detective, and a favorite among mystery fans, was not his ability to observe, but rather his ability to draw inferences from observations.

"I mean, a writer doesn't really live, he observes." Nelson Algren, author of *The Man with the Golden Arm*, came to that conclusion about his life as a writer (Cowley, 1958, p. 241). Many writers agree with Algren's conclusion. Accurate observation is prerequisite to good writing, whether fiction or nonfiction. Writers learn to penetrate the inner chambers of what they observe. Teachers can help children observe their subjects more keenly by reading excerpts from literature which illustrate the observations mature writers have made in their stories. They will soon see, for example, that effective description goes beyond cataloging what is immediately available to the senses. Description takes many forms. It may be accomplished through straight-forward narrative, conversation, manner of dress, behavior, other people's reactions. James Baldwin said, "Don't describe a purple sunset, make me see that it is purple." Use short selections from literature to present examples of what you want children to observe on their own. Examples drawn from literature can be the writing teacher's best friend, a sort of unpaid substitute teacher.

Mapping

Mapping is an outline in graphic form. It pictures graphically how topics are related to subtopics and how subtopics are related to subordinate details. Picturing ideas graphically appeals to children, and they usually enjoy doing it. Mapping has been done successfully as early as kindergarten. Mapping is easy to learn because its graphic form shows how ideas are related in a concrete, pictorial way. Outlining, on the other hand, is more difficult. An effective way of teaching outlining is to start with mapping and convert the mapped topic into an outline. This enables children to compare the visually obvious relationships to their outlined counterparts. Teaching mapping and outlining concurrently makes outlining more understandable than when outlining is taught alone.

Mapping can take different forms depending on the the type of writing envisioned. A map for story writing, for example, can be a simple affair representing only a topic and three subtopics: beginning, middle, and ending. Or a story map can be more complex, dealing with narrative structures such as story problem, setting, characters, events, and resolution. While visual maps are usually arranged in an hierarchical structure where there is a logical connection between topic, subtopic, and subordinate details, they can also be organized nonhierarchically. Nonhierarchical maps are useful when a topic is still being brainstormed, and its logical structure is not yet apparent. Such maps can be reorganized into a more logical hierarchical order later.

Ms. Sonntag's fourth grade class developed prewriting maps and outlines centering around the color green. The map and outline were done as a group prewriting activity. When the mapped topic, Green, had been converted to outline form, Ms. Sonntag explained some of the rules for outlining. For example, she told them that subtopics in an outline usually have two points rather than just one, as is the case in several places in the children's outline. What I like about this example is its lack of perfection, just what you might expect as children explore the mysteries of structuring their ideas for writing. Figure 3.2 shows the map the class created, and Group Map shows the outline derived from the map.

	Christmas			Spring	
Pine	Fresh	Sharp	Grass		Leaves
			Sweet/Sneeze		Rustle/Shapes
	Vegetables			**Ponds/Swamps**	
Lettuce		Cucumbers	Turtles	Frogs	Alligators
			Smelly	Kermit	Scary

Figure 3.2   Map of Greenness

GROUP MAP: CONVERTED TO OUTLINE FORM

Green

   I. Christmas
      A. Christmas Trees
         1. Pine
         2. Sharp
         3. Fresh
  II. Spring
      A. Grass
         1. Sweet
         2. Sneeze
      B. Leaves
         1. Rustle
         2. Shapes
 III. Vegetables
      A. Lettuce
      B. Cucumber
 IV. Water in Ponds
      A. Turtles
         1. Smelly
      B. Frogs
         1. Kermit
      C. Swamps
         1. Alligators

After the class had completed their group project, children chose their own colors, mapped and outlined their topics, and wrote poems about their favorite colors. Kelly chose the color blue, made a map, an outline, and wrote the poem "Blue" shown below.

Blue

Blue is a color,
A color very pretty.
It is very nice
Every boy likes it
Most of the girls hate it,
But I like it.
Most adults, like women, always use it
For flower arrangements.
Men wear tucksetoses in blue.
All I can say is
Everyone uses it.
So now you know about this fantastic color,
Blue is a wonderful color.
It is so nice.
There are things you can't think of
Yousing it for.
Kelly

Carol Sievert, a third grade teacher, describes in her "Voices" piece how she conducted a prewriting activity centering on letter writing to "Pen Pals."

VOICES FROM THE CLASSROOM: Carol Sievert

Writing Letters

I believe in modeling. It helps my students understand how prewriting helps them write. My third graders selected a fifth grade class to be our "Pen Pals." Since letter writing is part of our curriculum, I try to make it enjoyable and meaningful. I model the different letter writing forms.

I give each student a writing worksheet, a type or graphic organizer, and I work at the chalkboard. When writing a friendly letter, for example, I ask my kids to brainstorm possibilities for the content of the letter. We select the ideas we want to include in our letter and then write a group draft. As we move our letter through the writing process, students see what happens from prewriting through publishing.

After group writing, I have my students write their own individual letters, following the model. They have a form on which to create their own graphic organizer, just as we did for the group letter. The students are able to refer back to our group letter that is posted in our classroom for reference. I have found the students write better if they have a model.

For many of my third graders, this is their first experience with letter writing. My goal is to make sure they understand the process, the style of the letter, and the enjoyment that letter writing can bring.

Interviewing

Interviewing is a challenging way to gather information for writing. Primary grade children may benefit from group interviews where the person to be interviewed, such as the principal, visits the classroom. Preparation for interviewing can be simple and informal. Children think of questions they want to ask, and then write about the experience after the person has departed. For older children, interviewing can be done in pairs. Preparation for interviewing revolves around planning, interviewing, and writing. The outline below shows the preparation and planning needed for effective interviewing.

Planning for the Interview

1. Learn about the person to be interviewed ahead of time.
2. Contact the person and arrange for a time and place.
3. Prepare questions that invite detailed answers.
4. Organize the questions into categories or subtopics.

Conducting the Interview

1. Arrive on time and politely introduce yourself.
2. Have questions and equipment for recording answers ready.
3. Ask permission if you want to tape-record the interview.
4. Ask follow-up questions if more information is needed.
5. Ask everything you need to know before you leave.

Writing up the Interview

1. Organize notes according to the categories previously established.
2. Look for an interesting quote for the write-up.
3. Write a draft using the plan established prior to the interview.
4. Try drafting the write-up from different points of view.
5. Share the write-up with other members of the class.

Brainstorming

Brainstorming involves quick-paced calling out as many ideas as possible. Brainstorming allows creative ideas to emerge because an essential ground rule asserts that no idea will be rejected or criticized. Brainstorming must be conducted in a nonjudgmental atmosphere, and all ideas must be received without regard to merit. Members of a brainstorming group are encouraged to build on earlier ideas submitted by other group members, a practice called piggybacking.

Brainstorming is helpful when you want to make students aware of the range of options available. It is useful as a prewriting activity, and at other stages of the writing process. Initially, group brainstorming can be led by the teacher. After modeling it can be led by students. During brainstorming, several students can record responses on the board. Brainstorming aids topic selection, character development, poetic writing, and other components of writing. In poetry, for example, brainstorming can be used to prepare lists of rhyming words or in developing lists of opposing nouns for Cinquain. In story writing, brainstorming rapidly yields a ton of topics or a list of ideas for plotting a story.

Factstorming

Factstorming is a technique described by Hennings (1990) in which children are led to quickly call out facts related to a topic about which they are preparing to write. Unlike brainstorming, where creativity is the focus, factstorming elicits factual information about a writing topic. Factstorming is especially useful for expository writing. Factstorming can be conducted after research sources have been

Five minutes of brainstorming can yield a ton of topics. Emily keeps her own list of writing topics, some of which have come from class brainstorming sessions led by Ms. Webb.

consulted such as surveys, interviews, and library research. Factstorming prior to information gathering creates an interesting learning situation. It is a good way, for example, to help children compare what they think is factual with what they actually learn to be factual after consulting sources.

Procedures for engaging children in factstorming are similar to those used in brainstorming. The teacher asks content-centered questions while someone writes the facts on the board. After a sufficient number of facts are listed, the facts can be evaluated for accuracy and appropriateness and organized into maps or outlines to guide expository writing. Suppose, for example, the class has decided to study camels. The teacher could begin a factstorming session by asking: What do you know about camels? List facts derived from this question. As responses dwindle, ask more specific questions: What do camels do? Where are they used? Do they store water in their humps? How long can they go without water? In what countries would you expect to find camels? Are camels eaten for food, like cattle? Record the information. Then help children conduct research to find factual information about camels. Following the research, direct a factstorming session again. Have children compare their before and after factstorming information and eliminate inaccurate information. Organize the remaining facts into a map or outline. Then have children write.

SUMMARY OF PREWRITING STRATEGIES

1. *Drawing* increases fluency and stimulates ideas for writing. Drawing is especially helpful for younger, less experienced writers.
2. *Talking* with the teacher or peers helps children plan their writing.
3. *Reading* before writing provides information, ideas, and models useful for writing.
4. *Close observation* of the physical and human world enriches possibilities for effective poetic, narrative, and expository writing.
5. *Mapping* ideas for writing helps children see how ideas are related in a concrete, pictorial way.
6. *Interviewing* is an effective way to gather information useful for various types of writing.
7. *Brainstorming* involves quick-paced calling out of many divergent ideas and makes children aware of the range of options available for a given topic.
8. *Factstorming* focuses on eliciting children's prior factual knowledge about a topic, and it is conducted in a fashion similar to brainstorming.

IDEAS FOR WRITING

1. **Clustering.** Clustering is an important prewriting experience. Clustering starts with a nucleus word at the center. Then related words and ideas are brainstormed and linked to the nucleus word through webbing. Clustering helps visualize relationships and it shows how prior knowledge is used to plan writing. Here are some nucleus words around which clustering ideas can be brainstormed: gangs, cruelty, elephants, big cats, trucks, courage, Have children add their own nuclear words.

   characteristics   endangered

                                  elephants

   habitat   kinds

2. **Choosing topics.** Choosing a writing topic can be difficult and frustrating. But many everyday events can become a writing topic. Here's a way to use everyday ideas to find a writing topic. Play "What's On My Mind." Start by modeling. Write a list of "What's On My Mind" ideas on the board, thinking out loud as you do so. This might include: what's for dinner tonight, art fair this weekend, it's raining again. Choose one item from your list and make a web. Then have children make their own list of "What's On My Mind," create a web, and write an account.

3. **Observing details.** Many writers stress the importance of observing detail. Obtain color photographs of two or more members of the cat family: lion, tiger, lynx, leopard, mountain lion, house cat. List the distinct characteristics of each member of the cat family. Then list items that distinguish a lion from a tiger or a lynx and house cat. Organize the information into categories: size, coloration, shape, unique features. If done in groups, share the results. Follow up with a writing activity comparing and contrasting two or more members of the cat family.

4. **Writing a newspaper account.** Read the following account to your students: "Two men, returning from a night baseball game, reported seeing a flying saucer. The men, an engineer and a lawyer, reported that the object, shaped like a giant inverted cereal bowl, swooped low over a cornfield, hovered for nearly two minutes then swooped off, accelerating at an unbelievable speed. No other witnesses reported seeing an object in the night sky last evening." Take the details from this account and make a cluster, draw a picture, and write the rest of this report as it might continue in a newspaper account.

5. **Writing from art.** Make a collage with a theme: happy, funny, lazy, hungry, sleepy. List the details that can be observed in the collage. Brainstorm ideas for a title. Write a draft that describes the feeling that the collage suggests.

6. **Combining facts and fiction.** Events happen in classrooms that are worth writing about. Recall the facts of such an event and list them on the board. Write about the incident as a factual account. Later, brainstorm for fictional ideas to add to the facts. Write about the incident as a mixture of factual and fictional elements.

REFLECTION AND SUMMARY

Reflection

Many writers have their prewriting rituals. Ernest Hemingway sharpened a dozen pencils before starting to write. I arrange my desk neatly, even though I know it will soon be messy again. Prewriting rituals are second cousin to superstitions, akin perhaps to the good luck rituals common among athletes. These rituals may seem absurd, though they are not. They are merely the outward symbol of the interior preparation of the mind for the task ahead, writing and wishing for success.

Young writers may find such rituals interesting, so there is good reason to explain them to novice writers. But prewriting rituals are not the same as prewriting strategies. The prewriting strategies described in this chapter are more fundamental to writing than prewriting rituals. Successful writers do not substitute rituals for preparation. They rehearse, research, interview, collect, organize, in short, plan their writing according to their needs. Rituals are merely the icing on their prewriting cake.

Prewriting is the gestation period, a time for the birthing of ideas, rehearsing possibilities, planning, gathering, waiting. Prewriting is idiosyncratic. Every writer has a personal road map for the journey into writing. John Barth prepared for writing with great care, making outlines and planning the ending in detail. Isak Dinesen, on the other hand, said writing for her started, ". . . with a tingle, a kind of feeling of the story I will write." We can best help children prepare for writing, it seems, by knowing the possibilities for preparation, sharing this knowledge with children, and encouraging young writers to develop their own style of getting ready to write.

Summary

This chapter has presented the following main ideas.

1. Prewriting is the planning, collecting, and organizing stage of the writing process. Activities associated with prewriting occur before and throughout the writing process, reflecting the recursive nature of writing.

2. Collecting, planning, and organizing information for writing is time consuming. Some writers spend more time getting ready to write than they spend actually drafting.

3. Self-selected topics result in more and better writing. Even so, assigning topics is reasonable as long as we heighten interest, expand knowledge, and provide choice within an acceptable range.

4. Expand children's sensitivity to their audience by sharing and publishing writing, increasing peer audience opportunities, and seeking outside audiences for writing.

5. Expose children to a variety of writing forms. Nontraditional writing forms add interest to writing. Encouragement to use nontraditional forms is needed or traditional forms will always prevail.

6. Expose children to prewriting strategies that help them plan, collect, and organize ideas and information before and during writing. Eight strategies were described.
   - Drawing increases writing fluency for many children and stimulates ideas for writing that accompanies drawing.
   - Talking about writing helps children think about their writing. It is best stimulated when children talk to themselves, their peers, and their teacher.
   - Reading stimulates the mind and the imagination. It is a major resource and model for the aspiring writer.
   - Observing is a combination of what the senses detect and what the mind deduces. It plays a keen role in writers' work.
   - Mapping is a graphic way of showing how information is related. Mapping provides a kind of road map for the writer to follow.
   - Interviewing individuals who possess relevant information about a topic is an excellent way to gather realistic information for writing.
   - Brainstorming involves quick-paced calling out of ideas in a short period of time. All ideas are accepted without regard for their merit.
   - Factstorming is a technique in which children are led to call out facts related to a specific topic about which they are to write.

QUESTIONS FOR REFLECTIVE THINKING

1. Why would infrequent opportunities to write have an adverse effect on rehearsal for writing?

2. What influence is research likely to have on writing?

3. When children choose their own writing topics, it tends to have a positive effect on writing. Why might this be so?

4. Assigning writing topics is sometimes useful or even necessary. What precautions can teachers take to mitigate possible negative effect of assigned topics?

5. What activities or procedures are useful in developing audience sensitivity among young writers?

6. What is meant by the statement, "Form influences the content and organization of writing"?

7. Choose one of the prewriting strategies described and discuss how you might use it to help children plan their writing.

8. Choose the major topic discussed in this chapter that most piqued your curiosity or interest. Find another book or article that deals with this topic and compare and contrast the two presentations.

9. What topic in this chapter did you find least useful? What topic most useful? Explain your decisions.

10. Mini case study: You are teaching in a middle school and have a group of students with little writing experience. They are unfamiliar with writing process, and have seldom engaged in prewriting activities. Choose a writing topic that would interest your students, and describe a set of prewriting experiences you would plan for your students.

REFERENCES

Calkins, L. M. (1986). *The art of teaching writing.* Portsmouth, NH: Heinemann.
Calkins, L. M. (1994). *The art of teaching writing,* 2nd ed. Portsmouth, NH: Heinemann.
Clark, R. P. (1987). *Free to write: A journalist teaches young writers.* Portsmouth, NH: Heinemann Educational Books.
Cowley, M. (1958). *Writers at work: The Paris review interviews.* Middlesex, England: Penguin Press.
Doyle, A. C. (1985). "The adventure of the blue carbuncle." In *The complete works of Sherlock Holmes,* Philadelphia, PA: The Franklin Library.
Dyson, A. H. (1982). "The emergence of visible language: Interrelationships between drawing and early writing." *Visible Language,* 6, 360–381.
Dyson, A. H. (1986). "The imaginary world of childhood: A multimedia presentation." *Language Arts,* 63, 790–808.
Dyson, A. H. (1993). *Social worlds of children learning to write in an urban primary school.* New York: Teachers College Press.
Elson, P. (1990). *An investigation of the revision processes of fifth grade children.* Unpublished Dissertation, Oakland University, Rochester, MI.
Gilbar, S. (1989). *The open door: When writers first learned to read.* Boston: David R. Godine, Publisher, Inc.
Graves, D. H. (1983). *Writing: Teachers and children at work.* Exeter, NH: Heinemann.
Graves, D. H. (1994). *A fresh look at writing.* Portsmouth, NH: Heinemann.
Heimlich, J. E. and Pittelman, S. D. (1986). *Semantic mapping: Classroom applications.* Newark, DE: International Reading Association.
Hennings, D. G. (1990). *Communication in action: Teaching the language arts,* 3rd ed. Boston: Houghton Mifflin Co.
Kroll, B. M. (1978). "Developing a sense of audience." *Language Arts,* 55, No. 7, 828–831.
Langer, J. A. (1985). "Children's sense of genre." *Written Communication,* 12, 157–187.
Langer, J. A. and Applebee, A. N. (1987). *How writing shapes thinking: A study of teaching and learning.* Urbana, IL: National Council of Teachers of English.
Moffett, J. (1968). *Teaching the universe of discourse.* Boston: Houghton Mifflin.
Murray, D. M. (1982). *Learning by teaching: Selected articles on writing and teaching.* Portsmouth, NH: Boynton/Cook Publishers, Inc.
Murray, D. M. (1985). *A writer teaches writing,* 2nd ed. Boston: Houghton Mifflin Co.
Murray, D. M. (1990). *Shoptalk: Learning to write with writers.* Portsmouth, NH: Boynton/Cook Publishers.
Newkirk, T. and Atwell, N. (1986). *Understanding writing: Ways of observing, learning and teaching K-8.* Portsmouth, NH: Heinemann Educational Books.
Piaget, J. (1955). *The language and thought of the child.* Translated by Marjorie Gabain. New York: New American Library.
Smith, B. (1943). *A tree grows in Brooklyn.* New York: HarperCollins Publishers.

CHAPTER 4
Drafting: First Thoughts

The first part—the lead, the beginning—is the hardest part of all to write.

John McPhee

The writer's moment of truth arrives when all the collecting and planning
are completed and the writer faces the blank page.

Donald Murray

A WRITER'S STORY

*Aline, age nine, wrote some verses during her first week in a new school and offered them
to her teacher. "I was vain enough," she reflected years later, "to want to see them printed
in the school paper." Her teacher read them right before her eyes, and handed them back
with the cold comment, "They are not up to our standard." Not one to give up easily, she
trotted up to the third floor, occupied by "big" people, high school students, and headed for
Hughes Mearns' room. She gave her verses to Mearns and hurried back to the lower level
without waiting for comment.*

*Next day, Mearns went downstairs to visit Aline. They talked about her verses,
laughed, enjoyed themselves. Aline knew they were good the moment they came off of her
pen. Mearns knew they were good and told her so. The "telling her so" was the key to
opening the door to Aline's heart and mind: "I was testing you, to see if all that they said
here was true, to see if you were just like all the others." But, he wasn't or he wouldn't
have been Hughes Mearns, a man who knew about the creative power of youth, and wrote
about it so beautifully nearly four score years ago. Mearns printed her verses in the school
magazine. Soon, those who read the magazine knew they were good. Such was the beginning of a young writer. She went on to edit the school magazine and in her eleventh year
wrote this lovely "farewell" to childhood.*

Youth

I must laugh and dance and sing,
Youth is such a lovely thing.
Soon I shall be old and stately;
I shall promenade sedately

Down a narrow pavement street,
And the people that I meet
Will be stiff and narrow too,
Careful what they say and do;
It will be quite plain to see
They were never young like me.
When I walk where flowers grow
I shall have to stoop down low
If I want one for a prize;
Now I'm just the proper size.
Let me laugh and dance and sing,
Youth is such a lovely thing.
Aline Wechsler (Mearns, 1929, xvi)

INTRODUCTION

Aline was a fluent drafter, even at the age of nine. But this is not the case for all writers. Many writers find drafting more difficult than revising. This is not surprising. Beginnings are hard. But writers and teachers have discovered ways to facilitate drafting, although, for many writers, drafting may never be easy. Children draft more readily when they have spent time getting ready to write. Prewriting accomplishes this task. But, then the writer must face the blank page and start drafting. This is the "moment of truth" that Murray alludes to in the quote at the head of this chapter. Fluent first drafts flow from solid preparation, not from inspiration, a term professional writers shun. Jack London said, "You can't wait for inspiration. You have to go after it with a club."

Drafting is getting black on white as rapidly and as fluently as possible. Frank O'Connor had this in mind when he said, "I don't give a hoot what the writing's like, I write any sort of rubbish which will cover the main outlines of the story; then I can begin to see it." Drafting is not deliberate and precise like revising. Drafters need to splash words across the page as boldly as an abstract expressionist splashes paint on a canvas. Revisers behave quite differently. Revisers need to be as precise as pointillism, choosing words and sentences with deliberation and delicacy.

Drafting must be free of constraints. Freedom to draft means not worrying about spelling, punctuation, or grammar. It even means not worrying about content and meaning. This may seem contradictory, but it is not. Drafting is a search for meaning, not a guarantee of it. A writer may only vaguely sense the outlines of a topic, and this is what Frank O'Connor meant when he spoke of putting down "any sort of rubbish" that came to mind. The idea is to get something tangible on the page and work from that concrete beginning. Once words cover the page, content and meaning can be shaped through revision. Surprising things happen when drafting is free of constraint. Even throwing a draft away is not wasted effort, since the residue of a beginning remains.

STRATEGIES FOR SUCCESSFUL DRAFTING

John Steinbeck said, "When I face the desolate impossibility of writing 500 pages a sick sense of failure falls on me and I know I can never do it. Then gradually I write one page and then another." Drafters dare not think of the entire draft looming ahead. To do so induces paralysis or confusion. Instead, encourage children to think of their drafts in more manageable chunks. Steinbeck thought of his book not as a massive 500-page tome but as one page. Many writers think of their writing tasks in smaller units. This is sound psychology for young writers when they face a challenging drafting task. Drafters need, in addition to sound psychology, basic working strategies. The following strategies for drafting work for many writers, but certainly not all. Expose children to a variety of drafting strategies, and you increase the likelihood of finding a few strategies that will work for nearly every child.

Writing Leads

The heroes of the Persian fairy tale, *The Three Princes of Serendip*, possessed the marvelous gift of finding agreeable and valuable things not sought for. Some teachers have this gift, too. Ms. Elson, a fifth grade teacher, suggested to Mark that he might try *several* leads to his story, "Nikki and Me." Mark returned a half hour later and said, "Ms. Elson, here are the *seven* leads you wanted me to write." The leads Mark wrote are a superb example of the flexibility and imagination children possess.

Lead 1: One bright, sunny, day I walked into my moms room and asked her, "Mom, did I ever do something funny as a baby?"

Lead 2: "Mom, did I ever do something, that was real funny, as a baby?" I asked curiously.

"Why yes. Two things pop up from the top of my head."

Lead 3: There are two stories about me as a baby that are real funny.

Lead 4: One morning I crawled up to my dog's food, grasped as much as I could, and ate it.

Lead 5: I was sitting next to our big recliner resting. After awhile, I wanted to go somewhere else in the house. I tried to get up, but I couldn't. I struggled and struggled.

Lead 6: Ellerey and I were in my room shooting at the basket hooked up on my closet. "Say El, do you know anything you did, as a baby, that was funny?"

"No," he replied.

"Well I do. You want me to tell you about them?"

"Sure," he said anxiously.

Lead 7: I was lying in bed trying to go to sleep. "I'll never be able to fall asleep!" I whispered. I rested for awhile and then said to myself: "I might as well try what mom said to do. She always said, "If you can't fall asleep, think of something funny or happy." So I started to think about two funny things I did when I was a baby.

Good luck, some say, is the residue of preparation. This serendipity of leads happened in Ms. Elson's class because she had taught her children to write leads. She had developed an excellent writing program in her classroom. Consequently, Mark already had a writing history when he serendipitously confused *several* with *seven* and wrote seven leads to his story, "Nikki and Me." You can create an atmosphere where serendipities are possible. Start by teaching children to write leads. Consider starting with a demonstration. Go to the board or overhead projector and say, "Sometimes I have a hard time getting started writing. I thought I'd show you how I sometimes start a new piece. Suppose I'm writing a report about woodpeckers. I've read and collected information, and now I'm ready to start writing. Sometimes I start by writing three or four different beginnings, called leads." Then write a few leads on the board or overhead. Here is an example of different leads for a report on woodpeckers.

Lead 1: Alice leaned against a tree and gazed at the redheaded woodpecker.

Lead 2: Woodpeckers, looking for insects to eat, use their bills to chisel holes in trees.

Lead 3: Rat-a-tat-tat—the redheaded woodpecker clung to the rough bark drumming out a theme on a decaying oak tree.

Lead 4: "If that woodpecker doesn't let up, he'll beat his brains out," Alice said as she watched a redheaded woodpecker drilling holes in a dead oak tree.

Explain the value of writing leads. "After I've written a few leads, I decide which lead is best for starting the kind of report or story I'm writing." Encourage your children to try different leads for their pieces, but keep lead writing flexible. Not everyone needs to write different leads every time they work on a piece. Some primary grade children may not be ready to write leads. Writing leads is especially useful for children at the upper elementary and secondary level. Experiment and find what works best with your children.

Reviewing Notes

Writing often requires note taking. When children are writing book reports, articles, and essays based on research they have done, remind them to review their notes just prior to starting a draft. An opening sentence can often be taken from information contained in notes. Quotes, examples, or arresting facts are excellent ways to begin a draft. It is easy to illustrate how this works by taking a student's notes, sorting through them, and finding a fact or quote with which to begin a report. After you have illustrated how a fact or quote can be used in a lead, have children sort their notes into several categories for possible leads. Then have them follow your example by writing leads on their own.

Writing Discovery Drafts

"We write the first draft to discover what we have to say and how we may say it," is how Murray describes the purpose of the discovery draft (1985, p. 52). The dis-

Writing leads suggests different directions a story, essay, or report might go. Isaac is trying different leads for his story.

covery draft is experimental, a beginning. It has many aliases: test draft, zero draft, practice draft. The idea is to plunge ahead no matter what gaps are left when it is done. Exploration of your own thinking is the goal. A first draft does not usually march steadily toward its final destiny; it is more likely to stagger and stumble. Discovery drafting helps writers uncover what they know or do not know, to discover whether the topic is too broad or too narrow, to encounter a surprise or two, pleasant or unpleasant, that may inform writing.

Most young writers do not think of first drafts as experimental. On the contrary, they think of first drafts as permanent and complete. This is especially true if their writing history has bordered on the traditional. It is necessary, therefore, to entice young writers into the arena of discovery. Jeannil wrote a first draft of her story about Ginger, her cat (see Figure 4.1). The invented spelling is quite good for early first grade writing. She put dots where she thought sentences should end, though she was usually wrong. Jeannil's teacher, in a spontaneous conference, took a few minutes to explain sentence punctuation. She drew lines between the words in Jeannil's story, suggesting the need for better spacing. She eased the burden of rewriting by providing a generous amount of time for moving from a first to a second draft. Jeannil then wrote a second draft (Figure 4.2). In her second draft, she leaves lots of space between

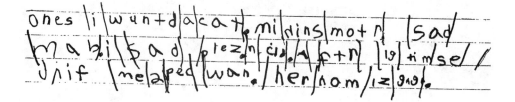

Jeannil.

Figure 4.1 **First Draft** Jeannil, Age 6

ones iGngr wunted a
cat, mi nis motr
sad maB.
i sad plez.
'n cid. aftr lo tm
se tk me to
pec wan. har
nam ez gh gr. i kat
lot r go eyh the
mod. i luv gngr e
luv ihovr. the end.
Jeannil

Figure 4.2 **Second Draft** Jeannil, Age 6

words and successfully punctuates several sentences. While Jeannil's spelling remains unchanged, she makes a substantial addition to her story in the second draft.

Freewriting

The idea in freewriting is to let your thoughts flow freely without regard for mechanics, sequence, relevance, or ultimate worth of the ideas recorded. Freewriting develops fluency and gives a start on a topic that may be developed later. The product does not have to meet traditional standards, though there is no intent to disregard standards. The procedures for freewriting include these steps:

1. Choose a topic.
2. Write for five to ten minutes without stopping to think at length on any aspect of the topic.
3. Do not worry about spelling, punctuation, sequence, or the worth of the ideas you are writing down.
4. When you cannot think of anything to say, write, "I can't think of anything to say," until another thought occurs to you.
5. Reread your freewrite, and circle any ideas that can be expanded upon later. If the freewrite is fully developed, treat it as a first draft.
6. Optional: Start another freewrite focusing only on the ideas that were circled after rereading the first freewrite.

Freewriting is useful for students who are convinced they have nothing to say or who imagine themselves unable to put words on paper. It develops confidence since the emphasis is on recording ideas freely while ignoring traditional concerns about correctness, organization, and relevance. Writing never has to be perfect, and it does not need to be correct in its initial stages. Thinking that it does keeps children from expressing their ideas freely and hinders creativity.

In her diary entry, Ms. DeWard tells how she drafted a story on the overhead projector for her fourth graders. Later, she revised the piece and read it to her students.

A TEACHER'S DIARY: Jennifer DeWard

My class has been working on a story about their family for the past few weeks. When I first introduced the idea, I used the overhead projector and modeled brainstorming. I wrote down all of my story ideas, and chose one. I told my students that I would take that idea and turn it into a finished piece to share with them. Last week, I shared two "sloppy copies" with them that I had written. They were complimentary, of course, even though my piece was not exceptional. To my fourth graders, however, the piece was fabulous. I told my kids that I would consider their questions and suggestions as I revised the piece one last time. Today, I read the final version, and they clapped for me when I was done. It felt so good, and I instantly knew what it was like to have a piece of writing accepted by others.

They were very specific in their compliments: *I like the way you used dialogue,* and *I like the details about the grilled cheese and tomato soup.* After reading my story, I gave them

30 minutes to work on their piece of writing. Without having suggested adding dialogue, four students added dialogue to their pieces. I was amazed! The kids probably didn't even know where their inspiration came from, and that is just as well.

I am by no means a brilliant writer, but teachers do not have to be outstanding writers for their students to benefit. Our writing only has to be a little better than our students' writing, in order for the kids to find something worthwhile to include in their own pieces.

Psyching-Up

Prior to a big game, many athletes indulge in rituals and routines to get themselves mentally prepared to compete. Sports psychologists believe that these rituals and routines work. Such rituals and routines are called *psyching-up*. Many writers have similar rituals and routines. I have my own prewriting routines, some of which are personal enough to keep to myself. Others I have described elsewhere in this book. Psyching myself up for writing is a comfort and confidence builder. Some writers set goals: "I'm going to write for thirty minutes without stopping; I'm going to write five hundred words this morning." Tell children of your own writing rituals and routines. Explain the purpose they serve in your writing. Encourage children to develop their own rituals and routines. Occasionally, have them share with their classmates.

Tuning Out Distractions

E. B. White said that, "A writer who waits for ideal conditions under which to work will die without putting a word on paper." It is not unusual for writers to seek distractions just so they can avoid the hard work of writing. You can't always avoid distractions, so you have to learn to tune them out. Ideal conditions for writing are not possible, yet you can tune out distractions as well as avoid them. E. B. White learned to tune out distractions because his wife and family made no special concessions to his work. When the distractions became too great he went elsewhere: "If I get sick of it, I have places I can go," he said. Classrooms and homes are often busy, distracting places. While it is wise to avoid distractions, it is also necessary to accommodate to them. Encourage children, for example, to avoid television while writing, but remember that tomb-like silence is not prerequisite to effective writing.

Rereading

Writers often find the initial rush of ideas quickly slowing to a trickle. After a few sentences or paragraphs, they may say, in the words of a song made famous by Peggy Lee, "Is that all there is?" Perhaps the most universal strategy for getting the stream of ideas moving again is to stop and reread what has been written.

Rereading is like pole vaulting. You can't vault high if you start your run too near the takeoff point. You have to back up and get a running start. Rereading gives the writer a running start. It stimulates reflection, revisits the road already traveled, and offers fresh ideas for the road ahead. Rereading aids revision as well as fluency.

Ms. Elson (1990) asked Mercedes, a fifth grader, if rereading helped her with her writing. Mercedes, articulate about rereading, said: "Well, I usually write a page and then I reread it, and then I write a page and then I reread everything and then I just keep rereading it." When asked why she rereads, Mercedes explained: "Well, as I reread it, it helps me think about the story more. If I get stuck, I always reread my story and that always gets me going again. If I have no idea what's going to happen next, I always reread my piece and it helps me get thinking again. I put it in a sentence and I change it. I think the sentence I'm going to write and then I write it and I read it. If it doesn't sound good, I make more changes."

Many writers revise as they are drafting. Patching up holes in the parts already completed helps them gather their thoughts for additional drafting. Other writers find that making changes while they are still drafting hinders the flow of ideas. Since every writer is different, children should be encouraged to deploy their strategies in ways that work best for them.

Talking

When you think you are about ready to write a draft, talk about your draft with a good listener. In classrooms, that good listener may be the teacher or a classmate. At home the good listener might be Mom, Dad, or a friend. If you talk through your writing, you may find yourself writing a draft aloud. Once you've *talked* a draft aloud, the drafting seems easier. Discussing your writing has other advantages as well. It may result in new ideas and information that would otherwise have been missed. Talking to yourself is also a good idea, sometimes it's as or more useful than talking to teachers, friends, and family.

Ms. Debbie Clark, who teaches middle school, describes the value of having her children talk before moving into a writing project.

VOICES FROM THE CLASSROOM: Debbie Clark

Talking and Writing

Have you ever walked into a middle school classroom and heard silence? Well, I hope not. Middle school students are social creatures. They need to socialize and communicate with friends as part of that dreaded "adolescent phase" we hear about all the time.

I have found that the best way to handle the social aspect of this age and still have learning take place in the classroom is to let them talk! I plan my lessons around talk time. I try to allow group or partner work every single day.

For example, I allow students to discuss any reading they complete with a partner before moving on to writing in their reading logs. This I accomplish by having students ask around the room until they find another student who has read the same selection. Then they move into the hallway for a five minute discussion of the story before beginning to write. This allows students to exchange ideas and socialize a bit before sitting down to tackle their next activity.

I have also changed my book reports to a game format this year. Students read a book, then apply for a book report. I schedule their book report for a convenient day in the near future. Students are given a game board with generic questions geared toward the type of book they have read. They go in the hallway and answer three questions on the game board. The group members grade their performance and write comments about how their book report went. The students love the game book report. In fact, my students are reading more books than they ever have because of this simple change in how they report on their reading choices.

So, what is my advice? Middle school students are going to talk whether you allow them to or not. Why not make their talk time a constructive part of your classroom activities?

Walking Away

When I find myself tied up in knots and unable to produce anything resembling a draft, I walk away from the draft. I don't usually stay away long. I might go outside and throw a rock at a tree or put some feed out for the birds. If I'm at the university, I might wander down the hall for a drink of water or stop at a friend's office to steal a jellybean or two. When I return, I'm usually able to resume the draft with greater ease than when I left. Of course, sometimes the problem is more fundamental than a walk away will solve. Drafting difficulty is often related to inadequate information. No amount of walking will cure this problem unless it is a walk to the library.

Do teachers dare tell children to walk away from a draft? Won't they take advantage of this freedom? Yes, some will. But when we treat children like real writers, something wonderful happens; they begin to behave like real writers. They'll walk back. Of course, you will have to deal with those who take license, but solving big and little problems is what teaching is all about.

Writing Inside-Out

For Katherine Porter, author of *Ship of Fools,* starting at the end was an article of faith: "If I didn't know the ending of a story, I wouldn't begin. I always write my last line, my last paragraphs, my last page first." Agatha Christy sometimes wrote the last chapter of her mysteries first. Other writers start in the middle and work inside-out. I often start at a place where I feel the greatest confidence or comfort, perhaps at a point where I feel my knowledge or experience is strongest. I have often found that my writing goes better when I start somewhere in the middle. Children need to know about this inside-out trick. Make them comfortable with the idea that they can try this strategy just to see how it works for them. Some children will find it works well. Others may be uncomfortable and confused with the idea of drafting parts of the whole nonsequentially. Experimenting with writing is an asset, and I have never known it to damage a writer's confidence, though it may be temporarily confusing.

SUMMARY OF DRAFTING STRATEGIES

1. Write two or three leads to a piece of writing before proceeding through the rest of the draft.

2. Review notes prior to starting a draft. This is especially useful in expository writing.

3. Write a "discovery draft" to learn what you already know or do not know about a writing topic.

4. Start a draft by freewriting for five or ten minutes. Ignore everything except getting your ideas down on paper.

5. Prior to writing, psych-up by setting goals or by observing prewriting rituals intended to get you into a drafting mood.

6. Practice tuning out distractions that interfere with drafting productivity.

7. Reread what you have written from time to time to help you stay on track or to stimulate new ideas.

8. Talk about your draft with a good listener to get an outside perspective. It is also useful to talk to yourself about your draft.

9. After an initial draft or during drafting, it sometimes helps to walk away from the draft for a period of time.

10. Write the middle or ending to your piece before you write the main body. This is called writing "inside-out."

THE TEACHER'S ROLE IN DRAFTING

As words flow onto the page writers must constantly make decisions about sequence, meaning, audience, what to leave in, what to leave out. If too much thought is given to a first draft, fluency will be slowed, perhaps crippled. Yet, fluency without deliberation is less than satisfactory. Learning to draft fluently means balancing these two competing demands. Teachers can help students avoid the pitfalls that impede fluent drafting. The role of teacher is crucial in showing children how drafting might proceed.

Model Drafting

"I am a writing man and not a teacher of writing; and there is a vast difference between these two sorts of creature," said Hughes Mearns (1929, p. 7). Perhaps Mearns states the case too strongly, but he makes an important point. Respect between athletes and their coaches rests partly on athletes' knowledge that their coach can play the game as well as coach it. Basketball coaches do not have to be all-stars; they do not have to do three kinds of slam dunks. But they do have to know the game as a participant. Without this qualification, they cannot command the respect from their players.

Similarly, a teacher's validation as a writer is rooted partly in the ability to teach writing, and partly in the ability to demonstrate participants' knowledge of the game of writing. When teachers write, children notice. Melissa, a first grader, asked, "Ms. Dalmage, did you really write that story for *us?*" Ms. Dalmage's answer reinforced what Melissa already suspected: "Yes, Melissa, I wrote that story just for you." Melissa returned to her seat with a pleased look on her face. This bit of intelligence impressed her mightily. It is good for teachers to write. It is good for them to write for their students. Writing for children is a way of saying, "You're special. Here's something I wrote, and I want to share it with you." Writing with and for children establishes your credibility as a writer; it provides a model that children respect and imitate; it keeps you in touch with the problems and pleasures of writing; it models the writing process.

Ms. Melissa DeClerck knows the value of writing for her third grade children. She describes her experience of writing for her children in the following "Voices" piece.

VOICES FROM THE CLASSROOM: Melissa DeClerck

Writing with Kids

I have found one of the best ways to introduce my third graders to writing fiction is to use a piece of writing that I have written especially for the lesson or one that I've written in the past. The first few times that I used my writing, I read my story aloud first and then I explained the process I went through to write my story. But, I found that since my students had already heard the "main act" (my story), they were not that interested in listening to the "opening act" (prewriting, drafting).

Now, I begin by telling my students that I have written a story and I want to share it with them, but first I want to show them how I wrote it. On the board I show them the prewriting process of brainstorming that I went through. If I don't have my original brainstorming outline, then I put down ideas that I can remember. As I write ideas under the headings: setting, characters, and problem, I talk to myself aloud as I would have done in my head when I brainstormed originally. Then, I talk aloud to myself as I eliminate ideas from the lists and make decisions as to the setting, the characters, the problem and sometimes the solution.

I try to impress upon my students that the order in which a writer comes up with possible ideas for a story can vary from story to story and from writer to writer. I explain that if I have already decided on the problem for a story, or the solution, or the characters, or the setting or any combination of these, I just brainstorm under the other headings. I also let my students know that even after they begin writing their first drafts, it is okay to change their mind and add a character or change the setting, etc.

After I have shared my process for brainstorming, I tell my students how I decided on the beginning of my story and then I read my first draft. After I have read it, I make comments about what I thought about as I was writing it and about any problems I had while I was writing. I ask my students for their comments too. If I have a second draft or a final draft, I may share it with my students at this time or I may wait and use it to illustrate revision at a later time.

Conference

"Probably the single most significant determinant of how children view the process of drafting is the teacher. The teacher who starts children writing by reminding them to use their best penmanship, to keep papers neat, and never to cross out is building an erroneous picture of first drafting" (Hennings, 1986, p. 288). Hennings is right. While children draft, help those who have stalled-out and encourage those who are drafting freely. Talk children through drafting difficulties. Listen as they describe their problems. Ask questions that will get the words and ideas flowing again: "What have you written so far? Can you tell me more about that idea? Yes, I see. Well, have you thought of. . . ?" Writers who have reached an impasse or settled into the "slough of despond" may need a specific suggestion that will move their writing off dead center. Do not allow legitimate concerns about student ownership of writing keep you from giving advice and counsel when it is desperately needed. Writers benefit from good ideas suggested at crucial moments in the drafting process, just as mature writers do. Young writers, like professional writers, benefit from the suggestions of a good editor, which is what a teacher must sometimes be.

Listen

Be the first audience for your children. Listen, suggest, comment. Writers need constructive criticism, but much more they need encouragement and praise. The primary value of an audience is to build confidence in the writer. John Irving, author of *The World According to Garp,* shared his drafts with friends because he wanted their approval not their critique. An appreciative audience celebrates writing. Consequently, the teacher's first role is appreciative listener; the teacher's second role is constructive critic. Both are important, though listening may be the more important of the two. Of course, grading is part of a teacher's professional responsibility, but this role should be insulated from the more important role of appreciative audience for student writing.

Instruct

Observe children's writing as they draft. You will discern certain writing tendencies. As you inform yourself about individual and class needs, consider ways in which you can provide appropriate instruction to meet the needs you have diagnosed. When you spot a specific writing need that a reasonable number of children can profit from, teach that need. You are in the best position to decide whether the instruction should be given to the entire class, a subgroup, or to an individual. Longer, formal lessons are sometimes needed, but it is better, in most instances, to teach five- to ten-minute informal lessons to the class or to give brief personal suggestions to an individual. If you notice a tendency, for example, to choose general rather than specific words, take five minutes to discuss precise word selection. If run-on sentences are a problem, show children how to correct this tendency. Our job is to teach, and there are many ways in which we can fulfill this professional responsibility.

In her "Voices" piece, Ms. Christie McVean describes the procedures she used to teach drafting to her bilingual fourth and fifth grade children.

VOICES FROM THE CLASSROOM: Christie McVean

Teaching Writing to Bilingual Children

The majority of my students are bilingual, often causing writing to be a laborious task for them. Even so, writing is something I must continue to stress throughout the school year. To facilitate drafting I always try to motivate them to want to write on the topic for a particular writing project. I usually do this by stating the purpose for the project during the prewriting phase. Whether it is holiday writing activities, reports, writing letters, creating class articles, or poetry lessons, I display and share examples of students' writing from previous years. Once the motivation and expectations are present, drafting becomes easier.

Placing our prewriting activity of webbing on the overhead, I display our class created web as a sample to model the drafting procedure. Using colored markers the students suggest ways for me to color code similar ideas on the web. This is done by outlining the circles of the web in various colors. By doing so, we are able to plan out paragraphs and organize our ideas. This provides an easy way for students to understand paragraph content and form. Using each idea one color at a time, we use our web to generate sentences for the piece.

Once the process has been modeled, the students are ready to implement the drafting procedure from their individual webs. Next, they color code related ideas and begin forming sentences for their pieces. Once all ideas have been written and paragraphs formed according to colors, the children reread their piece to insure their intended message was conveyed.

When the draft is completed, it is put away until we are able to revisit our piece. Using this simple modeling process has helped my students, bilingual or not, to be successful with drafting.

IDEAS FOR WRITING

1. Making lists. A man once made a list of 100 things he wanted to do, and by the time he was forty he had done all but five. Make a list of things you want to do in your lifetime. Look in travel magazines, encyclopedias, and talk with your writing group to get ideas. Choose one item on your list and freewrite about it for ten minutes.

2. Tall tales. Mountain Men loved to tell exaggerated accounts of their deeds, "Tall Tales" as they sometimes called them. Many of the Mountain Men would have made good members of a "Liar's Club." Pretend you are a member of a "Liar's Club." You are getting ready to attend the annual meeting at which you will tell one of your famous whoppers. Write an elaborate whopper that is creative and will entertain your friends.

3. What if . . . . Choose one of these "What if . . ." ideas and write a quick draft. After you have finished, rewrite the lead sentence three different ways.
   What if you owned a ranch in Montana
   What if you played lead guitar in a rock band

What if all cars were replaced by horses
What if you could fly like a bird

4. Making choices. You are on a one-person life raft and are the only survivor of a shipwreck. After a day on the raft, your food and water supply are running low. Then you see another survivor clinging to a tiny piece of driftwood. Write a quick draft explaining what you would do and why.

5. Loneliness. Think of all the words you associate with the idea of loneliness. Write these words in a box in the corner of a paper. Then write a poem or story. You may find that some of the words you wrote work well in your story or poem.

6. Who's in charge here? Judith Viorst wrote a poem called, "If I Were in Charge of the World." Suppose you were in charge of the world. What would you change? What would stay the same? First, write some statements telling what wouldn't be. For example, "If I were in charge of the world there would be no Mondays." Then write some statements telling what would be. For example, "If I were in charge of the world weekends would start on Thursday." Arrange your ideas into lines and verses and you have a poem.

7. Disappointment. All of us have been disappointed by such things as an unkept promise, a broken friendship, a trip not taken. Write a first draft of a story based on the keenest disappointment you have ever experienced.

REFLECTION AND SUMMARY

Reflection

Maxwell Perkins, a legendary editor, advised Marcia Davenport, "Just get it down on paper, and then we'll see what to do with it." I believe Perkins' advice to Davenport is good advice for young writers as well. Teachers have an editorial role in working with children. Getting children to the point where they are skillful drafters requires a deft touch. We have to walk that fine line between helpfulness and taking over a writer's work. It's an invisible line, so no one can tell you just when you've stepped over the line. If you've taught a while, you've certainly crossed over that line occasionally. But no permanent harm is done when there is trust between the writer and the teacher-editor. Strengthen the trusting relationship between yourself and your writers, and over the long haul you will succeed.

Summary

This chapter has presented the following main ideas.

1. Writers need strategies to help them move forward with drafting. Ten strategies for keeping drafting moving were suggested.
   - Practice writing leads to stories, reports, and essays.
   - Review notes prior to drafting looking for an interesting beginning.
   - Write discovery drafts, an experimental beginning to drafting.
   - Freewrite, allowing ideas to flow without regard to conventions.

- Psych-up prior to writing with personal rituals and routines.
- Learn to tune out distractions that interfere with writing
- Rereading refreshes the writer's mind about what has been written and stimulates fresh ideas for continued drafting.
- Talking through a draft with a good listener can give the writer additional ideas for continuing a draft.
- Walking away from a draft relieves tension so that the writer can return refreshed and ready to tackle the draft anew.
- Beginning at the end or middle of a draft may prove more effective than searching fruitlessly for an elusive beginning point.

2. Teachers can instruct and inspire children as they face the drafting by following these suggestions.

   - Model drafting for your students.
   - Confer with students about their drafting problems.
   - Listen and respond to writers as they face drafting problems.
   - Teach drafting strategies to the class, groups, and individuals.

QUESTIONS FOR REFLECTIVE THINKING

1. How can writing leads help facilitate drafting?

2. What is a discovery draft? How can a discovery draft help a writer?

3. Why should writers ignore concerns about correctness and organization during freewriting?

4. When drafting slows to a trickle, rereading often helps the writer begin to move forward again. Why might this be so?

5. What would you do to help a student who has gotten stuck while drafting and can't seem to move forward?

6. What single idea about drafting did you find most useful? How can you use this idea to improve drafting among your students?

7. Make a KWL chart about drafting. Make three columns using these headings: What do I **K**now? What do I **W**ant to know? What have I **L**earned?

8. Mini case study: You have successfully engaged your middle school students in a series of prewriting experiences, and they are ready to draft. Most are drafting successfully, but several of them seem unable to get started drafting. What instructional help can you give to the students who are having difficulty getting started?

REFERENCES

Elson, P. (1990). *An investigation of the revision processes of fifth grade children.* Unpublished Dissertation, Oakland University, Rochester, Michigan.

Hennings, D. H. (1986). *Communication in action: Teaching the language arts,* 3rd ed. Boston: Houghton Mifflin.

Mearns, H. (1929). *Creative power: The education of youth in the creative arts.* New York: Dover Publications.

Murray, D. M. (1985). *A writer teaches writing: Second edition.* Boston: Houghton Mifflin.

CHAPTER 5

Revising: Making Writing Better

> The beautiful part of writing is that you don't have to get
> it right the first time, unlike, say, a brain surgeon. You can always
> do it better, find the exact word, the apt phrase, the leaping simile.
>
> *Robert Cormier*

A WRITER'S STORY

Russell Baker grew up poor, but his mother kept telling "Buddy" that he had to "make something" of himself. Just what that something might be, Buddy had no idea. Everything he tried seemed not to work. He sold magazines door-to-door, but he seldom sold out his weekly allotment: "I moaned that I had rung every doorbell in town and knew there wasn't a single potential buyer left in Belleville that week." But his mother wouldn't hear of failure: "If at first you don't succeed, try, try, again." Buddy was sick of hearing these lectures on self-improvement. Finally, even his mother concluded that Buddy was not meant to be a business tycoon.

One evening Buddy brought home a composition on that perennial favorite, "What I Did on My Vacation." He had gotten an A. His mother, a former teacher, agreed that it was a fine composition. One evening she said, "Buddy, maybe you could be a writer." Buddy had never met a writer, had no idea how to become a writer, possessed no urge to become a writer. But mother had decided, and Buddy, after thinking it over, concluded that writing would be a vast improvement over peddling magazines: "Writers did not have to trudge through town peddling from canvas bags, defending themselves against angry dogs, being rejected by surly strangers. Writers did not have to ring doorbells. So far as I could make out, what writers did couldn't even be classified as work" (Baker, 1982, p. 16).

Lack of gumption *was another of Buddy's shortcomings, according to his mother, so he decided that he would enter a profession that didn't require it. Writers, Buddy thought, ". . . didn't have to have any gumption at all." So he decided, secretly, that he'd be a writer when he grew up (Baker, 1982, p. 17). Buddy got a job as a copy boy for the* Baltimore Sun, *where he eventually became a reporter. Russell Baker is best known for his humorous writing as a columnist for the* New York Times *and for his Pulitzer prize-winning autobiography,* Growing Up.

INTRODUCTION

Journalists, like Russell Baker, often write under strict deadlines. They learn to draft and revise rapidly, and often get help from copy editors who may make further revisions of deadline copy. Mr. Baker also wrote books where deadlines are more elastic, and one can sense in his autobiography, *Growing Up,* the hand of a master reviser. Revision is the heart and soul of writing. It is basic, and it is broad. Picture revision as a ship, anvil, and microscope, each metaphor reveals different facets of revision.

Revision is a ship. It is the vessel on which writers set sail to discover what they have to say. Writers voyage into a sea of uncertainty, searching for meaning and a message only dimly perceived in first draft writing. Revision takes the writer through uncharted waters and dangerous shoals. Eventually, meaning surfaces on the wings of revision. Murray says, "Non writers think of revision as a matter of tinkering, touching up, making presentable, but writers know it is central to the act of discovering" (Murray, 1985, p. 171). The compass of revision guides the writer into the safe harbor of meaning discovered.

Revision is an anvil. Ben Jonson, the great English poet and playwright, advised writers to, "Strike the second heat/ Upon the Muse's anvil." Revision is the hard surface on which writers shape their writing style and skill. Writers seldom select their best words and thoughts in first drafts; the exact wording or the best arrangement of ideas must be shaped and hammered on the anvil of revision. The writer's unique style and skill emerges in the shower of sparks produced by constant hammering on the Muse's anvil.

Revision is a microscope. It magnifies those inevitable craters, small and large, in our writing that are present but unrecognized in early drafts. Writing is rarely a steady flow of words and thoughts. More often it is a halting dribble. We accumulate words and thoughts, piled one upon the other, as they tumble from our minds. Saul Bellow, a Nobel laureate said, "I'm happy when the revisions are big. I'm not speaking of stylistic revisions, but of revision in my own understanding" (Murray, 1985, p. 181). First draft writing corrals our untamed words and thoughts. Revision tames and curries them.

Revision develops responsibility and independence in writing, and it is seldom easy. But we can move children in the right direction; we can teach them the techniques of revision; we can motivate them with the desire to improve their writing. Accomplishing these goals may be more difficult than correcting their writing for them, but if we accept the challenge we will have independent, responsible, competent writers.

WRITERS TALK ABOUT REVISION

We can learn something of importance about writing by knowing how writers go about their work—their writing habits, standards, procedures, even their biases. Outstanding writers, men and women who have achieved the highest accolades in their profession, can help us understand what it takes to be a writer. I believe we can rely, to a significant degree, upon what they offer by way of advice and example to those who want to become better writers.

William Butler Yeats, the Nobel prize-winning Irish poet, enjoyed the exquisite pleasures of revision. He often revised his own poems and saw this as a revision of himself, not just a revision of his poems. He replied to those who criticized his life-long devotion to revising his poems in this revealing verse:

My friends who have it I do wrong
Whenever I remake a song
Must know what issue is at stake
It is myself that I remake.

As Yeats grew older, he revised the poems of his youth to reflect the changes that time and experience had wrought. These changes are reflected in "The Old Pensioner," written in 1890. Yeats rewrote this poem in 1939, nearly fifty years later, and gave it a new title, "The Lamentation of the Old Pensioner" (Kennedy, 1986, p. 225). Yeats' revision of "The Old Pensioner" helps us understand what he meant by, "It is myself that I remake." Revision alters thinking, changing us as well as our writing. Revision causes us to reflect upon our thoughts and experiences; it extends our capacity to convey the meaning we intended but may not have achieved in our early drafts.

Tolstoy seemed unable to even imagine writing without revision: "I can't understand how anyone can write without rewriting anything over and over again. I scarcely ever re-read my published writing, but if by chance I come across a page, it always strikes me: all this must be rewritten . . ." (Murray, 1990, p. l6). Britton (1975) said, "Great writers and teachers of composition agree about very little, but a large proportion of both are fiercely insistent on the need for very careful revision" (p. 46). Hobson confirms Britton's insistence that writers devote an enormous amount of writing time to revision: "I rewrite everything, almost idiotically, I rewrite and work and work, and rewrite and rewrite some more" (Murray, 1975, p. 9). Many of the world's finest writers testify to the crucial role of revision. A few of their comments are listed below.

Toni Morrison: Because the best part of all, the absolutely most delicious part, is finishing it and then doing it over. That's the thrill of a lifetime for me: if I can just get done with that first phase and then have infinite time to fix it and change it. I rewrite a lot, over and over again, so that it looks like I never did. I try to make it look like I never touched it, and that takes a lot of time and a lot of sweat. (Murray, 1990, p. 186)

Vladimir Nabokov: I have rewritten—often several times—every word I have ever published. My pencils outlast their erasures. (Charlton, l980, p. 29)

James Dickey: I have endless drafts, one after another; and I try out 50, 75 or a hundred variations on a single line sometimes. I work on the process of refining low-grade ore. (Murray, 1990, p. 182)

Anne Sexton: Like a surgeon, right down to the bone. That's why I liked it. My method in writing a poem is to expand, expand, and then slice, and then expand, then slice, then slice, cut. And that's the way it always works. (Murray, 1990, p. 186)

Theodore Geisel (Dr. Seuss): To produce a 60-page book, I may easily write 1,000 pages before I'm satisfied. (Murray, 1990, p. 7)

Kurt Vonnegut, Jr.: This is what I find most encouraging about the writing trades: They allow mediocre people who are patient and industrious to revise their stupidity, to edit themselves into something like intelligence. (Charlton, 1980, p. 35)

Ernest Hemingway: I rewrote the ending to *Farewell to Arms,* the last page of it, thirty-nine times before I was satisfied. (Murray, 1990, p. 8)

Dylan Thomas: Almost any poem is fifty to a hundred revisions—and that's after it's well along. (Murray, 1990, p. l6)

Joan Didion: My writing is a process of rewriting, of going back and changing and filling in. In the rewriting process you discover what's going on, and you go back and bring it up to that point. (Murray, 1990, p. 182)

The revision practices of professional writers are relevant to teaching children to revise, but of course we must always consider the age and experience of those we teach. Clearly, young writers cannot revise a poem 100 times, as Dylan Thomas did. Nor can they revise story endings 39 times, as did Hemingway. Such expectations would be nonsensical. But we can expect young writers to learn the purpose and procedures of revision, and as they do, they gain greater command over their writing and confidence in themselves as writers. When revision is encouraged and nurtured, as it was in Ms. Elson's fifth grade classroom, children discover the pleasure, procedure, and purpose of revision. Kelly, a student in Ms. Elson's fifth grade classroom, puts this idea into simple but sincere words: "Well, I—I like to do revision, I mean I like to make my stories good when I write them, so I just like to revise them to make them good" (Elson, 1990, p. 87).

What we learn about revision from professional writers is this—revision is fundamental to successful writing. It is the ship on which writers set sail to discover meaning; it is the anvil on which writers shape their thinking; it is the microscope writers use to discover imperfections in their drafts.

The list below suggests some best practice tenets of revision that professional writers apply to their revising strategies.

REVISION PRACTICES AND CONCEPTS OF PROFESSIONAL WRITERS

1. Rewrite everything.
2. Discovering your best words and ideas requires constant rewriting.
3. Revise by expanding; then cut.
4. Don't stop revising until you are entirely satisfied. Don't be easily satisfied.
5. Extensive revision allows writers to move from nonsense to substance in their writing.
6. Understanding what's going on in your work comes through revision.

7. Revision not only remakes the piece; it remakes the writer as well.
8. Revision makes writing clear, true, and graceful.
9. Writers and teachers of writing disagree about many things, but the vast majority agree that revision is essential to effective writing.

RESEARCH ON REVISION

Braddock, Lloyd-Jones, and Schoer (1963) reviewed early revision research. Their review suggests two conclusions: (1) Researchers seldom studied revision during the first half of this century. (2) The few studies conducted during that time demonstrated that revision had a positive effect on writing. Hansen (1971) found that simply discussing revision with students resulted in overall improvement in writing. Odell and Cohick (1975) conducted a six-week revision program with ninth graders. They found that instruction centered around conferencing between drafts produced excellent results. Five out of six students improved the mechanical and substantive aspects of their writing. Beach (1979) evaluated three modes of revision and found that between-draft direct teacher evaluation led to more and better revision than two types of student self-evaluation.

A study conducted by the National Assessment of Educational Progress (1977) found that 9- and 13-year-olds revised mostly by making stylistic, mechanical, and informational changes; both 9- and 13-year-olds were less likely to revise by rearranging information or improving transitions between ideas; 13-year-olds made more substantive changes in their writing than did 9-year-olds. The study reported that students defined revision as adding and deleting information, substituting one word for another, and making mechanical changes.

Calkins (1979) reported a case study showing how teacher intervention shapes growth in revision. Initially, Andrea valued neatness and viewed writing as a one-step process. Over time, however, teacher intervention resulted in the development of substantive revision skills including revised content, added information, and other significant writing improvements. Emig (1971) used a case study approach to assess the composing processes of twelfth graders. She found that twelfth graders: (1) viewed school-sponsored revision as tedious and punishing, (2) revised self-sponsored writing more readily than school-sponsored writing, (3) reported that teachers offered few revision suggestions, and (4) viewed revision as the correction of minor faults in punctuation, spelling, and grammar. Graves (1979) reported five findings regarding young children's revision strategies: (1) personal experience topics make revision easier, (2) crossing out and drawing lines and arrows instead of erasing signals a new attitude toward revising, (3) rapid writers are more likely to revise in larger units than slow writers, (4) facility in topic listing and writing topic leads signals a strong capacity for revising, and (5) teachers can release children's revision potential.

Sommers (1980) examined the revision practices of student writers and experienced writers. She identified four revision operations (deletion, substitution, addition, and reordering) and four levels of change (word, phrase, sentence, and theme). Student writers described revision as a rewording and cleaning up process. They revised in a way consistent with their implicit definition of revision. Sommers described students as seeing ". . . their writing altogether passively through the eyes of former teachers or their surrogates, the textbooks, and are bound to the rules which they have been taught" (p. 383). Sommers (1980) also found that student writers revised to bring their essays into harmony with a pre-defined meaning, whereas experienced writers revised to discover and create meaning. Experienced writers envisioned their essay holistically, regarded revision as a recurring cycle of activities, and considered their audience. Sommers suggested that student writers need a new vision of revision: "Students need to seek the dissonance of discovery, utilizing in their writing, as the experienced writers do, the very difference between writing and speech—the possibility of revision" (p. 387).

Elson (1990) investigated fifth grade children's revision capabilities and practices. She found that students with *low revision profiles* revise in smaller linguistic units, focus mainly on form, view revising as correctness or incorrectness and not as a process aimed at improving the writing quality. When they do multiple drafts, the drafts closely resemble each other. On the other hand, students with *high revision profiles* think of revision as making changes in content, revise in larger linguistic units, exhibit a sense of ownership and control over their writing, see themselves as part of a writing community, and have confidence in themselves as writers. Lane (1993) explores the teaching of revision in his book, *After the End.* He starts with this excellent advice, "Traditionally, teachers have modeled perfection and students have struggled to meet that teacher's standards. Today, as teachers move toward individualized instruction and collaborative learning, students struggle to create and meet their own standards of excellence; teachers are learning to model the struggle" (p. 6).

Graves (1994) suggests that children need to understand the options available to them when they write. Writers' options are most clearly delineated by knowing what it means to revise. Teachers can illustrate writers' options through their own writing and through the instructional strategies they employ. Graves describes many ideas that foster effective revision, and argues that foremost among these ideas is the need for teachers to convey and children to understand the concept of revision. He summarizes his experience with teaching revision to children with this statement:

> Most of the focus in revision concerns the addition and deletion of information. In most traditional writing instruction, teachers have focused only on mechanics, the conventions of the craft, at the expense of what the writer is trying to communicate. They have required young writers to tinker with minor details in lieu of breathing new life into the piece. Make no mistake, conventions are important, and if they are poorly applied, both the writer and reader are ill served. But if teachers focused first on the children's intentions, then these young writers would connect more easily with themselves and be energized to continue writing. (Graves, 1983, p. 239)

The list on page 103 summarizes what research on revision reveals.

SUMMARY OF WHAT RESEARCH ON REVISION REVEALS

1. Early revision research usually found a positive effect. More recent research concurs with earlier results.

2. Student writers typically view revision narrowly. They think of revision as minor rewording and the correction of grammar, punctuation, and spelling.

3. Mature writers view revision broadly. They think of revision as discovery, rethinking, and making substantive changes.

4. In the past, revision instruction tended to emphasize correctness—form over substance. More recently, the emphasis has been on substance over form.

5. Revision is crucial to writing success.

6. Facility in topic selection and writing leads signals strong capacity for revising.

7. Teachers can release children's revision potential.

DEFINING REVISION

Many terms are used to describe revision and its related activities. Among the most common are: revising, editing, proofreading, rewriting, and reformulating. These terms are often loosely defined, if they are defined at all. This has led to some confusion, so I want to review the terms as they are used in the literature, and as I use them in this chapter. First, I will describe these terms as they are typically used in the literature. Then, I will give my own definitions of three key terms: revision, editing, and proofreading.

The Terminology of Revision

Revising: There are many definitions of revision. Faigley and Witte (1984) developed a taxonomy of revision with categories and subcategories describing the changes made in written text. Their taxonomy describes a set of revision operations that can be used to analyze written texts. Their taxonomy is thorough and thoughtful, and I have used it to guide my own thinking about revision. Graves (1983) and Calkins (1986) define revision as encompassing writing changes, ranging from mental rehearsal to actual changes in written text. Murray (1985) describes revision as collecting, planning, and developing drafts, an extraordinarily broad definition. Marder (1982) defines revision as discovering what you have to say. Still others describe revision as modifying point of view, adjustment in purpose or theme, making significant additions, deletions, or rearrangement of text. None of these definitions are necessarily wrong, but the tendency to define revision too broadly makes the term imprecise and renders it less useful.

Editing: Editing has a range of meanings in the literature. Sometimes it describes the polishing or refining stage of writing. Graves (1983), Murray (1985), and Fulwiler (1987) use the term in this sense. In this usage, editing includes stylistic changes, precise word selection, improving sentence structure, and other related language refinements. Hillerich (1985) and others use *editing* interchangeably with *revising.* In this usage, editing encompasses changes in writing of almost any sort.

Proofreading: There is general consensus on the meaning of proofreading. Proofreading is usually defined narrowly, as it should be. Typically, it involves correcting writing faults in grammar, usage, spelling, punctuation, format, and other infelicities of form. It is often used to describe writing changes that take place after substantive changes in content and language refinements have been completed.

Rewriting: Rewriting is a term some writers favor. It frequently describes broad, organic writing changes similar to uses of the term revision. Emig (1971), for instance, defines rewriting as changes that affect writing in organic ways.

Reformulation: Reformulation is a term that shows up only occasionally in the literature describing writing changes. Emig (1971) used this term in her classic study of twelfth graders' composing processes. She described reformulation as having three components: correcting, revising, and rewriting. Emig (1971) defined correcting as dealing with minor writing faults, revising as major changes that affect writing in organic ways, and rewriting as complete rethinking of a piece which might require scrapping a draft and starting over.

Revision terminology is often used loosely with little effort to define or restrict its parameters. Some researchers propose new terms, such as *reformulation.* There is nothing inherently wrong with this, but one may ask, "Are new terms needed?" Do they add anything meaningful to the discussion of revision?" I think not; they merely confuse the issue. We would be better off with fewer terms more carefully defined.

Revision Defined

An important criteria in defining revision is that revision deals only with changes in written text. If it does not involve written text, it is not revision. Any change in a written text constitutes revision whether it be large or small, form or substance, minor or major. Hence, editing and proofreading are revision of a specific sort, occurring and reoccurring at unpredictable times during writing, according to the habits of a given writer.

There are three phases of revision: revising, editing, and proofreading. Revising deals with broad organic changes primarily affecting content. Editing deals with language refinement. Proofreading deals with corrections of a more mechanical nature. This sounds like a sequence, first revise, then edit, then proofread. But this is not necessarily how writers actually work. Writers do not usually follow a revision sequence. It is not possible to specify exactly where revising ends and editing or proofreading begins. But there is usually a narrowing of changes in written text as succeeding drafts are written. Only in this sense can one think of moving from revising, to editing, to proofreading. It is a question of which activity, revising, editing, or proofreading, dominates as one proceeds from draft to draft. Three Faces of Revision illustrates, in an approximate sense, the relationship between revising, editing, and proofreading.

THREE FACES OF REVISION

Revising	Goal: Improve content
	Asks: What do I have to say?
Editing	Goal: Refine language
	Asks: How can I best say it?
Proofreading	Goal: Make final corrections
	Asks: What imperfections need correcting?

Revision has three faces: revising, editing, and proofreading. Writers return over and over again to improve their drafts. Each return refines the text so that gradually the writer's emphasis moves from establishing content to refining language and eventually proofreading. At any stage of revising, writers may modify content, refine language, and perfect the text in minor or major ways. Consequently, revision is recursive not linear.

Generally, one might expect the second draft to require more organic changes than the tenth draft. By the tenth draft more language refinement or proofreading might dominate the writer's work. But everything depends on the individual writer's sense of how satisfactory draft ten is. If satisfied, editing or proofreading might dominate in draft ten. If the writer is dissatisfied, perhaps revising will dominate the writer's work in draft ten.

Editing and proofreading are subcategories of revision. Editing can be defined as refining the language of a draft after the basic content is established. Proofreading can be defined as the correction of minor writing faults that remain after revising and editing are complete. Theoretically, editing commences after content is well established and proofreading happens just before publishing. But in real life, it doesn't happen that way for most writers.

Writers seldom revise in neat, sequential steps: revising, editing, and proofreading. Writers have many patterns of revision. Some writers do not edit or proofread until content is established; others edit and proofread as they go, almost line by line. Writers make changes, ranging from major content modifications to minor adjustments of punctuation, whenever it pleases them and in whatever order best serves their established revision habits.

Children show similar tendencies. Rose, for example, told her third grade teacher, Mrs. Stanley, "I like to revise after every four or five lines. Then I can keep track of what I'm doing. And I can figure out what I'm going to say next" (Stanley, 1988, p. 25). Rose doesn't distinguish between revising, editing, and proofreading. And it doesn't much matter that she doesn't. She has a strategy for making changes that works for her. For Rose, and many other writers, editing and proofreading are an integral and often indistinguishable part of revising.

A Revision Taxonomy

A taxonomy is a system for classifying ideas in some logical fashion. Faigley and Witte (1984) developed a parsimonious taxonomy of revision some years ago. The following taxonomy I have presented is closely related to the Faigley and Witte system of classifying concepts related to revision, though it differs in moderate ways from their work.

Revision occurs when any change is made in written text. There are two major revision changes: (1) changes in form, and (2) changes in substance. Changes in form typically involve the kind of corrections that a copy editor might make in preparing a piece just before publication. Changes in substance are more likely to alter meaning than changes in form, although changes in form can also alter meaning. Changes in either form or substance are brought about by completing any of four revision operations: adding, deleting, substituting, and rearranging.

Surface changes: Surface changes are concerned with the more mechanical aspects of writing such as spelling, punctuation, and format. But even the mechanical aspects of writing influence meaning to some degree. For example, the placement of a comma or the incorrect spelling of a word can make a trivial or a significant change in the meaning of a text. But, on the whole, the mechanical aspects of writing are more likely to change the surface of a text than the deeper meaning of it.

Meaning changes: Changes in meaning more frequently and more profoundly alter the substantive content of a text than surface changes. Meaning changes can be relatively minor such as substituting one synonym for another or changing tense. Or, they may be major such as adding or deleting sentences or paragraphs, a change in point of view, adjustment of purpose, and other organic changes that affect the deep structure meaning of a text. Meaning changes take place at three levels: word-phrase level, sentence-paragraph level, and whole composition level.

Four revision operations: There are four revision operations: adding, deleting, substituting and rearranging. Each operation requires different considerations. For young writers, adding is the easiest operation and rearranging text the most difficult. Substituting and deleting fall somewhere in between.

1. Adding: Good writing is complete without being wordy. Writers must learn to reread their drafts and ask: Have I left out important information? Will my readers need to know more? Children learn to respond to these questions through feedback from peers and teachers. Through instruction and practice, they learn to be an audience for their own writing. Adding information is probably the easiest revision operation for introducing children to content revision. Even first graders quickly grasp the idea of adding to their compositions.

2. Deleting: Good writing is concise. Sentences need no extra words, paragraphs no redundant sentences, compositions no irrelevant information. Writers must learn to delete redundant words and sentences, irrelevant

information, and cluttering detail. But this is a difficult operation for young writers. Teacher modeling, peer review, and other instructional methods are essential in guiding children to delete unneeded words, sentences, and paragraphs.

3. Substituting: Substitution is one of the most common revision operations. Revision often requires substituting one chunk of information for another, one sentence for another, one word for another. Substituting involves the simultaneous application of two operations, deleting and adding. There is a sense, therefore, in which substitution is not a separate operation, though I have treated substitution as though it were.

4. Rearranging: Order is crucial to all forms of writing. A paragraph's punch can be destroyed by misplacement of one sentence within it; a plot can be rendered useless by the premature disclosure of a crucial detail; an argument ruined by injudicious arrangement of reasons. Rearranging words and ideas into their most effective sequence is a complex skill. As writers mature, they must learn to rearrange sentences, paragraphs, and larger chunks of information within a composition. Writing on a computer facilitates rearranging text. Children who do not have access to a computer can be shown how to cut and paste and how to draw arrows to show how text can be rearranged.

Four levels of surface changes: Surface changes occur at four levels. Usually surface changes influence meaning in a minor way, though there may be exceptions to this general rule.

1. Spelling. The essential meaning of a text is seldom affected by spelling errors. For example, children's writing can almost always be understood completely even though there may be a substantial number of invented spellings. Even when spelling errors influence meaning, they usually do so in a minor way. Homophone misspellings may occasionally be an exception to this general rule.

2. Punctuation. Punctuation changes normally change meaning in a minor rather than in a major way. This does not mean that punctuation is unimportant. On the contrary, appropriate punctuation makes writing easier to read; consequently it is important to punctuate according to standard rules.

3. Format: Format has to do with arrangement of text on a page. Such matters as indenting, manner of using heading, margins, and other such matters come under this category. Like punctuation, formatting is intended to make the arrangements of text more convenient for the reader, though it seldom influences meaning at a substantive level.

4. Grammar and usage: Of the four surface changes outlined in the Revision Taxonomy on page 108, grammar is the most difficult to categorize as a surface change. There are grammatical changes in text which can have a significant influence on meaning. In most instances, however, such changes are more likely to have a minor influence.

Three levels of meaning changes: Changes that significantly influence meaning occur at three levels: word-phrase level, sentence-paragraph level, and whole composition level. Of course, such changes do not always change meaning in a substantive way.

1. Word-phrase: Changes at the word-phrase level are the most common. The operation most often performed is substituting one word or phrase for another. Words can also be added, deleted, or rearranged.

2. Sentence-paragraph: Rearranging sentences and paragraphs within a composition strengthens writing immeasurably, but immature writers seldom attempt it unless guided to do so.

3. Whole composition: Writing changes can take place at the level of the whole composition. One way this happens is to throw away a draft and start over. More commonly, whole composition changes evolve through addition and deletion of small and large chunks of information, changing point of view, reconceptualizing theme, and rearranging information within the composition.

From a teacher's perspective, there is a practical reason to understand the components of revision. For instance, some teachers are understandably reluctant to teach first graders to revise. But once they understand that adding to a composition is revising, it becomes obvious that first graders can revise, since they often add to their compositions spontaneously. Once first graders learn that adding is revising, the next challenge is to try deleting or substituting, perhaps at the word level initially. Rearranging is more challenging, but manageable for some first graders. However, it is of utmost importance to first establish fluency in writing before concepts about revising are considered. Below is a taxonomy summarizing revision operations and changes.

REVISION TAXONOMY

Operations	Surface Changes	Meaning Changes
Adding	Spelling	Word-phrase
Deleting	Punctuation	Sentence-paragraph
Substituting	Format	Whole composition
Rearranging	Grammar	

This taxonomy roughly categorizes the revision operations and the influence that various changes have on meaning. It is only a rough guide, since language and writing tasks are too complex to adequately classify. Major elements of this taxonomy were first described by Faigley and Witte (1984).

PRINCIPLES AND PRACTICES OF REVISION INSTRUCTION

Few things are more practical than a philosophy of instruction. A philosophy is a star to steer by, a compass on a dark night. A philosophy has a steadying influence. We must all develop our own philosophy; the best ones do not come ready made. I have a philosophy of revision, and it is set forth in the following statements of principles and practices. Perhaps you will find that we share a common philosophy, perhaps not. Undoubtedly, you will have principles and practices of your own to add to my list. Surely you will reject or modify some of mine. If it is going to be *your* philosophy, it must reflect your values, experience, and knowledge.

Focus on Content

Honor content above all else. Take content into account when you evaluate writing. Nobody buys books to marvel at the lovely sprinkling of commas and periods. But the presentation of wonderful ideas, well, that kind of book people will stand in line to buy. Children can learn to revise for form and substance. If this is to happen, however, revision instruction and practices must emphasize substantive revision changes while simultaneously deemphasizing the trivial revision focus that has come to prevail in the minds of many young writers.

Teachers and parents must also distinguish between changes involving substance and changes involving form. Megan, for instance, reveals how she has had to educate her father about what's important in revising a first draft: "I made a lot of mistakes and he kept telling me how to spell stuff and I said, 'Well, it's only a first draft and I don't need to be real perfect at it' " (Elson, 1990, p. 74). Ms. Elson has taught Megan the difference between form and substance, and now Megan explains to her father that her draft isn't at the stage where she is concerned about form. That will come later when she is ready to publish a final draft of her story. Megan knows that will be time enough to worry about matters of form. In the meanwhile, she is saying, in effect, "Right now I'm concerned about more important things, content not form."

Ms. DeWard's diary entry tells of her efforts to connect writing to content. She found that writing served a useful metacognitive purpose—it helped her fourth graders realize they don't know enough about their topic.

A TEACHER'S DIARY : Jennifer DeWard

I have been using writing more in the content areas lately because I know that when students write about something, they are more likely to remember it. If a fourth grade student can't write about photosynthesis, it is likely that he or she is not clear about the concept. However, if a student can write some details about photosynthesis, it probably means that he or she understands something about the topic.

In social studies we will be studying about the Pilgrims for the next couple of weeks. I asked my students today if they knew anything about the Pilgrims, and they stated that they knew a lot because they had learned about it since first grade. Instead of having the students orally tell me the facts they remembered, I asked them to write down anything they thought they knew about the Pilgrims. I explained that the assignment was not for a grade, and that they didn't even have to write in complete sentences. I gave them five minutes.

As I walked around the classroom, I noticed that many students were having trouble thinking of more than one or two things to write down. I also noticed that many of my students were confusing the Pilgrims' voyage with Columbus' voyage. I knew that I would correct the confusion immediately after the writing time.

The most important lesson my students learned through writing today is that they really don't know that much about the Pilgrims. While they thought they knew a lot, they realized that their knowledge was limited. They seemed more ready to learn because they knew that they did indeed have a lot to learn.

Seek Audiences for Writing

The teacher is an important audience for writing, and there are other audiences in addition to teachers and peers. Every time I visited Ms. Ayres third grade class, I was greeted with a lovely request: "Dr. Cramer, would you like to hear the story I wrote?" I enjoyed listening, and they loved to read to me. One reason Ms. Ayres invited me into her classroom was to provide an additional audience for her children's writing. Outside audiences are important. A headmistress I met in England encouraged teachers to send children to her office to read aloud their best pieces of writing. Afterwards, she displayed the children's writing on her office wall.

Billy, a fifth grader, is beginning to develop a sense of how he wants his writing to sound when his teacher or peers hear it or when he hears it himself as he rereads it.

MS. ELSON: How would you describe the kinds of changes you make?

BILLY: Well, in my "World War XVIII" draft, I crossed out a whole page.

MS. ELSON: Why did you cross out that page?

BILLY: 'Cause it didn't sound right.

MS. ELSON: Do you remember what was wrong with it or it just didn't fit?

BILLY: Well, it just, it mostly didn't fit, but some of the words were kind of low-grade words.

MS. ELSON: What do you mean by low-grade words?

BILLY: Well, they didn't sound right. It just said, "and left the room."

MS. ELSON: And what might you write instead?

BILLY: "and left the room as fast as a cheetah," or something. (Elson, 1990, p. 76)

Find interested audiences for children's writing and your writing program will be immeasurably strengthened.

Set Standards and Expectations

Writing is change, and this means substantial change, not merely changing a few surface features and making a neater copy. Unfortunately, many children have learned that revision means surface changes. Some of them even develop strategies to satisfy shallow expectations. Charles, a seventh grader, divulged his bankrupt, though admittedly practical, strategy in this revealing comment: "I always make a few mistakes in my first draft so that I will have something to change when the teacher has us make a second draft." Charles does not have a revision standard, but perhaps he has a philosophy. Perhaps he has never been taught or never learned a revision standard, but he desperately needs one. Teach children the right standard of revision: good writing nearly always requires changes in content as well as in language refinement, to say nothing of changes in form. It is wise to challenge children, but a challenge should be attainable. Learn what is reasonable to expect from each child. Gain a feel for children's writing experience, skills, and background knowledge. Gradually, you will sense the limits of editorial suggestion. Then hold children to standards that are within their reach.

Make Time for Revision

To revise a piece of writing in a substantive way may require stretching the work out over a period of weeks or, in some cases, even months. Kelly, a fifth grader, took five months to complete six drafts of her fiction story, "Snobby Star." Mercedes took two months to write and revise four drafts of her personal narrative, "Getting a Little Sister."

> MS. ELSON: A lot of changes. What kinds of things did you do?
>
> MERCEDES: I crossed out. I changed sentences all around. I deleted things . . . I added. I added dialogue. I did almost everything. . . (Still looking through drafts). I think it took me four drafts counting my final draft.
>
> MS. ELSON: What was the original date on the first piece? Let's look at that.
>
> MERCEDES: February 6th. (Laughs)
>
> MS. ELSON: Right. And then the last draft was . . .
>
> MERCEDES: April 3rd. (Elson, 1990, p. 79)

Ms. Elson runs a classroom where children write every day and often choose to write when they have free time. Of course, both Mercedes and Kelly wrote many other pieces while working on their drafts. Professional writers understand the need for time to draft, revise, and rethink a piece of writing. Teachers, under pressure of time and many responsibilities, are more accustomed to expecting writing assignments to be completed quickly. But good writing cannot be hurried. Determining the right amount of time to devote to writing is difficult and varies from situation to situation. Pliny's motto was, "Never a day without a line." This would be ideal, but the ideal is seldom achievable. An ideal to shoot for would be:

Kiley knows how to revise her own writing. She can work independently, with her teacher, or with her peers when she's ready to revise.

(1) write four or five days a week, (2) sustaining writing for 45 to 60 minutes at a time, and (3) make writing part of every school subject.

Give Access to Peers

Peer access is essential to an effective writing program. Once children have learned the rudiments of revision, they can help one another revise. Writing is inhibited in classrooms where children have little or no sanctioned access to their peers. A successful writing program comes about when the classroom becomes a writing community, a place to work out problems and seek advice from one's teacher or peers. Billy is a member of such a writing community, as this conversation suggests:

> Ms. ELSON: Sometimes I see you sitting there. You look like you're deep in thought. What are you doing when you're doing that?
>
> BILLY: Well, I'm sitting there thinking about, like, what I should write about, what a character should do, or what a better word is, so I usually sit there and think about it. Or sometimes when I get stuck and I'm really stuck, then I have to go and see Robbie or Ryan or a couple more people.
>
> Ms. ELSON: Did you do that in the past? Talk with your friends or have conferences about your writing?
>
> BILLY: I did that pretty much because sometimes I just go over to Robbie's or Ryan's desk and ask'em what a better title would be or I read it to them and I conference with them and then we decide if this sounds right or not. (Elson, 1990, pp. 67–68)

Publish Children's Writing

Publishing is the reward of effective revision. Grown-up writers and children are much alike. Both benefit from the powerful stimulus of publication. When I visit writing classrooms, I am often asked to listen to a recently written piece. Sometimes I am shown a classroom-published book, and asked to read it. Authors have tender feelings about their pieces. Pride of authorship is a wonderful emotion, and one that should be celebrated. I've never forgotten the day I received copies of my first book. It seemed wonderful to just look at it, feel it, read a few paragraphs. Book making is a wonderful outlet for publishing children's writing. And there are other possibilities, such as a class newspaper, and magazines that publish children's writing.

Christy, a third grader, wrote a story, "The Dragon Who Couldn't Breathe Fire" (Figures 5.1, 5.2, and 5.3). The story and how it came about is a case study in how excellent teaching can bring out the best in a young writer. Read the first draft (Figure 5.1). Christy misspelled 10 words in her original draft (breave for breathe, apone for upon, excpt for except, breave for breathe, word for worried, lefted for left and brong for brought). Her teacher, Mrs. Palmer, helped Christy correct the errors in preparation for publishing her story in a book.

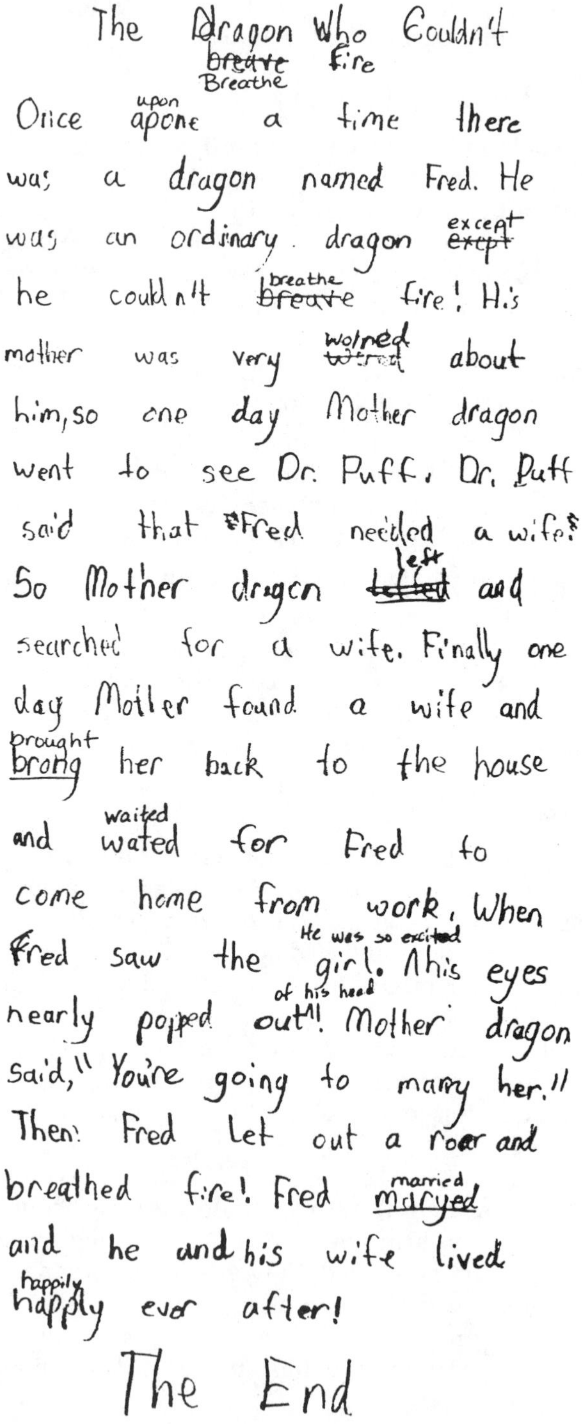

The Dragon Who Couldn't
~~breave~~ Fire
Breathe

Once a~~p~~one a time there
    upon
was a dragon named Fred. He
was an ordinary dragon ~~exept~~
                              except
he couldn't ~~breave~~ fire! His
            breathe
mother was very ~~worred~~ about
                  wolried
him, so one day Mother dragon
went to see Dr. Puff. Dr. Puff
said that Fred needed a wife!
So Mother dragon ~~toffed~~ and
                   left
searched for a wife. Finally one
day Mother found a wife and
~~brong~~ her back to the house
brought
and ~~wated~~ for Fred to
    waited
come home from work. When
                He was so excited
Fred saw the girl. His eyes
                of his head
nearly popped out! Mother dragon
said," You're going to marry her."
Then Fred let out a roar and
breathed fire! Fred ~~maryed~~
                     married
and he and his wife lived
happily
~~happly~~ ever after!

The End

Figure 5.1   Christy's Original Story: The Dragon Who Couldn't Breathe Fire

Caps for Sale by Esphyr Slobodkina

Character: Peddler
Problem: How to get the peddler's caps back from the monkeys
Trials: 1. Shook 1 finger
               2. Shook 2 fingers
               3. Stamped his feet
Solution: Threw his caps on ground
Resolution: Got his caps back
Ending: "Caps for Sale"

The Dragon Who Couldn't Breathe Fire by Christy

Character: Fred
Problem: Couldn't breathe fire
Trials: None
Solution: Got a wife
Resolution: Breathed fire
Ending: Lived happily ever after

Figure 5.2   Story Grammar Chart

Christy and Mrs. Palmer had a revision conference. As they discussed the first draft, Mrs. Palmer realized Christy could improve her story. How to do this without upsetting the young writer? Mrs. Palmer read *Caps for Sale,* by Esphyr Slobodkina, to the class. Together, they filled in the elements of the story grammar of Slobodkina's book (see Figure 5.2). Then they did the same thing with Christy's book. Comparing the story grammars of the two books, they discovered one story grammar element missing in Christy's story. Christy's story had everything except trials—sometimes called events. Christy's book had a main character (Fred), a problem (Fred couldn't breathe fire), a solution (Fred got a wife), a resolution (Fred breathed fire) and an ending (Fred and his new wife lived happily ever after) but no trials. Mrs. Palmer suggested that Christy might want to add some trials to her story. Christy added several trials and added other details to her story. Then Christy published her book (Figure 5.3). It had 14 beautifully illustrated pages. Peruse figures 5.1, 5.2, and 5.3.

The instructional events leading to the production of Christy's book illustrate two important revision concepts. First, young children can revise. Adding to a piece of writing is the easiest and perhaps the best place to begin revision instruction. Second, excellent instruction works. Mrs. Palmer used conferences, mini-lessons, and modeling to help Christy produce an outstanding published piece of writing.

**The Dragon Who Couldn't Breathe Fire
by Christy**

Dedicated to Katie

Page 1: Once upon a time there was a dragon named Fred.

Page 2: He was an ordinary dragon except he couldn't breath fire.

Page 3: His mother was very worried about him, so one day Mother dragon went to see Dr. Puff. Dr. Puff said that Fred needed a wife.

Page 4: So Mother dragon left and searched for a wife.

Page 5: She looked in caves, she found old ladies.

Page 6: She looked in a mountain, she found men watching TV.

Page 7: She looked underground. She found a nursery for baby dragons.

Page 8: She finally looked up in the clouds, she found a prom!

Page 9: There were young dragons everywhere! Mother dragon found a picture of Fred. She got everyone's attention. She showed all of the girls the picture.

Page 10: One dragon named Shirley volunteered to be his wife. She was the prettiest dragon there! She was pink with purple plates and eye lids, and had light blue eyes.

Page 11: Mother dragon brought her home and waited for Fred to come home from work.

Page 12: Fred saw the girl. He was so excited his eyes nearly popped out of his head.

Page 13: Mother dragon said, "You're going to marry her!" Then Fred let out a roar and breathed fire!

Page 14: Fred married and he and his wife lived happily ever after!

About the Author
The author of this book is Christy. She is 9 years old and in third grade. She loves to dance and has one brother.

Figure 5.3 **Published book**

Collect and Study Children's Writing

Years ago, I began collecting children's writing. This literature had a profound influence on my understanding of what children are capable of writing. It is so easy to underestimate children's writing potential. Teachers can start their own collection of children's writing. Collect pieces from your students as well as pieces from students outside of your classroom. Children's compositions can be found in newspapers, magazines, and professional books. Read this extraordinary literature, and you will gain new insight into children's creative capabilities. The following poem appeared in an annual publication sponsored by a local community group in Northern Michigan. Their publication, *Exposures,* (Hungerford, Landry, Smith, and Stowe, 1992) is a labor of love honoring the creativity of children in their community.

Need We Say More?

Violence
I must forget
What's the meaning of life?
Nothing matters
Death
Why care?
Things attacking
Anger
Lost
Entrapped
Suicide
Emptiness of life
'   Engulfed
Black hole of reality
No hope
YOW! I'M ON A ROLL!!
Confusion
Rejection
Frustration
No reason
Hopeless
Darkness
Nothingness
Loneliness
Emptiness
Choking
Drowning
I want to escape
It's just a waste
Cold dark places

ugly faces
Why?
Die
Heart cried
Eternal sorrow
No tomorrow
IT IS WRITTEN IN A HANDBOOK?
(NOW I'M JUST GUESSING)
THAT POETRY MUST BE SO DAMN DEPRESSING?!
Aerin, Grade 12

Revise All Types of Writing

All types of writing may be revised, but not all writing need be revised. A poem is just as likely to require change as a business letter, perhaps even more so. When I first started teaching I thought that personal writing was too delicate for the rigors of revision. That, I am afraid, was a notion borne on the wings of distrust and nurtured in the halls of ignorance. I know better now. Sensitivity and selectivity are essential, but there is no a priori reason for exempting any type of writing from revision. Poetry, stories, personal narratives, essays, reports, letters—any and all may be revised. The decision to revise must always take into account the writer's pur-

You're never too young to revise. Young children, like Benjamin, find adding the easiest revision operation.

pose and the circumstance under which a piece came to be drafted in the first instance. In a classroom where many pieces are written, many options are available. Let the teacher and the writer confer, but let the final decision rest with the writer.

SUMMARY OF REVISION PRINCIPLES AND PRACTICES

1. Focus on content. While correctness is important, the first premise of revision is to rethink one's ideas by striving for the simple, clear, and precise use of language.

2. Writers need an audience capable of appreciating and evaluating the writer's work.

3. Set fair and reasonable standards for good writing and expect your students to meet those standards. Challenges are necessary but they must be attainable.

4. Revision requires a heavy investment of the writer's time, and instruction must be organized to accommodate this requirement.

5. Give children access to their peers so that, over time, a community of writers can develop the camaraderie and spirit needed to foster effective writing.

6. Publish children's writing in a variety of forums, including books, children's magazines, young authors' conferences, bulletin boards, and other forums.

7. Collect and study children's writing.

8. Revise all types of writing. Any piece of writing may be revised. Purpose and audience is the key to decisions about what shall be revised and what need not be revised.

REVISION STRATEGIES

Teach revision. It may be the most important instruction you can provide to improve children's writing. Some revision skills are relatively easy to teach at an introductory level, but they require constant monitoring and instruction in order to develop more complex layers of revision knowledge. Occasional episodes of revision experience will not be sufficient to develop the skills and strategies needed to revise well. Children need instruction and practice in revising throughout their school career. The strategies described will help you teach the revision skills children need to write well.

Revision Conferences

Revision conferences help children reconsider their words and ideas. Three kinds of revision conferences are described: content, editing, and proofreading. Each has its own features: (1) content conferences focus on ideas and information; (2) editing conferences focus on language refinement; (3) proofreading conferences focus on correcting minor errors in a final or near final draft.

Content conference: Get children talking about their writing, listen carefully, and provide helpful suggestions and encouragement. Below is a list of guidelines for revision conferences that focus on content.

CONTENT CONFERENCES

1. Effective response starts with critical listening. Ask questions, make suggestions, give encouragement. Three resources help guide your decisions: the writer's spoken words, the writer's written words, and your experience as a teacher.

2. Focus on the central meaning of the piece, not on the details, language, or writing conventions. A content conference deals with ideas, information, organization, direction, intention. Ask writers to tell you about their pieces; encourage them to summarize the whole, explain a troublesome part, or read a part that is not working.

3. Keep the conference brief. Long conferences offer the temptation of doing more than you should. Three or four minutes will usually suffice. You are there to be a sounding board. You are not there to rewrite the piece or take it over.

4. Respond to student writing honestly and sincerely. Your goal is to influence and enlarge the native gifts children possess.

5. Ask questions that are likely to elicit expansive responses. Open ended questions and comments are likely to elicit elaborated responses:
   Tell me more about this character.
   I didn't quite follow this part. Can you explain it to me?
   What additional ideas do you have for this story?
   What do you like about your story?
   Is there anything you don't like about what you've written?

6. Choose the conference location that best suits your personality and circumstances. Some teachers prefer to circulate among children to conduct conferences. But you may be more comfortable working at your desk. Choose the procedure that works best for you.

7. End a conference gracefully and promptly. Sometimes a simple question will do: "What will you do next?" Sometimes a word of encouragement is best: "You're making progress; you have good ideas; keep working."

Brittany's story, shown in Figure 5.4, is an example of a revision conference that worked well. Brittany, a first grader, wrote a story about a witch. The Language Arts consultant read it and told Brittany it was a fine story. Then she asked Brittany a few questions about her story during a revision conference. As a result, Brittany decided to add some details in a second draft of her story. Figure 5.4

Brittany's Original Text	Brittany's Translated Text
Once a witch livd in a old seah.	Once a witch lived in an old shack.
The witch was prite.	The witch was pretty.
She had loeg brown haer to her	*She had long brown hair to her*
knees. She was scine and she	*knees and she was skinny and she*
wore a bottef goen	*wore a beautiful gown.*
She wotia to be ugley	She wanted to be ugly
because she was a witch's	*because she was a witch*
and ather witch's were uogly	*and other witches were ugly.*
She scerem, I want to be ugley!	She screamed, "I want to be ugly!"
The frog that lved near hered her	The frog that lived near heard her
and he was a majic frog.	*and he was a magic frog.*
He came over to help the witch.	*He came over to help the witch.*
He aset her "wy are you	He asked her, "Why are you
scremen?"	screaming?"
I wont to be ugly.	I want to be ugly.
The frog said he wood help her	*The frog said he would help her.*
You need gren haer.	You need green hair.
"Thac you" sied the witch.	*"Thank you," said the witch.*
"You need seom hole's in your bots	"You need some holes in your boots
and a triagel hat" sied the witch	and a triangle hat"
sied the frog.	*said the frog.*
Oh thac you	"Oh thank you,"
sied the witch.	said the witch.
You most lose the manr.	"You must lose the manners.
Necs tiem you want to chage uos	Next time you want to change, use
the pheon, OK?" seid the frog	the phone, OK?" said the frog.
She woen the uglgts witch contes	She won the ugliest witch contest.
The End	The End

Figure 5.4   Brittany's First and Second Drafts of Her Witch Story

shows the first draft text in plain font. Brittany's revisions are shown in italic font. First graders can revise. They are most adept at adding to their drafts since adding is the easiest of the four revision operations.

Editing conference: After writers have discovered what they have to say, they need to ponder how to say it more effectively. This is where editing enters the picture. Children may not take naturally to editing. It is difficult, and more often than not, tedious. Try to inject a sense of excitement about the eventual product, even if the process itself is sometimes tedious.

Editing focuses primarily on perfecting word choice, writing sentences with clarity and economy, developing coherent paragraphs, unifying the whole composition, and expressing ideas in a style unique to the individual writer. Nobody has described the skills of editing more succinctly and eloquently than Strunk and White (1979) in their famous little book, *The Elements of Style.* Every teacher should have a copy of this book. It is considerate of your time as well as your pocketbook. In fewer than 100 pages, you can learn much of what you need to know of the skills of editing. Teaching children to edit their own writing is a tall order. It takes enormous effort to achieve even modest results. No one ever said teaching was going to be easy, but it can be exciting and rewarding.

An editing conference deals primarily with language refinement, but the line between content and language refinement is narrow. As language is refined content is inevitably modified in subtle but important ways. Murray (1985) suggests think-aloud modeling as one approach to teaching editing: "Then I have the student move over beside me and I go to work on the text in front of the student, talking out loud about what I'm doing: 'I wonder what would happen if I cut up these sentences here. Hmn. Doesn't seem to do it. Maybe I've just got to make these clauses parallel' " (p. 168). Murray is thinking out loud about editing while the student watches. Only a few moments of such modeling is done in one sitting, and there is no intention of editing the piece for the student. Rather, the goal is to model how the work of editing proceeds.

Proofreading conference: Separate conferences for proofreading may not be necessary. Some changes made during an editing conference may be of a proofreading nature—spelling, punctuation, format. If a separate proofreading conference is desired, however, it could be conducted in a manner similar to an editing conference except the focus is more narrow. Proofreading is the final stage of the revision process—the perfecting of a piece of writing just prior to publication or public display. Typically, proofreaders are looking for minor writing faults such as punctuation and spelling. But, as experienced writers know, larger writing problems are sometimes discovered at the last minute. When this happens changes should be made. The standards of proofreading must be flexible. Inexperienced writers are not able to achieve the same results as experienced writers. The goal is to help children take a piece of writing as far as their capabilities will allow. To push beyond this point will do more harm than good. Only the teacher, sensitive to the context in which writing is produced, can know when this point has been reached.

Peer Revision Conferences

There is one potential drawback to peer revision. Students who know little about revision cannot provide useful information to their peers. They have little to share except their uncertainty. Before organizing peer revision conferences, make sure students have acquired adequate revision knowledge. As students gain experience in revising their own writing, their ability to share this knowledge with peers becomes credible. Revision knowledge comes from practical experience such as revision workshops, conferences, and modeling. Participating in teacher-directed revision experiences gives children the practical knowledge they need to participate in similar conferences with their peers.

After students have acquired sufficient revision experience, organize small-group peer conferences. Initially, peer revision groups should be small. Pairing two or three students is sufficient for initialing peer conferences. Give specific instructions for helping one another and monitor performance.

Later, organize larger revision support groups. Revision support groups have several purposes. The members encourage each other's writing efforts, serve as an additional resource for writing, provide a real audience for writing, and critique each other's drafts at various stages of development. Revision support groups may gradually evolve their own operating procedures. Five effective practices for peer conferences are listed below.

PEER CONFERENCING

1. Encouraging: Writers read their drafts to the group. The first comments should be supportive, centering around what the listeners find positive about the piece.

2. Summarizing: Listeners summarize the piece back to the writer. This helps writers know whether they have communicated what they intended to communicate, and whether their writing is coherent to others.

3. Suggesting: Listeners make specific suggestions for improving the draft. They may, for example, suggest that more information is needed.

4. Questioning: After listening to group members, the writer may have questions. A writer may, for instance, ask for clarification of suggestions the group has made or ask about an issue not raised.

5. Owning: Authors decide what advice to use and how to use it. The group offers advice, but they do not make revision decisions. Writers remain in charge of their own writing.

Cooperative learning can be an important part of writing. Peer revision benefits writing in three ways: (1) it improves writing, (2) it helps students develop standards for judging the quality of their own writing, and (3) it broadens the audience for writing.

Jennifer DeWard describes her experience with peer conferencing among her fourth graders in her "Voices" piece.

VOICES FROM THE CLASSROOM: Jennifer DeWard

Peer Revision Groups

One of the most important aspects of writers' workshop in my classroom is the use of peer revision groups. I believe that my students produce better writing when they discuss their writing with peers. Before beginning peer revision, I model the types of interactions I want to see occur. Early in the year, I select a few students and we role play peer revision procedures. I give my students a list of focus questions to use when they are beginning peer revision work.

In my classroom, peer revision groups consist of 2–4 students. My students are not assigned to groups; rather students form their own groups when the need arises. When a student needs a sounding board for a piece of writing, he or she asks other students to listen to the writing in a peer revision group. Students may choose to read part of their writing or the whole piece to the group. I am not present during all these peer interactions.

Before reading a piece, the author asks the other students one or more questions he or she wants answered. For example, "Do I give enough detail about. . . ?" or "Can you picture this scene in your head?" These types of questions give the audience a focus. Audience members are asked not to interrupt the reading of the story but to give their comments at the end.

After a piece is read, peers usually give a compliment then answer the focus questions. I am amazed at how perceptive my fourth graders are about writing, and what good suggestions they have for their peers. Students are usually receptive to ideas given by peers. Oftentimes peer revision groups end after a few suggestions have been given, but sometimes a group will meet for 20 to 30 minutes. This occurs because the students in the group feel so comfortable together they may revise sentence by sentence, even word by word. I am pleased when this occurs because I know that those students will choose to meet again.

Rereading

Rereading is a revision strategy. Like Poe's purloined letter, it is so obvious that its fundamental importance in revision may be overlooked. There are two good reasons for rereading a draft: to make changes in the draft and to get new ideas for continuing the draft.

Making changes: When a draft has reached a certain stage, some writers get an itch to make changes. This itch occurs at different times for different writers. Kate, a third grade writer, gets the itch early: "I like to revise as I go. Sometimes I know I've written an absolutely horrible-sounding word and I like to stop every now and then to read my piece to see how it's going. So I revise at the same time" (Stanley, 1988, p. 21). Kate tells us she rereads for two reasons: to make changes and to get new ideas.

Kate's strategy of revising as she goes is perfectly acceptable. She revises in a way that works best for her. Each writer is different. Recognize this. Indeed, encourage it. As a draft is building, some writers, like Kate, can't resist changing it as they go, so they reread and patch potholes, or they find curves in the road that need straightening. When they have filled in the potholes and straightened the curves, they return to building the draft, often with new ideas. Some writers are only comfortable going back and forth from building to repairing. Others operate differently. Steve, a sixth grader, said, "I usually write three or four pages before I reread. I like to keep writing while things are going good." Whatever works best for an individual child is a good revision strategy. *If it ain't broke, don't fix it.* Of course, young writers need to be exposed to alternative strategies. I have found that young writers will adjust their revision strategies when they are introduced to new and better ones. Children are often more flexible than adults when it comes to learning new strategies.

Getting new ideas: Sometimes we should reread just to get new ideas for moving forward with a draft. Every writer has faced the perils of a partial draft. After a few sentences or paragraphs, we have nothing left to say, or so we think. Whenever this happens, reread the draft. Rereading helps writers discover new ideas. Mercedes, a fifth grader, explains how this works for her:

> Well, as I reread it, it helps me think about the story more. If I get stuck, I always reread my story and that always gets me going again. If I have no idea what's going to happen next, I always reread my piece and it helps me get thinking again. I put it in a sentence and I change it. I think the sentence I'm going to write and then I write it, and I read it. If it doesn't sound good, I make more changes. (Elson, 1990, p. 78)

Margaret, a third grader, finds that rereading also helps her get new ideas for continuing a draft. Rereading she said, ". . . gives me new ideas to go on and write the next part" (Stanley, 1988, p. 25). Broad jumpers can leap further when they back up and take another run at the pit. Rereading gives writers a running start on new ideas and directions.

Read Writing Aloud

Experienced writing teachers report that some writers seem to hear their writing problems more easily when they read their writing aloud than when they read it silently. Martha, a fourth grader, said to her teacher, "I can hear myself better when I read it out loud than when I read it to myself." Reading a draft aloud is a revision strategy that works well for some writers. Hearing the rhythm of your own words may stimulate new ideas and help you discover writing problems.

It is also helpful to have someone else read your writing to you. One of the advantages of working with a revision partner is that partners can read their pieces to each other. Encourage children to experiment with different revision strategies so they can, like Kate and Margaret, discover which strategies work best for them. Writers welcome a change of pace because writing is often lonely and tedious. Don't be shocked at this candid admission. Most writers will recognize the truth of this observation.

Think-Aloud Modeling

There are many ways to model writing to children. Murray (1985) recommends think-aloud modeling as a powerful way to help writers rethink their drafts. In think-aloud modeling, teachers talk aloud about what they are thinking as they revise in front of the class or in a personal conference. The idea is to demonstrate revision while students observe the decisions and considerations that go into making writing changes. The procedure is simple. Secure a piece of writing, preferably your own. Make a transparency and project the rough draft onto a screen. Start by reading a portion of the piece aloud. Talk in a natural way about changes you are considering. Then make the changes directly on the transparency so that the students can observe the connection between thinking aloud and the actual revision operation you perform.

As you make changes, use the proofreader's symbols shown below. These symbols communicate the revision changes that are intended, and they provide a common code that everyone can interpret. Even first graders have little trouble learning the basic proofreader's symbols, and they enjoy the professional touch these symbols lend to writing.

Follow up think-aloud modeling by having students perform think-aloud revision operations on their own writing or on a piece you have prepared for the occasion. The advantage of a prepared text is that you can deal directly with specific writing problems. On the other hand, the goal of revision is to teach children to revise their own writing. Use prepared text for specific purposes, but be sure that the preponderance of revision practice focuses on students' actual writing. Circulate among the students as they revise, listening to their think-aloud descriptions. Give instruction and encouragement as needed. In the "Voices" piece, Ms. Cohen, a first grade teacher, describes how she directed a think-aloud revision lesson.

PROOFREADER'S MARKS

make capital. (cap)   Take something out.

Make a sMall letter. (lc)   Add something. e

Add a period.   Transpose. (tr)

Add a comma   ¶ Make a new paragraph.

VOICES FROM THE CLASSROOM: Nancy Cohen

Adding Details to Writing

This year I have devoted more time to revision. I often use modeling to demonstrate revision. Here is a revision lesson I recently taught. I presented the following passage on the overhead projector:

> I went to my nephew's birthday party. It was fun.
> We played games and ate good food.

After reading this passage, I asked my students to make comments and ask questions. They began to ask questions about my nephew: How old is he? What presents did he get? What games did you play? What food did you have? We talked about how we could revise this passage to make it more interesting. Together we discovered how questioning leads to better writing. Following this lesson, we revised the passage by adding new information. This is how we changed the passage.

> My nephew's birthday was on October 13th. His name is Aaron and he turned four years old. It was at the Discovery Zone. There we played Hot Potato and ran through the crazy tunnels. For lunch, we ate pepperoni pizza and chocolate cake with oreo ice cream too. Aaron was excited by all of his presents. His favorite ones were the Tyco Race Track and Batman computer disk.

For several weeks I did similar activities. My students' revision strategies are beginning to show up in their writing. For example, my better writers are independently thinking of revision questions and are putting more details in their writing. During conferencing, I help my students think of content which will enhance their writing. Although my students are only in first grade, they are acquiring skills which will enable them to become independent writers.

WRITERS' WORKSHOP ON REVISION

Children need direct instruction in revision, although they seldom get it, as Emig's (1971) twelfth graders clearly stated. An excellent way to give direct instruction in revision is through revision workshops where revision is regularly taught (Cramer, 1973). The purpose of the workshop is to teach young writers to revise their own writing, and to enable them to gain independent revision skill. In order to gain independence, children must learn to change their own writing. Revision capability can grow if a variety of revision strategies and activities are part of the writing curriculum. Here is one way to conduct a revision workshop, though there are certainly other possibilities.

1. The materials needed are an overhead projector, chalkboard, transparency overlay, and grease pencil. Students will need a recently written draft. This draft may be written the day before the workshop, or it may be taken from children's writing folders.

2. For the first few revision workshop demonstrations, use pieces of your own writing. Later, after children become familiar with workshop procedures, conduct the workshop with anonymous pieces of student writing.

3. Project the writing onto the screen. Ask students to read the material. Then say, "What do you like about this piece?" List responses on the board in abbreviated form.

4. Ask the students to read the story again. Then ask, "Can anyone find something that could be changed? What improvements can you suggest?" Avoid telling students to find mistakes. Writing is about *change and improvement*. It is not a search for errors.

5. Make the changes students suggest directly onto the transparency. Comment on each suggestion, conveying praise for thoughtful suggestions and instructional advice as appropriate. In the beginning, children may tend to focus on punctuation, spelling, grammar, and other minor writing faults. Do not worry about this inclination. As children gain understanding of revision, their focus shifts to more substantive issues. You can also shift the focus yourself during the latter part of the revision workshop.

6. Select one item from the list, and ask students to apply it to their compositions. For example, you might say: "Read through your draft. Choose one sentence that could be improved. Write that sentence two or three different ways, and decide which one you like best."

7. Circulate among the children offering advice. This is a crucial step since it gives you an opportunity to give on-the-spot instruction and to evaluate student progress. Students will sometimes revise for more than the assigned task. Single out that behavior for recognition.

8. As revision skill grows, increase the number of revision tasks assigned in one session. Start with one. When students are able, assign an additional task or two. As confidence grows, focus on more substantive revision concerns by directing attention to content and language changes.

The following example will guide you through your first workshop. The example describes a revision workshop with sixth graders. These students had some revision background, mostly of a superficial nature. Students wrote on Monday. The teacher, Ms. Anderson, asked permission to use the story, "If I Were Rich," and conducted the workshop on the following day. For illustrative purposes, the workshop I have described covers much more ground than would normally be covered in a single workshop session. Start by reading "If I Were Rich."

If I Were Rich

If I had a lot of money I would be rich I would not buy a car motrsikl house and all the candy I could eat.

My mom and dad woulnt have to work any more either they would have their own house and all they needed to live. I would give money to poor people to I would not waste the money like some people. going to coledg is what I want to do with some of the money.

That is what I would do if I were rich

Getting started; looking at what is Ms. Anderson projected the story on to a screen. She instructed the children as follows: "Read the story carefully. Then tell me what you like about it." The students gave the following responses.

Words in the title are capitalized.

The word "I" is always capitalized.

Paragraphs are indented.

Most sentences start with a capital letter.

Several sentences have a period after them.

As Ms. Anderson wrote their comments on the board, she commented briefly on each. Notice that students' responses focused on the mechanical aspects of writing. This is a common pattern in the early stages of revision awareness. After the last comment, Ms. Anderson changed the focus by saying, "Think about the ideas in this story. What do you like about the ideas in this piece?" This elicited the following responses.

I like the things the writer wants to do with the money.

I think it's a good idea to share the money.

I thought the last sentence was good.

Sharing with Mom and Dad was the right thing to do.

The writer does not want to use the money foolishly.

Saving for college is a good idea.

Refocusing; considering improvements Up to this point, Ms. Anderson had focused on what the students liked about the piece. However, revision implies change. Revisers must find ways to improve writing. Ms. Anderson reoriented their thinking by saying: "You've done a good job looking at what was done well. Now, how can we make changes? How can we improve this piece?" Ms. Anderson's questions elicited these responses.

There should be a period after rich in the first sentence.

I don't think motorcycle and college are spelled right.

The word going should have a capital.

There should be commas after car and motorcycle.

There could be a period after either. They should be capitalized.

It should be t-o-o, not t-o, and it should have a period after it.

It is interesting, but not surprising, that these sixth graders recognized minor writing faults so readily. We sometimes think that because children fail to apply the conventions of writing that they have no knowledge of them. Often this is not true. These sixth graders knew more than they applied. Many children lack strategies for applying their knowledge. The revision workshop creates a context for applying writing knowledge while instruction and supervision are readily available.

Ms. Anderson's final question was, "Is there one sentence we could look at more closely and try to say the same thing another way?" One student suggested looking at the last sentence in the third paragraph which says: "going to coledg is what I want to do with some of the money." Students suggested five alternatives which Ms. Anderson wrote on the board.

I want to go to college with the money.

I'll use some of the money to go to college.

A good way to use some of the money would be going to college.

Since I want to go to college, I'll use some of the money for that.

I want to go to college. I'll use some of the money for that.

When they had finished Ms. Anderson commented: "Good, you've made some interesting suggestions, and you've shown me that you can think of different ways to write the same idea. This is what good writers do." Her remarks reinforced the importance of alternative ways of stating an idea, and she associated revision with what good writers do. In this session, she focused on alternative ways of stating an idea. She covered other writing concerns in subsequent sessions. Many revision skills can be taught in a workshop session. Over the course of the school year, Ms. Anderson taught many important writing skills and dealt with many writing issues in workshop sessions.

The final step; applying revision to personal writing The discussion had been completed, but one important instructional activity remained. Ms. Anderson instructed the students as follows: "Get out a piece of writing you've worked on before. Rewrite the lead sentence two or three different ways, and decide which one you like best. I'll be around to help you as you revise." As the students worked, Ms. Anderson circulated among them offering advice, instruction, and encouragement.

COMPOSING ON THE COMPUTER

I read an article in the *The New York Times Book Review* in which a poet claimed that poetry cannot be written on a computer. Poets, he argued, must feel the pencil in their hand and experience the rhythm of the words flowing from the tips of their fingers. A few weeks later, in the same publication, another poet ridiculed this notion as nostalgic nonsense. Writers love a good argument. I imagine similar arguments raged in ancient times as well. Centuries ago the argument may have gone something like this: "Poetry can't be written on papyrus. All this scratching with a quill and slopping ink all over your fingers destroys the rhythm you need to write poetry. Poetry can only be written on clay tablets using a stylus so you can feel the rhythm and flow of the words as the stylus slides over the wet clay."

There is a little bit of the Luddite in all of us. I admit, I was a computer Luddite. I did not want this labor saving device in my office. My computer literate colleague, Ann Porter, urged me to get a computer. The more she urged, the more I resisted. "I can write perfectly well without a computer, Ann," I claimed. "Fact is, I'd still be using a pencil instead of a typewriter if I hadn't injured my hand." Actually, I found it difficult to change, as many of us do. We are comfortable with familiar ways; new devices mean learning new ways; we suspect that that old way is best, or at least good enough. And sometimes we are right. But in the case of writing, the old way is not the best way. Computers are an extraordinarily valuable tool for improving writing, and they are uniquely valuable for revision.

We've all heard how technology is going to revolutionize teaching. We are rightfully skeptical. Some of us remember the teaching machines of the 1960s and wonder if the computer is nothing more than a fancy teaching machine. Well, the teaching machine and today's computers are as different as the Spirit of St. Louis is from the Concorde. I am not predicting that technology is about to revolutionize writing. Computers have influenced writing, though perhaps only modestly in many schools.

Computers are particularly valuable in teaching revision skills, and they make publication easy. Revising involves adding, deleting, substituting, and rearranging information. Any one of these operations can be simple or complex. A computer does not make writing decisions less complex, but once a decision has been made the computer makes the execution of that decision simpler. Moving text, for example, is a difficult chore to manage with pencil and paper, and it is not any easier on a typewriter. The computer makes moving text so simple even a writer can do it. Move a sentence or paragraph to a new spot. Read it. If you don't like it you can move it somewhere else, perhaps back to where you started. Young writers seldom rearrange text. Writing on a computer develops the skill of reorganizing information, an important skill that can improve writing substantially. The computer is an ideal tool for learning to organize and reorganize text since it provides the means by which it can be easily practiced.

Computers make it easier to experiment with writing ideas. This ease of manipulating text gives that advantage that E. M. Forster spoke of when he said, "How can I know what I think until I see what I say." Computers make "seeing what you say" easier. Visualization of thought is enhanced because computers have made the visualization of thought and the manipulation of written text simpler. Young writers get discouraged when they have to spend too much time recopying written work. Unless a piece is to be published or displayed, recopying is wasteful of children's time. There are ways around this problem. You can, for example, have children show revision changes by using proofreading symbols, double spacing so changes can be easily made, and marking changes with colored pens or pencils. But even these methods have limitations. Revision changes are easily made on a computer. After writing you are only a click away from producing a hard copy of what you have written.

Software programs designed to teach writing are available. Some of these programs are faithful to the writing process. They are interactive and lead students step-by-step through prewriting, drafting, revising, and publication. Computer assisted composition programs are more valuable, I believe, after children have experienced the writing process in the traditional fashion. There is no substitute for an excellent writing teacher. Writers need human interaction, especially in the formative stages of learning to write. However, once children have gained a foothold on the writing process, the computer can supplement writing instruction and provide useful practice.

Here are three examples of software, among many, for teaching students to write using computers. These programs provide for writing to be printed or presented through a slide show.

1. Microsoft Office: Published by Microsoft Corporation and available in Apple and IBM format. This software is made up of Microsoft Word for word processing, Microsoft Excel for spreadsheet and graphing, and Power Point for presentation capabilities. This software would be difficult for young students. Students use Microsoft Word for all of their writing, revising, and editing. They can scan pictures into their writing, create their own art work, and create tables and graphs for reports and insert them into their written text. Power Point allows the student to create a formal presentation using their writing whether it be a story they have written or a report they have researched. This software can be used in each of the curriculum disciplines. The Excel part of the program allows students to develop charts and spreadsheets which may be used for calculating results on a stock market unit. The spreadsheet can also be used by the teacher to calculate student grades.

2. HyperStudio: Published by Roger Wagner. A hypermedia developed for Apple and IBM format. This program has unlimited capabilities for student writing, animation, graphics enhancement, student drawing, and presentations. It can also be used by the teacher to develop portfolios in each class and have the students present their work to any audience. The writing can be presented in scrolling form. All writing such as reports, narratives, poems, and student books may be published and/or saved in a portfolio record. As good as this program is, it does take time and patience to learn. Students enjoy the challenge of this software.

3. Children's Writing and Publishing Center: Published by The Learning Company for Apple and IBM format. This is a writing program that is less challenging and is especially useful for younger students. It has simple graphics and easy to follow directions. Students in middle school may find this software too simplistic. There is a software available by the same company for older students.

Ms. Barbara Head, a middle school English teacher, has been conducting a research project for the past two years, comparing computer revision with paper and pencil revision. In her "Voices" piece, she describes some of the problems and opportunities associated with teaching middle schoolers to compose and revise on a computer.

VOICES FROM THE CLASSROOM: Barbara Head

Composing on a Computer

I teach writing in a middle school. I have used computers to teach writing, and I have used traditional methods. I am currently conducting research comparing computer assisted writing with traditional methods. I have found computers to be a wonderful tool for teaching writing, but there are instructional issues that must be faced if one is to succeed.

When students use computers for writing, ideas flow more fluently and writing is often improved. Computers make revising easier than the more tedious process of revising with pencil and paper. Three computer skills must be acquired before writing on a computer can be effective: (1) keyboarding, (2) the mechanics of revising text on a computer, and (3) spell checking.

Keyboarding involves learning the placement of keys on a keyboard and using correct finger placement to find the keys. Keyboarding is simply learning to type, using the standard typewriter keyboard.

Revising text requires learning keyboard functions for adding, deleting, rearranging, and substituting. Each of these functions are also revision operations and require substantial revision knowledge. Keyboard functions and revising skills can be taught simultaneously, and both are essential. Some of my students tell me that moving text interrupts their composing thoughts, but this problem disappears as they gain more skill in revising and more automaticity in applying keyboard functions.

Spell checking is a boon to writing, but students need spelling knowledge as well as knowledge of how to best use a spell checker. They need to learn spelling patterns as well as word meanings. Homophones are a particular spell checking problem. I have found usage to be the biggest issue.

Once students learn to compose on a computer they are ready to learn how to use graphics, insert tables, and use spreadsheets. These skills are particularly important in report writing. My students find writing with paper and pencil tedious, even quaint, once they have learned to compose on a computer.

IDEAS FOR WRITING

1. Revising a play. If you have written a play or skit, organize a group to act out the play. Listen carefully to the story, dialogue, and sequence of events in the play. Ask the actors for suggestions. Make changes that will improve the play or skit.

2. Precise words. Choosing more precise words improves writing. Look for imprecise words in your writing such as *stuff* and *things*. Replace such words with more precise ones. For example, if you have said, "All kinds of *stuff* sat on the garage shelves" replace *stuff* with a more specific description such as: "Paint and cans, bolts and nails, jars and rope sat on the garage shelves."

3. Conference partners. Ask your teacher to make arrangements for you to work with conference partners in a lower grade. Prepare for your peer

conference carefully. Take a piece of your best writing to read to your younger friends. Then have them read a piece of their writing. Make suggestions that will help them revise their writing.

4. Make a revision chart with two parts: content and mechanics. Use the chart to help you with revising, editing, and proofreading. Work with a small group or the whole class. As you learn a new writing skill, add it to your chart. Eventually your charts may look something like the two charts outlined below.

CONTENT: Revising and Editing

Did I say what I wanted to say?

Did I say it clearly, accurately, and completely?

Did I arrange paragraphs in a logical and interesting way?

Did I choose precise and interesting words?

Did I try more than one beginning to my piece?

Did I develop the middle of my piece well?

Did I write an interesting ending?

Did I make the characters seem real?

Did I use conversation to advance the story?

MECHANICS: Proofreading

Did I end each sentence with correct punctuation?

Did I include punctuation within each sentence, as needed?

Did I start each sentence with a capital letter?

Did I check each word for correct spelling?

Did I use good form: margins, indenting, titles?

Did I get word endings right?

5. Working with a partner. Work in pairs to help each other revise and edit writing. Start with positive comments. Help your partner see how the piece can be made better without making them feel badly about their writing.

6. Writing a story. Many people read stories because they identify with the main characters in a story. It is important, therefore, that your characters appeal to your readers. Next time you write a story ask yourself these questions about your characters:

Do your characters have an unusual habit or trait?

What weaknesses and strengths does your character show?

Is there something unusual about the way your character talks?

Have you shown, not just told, how your character behaves?

What is there about your main character that would make readers want to read more stories with this person in it?

7. Retelling. Retell a story, essay, or report you have written without looking at the written draft. Do this with a peer partner. Compare the retelling with the written draft. If important ideas or details were omitted from the draft, add them to the draft after consulting with the peer partner.

REFLECTION AND SUMMARY

Reflection

Writers have opinions on everything from aardvarks to zygotes. Poll a hundred writers on any topic, and you'll find two hundred opinions—or more. On revision, however, writers from W. H. Auden to William Butler Yeats hold similar views; revision is the heart and soul of writing. Of course, writers go about revising in their own idiosyncratic fashion. They disagree about one aspect of revision or another. But, like Tolstoy, most writers find it difficult to imagine writing without revising. John Irving said simply, "Half my life is an act of revision."

When I started this chapter I said, "Revision is the heart and soul of writing." I still cling to this fundamental premise. But I have had to modify and even reject other ideas I started out with. Like Yeats, I learned that when I revise, "It is myself that I remake." I have added some new ideas to my revision repertoire; I have also deleted, substituted, and rearranged ideas previously held.

I have also learned that I have a lot in common with my third grade friends, Rose, Kate, and Margaret. Sometimes I revise after a few lines have been drafted. Sometimes I revise after a few pages, sometimes I revise just for content, and sometimes I edit just to refine language. Yet, most often I do everything at once: revising for content, refining language, proofreading for minor faults. When I see something I am not satisfied with, I want to change it right now, whether a missing comma or a poorly structured paragraph.

I know my revision strategies are idiosyncratic, yet everything I know about writers and revising tells me I am in good company. I want children to have the same freedoms I allow myself, the freedom to do it their way. Yes, they must learn the basic rules of this complex game: why revising is important; how to go about it. But even though revising is complex, I have no doubt children can handle it. Move them beyond a surface view of revision. Let them experience the exquisite pleasures and the inevitable tedium of real revision. Teach them that revision is the heart and soul of writing.

Summary

This chapter has presented the following main ideas.

1. Professional writers almost universally regard revision as essential to writing well.
2. Research on revision, while limited, has provided useful information for teachers of writing.
   - Children seldom revise, and when they do, they tend to make surface changes rather than deep structure meaning changes.

- Revision instruction has a positive influence on writing growth.
- Children can learn to revise when given appropriate instruction.

3. Revision has many terms, most of them loosely defined. Revision deals with written text; if it does not deal with written text, it is not revision.

- Revision is an inclusive term. It encompasses all changes in written text, including editing and proofreading.
- Rehearsal is not revision, though it is closely related.
- There are three phases of revision—revising, editing, and proofreading.
- Revising focuses on content, editing on language refinement, and proofreading on final corrections. However, these distinctions are arbitrary since, in actual practice, writers do not necessarily follow a defined revision sequence.

4. Nine principles and practices of revision instruction were suggested.

- Focus on content when evaluating effective revision practices.
- Seek outside audience for children's writing.
- Set high standards and expectations
- Revision is time consuming, so plan writing instruction with this in mind.
- Revise your own writing and share the results with your children.
- Peers can help one another revise their writing.
- Publishing is the reward of effective revision.
- Collect and study children's writings.
- All types of writing may be revised, but not all writing need be revised.

5. Expose children to a broad array of revision strategies. Five strategies were suggested.

- Teach revision through content, editing, and proofreading conferences.
- Have children aid one another in peer revising conferences.
- Teach rereading as a revision strategy.
- Reading writing aloud to oneself or others helps spot writing problems.
- Teach revision by modeling your own revision practices aloud.

6. Children need instruction in revision and the "Writers' Workshop on Revision" was described as an effective way to provide this instruction.

7. Computers are particularly useful for teaching revision skills.

QUESTIONS FOR REFLECTIVE THINKING

1. Professional writers describe revision as the key to writing success. Why might this be so?

2. Elson found that fifth graders with high revision profiles differed from fifth graders with low revision profiles. What major differences did she find?

3. Lane recommends that teachers "create some of their own rules for revising." What three rules would you create?

4. Reread the definition of revision given in this chapter. Now write your own definition. How is it similar to or different from the author's definition?

5. The author cited four revision operations: adding, deleting, rearranging, and substituting. Which operation might be easiest for young writers? Which hardest? Why?

6. Choose one of the eight principles and practices of revision and defend it or disagree with it.

7. What important revision objectives would you try to accomplish while conducting a content conference with a first grader?

8. How does rereading what you have written facilitate revision?

9. Do you agree or disagree with the idea that computers aid writing? Support your decision with sound arguments.

10. What was the most important idea you learned from this chapter? Explain your choice.

11. Mini case study: You are a first grade teacher. You have succeeded in getting your first graders to write rather fluently, but have noticed that they seldom revise their writing. Suggest an approach that might help them begin to revise their writing. What operation of revision would you try to get them to try first? How would you begin to model revision for your first graders?

REFERENCES

Baker, R. (1982). *Growing up.* New York: Congdon & Weed.

Beach, R. (1979). "The effects of between-draft teacher-evaluation versus student self-evaluation on high school students' revising of rough drafts." *Research in the Teaching of English*, 13, May, 111–119.

Braddock, R., Lloyd-Jones, R., and Schoer, L. (1963). *Research in written composition.* Champaign, IL: National Council of Teachers of English.

Britton, J., Burgess, T., Martin, N., McLeod, A., Rosen, H. (1975). *The development of writing abilities.* (11 to 18). London: Macmillan Education.

Calkins, L. M. (1979). "Andrea learns to make writing hard." *Language Arts*, 56, May, 569–576.

Calkins, L. M. (1986). *The art of teaching writing.* Portsmouth, NH: Heinemann.

Charlton, J. (1980). *The writer's quotation book: A literary companion.* Middlesex, England: Penguin Books.

Cramer, R. L. (1973). "Pass out the red pencils." *Instructor Magazine.* Danville, NY: Instructor Publications, January, 81–84.

Elson, P. D. (1990). *An investigation of the revision processes of fifth grade children.* Unpublished Doctoral Dissertation, Oakland University Rochester, MI.

Emig, J. (1971). *The composing processes of twelfth graders.* NCTE, Urbana, IL.

Faigley, L. and Witte, S. P. (1984). "Measuring the effects of revision on text structure." In *New Directions in Composition Research*, R. Beach and L. Birdwell (Eds). New York: The Guilford Press.

Fulwiler, T. (1987). *Teaching with writing.* Upper Montclair NJ: Boynton/Cook.

Graves, D. M. (1979). "Research update: What children show us about revision." *Language Arts*, 56, May, 312–319.

Graves, D. M. (1983). *Writing: Teachers and children at work.* Portsmouth, NH: Heinemann.

Graves, D. M. (1994). *A fresh look at writing.* Portsmouth, NH: Heinemann.

Hansen, B. (1971). *The effect of teacher-guided theme-revision on composition performance of university freshmen.* Unpublished Dissertation. Ball State University.

Hillerich, R. L. (1985). *Teaching children to write, K-8.* Englewood Cliffs, NJ: Prentice-Hall.

Hungerford, A. H., Landry, M. L., Smith, L., and Stowe, D. (1992). Exposures. Leelanau County, Chamber Arts North.

Kennedy, X. J. (1986). *An introduction to poetry: Sixth edition.* Glenview, IL: Scott, Foresman.

Lane, B. (1993). *After the end: Teaching and learning creative revision.* Portsmouth, NH: Heinemann.

Marder, D. (1982). "Revision as discovery and the reduction of entropy." In *Revising: New essays for teachers of writing,* R. Sudol (Ed). Urbana, IL: National Council of Teachers of English.

Murray, D. M. (1975). "What writers say about writing." Unpublished Mimeographed Material, University of Vermont.

Murray, D. M. (1985). *A writer teaches writing: Second edition.* Boston: Houghton Mifflin.

Murray, D. M. (1990). *Shoptalk: Learning to write with writers.* Portsmouth, NH: Boynton/Cook Publishers.

National Assessment of Educational Progress. (1977). *Write/Rewrite: An assessment of revision skills.* Princeton, NJ: Educational Testing Service.

Odell, L. and Cohick, J. (1975). "You mean, write it over in ink." *English Journal,* December, 48–53.

Slobodkina, E. (1940). *Caps for sale.* New York: Harper Trophy.

Sommers, N. I. (1980). "Revision strategies of student writers and experienced adult writers." *College Composition and Communication,.* 31, December, 378–387.

Stanley, A. G. (1988). *Revision in third grade.* Unpublished Master's Thesis. Oakland University, Rochester, MI.

Strunk, W. and White, E. B. (1979). *The elements of style,* 3rd ed. New York: MacMillan.

CHAPTER 6

Post Writing: Sharing and Publishing

> It requires a special kind of courage, which the creative
> life does not cultivate, to walk up to any person
> and present the things of one's private endeavor.
>
> *Hughes Mearns*

A WRITER'S STORY

The creative life is fragile. Writers fear adverse judgment. It matters not whether you are a kindergarten child or a Ph.D. candidate, fear inhibits writers from using their talents. But when writing is respectfully received, fear is diminished, if not banished.

I remember experiences I endured or enjoyed as a child. I am grateful for a few good teachers who threw me a lifeline. In retrospect, I now see their efforts as heroic. Now and then, though, I think about "experiences" that never happened. What might my life be like today if I had known just one marvelous writing teacher in high school? Suppose Mr. Smith had taught us to write poetry, not just read it. Suppose further that I had written a poem in Mr. Smith's English class and he had said, "This is great. You should write more often." What ripples might have spread from such a remark? Teachers throw pebbles into life's pond that ripple throughout a lifetime. Seldom do we realize that these ripples splash on distant shores. But splash they do, gently or harshly, a life's work chosen, a career inspired, a dream unrealized.

I know a teacher who's been throwing pebbles into life's pond for 25 years, Peggy Elson. She's a wise teacher, and a fine writer. As a writing teacher, she has few peers. Former fifth graders come visiting these days. Hear their laughter? They're telling war stories; things they thought Ms. Elson never knew, though usually she did. Eventually, the talk turns to writing. Listen carefully, and you'll hear a few heart-felt testimonials. Nothing eloquent, just sincere:

> *"You're the only teacher who ever* really *taught me to revise."*
>
> *"We wrote chapter books and published them. Remember, Ms. Elson? I wrote one with 12 chapters, and* you *loved it!"*

"You gave me confidence to write. I loved writing for you. I'm studying journalism at the University of Michigan now."

Peggy Elson, writer and writing teacher, has thrown lots of pebbles into life's pond. They'll ripple silently on distant shores she'll probably never know about—this writer and writing teacher's unknown stories.

INTRODUCTION

Ms. Elson ran a first class writing program. Her children did lots of publishing, sometimes with the help of volunteer parents. She knew how to motivate writing before, during, and after writing. This chapter focuses on what happens after writing has occurred—publishing and sharing writing.

Murray (1985) captured the essence of why writers write and what keeps them writing when he said, "We write for power—to persuade and influence others; we write to entertain, for applause; we write to share, to escape our loneliness; and we write to retreat to loneliness and mine it" (Murray, p. 85). Most of the reasons Murray gives for writing depend, to a significant degree, on post writing experiences for their fulfillment: sharing, gaining applause, persuading, influencing, entertaining. While professional writers have an urge to express themselves, young writers may not feel this urge, at least not initially. Effective post writing experiences, however, help create an urge to express that is not easily extinguished. This chapter describes values, strategies, and ideas for sharing and publishing writing.

REASONS FOR SHARING AND PUBLISHING CHILDREN'S WRITING

The final stage of the writing process is sharing and publishing writing. In a sense it is a crucible, a time and place to submit one's work to the trial of public acceptance or rejection. It is the time when writing moves onto the public stage and, for the first time, beyond the author's full control. It is a frightening as well as a joyful time. Writers exist in a world of tension. They fear rejection and ridicule; yet they yearn for acceptance and applause. Writers thirst for personal satisfaction, yet long for public acknowledgment. Sharing and publishing is the ultimate reward of the hard work of writing. In this section, I describe four values associated with sharing and publishing.

Integrates Writing with Broader Curricular Goals

Integration is a strategy for combining the teaching of two or more subjects or skills simultaneously. Sharing and publishing writing is one of several places within the writing process where integrating writing with reading, speaking, and listening, and content subjects occurs naturally.

Writing influences the development of a broad range of skills within the language arts. It improves comprehension, word knowledge, and spelling. It provides a meaningful context for improving handwriting, grammar and mechanics, talking with assurance, and listening with a purpose. Sharing and publishing moves children naturally into library research, note taking, organizing information, discussing, and collaborative learning situations. The interrelationships and interdependence of the skills of literacy reinforce one another when the language arts function as one entity with a common goal, communication of one's ideas.

Sharing and publishing can be integrated with content subjects, indeed should be. Connections with content subjects are almost unavoidable in a writing program culminating in sharing and publishing. One of the most memorable science reports I've ever heard was given by Sherry, a first grader, who had read a book about hummingbirds. Ms. Smart, Sherry's teacher, had asked her children to choose a book about animals, read it, write about it, and tell what they had learned to the class—reading, writing, listening, speaking, and science all connected in one piece. Five curricular goals served in one assignment. Sharing with her classmates, Sherry gave a mini-lecture on hummingbirds. Years have passed, and I still recall her memorable illustrations. She held up a penny and said, "A hummingbird weighs about as much as this penny." Next, she held up a thimble and said, "You could fit two baby hummingbirds into this thimble." She continued in this vein, talking and illustrating for four or five minutes. Integrating writing with the language arts and content subjects not only sparked Sherry's interest, but many of her classmates wanted to read Sherry's book.

Fosters Acceptance and Acknowledgment of Children's Writing

In Russia, poets are heroes. When Russian poets read their poetry, a large auditorium may not accommodate all who want to attend. It is a different story for American poets. An American poet is fortunate to gather fifty brave souls to a poetry reading. Writers yearn for public acceptance and acknowledge of their work. Likewise, young writers need acceptance and acknowledgment of their writing. Broad public recognition for young writers is not necessary nor is it likely. But it is important to acknowledge young writers' work because a healthy view of one's worth as a writer enables children to believe in their writing and in themselves. There are many ways of accomplishing this goal, and they are described in detail later in this chapter.

Improves the Written Product

Motivation for producing one's best work is inherent in the publishing and sharing process. Publishing is a form of review of a writer's work. While there may be no formal review, the steps in the process of publishing establish a type of review that ensures opportunity to consider and reconsider first draft words and ideas. Publicly presented writing, under most circumstances, passes through stages of planning, drafting, and revising. When it does, writing moves closer to acceptable standards of substance and form. Peer review, for instance, gives writers an opportunity to monitor their own writing through the eyes and perspective of a valid audience. Of course, for beginning writers, standards must be flexible

Michael has written a dinosaur story which he is about to share with his teacher and classmates.

enough to accommodate invented spelling and an imperfect adherence to the mechanics of writing. But even beginning writers can be motivated to put their best foot forward when their writing reaches a public audience. In the end, we are not looking for perfect writing, but we must always look for ways to help children understand that improving their writing is fundamental to becoming mature writers.

Strengthens Writers' Understanding of Their Capabilities

Interested audiences provide a marketplace in which children can assess the progress they are making. As children grow in writing skill, they become more aware of their capabilities. Experiences that make children aware of their growing skill at telling stories, choosing words, and organizing ideas strengthen the emerging writer's command of the writing craft. Confidence grows as writing is acknowledged by others. I visited in a fifth grade classroom where I asked Lonnie, "Would you mind reading your story to me?" He seemed reluctant, perhaps because he didn't know me well and had no reason to trust me. Nevertheless, Lonnie began to read. He sensed that I liked his story, for I had listened carefully. His voice registered excitement as he approached the climax of his story. When he had finished, I said, "Lonnie, that's a wonderful story. Where did you get the idea to have a spider weave the message that saved Andy's life?"

"Oh," he said loftily, "I imagined it. I have plenty of ideas for stories. As soon as I finish this one, I've got another story I'm going to write. I'm pretty good at writing stories."

I know where much of Lonnie's confidence came from, and it wasn't my response to his story. His teacher and classmates share writing regularly. Positive experience in sharing and publishing had nourished Lonnie's view of himself as a writer. His teacher, Ms. Wilson, had created a healthy climate for sharing and publishing writing. I was part of that climate, a visitor, just one among many, who Ms. Wilson invited into her classroom. She wanted visitors who would validate her writers and the work they were producing.

STRATEGIES FOR SHARING AND PUBLISHING WRITING

Sharing can start as early as the prewriting stage or as late as reading a published book aloud. While sharing can start at any stage of the writing process, publication is often a culminating experience that occurs after a work has been revised. This section describes ways to share or publish children's writing by publishing books, sponsoring a young authors' conference, using the author's chair, working with classmates, and publishing in children's magazines and other public forums.

Publish Books

"Books are a delightful society. If you go into a room filled with books, even without taking them down from their shelves, they seem to speak to you, to welcome you," William Gladstone said. Books symbolize the human desire to place our footprints in the sands of time, a hope that our words and ideas may have some permanence amidst the flux of human events. Few things are as exciting as publishing your own book. Winston Churchill, who wrote many books, said, "Writing is an adventure. To begin with, it is a toy and an amusement. Then it becomes a mistress, then it becomes a master, then it becomes a tyrant. The last phase is that just as you are about to be reconciled to your servitude, you kill the monster and fling him to the public."

What an adventure it is to be an author of a book. The book is your baby! You have brought it into this world through the tumult and toil of thought and will. An author prays that her book will be recognized for its merit; she anticipates that it will delight her readers. She may even fantasize that it will be a best seller. And, while disappointment is no stranger to writers, there is always hope. Children who have been nourished on a feast of literature, who have heard or read books, who have been inoculated with the needle of the written word, may want to record their words and ideas in books. Children who are not acquainted with the delightful society of books can be ushered into their presence. Helping children publish their writing plants the seeds of authorship in fertile ground that may yield an abundant harvest in years to come.

There are simple and efficient ways to help children publish books. More elaborate bookmaking can be reserved for special purposes. If bookmaking becomes so complex that only teachers or parents can make books, some of the pleasure and spontaneity of bookmaking may disappear. Parents and volunteers can certainly be helpful in making books for special purposes. But for everyday purposes, keep it simple. Below are suggestions for several different types of easy-to-make books.

Cardboard books: A simple book cover can be made from pieces of cardboard cut to the same size as the pages on which a story, poem, or report has been written. The directions below can be duplicated and given to children so they can make their own books.

1. Gather the following materials: cardboard, metal rings, paper, art supplies, and a hole puncher.
2. Decide how many pages your book will have and what will be on each page. Break your writing into pages, and add pictures or illustrations.
3. Cut two pieces of cardboard for the cover and one piece for every two pages in your book.
4. Make the final copy of your story, poem, or article. Paste each page onto the cardboard in sequential order.
5. Write the book title and author's name on the cover.
6. Punch three holes along the left side of each page and cover piece. Then bind them all together with metal rings.
7. Add an author's page if you would like your readers to know more about you. Write a few comments about yourself, and add the author's page to your book.

Shape books: Shape books are books cut into shapes that symbolize a book's content or theme. To make shape books follow the directions for the cardboard book only cut the pieces into appropriate shapes. For example, suppose you've written a book about pyramids. Cut your pieces into the shape of a pyramid. Be sure that the shape you choose stands for the theme or content of your book.

Folded paper books: Take six or so sheets of paper and place a piece of colored construction paper the same size on top. Now fold the stack of paper in half, and staple the pages together along the fold. Hide the staples by covering them with a strip of tape.

Accordion books: Cut strips of paper to a desired width and length. The longer the length, the more pages you can have in your accordion book. Fold the pages accordion fashion to make a book. You can also tape pages together to make an accordion book. Accordion books are excellent for writing long, narrative stories and chapter books. They may also be used for a series of poems, jokes, or sayings.

Canned books: Write stories on adding machine tape, roll up the tape and insert it into an orange juice can. Decorate the can with an appropriate illustration and title. Arrange the "canned" books on a shelf.

Scrapbooks: A scrapbook includes items that help you recall special occasions and important events. A scrapbook can contain photographs, ticket stubs, report cards—anything that helps you remember events in your life. Of course, a scrapbook can also include your own writing—poems, stories, and notes you've written to yourself or to a friend. Scrapbooks can be purchased in stores, but you make it personal with the items and decorations you add to it. Save items that you think will be appropriate for your scrapbook. For example, if you've gone to a concert and want to remember it, save the ticket stubs. Paste them into your scrapbook along with your description of the concert.

In her "Voices" piece, Ms. Christie McVean describes her experience with book publishing. She often uses a computer to print out the books her children have written.

VOICES FROM THE CLASSROOM: Christie McVean

Publishing and Sharing

I teach 28 students in a fourth and fifth grade split classroom. My students have always enjoyed publishing their writing in books. When we are ready to make books, we decide what type of book we will make first: flap book, shape book, mini book, pop-up, etc. We make many different kinds of books throughout the year.

After completing the writing we are ready to publish. The students take their handwritten copy and type it into the computer. I allow 30 minutes for each student to type their story. If they are unable to complete typing their story in the half hour, I make time to complete the remaining portion. The children are always excited when their name is called to come to the computer. I have found that typing their story themselves keeps them familiar with the keyboard and motivates them to continue writing. It also gives them sole ownership of their piece. I have only one computer in my room, and I can get ten students done in one day.

Once the typing is completed, we print their stories out. The children are responsible for deciding how many pages their book will contain. To figure out the page breaks, the children use a pencil to number the sentences to show where the pages will begin and end. After deciding the number of pages, they cut and paste their typewritten version onto the pages, draw illustrations, and bind their story into a book cover. Now they are ready to share their book with the class.

We have an author's chair in my room, and the students share their books with their classmates. Even my shiest children cannot resist going to the author's chair. My students never get tired of hearing stories from the author's chair.

Sponsor Young Authors' Conference

A Young Authors' Conference is an idea first initiated by Professor Harry Hahn, of Oakland University in Rochester, Michigan. Hahn brought young writers together to share their writing. His idea was to celebrate writing and writers. He also wanted to put young authors in touch with other young authors, as well as the authors and illustrators of the books young writers read. What a celebration

Young Authors' Conferences have been. At one of Professor Hahn's conferences, a sixth grader said to his teacher, "Before this conference, I thought I was the only sixth grade boy who wrote poetry." At the conference he met dozens of others who also wrote poetry.

A few years ago, a college freshman stood in the office doorway of Gerry Palmer Coon, longtime coordinator of Oakland University's annual Young Authors' Conference. The following conversation took place.

GERRY: Can I help you?

YOUNG MAN: Well, yes. I was wondering, Can I see my book?

GERRY: What book?

YOUNG MAN: My Young Authors' Book. You see, I attended a Young Authors' Conference here when I was in fifth grade, and I wanted to look at the book I submitted once again. Can I see it?

GERRY: You bet!

The first Young Authors' Conference was held at Oakland University over three decades ago. It was a semi-annual affair for years. Professor Hahn, along with his associates and students, soon expanded the idea. Young Authors' Conferences were held in school districts, schools, and classrooms. Today, Young Authors' Conferences are held all over the world. They differ as widely as teachers and schools differ, but they retain one common characteristic. They celebrate young writers and their writing.

Some schools organize elaborate celebrations, others simple ones. For instance, the following Young Authors' Program illustrates an elaborate series of activities organized to celebrate Authors' Week in one Michigan school:

Monday, March 23: Balloon Launch: Balloons carry messages about Authors' Week. Replies requested.

Tuesday, March 24: Story builders Theater: Professional actors put on plays written by the children.

Tuesday, March 24: Read-In: Students bring sleeping bags and pillows for a Read-In.

Wednesday, March 25: Book Sharing: Students share a book they have written with other students.

Wednesday, March 25: Open House and Ice Cream Social: Students show off their writing to parents and invited guests.

Thursday, March 26: Storyteller: Local storyteller entertains students with original tales.

Friday, March 27: Poetry Reading: Local poet shares poetry and talks about writing poems.

Tuesday, March 31: Author/Illustrator: Talks about writing and illustrating books.

Friday, April 3: Professional Storyteller: Tells original folk tales and legends.

Few Young Authors' Conferences are as elaborate as the one described, and none need be. Teachers and administrators can organize writing celebrations in whatever manner works best for their circumstances. They are an excellent way to celebrate writing and reward children's writing efforts in a special way.

Perhaps a word of caution is in order, however. Young Authors' Conferences are no substitute for a solid writing program. Writing must be an everyday affair. It is a mistake to organize a special writing celebration when writing is not celebrated as part of the daily curriculum. Sharing and publishing children's writing and celebrating it must be motivated by successful classroom writing experiences. It is a mistake to dragoon teachers into participating in Young Authors' Conferences when there are no daily writing experiences to validate a conference. It creates resentment among teachers and fosters hypocrisy. It promotes the unhealthy notion that public display is a satisfactory substitute for genuine accomplishment.

Establish a Sharing and Publishing Center

What child has not built a fort to satisfy a need for a special place with a little magic of its own? You can respond to this need by creating a special place, such as an author's chair, from which writing is shared with the class. Of course, it need not be a chair; a podium or special place within a room will do as well. Teachers can use the author's chair for a variety of purposes. Some teachers use the chair as a forum where young writers seek suggestions for improving their writing. Others use the author's chair for sharing writing as it develops through the various stages of completion. The uses of the author's chair depend on the framework of your writing program.

Ms. Bennett's classroom has an author's chair and a bookmaking center. The author's chair is the hub of daily sharing of writing. From this chair, children read selected portions from pieces they are working on. Ms. Bennett has chosen to make the author's chair a forum for celebrating writing rather than a forum for exploring the need for writing improvement. While suggestions for changing writing are sometimes made, it is more common in Ms. Bennett's classroom to use conferences and collaborative learning strategies to stimulate changes in writing.

Most of Ms. Bennett's children work on several pieces of writing within the same time frame. Martha, a voracious reader and elegant writer, is an example. One of Martha's several writing projects is a novel, an extended story of many chapters. Martha sometimes discusses ideas for her novels before starting to draft, usually with Ms. Bennett or in collaborative learning settings with other students. Martha shares her writing from the author's chair as it traverses the stages of development from planning to a much revised final draft. As her novel develops, she reads excerpts from it three or four times over the six or eight weeks it takes her to write a novel. As her novel proceeds from planning to drafting to revising, Martha's sharing occurs in a recursive fashion similar to the manner in which the writing process itself unfolds. Eventually, Martha completes her novel. When she does, she may choose to publish it or not. Usually she does, and then the action moves to Ms. Bennett's publishing center.

The author's chair and the publishing center of Ms. Bennett's classroom are closely related components of the post writing phase of writing. Ms. Bennett's students may choose from a number of publishing options. They may make their own books, handwritten and illustrated, using the resources available in the classroom publishing center; they may also publish their book using the facilities of a computer center available in Ms. Bennett's school; they may request assistance from parent volunteers who help students produce more elaborate published books. There are additional publishing options available as well including: display, school newspaper, Young Authors' Conference, and publishing in magazines and other children's writing outlets. Which option is chosen depends on the student's wishes and the merits of the written piece.

Establishing an author's chair within your classroom is easy enough. Get a chair, stool, podium, or platform. Explain the idea of the author's chair to your children. Establish rules for sharing that serve your teaching goals. Rules and procedures for sharing can be made jointly by the teacher and the children. Then be the first writer to share from the author's chair. Model sharing techniques by reading your writing to the children. When teachers take the first risk, children willingly follow. Set an example for critical listening by giving respectful and thoughtful attention to the writing children share. Make comments that serve your teaching goals. What you say and how you say it will be remembered and imitated. Give praise, recognition, and respect. Above all, make sharing pleasant and safe.

It is particularly important that sharing be pleasant and safe for children who have special needs. Bilingual children face challenges that native speakers do not face. The need for a safe and pleasant sharing and publishing experience is especially important for such children. Ms. McVean has provided just such an environment for the bilingual children she teaches, as she describes in her "Voices" piece.

VOICES FROM THE CLASSROOM: Christie McVean

Publishing and Sharing

I teach 30 fourth and fifth graders. The majority of my students are bilingual and are working at various levels. Writing is new to many of them and they struggle with writing due to their lack of experience with the English language. This explains the excitement I felt this year when my new student, Atemad, asked, "Mrs. McVean, do we get to make books this year like the kids last year?" This meant that the students I had the previous year had shared their writing with other children and now they too wanted to experience that same sense of accomplishment. Due to our need for exposure with the English language, my school celebrates writing through contests, students reading over the PA, and publication in newsletters.

I introduce my students to an assortment of writing formats which we use to develop pieces for publication. We are constantly working on books in a variety of forms. Sometimes we exercise our writing pride by displaying copies of books in the hallway or on our bulletin boards.

To integrate the content areas with writing, newspaper articles are written and typed to explain ideas found in Social Studies or Science. Sometimes we write to audiences outside our classroom such as writing letters to our family and friends. Persuasive letters are also written, their favorite being sent to the President concerning issues about which they feel strongly. At times we create humorous tales to share with younger grades. Whatever format we use, my students get excited about writing when they know it will be taken through the publishing process.

Share Writing with Classmates

It can be difficult to share your writing with others. Some writing is private, and there are pieces of writing that cannot be shared with others. On the other hand, there are excellent reasons for sharing writing among classmates. Initial reluctance to sharing gradually melts as group cohesion increases. It is important, therefore, to build cohesion within your classroom. Children work well within a classroom that has the comfortable feeling of family. A family is a place where intimacy is possible, even though perfect harmony does not always prevail. Sharing writing with classmates will accomplish five writing goals:

1. Sharing writing in peer conferences improves writing. Conference partners help each other develop an awareness of one's own writing that is difficult to learn independently. We are not always our own best audience.

2. Sharing gives writers a sense of how others understand and react to what they write. This helps writers to understand how an audience understands what has been written.

3. Sharing writing fosters pride. Conference partners must learn to evaluate each other's writing within a positive framework. If they do not, they must be shown the value of a positive approach. Learning how to be critical in constructive ways not only helps your writing partner, but it also adds to a writer's repertoire of self-monitoring capabilities.

4. Sharing helps children prepare their writing for a public presentation of their writing outside of the classroom. Children need to share their writing with the outside world, but before this happens it is instructive to have been exposed to friendly fire from within the family.

5. Sharing helps convince children that they have worthy ideas that should be shared with the rest of the world. Believing you have something worth saying is a basic motive for writing. This is as true for young writers as it is for professional writers.

Ms. DeWard has developed effective sharing experience in her fourth grade classroom, and she describes one such experience in her diary entry.

A TEACHER'S DIARY: Jennifer DeWard

Today we started writers' workshop with a student reading a story from the author's chair. Usually I end writers' workshop time with students reading stories from the author's chair, but I decided to try something different today. It was a great change. One boy read a story about Paul Bunyan that he had written. We have been studying Paul Bunyan in social studies, and he liked the character so much he decided to write a legend of his own. The kids really seemed charged and ready to write after hearing the story. Some kids even asked if they could try a Paul Bunyan story of their own, and I said that it would be a good idea. Hearing the student's story seemed to give the kids inspiration as they began writing. I know that I will start writers' workshop in this way more often from now on.

Publish in Kids' Magazines and Other Forums

A teacher I know went to the local newspaper with an idea. She asked if they would publish her children's writing. To her surprise, they said yes, and did so for most of the school year. The newspaper as a forum gave her a reason for stressing the idea that newspapers try to avoid mechanical errors in punctuation, spelling, and grammar. Also, newspapers prefer stories and reports that people are interested in reading. Perhaps not many newspapers are likely to publish children's writing, but you may live in a neighborhood where something of this sort is possible.

There are many magazines and organizations which publish children's writing, many of them specifically for children's writing. Your local librarian can help you locate names and addresses of organizations which publish children's writing. Kathy Henderson has written a guide for publishing children's writing, *Market Guide for Young Writers: Third Edition*. This book is useful for teachers or administrators interested in encouraging student writing. The guide is published by Shoe Tree Press. Henderson's guide gives suggestions for manuscript preparation as well as detailed information about submitting writing for publication.

The two poems below were written by Markila and Jaquita and published in a student magazine called *Nautica*. The publication was sponsored by the Inside-Out Writing Project and Chadsey High School in Detroit, Michigan. InsideOut provides opportunities for students to publish and perform their work and is directed by Dr. Terry Blackhawk.

Memory

I love looking
into my grandmother's face

trying to capture
just one unique feature

I'll remember
when she is gone.
Markila

If You Knew

Have you ever seen the sun rise?
Did you ever hear an angel cry?
Well, I have.
I saw the sun rise in your eyes;
that's when you loved me.
And when I heard an angel cry
was when you lied.
Jaquita

Create Interested Audiences within Schools

Seek out interested audiences for children's writing within your school district or building. Audiences may include classmates, principals, school administrators, children in nearby classrooms—even the janitor can be an audience for children's writing. Ms. Smith, a high school creative writing teacher, encouraged her students to write books for kindergarten children. First, she provided them with books appropriate for kindergarten children. Next, she had her students read selected books to kindergarten-age children. She wanted them to gain first-hand knowledge of how kindergarten children reacted to these books. Back in class, Ms. Smith helped her students develop a list of audience characteristics. The list included these statements about the kindergarten audience:

1. Kindergartners are usually five years old.
2. They have lively imaginations.
3. They love having someone read books to them.
4. They like: fairy tales, books about animals and pets, stories about families and friends, scary books, funny books.
5. They are curious; they like to know how things work.
6. They are innocent. For example, they believe in Santa Claus, the Tooth Fairy, and other make believe characters.
7. They may not distinguish between fantasy and reality.

Then book writing began. It was wonderful to see twelfth grade students writing and illustrating children's books. They asked questions of one another and read drafts aloud to get reactions to their words and ideas: Is this word too hard? Is this sentence too complicated? Will five-year-olds understand this idea? They laid on the floor and used crayons as in their own kindergarten days, and with obvious relish. They had a real purpose. When books were finished and bound, the day came when the twelfth graders descended upon the kindergarten classes of a nearby school. They read to children in small groups and one-to-one. How pleased they were to find themselves the heroes of five-year-old children who loved their books and looked upon these twelfth graders as real authors—as indeed they were.

SUMMARY OF STRATEGIES FOR SHARING AND PUBLISHING WRITING

1. Publish children's writing in a variety of interesting and easy-to-make book formats.
2. Organize a Young Authors' Conference within your school or district.
3. Establish a sharing and publishing center within your classroom.
4. Develop a variety of ways in which children can share their writing within the classroom.
5. Publish writing in kids' magazines, newspapers, and other similar forums.
6. Create interested audiences for writing with your school or district.

IDEAS FOR WRITING

1. Radio play. Turn a story you have written into a radio play complete with sound effects. Does your story have dialogue? Dialogue is the talk that occurs among the characters in your story. If not, dialogue can be added. Find classmates to read the different parts. Think of sounds that help tell the story and gather the materials needed to make the sounds. Practice your play until it runs smoothly. Then record it on tape and play it for the class.

2. Story hour. Organize a story writing project in your class with the idea that the stories will be shared with other children in your school. Arrange to read your stories to children in other classes in your school. Invite them to your classroom or visit theirs.

3. Writers' library. Look around your room. Undoubtedly, there are books lying here and there. Are any of these books written by someone you know? Perhaps not. You can change that quickly. Start a class project that will make the writing done in your classroom available to everyone. Make bound books, and start a class library featuring writing produced in your classroom.

4. Class mural. Arrange your writing on large sheets of paper taped together. Draw pictures or make collages to illustrate the writing. Display your mural where others can see it and read what you have written.

5. Exchange writing. Find other classes in your school or nearby schools with whom you can exchange writing. If the other school is in another city, send your writing through the mail. Ask your teacher to help you arrange the exchange.

6. Display writing. Make a neat final copy of your work and display it in the hallway or on the class bulletin board. Taping or stapling your piece onto construction paper makes an attractive frame.

7. Class newspaper. If your school does not publish a newspaper, start one. First, decide when and how often to publish. Second, choose people to edit the stories, handle the expenses, and circulate the paper. Make sure everyone has an opportunity to contribute to the newspaper. Get your newspaper out to as large an audience as possible. Ask your teacher to be the publisher, the one who arranges the financing of the paper.

8. Class books. Write a poem, story, or article, and put these pieces into a class book. A class book can be about the same topic, for example, a book of jokes. You can also make class books of individual student poems and short stories.

9. Pen pals. Pen pals can give you a good reason to write about many topics. Share your writing with other individuals or classes within your school or with schools in other areas. If you know someone your age in another school, write to see if you can arrange an exchange between classes.

10. Plays and skits. Produce a play, skit, or story you have written. You don't have to make a big deal out of your play. It can be as simple or fancy as you wish to make it. Choose players; get together to make costumes, sets, and props. Rehearse the play and put it on in your own class or for students in other classes.

11. Reports and demonstrations. Write an essay on how to do something—make popcorn, for instance. Make notes on the steps needed to make popcorn (or whatever you have chosen) and turn them into an illustrated essay. Practice your talk as you actually do the steps involved. Give your talk to the class, demonstrating with the materials as you speak.

12. Class made books. Develop a library of individual or class made books. Keep these books in a designated place in the classroom, and provide a means for checking them in and out. At the end of each book, add blank pages for "Readers' Comments." Invite readers, including parents, to comment on their enjoyment of the book. Here is a comment made by parents who read a book written by Ms. DeWard's fourth grade class. "The important thing about *The Important Book* is that it was creative and enjoyable and done by Ms. DeWard's 4th graders! Twenty-five students authored the book. Readers' comments are in the back. But the important thing about *The Important Book* is that it was creative and enjoyable and written by Ms. DeWard's 4th graders."

REFLECTION AND SUMMARY

Reflection

I once heard a writer say, "I don't like writing." After a brief pause, she added, "But I love having written." Over the years, I have came to appreciate the complexity of this remark. It suggests a number of possibilities about writers and writing. Writing is difficult, lonely work. Sports writer, Red Smith, said, "There's nothing to writing. All you do is sit down at a typewriter and open a vein." You don't have to love writing. There is nothing wrong with deriving your satisfaction from *having* written. There is a wonderful freedom in this idea.

On the other hand, some writers derive their satisfaction from the writing itself. Alfred Kazin said, "In a very real sense, the writer writes in order to teach himself, to understand himself, to satisfy himself; the publishing of his ideas, though it brings gratifications, is a curious anticlimax." Every writer is different. Some thirst for public acknowledgment. Others withdraw from the public forum, J. D. Salinger and Beatrix Potter withdrew from public scrutiny, shunning interviews. But young writers need experiences and forums for sharing and publishing their writing that will help them grow and prosper as writers.

Summary

This chapter has presented the following main ideas:

1. There are four reasons why sharing and publishing writing is an essential component of the post writing experience.

   • Sharing and publishing writing builds and strengthens writers' confidence.

   • Sharing and publishing connects writing to wider curricular goals in the language arts and in content subjects.

- Public acceptance acknowledges the value of writers and writing.
- Sharing and publishing improves the written product and provides the rational and the means for critical review.

2. Five strategies for sharing and publishing writing were presented along with a set of briefly described ideas.

- Publish children's writing in books made by children.
- Organize Young Authors' Conferences to celebrate writing.
- Use the author's chair concept for sharing writing.
- Share writing with classmates in peer review sessions.
- Publish writing in kids' magazines, newspapers, and other forums.

QUESTIONS FOR REFLECTIVE THINKING

1. How can sharing and publishing contribute to integrating the language arts?

2. How can sharing and publishing writing nourish children's sense of themselves as writers?

3. There are many kinds of books suitable for classroom publishing. Describe one type and tell how you would use it in a classroom setting.

4. How can a Young Authors' Conference contribute to children's understanding of what it means to be a writer?

5. What writing goals can sharing help accomplish in a writing program?

6. Assume you are a middle school teacher. What audiences for writing could you generate within your school or district?

7. What do you see as the most important outcome of sharing and publishing children's writing?

8. What would you like to know about sharing and publishing children's writing that this chapter has not covered?

9. Mini case study: You are a high school English teacher. You have a group of talented writers who have come to enjoy writing. You would like your principal, colleagues, and parents to become more aware of your students' writing talents. What ideas can you suggest that might accomplish this goal?

REFERENCES

Henderson, K. 1990. *Market guide for young writers*, 3rd ed. White Hall, VA: Shoe Tree Press.
Murray, D. (1985). *A writer teaches writing: Second edition.* Boston: Houghton Mifflin.
Nautica (1999). Chadsey High School, InsideOut Writing Project, Detroit, MI.

CHAPTER 7
Literature and Writing

Every man who knows how to read has it in his power to
magnify himself, to multiply the ways in which he exists, to make his
life full, significant and interesting.

Aldous Huxley

A WRITER'S STORY

*Kate, a fluent third grade writer, volunteered this comment to her teacher, Mrs. Stanley,
"The Midnight Folk keeps running through my head." Later, when Mrs. Stanley read
Kate's latest draft, it became obvious to Mrs. Stanley that John Masefield's book, The
Midnight Folk, had heavily influenced Kate's latest piece, as this passage from Kate's
draft, which she called "Frederick," indicates.*

> *He could see the grey, dreary sky through the bare trees. Some of the brownish leaves
> still clung onto the branches fervently, but the wind was whipping them off one by
> one, with a gesture that reminded Frederick of the schoolteacher, shooing the children
> off the playground at the last bell. (Stanley, 1988, p. 25)*

*A few weeks later, Mrs. Stanley asked Kate, "Who are you reading these days?" Kate
replied that she was reading Enid Blyton. "I've read two of them so far," she said. When
Kate turned in her next draft, which she called "Canorama," Mrs. Stanley thought she de-
tected a resemblance between Kate's writing and Enid Blyton's writing. Here is an excerpt
from Kate's "Canorama" draft.*

> *Now she had a suggestion to make. If Mrs. Canorama heard, though, it wouldn't be so
> great. "How about this," she whispered when the woman turned back to her orna-
> ments. "Tonight at eleven o'clock, we'll sneak over here and—um—catch the thief.
> Then we might find out some more about this thing." Beryl glanced at her in disbelief.
> "You're crazy," she concluded. "No, Beryl. I'm serious. Please?" (Stanley, 1988, p. 25)*

*Kate made an interesting comment after the "Frederick" and "Canorama" drafts had
been completed. "It's hard to write in the style of another author," she said. Her comment
made it clear that Kate had been "borrowing" from the authors she had been reading. Kate
may have borrowed too freely, but Mrs. Stanley also realized that Kate was developing
into an excellent writer. Her success, Mrs. Stanley thought, was due to the many books
Kate had read and her attempts to model her writing after the writers she most admired.*

INTRODUCTION

Literature and writing are the Siamese Twins of literacy. Literature has a beneficial influence on writing, as Kate's experience illustrates. It helps children internalize the conventions of writing and the structure of stories. It provides language, ideas, and information that gradually seep into children's writing.

I once heard a renowned editor of high school literature anthologies speak to teachers on his assigned topic: "Why Teach Literature to Children?" After the introduction, he approached the podium and, without a word of explanation, began reading poems and stories. Twenty minutes passed rapidly by and those who had invited him grew restless: "Why hadn't he yet uttered a single word on his assigned topic?" But he was taking no cues from his handlers. He continued to read. After 40 minutes he paused, looked up at his audience and said, "And you ask, 'Why teach literature to children?'" A stunned moment of silence followed as the teachers realized they weren't going to hear another word. Then a spontaneous ovation erupted as he returned to his seat. His message was simple and elegant: literature speaks for itself. But not everyone has heard the message. Of course, literature has its own value independent of writing, but as an adjunct to writing it has no equal. This chapter speaks of the contribution of literature to writing.

WHAT LITERATURE DOES FOR WRITING

Literature Models Writing

Richard Lewis (1966) collected children's poems from around the English-speaking world and published them in a book called *Miracles*. Lewis wanted his book to be read as poetry, not as a sampling of precociousness. The young poets came from around the world—different countries, cultures, and circumstances. He said they had one thing in common: "They are all children—no different from the ones we see every day jumping, singing, yelling, discovering—who for the very brief moment of a poem, have spoken with the intense clarity, vision and artistry of the poet." (Lewis, 1966, p. 7).

From where do the "miracles" of childhood writing come? *Ex nihilo*, arising out of nothing? Hardly. Miracles arise out of classrooms and homes where love and literature mingle. Miracles also arise out of circumstances too depraved and deprived to imagine. When you encounter a miracle of childhood writing you say to yourself, "How wonderful; how lovely; how extraordinary." *Miracle*, as I am using the word, describes a moment when a child captures a word or a line, a poem or a story so powerful or poignant as to excite our admiration, arouse our interest, inform our imagination.

Most often parents and teachers create the conditions in which miracles happen. Usually, miracles can not be planned. Most often, they arise spontaneously. They may arrive abruptly, like the sharp bark of a rifle; they may arrive gradually, like the dawning of a new day. They arise from homes and schools where children are read to—where children are encouraged to draw and write. They arise in homes where children's miracles hang on refrigerator doors—where hand-molded ceramics are adored and displayed, even if the object more closely resembles a rock than a vase. But most often the miracles of childhood writing are the residue of literature—read aloud, read independently, read voraciously, read greedily, read lovingly. Literature is the catalyst that creates the miracles of childhood writing.

Literature Develops a Love for Reading

Kathleen Norris said, "Just the knowledge that a good book is waiting one at the end of a long day makes that day happier." I know the truth of that remark. My own discovery of books happened in a small library in South Gate, California. One summer day I walked into the library and emerged with a book that set my feet on the path to literacy. I had discovered Joseph A. Altsheler's, *The Young Trailers*. The door opened, and I entered. I fell in love with Henry Ware and his fellow scouts, Paul Cotter, Shif'less Sol Hyde, Silent Tom Ross, and Long Jim Hart. I traveled with them in their grand adventures of scouting on the "Kaintuckee" frontier.

A few days later I returned to the library and discovered the other books in *The Young Trailers* series. In no time, it seemed, I had read them all. As I read the last book in the series, a dreadful fear entered my mind: "What will I do when I have finished this last book?" I soon found an answer, one I had never previously imagined. *I read them all again.* Finally, I realized I had to look for other books. Thus began the first broadening of my literary interests. Admittedly, I didn't venture far from my initial interests. Broadening literary tastes takes years and continues, if we are fortunate, for a lifetime.

Some critics might call Altsheler's books "trash" or "junk" literature, though I would not. I will concede that Altsheler's books may not be literature of the highest quality. But literature need not be classic to whet the appetite for reading and writing. William Faulkner expresses this idea pungently: "Read, read, read. Read everything—trash, classics, good and bad, and see how they do it. Just like a carpenter who works as an apprentice and studies the master. Read! You'll absorb it. Then write." Some children are introduced to good literature early. Perhaps more of us were introduced to reading through literature of a lesser quality, but exciting to young readers—*The Hardy Boys, Nancy Drew,* and *Goose Bumps* come to mind. Literature of this sort, I suspect, has hooked more children on books than classic literature. A love of reading often precedes awareness of literary quality. But for Altsheler, I might never have read Tolstoy, Steinbeck, Davies, Potok, Dickens, or Poe.

Literature Extends Language

Abraham Cahan, founder and long-time editor of "The Jewish Daily Forward," wrote a book called, *The Rise of David Levinsky,* a pushcart peddler. Levinsky is given a copy of *Dombey and Son* and a small dictionary by his evening schoolteacher, who extracts a promise that he will read Dickens' novel. Levinsky immediately discovers that his vocabulary is not up to the task. But he is hungry for knowledge, so with the aid of his dictionary, looking up "every third word," he begins reading. Some words were not in his dictionary, some definitions were inscrutable, but Levinsky persists. He finds the language of Dickens intoxicating; he delays going to work, falls into debt, and finally gives up his pushcart business. He cannot stop reading. Literature and language have him in an implacable hold.

Here is a man with little education but a hunger to know the "secret of life." That secret, he suspects, is contained in books. Levinsky's experience is reminiscent of Issac Bashevis Singer who, on his first visit to a library, asked the librarian for a book of philosophy because he wanted to know "the secret of life." For both men, one fictional and the other real, literature implanted the seed that grew into that sacred inward desire to know what literature and language have to offer.

Literature is a cornucopia of treasures, and language is the medium through which much of our world knowledge is expressed. Multitudes of common words, names, characters, and concepts derive from literature: Holy grail, Gordian Knot, burning bush, leprechauns, Solomon, Little Red Riding Hood, Tower of Babel, Pandora's Box, David and Goliath, Cinderella, Trojan Horse, unicorn, trolls, Babylon, Utopia, Torah, Chicken Little. Knowledge of these concepts, perceived through literature, opens the door to further knowledge. Unfamiliarity with the language of literature handicaps communication, whereas familiarity enhances children's ability to function in a literate society.

Literature Enlightens and Entertains the Mind

Richard Wright, author of *Native Son*, tells how reading H. L. Mencken reawakened his impulse to dream: "Yes, this man was fighting, fighting with words. He was using words as a weapon, using them as one would use a club. Could words be weapons? Well, yes, for here they were. Then, maybe, perhaps, I could use them as a weapon?" (Gilbar, 1989, p. 79). Soon, reading had grown into an unquenchable thirst. Wright got into the habit of taking books wrapped in newspaper to work. Some white workers pried into Wright's packet of books when he was absent and questioned him:

"Boy what are you reading those books for?"
"Oh, I don't know, sir."
"That's deep stuff you're reading, boy."
"I'm just killing time, sir."
"You'll addle your brains if you don't watch out." (Gilbar, 1989, p. 81)

Of course, rather than addle Wright's brain, literature enlightened it. The words of H. L. Mencken and Dreiser, among others, had enlightened his mind and fired his imagination.

Bettelheim (1976) could have been speaking for all of literature when he wrote of the influence of fairy tales on children's lives: "While it entertains the child, the fairy tale enlightens him about himself, and fosters his personality development. It offers meaning on so many different levels, and enriches the child's existence in so many ways, that no one book can do justice to the multitude and diversity of the contributions such tales make to the child's life" (p. 12).

Langer (1995) maintains that: "Through literature, students learn to explore possibilities and consider options for themselves and humankind. They come to find themselves, imagine others, value differences, and search for justice. They gain connnectedness and seek vision. They become the literate thinkers we need to shape the decisions of tomorrow" (p. 1). If even half of Langer's vision for literature in the lives of children is possible, how enriched would be the lives and minds of our children. Literature shapes and reshapes thought. It empowers children to create their own texts. It can ennoble the aspirations of readers, though this is assuredly not an inevitable outcome. Much depends on the nature of instruction and the nonschool influences that accompany the reading of literature.

Literature Enriches Cultural Knowledge

Literature is crucial to increasing cultural knowledge. Successful reading requires knowledge that may not be present in the text we are reading. We comprehend best when we connect new information and ideas with what we already know; what we already know determines, to a large degree, what new information and ideas will be learned or understood.

Readers and writers, speakers and listeners communicate best when they have shared cultural knowledge. Shared cultural knowledge is dependent on acquisition of a substantial body of cultural referents. Cultural referents may be current or embedded in our literature and history. Comedians, for example, assume that their audience knows the referents of their jokes. If a comedic referent is not immediately understood, the joke fails and the comedian gets no laugh, a disaster for a comedian. Seinfeld, the famous American comedian, recently gave a stand-up comedy routine in Australia. One of his jokes referred to an issue only relevant to current American politics. No one laughed. The joke's referent was unfamiliar to this Australian audience. On the other hand, the audience laughed uproariously when Seinfeld referred to Australia as a penal colony. Australians know Australian history, but do not necessarily know current American politics.

The more we share of a broad literary heritage, the more we increase our cultural literacy quotient. In a multicultural world, it is essential for people of all cultures and ethnic groups to know each other's literature, for our literature helps connect us to one another.

Literature Depicts the Human Condition

I recently reread *Darkness at Noon* by Arthur Koestler (1941). I have in my mind unforgettable pictures of a cramped cell with a straw mattress, a high barred-window overlooking the exercise yard, the brightly lit interrogation room, the dark stairwell where death awaits me. Were I to see a movie depicting these scenes, I should be disappointed, for I would surely discover variance between my imagined images and the movie's portrayal of them. I have no desire to see such a movie. I have my own reel of film that I can play back at any time. For me, Koestler's book depicts depravity and idealism, hardship and heroism better than any other medium could hope to portray it. Andre Maurois expressed this idea when he said, "The art of reading is in great part that of acquiring a better understanding of life from one's encounter with it in a book" (Charlton, 1986, p. 12).

Literature is not a movie screen flashing someone else's pictures. It is sentence upon sentence rubbing our little gray cells together until they spark their own pictures. Literature depicts the human condition in all of its lovely and ugly dimensions. Who has ever drawn a more vivid picture of depression America than Steinbeck in *The Grapes of Wrath?* Steinbeck takes us traveling with the Joad family as they journey across America, discovering again and again the naked realities of America divided along lines of class and wealth. As Steinbeck describes the hardships of the farm families migrating across the country during the great depression, readers generate their own images of rattletrap cars, evening campfires, hungry children, haunted men and women pursuing their uncertain dreams of California, the promised land.

The images that readers project onto the screens of their minds are superior to most films created for us. Maisha, a high school student, created vivid images of a daily experience at her school in a poem she wrote and published in *Style! Mumford's Literary Magazine.* Her poem is rich in imagery, and it sparked graphic pictures in my mind as I read it. Perhaps Maisha's poem will stimulate pictures in your mind as well.

Daily

I stand on the broken pavement
in front of Mumford High School
at the end of a long day

Gang bangers, weed slangers, thugs and haters
surround the parking lot.
The air fills with gang chants and weed smoke.

Security guards caution kids about loitering
on school grounds. All six guards flock
to harass the square smokers

The charcoal grey smoke of their cigarettes
billows unabashedly from a crowd of students,
"Hey, man, let's go to Ray-Ray's."

Illegally parked cars obstruct the traffic
as frustrated parents pick up handsome or beautiful
ne'er-do-wells. I can't proceed to my destination.

Bumper to bumper chaos, police cars block the traffic.
Big busses over power my Pioneer and an officer tells me to
 move. I'm
vibrating in my seat, to the rumble of a lowrider next to me.
Maisha

Literature explores life's great themes: love, death, friendship, family, hardship, courage, coping, evil, cruelty, compassion. Children identify with the feelings, thoughts, and events described in literature which match their own interests and concerns. Literature enables children to cry with the boxcar children, laugh with Charlotte at the obtuseness of Wilbur, or reconsider the consequences of getting three wishes. Lester, you may recall from Shel Silverstein's poem, had three wishes. But Lester became so obsessed with wishing for more wishes that he died with his wishes piled around him and, "not a single one was missing." Silverstein (1974) tells us that, "In a world of apples and kisses and shoes/ He wasted his wishes on wishes" (p. 69).

When I was young, I thought wishing for three more wishes an exceedingly clever idea. Lester's dilemma never occurred to me. Literature, through Silverstein's simple poem, gave me an alternative perspective. Literature helps us see the world and ourselves anew. That is what literature does so well, and that is why it is so essential in the lives of our children.

Literature Develops a Sense of Story

Every culture has its stories, and these stories are told to children. Hirsch, Kett, and Trefil (1988) make an interesting observation about such stories: "The tales we tell our children define what kind of people we shall be" (p. 27). Stories define us in more ways than we might expect. They tell of our fears and frivolities, values and traditions, prejudices and ideals. *Story* is an up-beat word. Its synonyms include tale, yarn, anecdote, narrative, and history. *Story* also carries the negative meaning of falsehood or lie. Stories may be written or oral, factual or fiction, prose or verse. In a more literary sense, story suggests characters, settings, plots, events, and resolutions.

Stories are as old as human history, and storytellers have always held an honored place in human affairs. Stories constitute an important part of the collective memory of a culture. The fabled Mountain Men of American frontier folklore were great storytellers. A mountain man wore his reputation as a storyteller as a badge of honor. Once a year, these rough and tumble men traveled hundreds of miles across mountains and plains to gather in their annual Roundup. They traded skins, fought, drank, and swapped stories. The stories they told one another were a duke's mixture of fact and fiction, exaggerated accounts of dangers faced, deeds done, victories won. If they bragged too much and misrepresented the truth more than just a little, well, that was part of the storyteller's art. Their storytelling filled a need lonely men have for narrative, a need common among adults and children at all times and in all places.

Stories have a transforming, almost magical, effect on children. Story time is often children's favorite time in school. And, stories have a practical, academic purpose. Stories are a powerful way of conveying information to children. Flood (1986) has shown that the best way to convey historical information to children is through a combination of story and expository text. The next most effective way is through story text. The least effective way is through expository text. Unfortunately, the least effective way is the primary way we convey history to children.

It is not just fiction writers who need a sense of story; writers of expository text need it as well. It is a sense of story that lays the foundation for reading and writing. Exposure to literature develops a sense of story. In a literate culture such as ours, literature is the most important repository of the tales our children need. Listening to and reading stories develop a cognitive map for how a story goes. Virtually all stories have certain components in common: character, setting, problem, attempts to resolve the problem, and a resolution. Researchers call this story grammar (Mandler and Johnson, 1987; Stein, 1979; Applebee, 1978). Having story grammars or cognitive maps for stories enables children to anticipate problems, events, and resolutions of stories they have not yet encountered. Repeated exposure to literature enables children's sense of story to grow.

Literature is the fountainhead. Every writer owes a debt to those who wrote the literature on which today's writers are nourished. Faulkner pointed out that quality literature is not the only source of useful information; one can learn from any genre or classification of literature. Nonfiction, for example, is a rich vein to be mined by serious students of writing. Writers need a storehouse of knowledge, a world of experience, an arsenal of language, and an archive of resources. Literature is the goddess who provides many of these treasures.

SUMMARY OF WHAT LITERATURE DOES FOR WRITING

1. Literature provides models for writing. Through wide exposure to literature children gain knowledge of the writer's craft.

2. Literature enlightens and entertains. Through literature children explore options for themselves, value differences, and gain connnectedness to their world.

3. Literature expands vocabulary and adds to children's general knowledge of the language.

4. Literature imparts shared cultural knowledge and provides cultural referents essential to comprehending oral and written language.

5. Literature depicts the human condition, helps us see the world and ourselves anew, and exposes us to life's great themes.

6. Literature imparts a sense of story which is crucial to effective poetic, narrative, and expository writing.

READING LITERATURE TO CHILDREN

"I lay voluptuously on my stomach on the big bed, blissfully alone, and I felt a thrill which has never left me as I realized that the words coming magically from my lips were mine to say or not say, read or not. It was one of the peaks of my whole life (Gilbar, 1989, p. 84). When I read M. F. K. Fisher's words, I recalled just" such an experience. I am sitting under an apricot tree, chores completed, with nothing but pleasure stretching ahead of me. I have been to the library, and I have a new book. I have graduated from Joseph Altsheler to Zane Grey. I have read other books by this most famous of all western writers. I know I am about to encounter good and bad guys. I am ready for the journey. Perhaps I'll travel into the Badlands of the Dakotas or onto the High Plains of Montana. Avid readers can recall a time when words from a book engrossed them completely. Every child deserves to experience the same pleasure.

It is well established that reading to children supports learning to read. It is less well recognized that reading aloud also supports writing, since it supplies models for writing and enriches the store of language available for writing. Chomsky (1972) found that children who were read many linguistically complex books developed greater linguistic capabilities than children who were not read to. Trelease (1995) cites dozens of highly successful read-aloud school and community programs that have been organized throughout the United States. After an extensive review of the literature, Anderson, Hiebert, Scott, and Wilkinson (1985) concluded that reading aloud to children constituted the single most important experience for reading success. Elley (1992) collected data from 32 countries looking for factors that influence learning to read. He found that factors which differentiated high- from low-scoring countries included, ". . . large school libraries, large classroom libraries, regular book borrowing, frequent silent reading in class, *frequent story reading aloud by teachers* (italics mine), and more scheduled hours spent teaching the language" (p. xii). Light (1991) found that parents who regularly read aloud had a significant positive effect on their children's attitude toward reading. The common denominator in all these read-aloud programs and experiments is the beneficial influence they exert on literacy and learning. The evidence is solid; reading aloud ranks among the most valuable of all educational experiences.

I believe that having books read to us when we are young has a lasting and profound influence. I have never forgotten Ms. Brown who always started her class by reading aloud. I loved going to her class and listening to the stories she read. The storyteller's art drew me into its sticky web. Here a boy's imagination caught fire; here a boy's spirit soared free. I've often wondered why reading aloud had such an impact on me. Of course, I haven't got an answer, but reading aloud certainly entertained me, informed me, and aroused my interest. I know now just how fine Ms. Brown's teaching instincts were. Research has caught up with her intuition.

Receptivity to Reading Aloud

Reading to children requires a climate of receptivity. Every farmer knows that seeds thrive in well-prepared soil. Just as a farmer prepares the ground for planting, so teachers prepare children's minds to absorb the spoken and written word. Best Practices provides four suggestions for enhancing the receptivity of children to the reading aloud experience.

RECEPTIVITY TO READING ALOUD

1. Make reading aloud a time for enjoyment and relaxation. If children are more comfortable resting their heads on their desks, encourage this. If cushions and rugs are available, younger children may wish to sit or lie on them. Textbooks and other working materials can be kept in desks so as not to distract attention. Set the stage for pleasure.

2. Schedule time for reading aloud. Some teachers schedule reading aloud just before writing time to make the literature-writing connection more direct. But there are other options. Reading aloud during the last twenty minutes of the day sends children home with a pleasant conclusion to the day's activities. The beginning of the day, on the other hand, has the advantage of getting the children off to a good start.

3. Jointly establish a few simple rules. Only a few rules are needed, and they are intended to create a relaxed and pleasant atmosphere. Have your children participate in making the rules as this gives them a sense of ownership, and they are more likely to comply with rules they helped create.

4. When children misbehave, it is reasonable to discipline them, but reading aloud should seldom, if ever, be withdrawn. Reading aloud may be the single most important adjunct to learning to read and write. Withdrawal, then, should be a last resort and then only in unique circumstances.

Ms. Dudzinski, who teaches fourth grade, has found that reading aloud is a crucial adjunct to her reading and writing program. She describes her experience with reading aloud in the "Voices" piece.

VOICES FROM THE CLASSROOM: Sheri Dudzinski

Reading Aloud

I have 35 children in my class, and this is my fourth year as a teacher. I've learned how important it is to read aloud to children. At first, I was a little skeptical, but not any longer. I've learned just how much my children love hearing me read to them, and I've discovered that reading aloud is time well spent. I'm convinced it's good for my kids. While I don't have what you might call scientific evidence to prove it, I've seen good things happen because of it. For example, my kids always ask to read, independently, the books I've read to them. They share more now that I read to them every day. They talk more often now about authors they like and books or stories they've read. Often they'll come to me to read aloud a passage they like. I couldn't prove it, but I think my kids are writing better now that I read to them every day.

Recently, I've been reading *Ziggie and the Black Dinosaur* by Sharon Draper. My kids love this book. Usually, I can end the day's reading at an exciting place where they can't wait to hear the next part. After I finished this book, many of my kids asked to read it on their own. They're always asking me when Sharon Draper is going to write another book. They can't wait to hear the next one.

I read a lot of narrative selections, especially ones with dialogue. I believe this helps them in their writing. I believe that narrative models for children dialects, sarcasm, and tone of the text. I now see my children writing more conversation and with more personal voice as the year goes on in our Writers' Workshop. I try to choose books that deal with topics that will elicit discussion, and I look for stories that have cliff hanger endings to the chapters. This stimulates their interest in the next day's selections, and they like to predict what will happen in the next chapter.

I read to my kids every day, without fail. We agreed on three rules. They're simple rules and I have no trouble getting my kids to follow them. Of course, I have to remind them once in a while. You know how that goes. Our rules are:

1. Heads down
2. Lights out
3. No drawing or reading

I read for twenty minutes every day just after lunch. This works out best for me, given the interruptions that occur during other times of the day. It also settles the kids down after their lunch break. My kids always beg me to read a little longer than twenty minutes. Sometimes I do, but this depends on where we are in the book and what other things we have to do that day.

What to Read

There are more excellent books for children today than there have ever been. Recent data indicate that more children's books were sold in 1998 than in any preceding year. This is good news for teachers and children. Taking advantage of the burgeoning of available children's literature requires planning. Guidelines for selecting books to be read aloud are suggested below.

SELECTING BOOKS TO READ ALOUD

1. Age and interest levels are pertinent guidelines in selecting literature to read aloud. But, nobody knows your children as well as you do, so trust your judgment in selecting read-aloud literature.

2. Read traditional and modern literature. Traditional or folk literature links the present generation with its cultural heritage. Justice, equality, courage, honesty, and a sense of humor are values in traditional literature, and these concepts remain important in a modern age. At the same time, modern literature with its contemporary language, settings, and situations delights and enlightens children. Strive for a balance between traditional and modern selections.

3. Read fiction and nonfiction. The balance of reading selections should tip in the direction of fiction. Children identify with the characters and

situations portrayed in fiction. It gives them an opportunity to be someone else, to imagine and to fantasize. On the other hand, children need to build a store of information from nonfiction works. The information thus obtained helps children formulate new ideas and expands their understanding of the physical world.

4. Read prose and poetry. Most children read prose, fewer read poetry. Reading poetry aloud provides the exposure that develops understanding and appreciation of poetry. Ms. Jonella Mongo teaches in Detroit. Since most of her children are African American, she reads poems from Langston Hughes, Nikki Giovanni, Paul Dunbar, and other gifted African American poets. She tells her children about the lives of these writers. Then she invites them to read and write, and they do.

5. Read books that represent the cultural and ethnic heritage of America. The past several decades has seen an increase in the publication of books written by and about African, Asian, Latino, and Native Americans. Walters, Webster, and Cramer (1998) have compiled an extensive multicultural bibliography of literature for younger and older children containing over 700 listings (ERIC document ED 407-388).

6. Select some challenging readings. Some read-aloud books should extend children's literary experience beyond their independent reading capability. Keep the challenge you present within an acceptable interest and listening range. Fortunately, when we go beyond an acceptable level, children usually let us know. Some of the books you read aloud may be appropriate for children to read independently. Encourage this, since hearing a book read aloud makes independent reading more manageable.

7. Read books with which readers can identify. Paule Marshall, an African American novelist and poet, discovered Paul Laurence Dunbar's poetry books in a Brooklyn library. She was just a child, but reading his poems gave her a goal, a dream, and an identity. Dunbar's poems permitted Marshall to dream that someday she too could write with something of the power with words her mother and her friends seemed to possess.

8. Study bibliographies available on children's literature, and choose those books that seem best suited to fulfill the needs of your children. Children love stories where the characters' emotions and problems parallel their own. They enjoy literature that tells of the human struggle against the forces of nature and the confrontation of good with evil. They especially like stories that enable them to imagine and dream of their future, as Paule Marshall did. Bibliographies for reading aloud can be found in *The Read-Aloud Handbook* by Jim Trelease (1995), *Best Books for Children: Fourth Edition* by Gillespie and Naden (1990), and "Children's Choices" which appears annually in *The Reading Teacher.*

Reading the Selection

Select appropriate materials and read them well. These guidelines may be helpful.

Plan each day's selection in advance: Certain days can be reserved for reading continuing books such as *Charlotte's Web, The Secret Garden,* or *James and the Giant Peach.* It is also useful to reserve some time for special selections such as poetry or readings intended to mesh with classroom projects.

Interpret the mood, tone, and action of the passage being read: I once heard Bill Martin, Jr., a consummate teacher-actor, say that all teachers would benefit by taking a course in acting. I've often regretted that I never took his advice. I see now how acting can serve a teacher. For instance, reading aloud is a good time to do a little acting. Younger children will appreciate *Jack and the Beanstalk* more if you let your voice rise and fall with the natural rhythms and emotions evoked by the story. Older children will also enjoy the extra dimension that dramatic interpretation adds to books such as *The Lion the Witch and the Wardrobe* by C. S. Lewis, *Harriet the Spy* by Louise Fitzhugh, or *A Wrinkle in Time* by Madeleine L'Engle. Self-consciousness sometimes makes us hesitant to dramatize stories as we read. However, children are a generous audience. They will appreciate your efforts to dramatize literature.

Distinguish between reading aloud and directed reading instruction: It is neither necessary nor desirable to turn reading aloud into a directed reading lesson, unless that is the specific purpose of a read-aloud session. Enjoyment is the major and distinctive purpose of reading aloud. When enjoyment is paramount, other important purposes are also accomplished. For example, reading aloud often leads to sharing the special passages that literature inevitably contains. Sharing literary gems makes literature special. If a sentence is especially well written, point it out; if a paragraph gives a marvelous vignette, mention it; if a passage has special meaning to you, tell about it. Encourage your students to reciprocate. Ask them to share favorite passages with you and their fellow students. The pleasures of literature are always sweeter when you have someone to share them with.

Choose strategic stopping points: When reading a continuing narrative, stop at a point that will build anticipation for the next episode. Avid readers know the pleasure of anticipation when they have a good book awaiting them at home in the evening. Anticipation is one of the great pleasures of life, and this doubly applies to reading. Anticipating the next day's reading can have a positive effect on attendance, although its primary benefit is to sustain interest in the selection.

Research has shown the importance of reading aloud. Adams (1990) identifies reading aloud as the single most important means of preparing children for entrance into literacy. Reading aloud provides writing models and enriches the store of language and ideas available for writing. Read to children every day. Read poems and prose, fiction and nonfiction, adventure and fantasy, myths and fairy tales, legends and folk tales. Read about heroes and villains, gods and ghosts, traders and trappers, cultures and creatures. Perhaps the most important result of your efforts will be to bequeath an enduring love for literature. No gift could be more precious, no legacy of greater value.

MODELING LITERATURE WITH CHILDREN

Teachers are models; literature is a model. Both play important roles in learning to write. A model is a standard of excellence to be imitated. Modeling is based on the premise that exposure to literature is one of the best ways to teach and learn writing. For example, if you want to expose children to elegant sentence writing, E. B. White is the master. Read aloud or have children read *Trumpet of the Swan, Stuart Little,* or *Charlotte's Web*. White has set a standard worthy of imitation, or modeling if you prefer.

Jack London, Winston Churchill, and Somerset Maugham owe a debt to writers who preceded them. These writers, along with countless others, deliberately imitated other writers as a means of learning their craft. To put it more euphemistically, we could say they modeled their writing after the writers they admired. London, Churchill, and Maugham acknowledged their indebtedness to other writers, and were not ashamed to do so. Imitation is widely practiced among writers, though not always acknowledged. Writers prefer the term *influenced by*, but this is merely a euphemism for imitation. Imitation has an honorable history but a bad reputation.

Bandura (1967) suggests that imitation is observing how someone else has done something and modeling your behavior on that standard. In spite of the honorable role imitation has played in learning to write, some question its benefits. They argue that imitation erodes integrity, compromises originality, or diminishes individuality. Is this true, or is this reluctance to acknowledge that talent is never entirely self-generated? The evidence suggests the latter; imitation is a natural, unavoidable component of learning. Imitation happens at conscious and unconscious levels.

Consider the arts as an example. Visit any great museum and you will see art students copying the paintings of the masters. There is style and technique to be learned in this fashion. The same is true of writing. Imitation does not erode integrity or destroy creativity. Rather, imitation is one way to learn the craft of writing. Writing is a craft just as cabinetmaking is a craft. Like cabinetmakers, writers serve an apprenticeship. Imitation is part of that apprenticeship. For those who pursue the craft of writing, there comes a stage when craft passes over into the realm of art. The art of writing cannot be imitated, but the craft of writing benefits from imitation. Churchill served his apprenticeship on the writings of Edward Gibbon and Thomas Babington Macaulay, eminent English historians. He describes his efforts to imitate the sentence structures of his writing models. His writing was the better for it. Of course, Churchill's own unique personality and voice surfaced as he mastered the art and craft of writing. Children, too, will benefit from whatever they absorb from the excellent models of writing that literature provides.

Fortunately, children assimilate ideas and information as they read. They absorb words and phrases, content and mechanics, topics and techniques from the stories they hear and read. Later, these assimilated elements appear in their writing. Teachers sometimes admonish children for imitating or modeling, but admonitions are seldom necessary and may do more harm than good. Imitation and modeling are not plagiarism, the deliberate appropriation of someone else's writing and passing it off as your own. The key is intent. Sometimes children retell familiar stories, as if these stories were their own inventions. A child may turn in a composition, for instance, that closely resembles *Goldilocks and the Three Bears.* This is especially likely if the child has recently read or heard the story. Young children are not necessarily aware of the closeness of their retelling to the original story. From their perspective, they are simply *telling a story.* In effect, they say to themselves, "Well, here is a story I know. I'll tell this one." Retelling is common in the storytelling and writing of young children. This need not worry teachers, and it must not be punished. Rather, regard it as a natural starting point for storytelling and writing. Children soon move beyond retellings to stories of their own making, as Ted soon did. But one of his first stories was the well-known folk tale, *Goldilocks and the Three Bears,* as Ted, a second grader, remembered it.

Golde Lox and The Three Bears

The three bears lived in the woods Thare was father bear and mother bear and baby bear. Thare house was made out of wood. And thare was a girl named Golde Lox. She went to the three bears house when the bears wer away from the house because they wer wateing for thare pareg to ceool.
Ted, Age 7

Ms. Nancy Cohen teaches first grade in Detroit. She has found that using literature as models for poetry and prose enhances the writing of her children. She describes how she uses literature to model writing in the "Voices" piece.

VOICES FROM THE CLASSROOM: Nancy Cohen

Sharing Literature

At the beginning of the school year, I establish a designated time which is used strictly for story time. I read stories which will stimulate my students' interests. I want my students to hear all kinds of literature which expands their knowledge of genres and widens their appreciation for reading. After I read a book, my students usually are excited to grab it from the shelf. They love to discover other books by the same authors as well.

Whenever literature is read, I strive to model reading and writing strategies. Before starting a book, I want to access my students' prior knowledge of the subject matter. I usually ask them to predict what the story may be about. They always want me to read on to see if their guesses are accurate.

My students are learning about the essential elements of a story. They know how to identify the characters, setting, and plot. Currently, we are discussing the main idea, problem, and solution. While reading, we talk about these components and frequently will write them down in a web. I also share information about the author and illustrator. My students are fascinated to learn of their backgrounds and are thrilled when I have photographs of them. They can see that authors and illustrators are "real" people too.

Modeling literature improves my students' writing abilities. When good literature is brought into the classroom, children are definitely more inspired to write. My students love to write classroom books which are modeled after real stories that we have read. Sharing different types of literature gives them opportunities to experiment with varied writing styles. Using the elements of stories, I plan creative writing assignments. For example, my students write their own endings for stories, write as if they are the main character in a book, and even develop their own conflict and solution. The ideas can be endless when writing activities are integrated with quality literature.

Procedures for Modeling Literature

Modeling a story or poem can be done with the whole class or a smaller group within the class. After the procedures are understood, have children try modeling poems and stories on their own. The following guidelines for modeling stories, poems, and skills are suggested, although you may wish to modify them to suit your own circumstances and approach to modeling writing. Guidelines for modeling literature for writing are suggested below.

MODELING LITERATURE

1. Select a story or poem with a predictable pattern which will interest your children.
2. Read the story or poem to establish the pattern in memory. Then have children identify and chorus the repeated parts of the selection.
3. Invite children to describe the images and ideas the selection arouses. Point out specific words, images, and patterns not mentioned by children.
4. Write a class composition. Start by inviting children to offer the first line. If the children are hesitant, offer the first line yourself.
5. Record the composition on a large piece of paper or on the blackboard.
6. Refine the first draft. Add or delete lines, improve word selection, and rearrange lines and verses as needed.
7. Make copies for each child, and have them illustrate the composition. If this is the first patterned story or poem your class has done, give the event special treatment.
8. Have children write their own stories or poems using the same or a similar model.

Modeling Stories

Modeling helps children make the connection between literature and writing. Look for stories and poems that have a linguistic or structural feature that will benefit your children. There are many features to look for. Stories and poems with a characteristic rhyme, rhythm, or catchy refrain work well. Some stories and poems have a predictable language pattern, or the content may be elegant and interesting. Patterns of this sort make a story or poem especially suitable for modeling. Some stories and poems are perfect vehicles for motivating writing and for enabling children to follow the pattern established in the piece. Children seem to love the sounds of language.

Start with the oral experience of a story or poem, and then move to the writing experience. A story I have used is Bill Martin's (1971) *David Was Mad*. It is a lovely story about getting angry and getting over being angry. I like this story because it says, "Yes, it's okay to be angry, but there are ways of getting over anger"—a good message for children. I used Martin's book in a modeling experiment with third grade children. First, children wrote a group story. Then they wrote their own individual stories, using the original model. The story, *David Was Mean*, was written by Amy, a third grader. She modeled her story on Martin's original story, *David Was Mad*.

David Was Mean

David was mean.
MEAN! MEAN! BAD!
He was so mean that he kicked the cat.
He felt all black inside.
Mother and Father knew that David was mean.
They knew because David yelled at them.
Grandpa knew that David was mean.
He knew because David wouldn't get the paper for him.
The teacher knew that David was mean.
She knew because David was hitting the kids.
Big brother knew that David was mean.
He knew because David tore up his room.
Little sister knew that David was mean.
She knew because David spit on her.
Everybody hated it. Everybody got meaner and meaner.
They all began to get mean.
They began to feel all black inside.
They were so mean that they began to fight.
They fought and fought.
Everyone had a terrible time.
It was one of the horriblest days they ever had.
"This was a terrible day," David said.

And he began to cry.
He cried and cried.
"Yes, that's how it is," Mother said.
"Meanness is like the wind. It blows on everybody that's near."
Already David was feeling better.
He was beginning to feel all white and warm inside.
His meanness had passed.
Amy, Age 9

Henry Ritchett Wing (1966) wrote a story called *What Is Big?*, an excellent concept story. In Wing's story, a young boy compares himself to a goat, horse, elephant, whale, and dinosaur. This story is perfect for developing the comparison-contrast concept and engaging children in a writing task they can easily manage. *What is Smelly?* was written by Jim, a fourth grader.

What is Smelly?

My name is Skunky. I am not very smelly.
I am not as smelly as a sock.
A sock is smellier than I am.
I am not as smelly as sour milk.
Sour milk is smellier than I am.
I am not as smelly as a diaper.
A diaper is smellier than I am.
I am not as smelly as a wet onion.
A wet onion is smellier than I am.
I am not as smelly as garbage.
Garbage is the smelliest thing I know.
Jim, Fourth Grade

A Maker of Boxes, by Bill Martin, Jr. (1966), is a wonderful story for modeling. Like many patterned stories, it can be adapted to multiple purposes. The first example, "An Observer of Animals," shows how this story can be adapted to writing across the curriculum, in this case science. The second example, *A Maker of Cards,* was a marvelously illustrated book written by Heather, a fourth grader, and submitted as her entry in Oakland University's Young Authors' Conference.

An Observer of Animals—Adapted to Science

Hello, I am an observer of Animals.
On Monday I observe birds.
They have wings.
They're warm blooded.
They eat worms, bugs, and seeds.
Some birds are: robins, sparrows, hawks, and eagles.

On Tuesday I observe mammals.
Mammals have fur or hair.
They produce milk for their young.
Mammals have a backbone and a four-chambered heart.
Some mammals are: humans, dogs, pigs, and bats.
The blue whale is the largest mammal.

(The poem continues with a verse for Wednesday,
Thursday, and Friday, dealing, respectively, with
reptiles, amphibians, and fish. The story summarizes
a science unit on vertebrates.)

Fifth Grade Class

A Maker of Cards

Hi, my name is Mrs. Hallmark.
I'm the maker of cards.
I make big cards, small cards, happy cards, and sad cards.
And white cards, and rainbow cards, and old cards, and new cards.
And all of them are good!

On Monday I make blue cards, red cards, and green cards.
On Tuesday I make baby cards, funny and anniversary cards.
On Wednesday I make dog cards, cat cards, and bird cards.
On Thursday I make orange cards, yellow cards, and purple cards.
On Friday I make dull cards, fancy, funny, and singing cards.
On Saturday I don't make cards, I make envelopes.
I make big envelopes, little envelopes, pink envelopes,
and purple envelopes.
On Sunday I don't make cards. I send them, and all to
my friends.

Heather, Fourth Grade

Another interesting type of imitation is the writing of parodies. Parody is the imitation of the characteristic style of a literary composition. A parody borrows the structure of a literary work and adds humorous and often modern contributions not contained in the original. Writers use parody to produce a specific effect. Pam, a fourth grader, rewrote *Little Red Riding Hood.* Her story recast the Wolf as the hero. Little Red Riding Hood became Little Red, the villain, who harassed the innocent Wolf. Writing parodies is a good way to teach point of view.

The story, *Groovylocks,* is a parody of *Goldilocks and the Three Bears.* The sixth grade author gives the story a modern setting but uses the style and structure of the original story.

Groovylocks

Once upon a time there was a pad located smack-dab in the middle of the sticks, which had air conditioning, console stereo, and a color tv. In this pad lived Big Daddy, Big Mama, and Big Baby, in that order. One bright sunshiney spring morn Big Daddy and Big Baby woke up to a tang and bagel breakfast. Big daddy, slumping down in his big chair took a bite out of the steaming bagel. Big Daddy yelped, "Don't you think this bagel is just a bit too hot to eat!" So then Big Mama and Big Baby tried theirs and agreed. Big Mama suggested that they take a walk to give the bagels a chance to cool.

Groovylocks, a girl wearing cutoffs and beads came walking down the street looking for a place to rest. She went up the walk and knocked on the door. No one answered. So she knocked again, the door creaked open a little bit. She called and when no one answered she walked right in. When she saw the Tang and bagels she exclaimed "Far out, finally I can get some good grub." She sat down in Big Daddy's chair and took a bite out of the bagel and yelled "Ouch, man this bagel is hot!" Then she went over to Big Mama's bagel and took a bite out of the bagel but it was too cold so she then went over to Big Baby's and found it was just groovy and ate it all up. . . .

(The story continues in this modern vein and concludes with the following paragraph.)

Then on the day she was to leave (the three bears house) they asked Groovylocks to stay, but she said no that she couldn't because she wanted to go live with her swinging aunt, GOLDILOCKS.

Mary, Grade 6

Remy Charlip (1964) wrote a book called *Fortunately*. Charlip's book features a series of events alternately characterized as fortunate and unfortunate. This theme can be modified in many ways. Some alternatives are: How wonderful, How horrible; What good luck, What bad luck; How exciting, How boring; How generous, How stingy; How wise, How foolish; How happy, How sad; How kind, How mean; How likely, How unlikely; How childish, How grown-up; How beautiful, How ugly. The piece below was written by Andy, a fourth grader.

Fortunately, Mom sent us out to play.
Unfortunately, it started to rain.
Fortunately, I had an umbrella.
Unfortunately, the umbrella had a hole in it.
Fortunately, I had a hat.
Unfortunately, I couldn't find it.
Fortunately, it stopped raining.
Unfortunately, I slipped on the wet grass.
Fortunately, I didn't hurt myself.

Andy, Grade 4

There are other good books that have a chain-like story theme that children are able to use for modeled writing. You may want to try these books:

1. Laura Joffe Numeroff and Felicia Bond (1985). *If You Give a Mouse a Cookie*. New York: HarperCollins Juvenile Books.

2. Laura Joffe Numeroff and Felicia Bond (1998). *If You Give a Pig a Pancake*. New York: HarperCollins Juvenile Books.

3. Laura Joffe Numeroff and Felicia Bond (1991). *If You Give a Moose a Muffin*. New York: HarperCollins Juvenile Books.

Children can use literature as a springboard to writing when given good models. Children need the comfort of knowing that it is all right to borrow structures and concepts when modeling their writing on another writer's work. There are many books and stories for modeling writing. A list of books suitable for modeling appears in the appendices of this book.

Ms. Jonella Mongo teaches kindergarten in a private academy for African American boys. She brings a missionary zeal to her work, and her "boys" succeed far beyond the expectations many have for them. In her "Voices" piece she describes her journal writing program.

VOICES FROM THE CLASSROOM: Jonella Mongo

Journal Time

I teach kindergarten boys in Detroit. Five-year-old Antonio often asked, "Miss Mongo, is it journal time? Is it journal time?" This was Antonio's endearing way of letting me know he was ready to write in "My Kindergarten Writing Journal." Antonio stopped asking about journal time as soon as he realized we wrote every day.

Most of my students enter kindergarten with a variety of writing capabilities. Some can scribble, some can write words or phrases, a few can write a sentence. For example, Charles' first journal entry consisted of black marks all over the page. He told me about his writing in these words: "a dog getting hit by a car I called 911." Mark's first story was about "Home and Dad." Through their journals, my boys discovered they had important things to write about. They could record their ideas through scribbles, pictures, words, phrases, or sentences. We call ourselves "inside our room authors." Our journal writing routine is simple:

1. Table captains distribute journal boxes: pencils, crayons, journals.
2. Children who can, copy the day's date at the top of the page.
3. Children select their own topics. I help when asked.
4. We write for a sustained period. I write, too. Spellings are invented.
5. We share our pieces with a partner, table mate, or the entire class.

I still have one of Antonio's dictated journal entries along with a touching illustration of his grandmother in a coffin surrounded by flowers. Antonio is standing in the background. Here is the story he dictated to me: "My grandma Eula died. She had a heart attack. My great grandma and me came to the funeral."

It is sometimes disturbing, yet heartwarming, when the realities of "my boys" life experiences come through in their journal writing. But then, I say to myself, isn't that what writing is all about—evoking feelings, thoughts, and reflections.

Modeling Poems

Langston Hughes wrote a wonderful poem called, "Mother to Son" (Rampersad and Roessel, 1994). The poem begins with these two lines: "Well, son, I'll tell you/Life for me ain't been no crystal stair." These opening lines set up the content and structure of the lines that follow. Hughes follows the metaphor of the crystal stair throughout his poem.

Ms. Johnson teaches in Detroit. She used Hughes' poem as a model. She talked about Hughes' poem, discussed the metaphor of the crystal stair and the structure of the poem. Students then brainstormed for possible metaphors around which their poem could be written. Here are some metaphors that were suggested:

Life for me ain't been no bed of roses

Life for me ain't been no book of prayer

Life for me ain't been no easy ride

Life for me ain't been no hallelujah chorus

Life for me ain't been no baseball game

Life for me ain't been no spring shower

Life for me ain't been no bowl of popcorn

Life for me ain't been no trip to the beach

Life for me ain't been no rock and roll concert

Mrs. Johnson started with a group poem. Then, children wrote their own "Mother to Son" poems. Hughes' poem is a challenging one, and beautifully fitting to convey genuine feelings. I would not recommend it as a starting point for modeling poetry, but once children have had some experience with modeling, this is a fine poem to use. Tara, a fifth grader, wrote her own "Mother to Son" poem. It is a lovely effort.

Mother to Son

Well, son, I'll tell you:
Life for me ain't been full of sunshine.
It's had thunderstorms,
And lightning strikes,
And sloppy wet clothing,
And booming loud lightning.
Burr.
But all the time,
I'se been tramping on,
And reaching farther stations,
And getting closer to freedom.
So, boy, don't you turn back
'Cause your legs are getting tired.
For I'se still trying for freedom,
I'se still walking through the rain.
And life for me ain't been full of sunshine.
Tara, Fifth Grade

Judith Viorst wrote a poem called, "If I Were in Charge of the World." There is something about this idea that strikes fire with children. Perhaps because they see adults as being in charge all the time, and they don't always see this as fair. When they write their own poems, it is as if they were saying, "Now, if I were in charge of the world . . ." Below is Jenny's, "If I Were in Charge of the World" poem.

If I Were in Charge of the World

If I were in charge of the world
I would cancel cleaning my room,
Smoking, wars, boys.
If I were in charge of the world
There would be more animals,
Rainbows, candy, books.

If I were in charge of the world
You wouldn't have sisters, brothers,
Vegetables, spiders, school.

If I were in charge of the world
Dreams would come true,
And things would come to life if you
Wanted them to.

Jenny, Third Grade

Shel Silverstein (1981) wrote "Crowded Tub." It is a hilarious description of too many kids in a tub. The poem "Crowded Bed" was modeled on Silverstein's poem, "Crowded Tub." Ms. Frazzini, a teacher, wrote it for her children. This is a wonderful way to initiate modeling. Children are reassured and inspired when their teachers participate with them as writers.

Crowded Bed

There's too many kids in this bed,
Someone keeps bumping my head.
I just picked some toes,
Whose were they?
Who knows?
There's too many kids in this bed.

Ms. Frazzini, Teacher

William Carlos Williams wrote a poem called "This Is Just to Say." In this poem, he apologizes for eating the plums that were in the icebox. It is a thirteen-line, free verse poem. It is so brief and so simple that even first graders can write, "I'm sorry to say . . ." poems. First, read the poem a few times. Ask the children what the author meant and how he felt about eating the plums. Ask if they have ever done something for which they felt like saying, "I'm sorry." Perhaps you could write your own, "I'm sorry to say . . ." poem and read it to your children.

Then have the children write their poems. Below is Eddie's poem modeled on William Carlos Williams' classic poem, This Is Just to Say.

I Am Sorry to Say

Dear Zak
I am sory to say
that I ate your
dog biskit
that you left on the
flor
I hope you
don't mind
It was hrd
and tastd so
good
Eddie, Grade 2

Ethel and Leonard Kessler wrote a poem called, "Do Little Chicks Pick up Sticks?" It is one of those poems that primary grade children seem to love. Mrs. Ruszkowski read this poem to her first graders and they loved it. So she decided to have them write a group poem modeled on the Kesslers' poem. Below is the poem her children wrote called, "Can Little Tadpoles Live in Bowls?"

Can Little Tadpoles Live in Bowls?

Can little tadpoles
live in bowls, eat
rolls, have goals?
Yes, they can.
Can they ride a
bike, just as I
can?
No, no, no!
Can hopping frogs
climb on logs, live
in bogs?
Yes . . .
But can they ride
on skateboards,
just as I can?
No, no, no!
Can babies, girls,
boys, moms, dads,
aunts, uncles,
grandmothers or

grandfathers eat
insects, worms,
tadpoles, or little
fish?
No, no, no!
But frogs can.
Mrs. Ruszkowski's First Grade Class

While almost any poem can be modeled, it is a good idea to choose poems that appeal in some special way. Perhaps the poem presents a special challenge, as "Mother to Son" does; or the poem makes children laugh, as "Crowded Tub" does; perhaps the poem empowers children in a unique way as, "If I Were in Charge of the World" does; possibly the poem has a universal appeal, as William Carlos Williams' poem has. There are many fine poems to choose from, but the important thing about a poem is that it must appeal to children. Once you've got a good poem, follow the procedures outlined or devise your own. You will have a wonderful writing experience. You will find a list of poems for modeling in the appendices of this book.

Modeling Writing Skills

Modeling is an effective instructional strategy (Cramer, 1976; Cramer, 1984). As such, it gives teachers a concrete way of demonstrating writing concepts and skills. Any writing concept or skill can be modeled, either directly or indirectly, through literature. Teachers can use literary models, for example, to demonstrate skills such as writing dialogue. Below are examples of how two teachers, Ms. Elson and Mrs. Stanley, used modeling in their classrooms to teach dialogue.

Dialogue: Ms. Elson, a successful fifth grade writing teacher, uses modeling routinely. Here is an example of a modeling episode. Ms. Elson was conducting a writing conference with Kristen about her most recent piece of fiction. Kristen's first draft is several pages of continuous dialogue. She hasn't interspersed narrative with dialogue, she hasn't used quotation marks properly, and she hasn't indented in the conventional manner. Still, she had an interesting piece of writing going. Ms. Elson simply said, "Kristen, find some passages in the book you are reading where the author has used dialogue. Read it. Think about it. Then let's talk about it." Kristen was reading *The Great Gilly Hopkins* by Katherine Paterson. Reading good books is a key component in Ms. Elson's reading-writing program. Ms. Elson knows, and so do her children, that literature is a valuable source of information for solving writing problems. Ms. Elson's suggestion enabled Kristen to return to her book with the clear purpose of learning how Paterson used dialogue. Later, Ms. Elson discussed with Kristen what she had learned about using dialogue. When Kristen revised her piece, something new appeared in her story. She had interspersed narrative in the dialogue. She had also indented paragraphs and used quotation marks, usually correctly, though not always. Ms. Elson used literature as a model for improving a specific writing skill.

Later, she taught dialogue writing in a mini-lesson to the entire class. She will teach dialogue writing again at other times and in other ways. Using examples from literature and from children's writing helps her solve writing problems that children encounter every day.

Descriptive Detail: Mrs. Stanley (1988) wanted her third graders to understand the connection between literature and writing. She read good literature to them constantly. She discussed how writers handled certain writing problems in their books. For example, she had just read aloud Roald Dahl's *George's Marvelous Medicine.* Together they discussed the wonderful descriptive passages in Dahl's book. Mrs. Stanley remarked, ". . . how chock full of information the story is." She reread several passages to illustrate her point. A few days later, Gretchen approached Mrs. Stanley carrying a library book: "Listen to this," she said. Then Gretchen read several passages from a book she was reading. "How's this for tons of information, Mrs. Stanley?" Gretchen, and Mrs. Stanley's other third graders, are gradually acquiring an insider's view of how writers work and how literature helps solve writing problems. Mrs. Stanley's third graders are beginning to understand what authors do and how they do it. This understanding gradually shows itself in the writing her children produce.

There are all of kinds of models and modeling. Sometimes the writing children produce can be an excellent model. In her diary entry, Jennifer DeWard tells how she used a former student's writing as a model to help her current fourth graders get a better grasp on certain fiction writing skills.

DIARY OF A TEACHER: Jennifer DeWard

My students have been coming along nicely in writers' workshop the past three months. However, something has been troubling me lately. Most of my students are writing stories about real events that happened to them, which is fine. However, they are not writing fiction. I have been reading good literature, and I hoped they would try a fiction story on their own. This has not yet happened. So, I asked a former student to come to my classroom and read a fictional story that she had written last year. I told my class that Jacquelyn had written a great story when she was in fourth grade, and I wanted her to share it with the class.

After Jacquelyn read her story, my students showered her with compliments. They loved her story; they liked the characters; they liked her story problem. Someone said they liked how, "someone else told the story." I gave my students an opportunity to listen to a great story written by a peer, and I'm confident that a few of them will take the bait and begin writing their own fiction.

USING LITERATURE IN WRITING FICTION

Many children think that fiction is writing that is untrue. Indeed, this is a classic definition of fiction in many children's textbooks. At best, this is a half-truth which inadequately represents the marvelously varied texture of fiction. Most fiction, and certainly the best fiction, is about real life, and it has more than a dollop of truth. Good fiction is a microscope that reveals the world in all its beauty and ugliness, wisdom and ignorance, decency and vulgarity. Even such popular genres as mystery, science fiction, and romance deal with real-life issues. But many children have been led to believe that fiction has little to do with real life. Few cultural resources represent life experiences more vividly and realistically than fiction. John Steinbeck's *The Grapes of Wrath* informed us of the hardships and travails of dust bowl America more vividly and realistically than any history book has ever informed us. Joad, the main character, lives only in the minds of Steinbeck's readers, yet he represents every man and woman who ever suffered a hardship or endured an injustice.

Writing fiction starts with observation of personal experience and diligent research. While fiction writers do not usually use the names of living people, they often write about life as it is actually lived. Fiction deals with representational truth, just as art does. Picasso painted his great masterpiece, *Guernica*, as a protest against the bombing of a Spanish town by the Nazis. *Guernica* is not a photograph of Nazi atrocities, but it represents the truth of atrocities better than any photograph could. *Guernica* is a symbolic representation of truth.

Fiction writers also represent truth symbolically. The plots, settings, characters, events, and resolutions of fiction are of the same genre of truth as that of art. Norman Mailer makes this point explicitly in the epilogue to his novel about the CIA, *Harlot's Ghost.*

> My hope is that the imaginary world of *Harlot's Ghost* will bear more relation to the reality of these historical events than the spectrum of facts and often calculated misinformation that still surrounds them. It is a sizable claim, but then I have the advantage of believing that novelists have a unique opportunity—they can create superior histories out of an enhancement of the real, the unverified, and the wholly fictional. (p. 1288)

Encourage your children to read and write fiction. They can do it. You need only show them the pathway: share literature with them, suggest a few ideas, and get out of their way. They have experiences and they can use them in their writing. The following suggestions may help you direct children along the pathway of effective fiction writing.

Write about Real People, Problems, and Events

The best fiction is about real people, problems, and events. The best topics are often rather ordinary, at least on the surface. For example, Robertson Davies, the great Canadian novelist, starts *The Deptford Trilogy* with a snowball throwing incident. A young boy throws a rock-laden snowball at his best friend, misses, and accidentally hits a young woman. This seemingly insignificant incident sets off a chain of events that tosses the novel's characters about in life like a raft in white water. A book more appropriate for children, *The Rifle,* by Gary Paulsen has a somewhat similar theme. The history of a rifle, passed from generation to generation, is tracked to its present owner. A tragic accident involving the rifle occurs and this sets off a series of events that provide the conclusion and message of Paulsen's book.

Children can write fiction, but first they must know what it is. Instead of using contrived topics such as "The Thoughts of a Pencil," help your children take the crucial first steps in writing fiction based on their own concerns and experiences. Contrived fiction is not creative, it is merely cute. And while I do not object to some writing of this sort, too much of it can give children a distorted notion of fiction.

Fiction writers write about life. Katherine Paterson put it this way: "My job is to tell a story about real people who live in the world as it is." Children can do the same if they learn to keep company with books, and are shown how literature can inform their own writing. Paterson's Newbery Award winning book, *The Bridge to Terabithia,* is realistic fiction. In Paterson's book, two lonesome children from different backgrounds become friends, and create a secret kingdom of the imagination. While Jess goes off to an art museum, his friend, Leslie, drowns. Jess feels guilty about her death, but learns to cope and to look toward the future with hope. Paterson deals with real emotions children experience: lonesomeness, friendship, guilt, disappointment, hope. The central events and characters in her book are loosely based on the experiences of Katherine Paterson.

Nothing But the Truth, a 1992 Newbery Honor Book, is a documentary novel. Ninth grader, Phillip Malloy, irritates his English teacher, who he blames for keeping him off the track team, by humming along with the daily audiotape of "The Star Spangled Banner." This seemingly minor incident escalates into a national controversy.

Children relate to fiction that resonates with their own feelings, thoughts, and experiences. The books cited above deal with real people, problems, and events in a fictional mode. When children understand that fiction is a combination of experience and imagination, they can begin to see that what they have lived and experienced can become the source of their own fiction.

Incorporate Real-Life Experiences into Fiction

Fiction is not simply thinking up imaginary events and people that never existed anywhere in the world before. If this were the basis for fiction, there would be no fiction. Even science fiction depends upon familiar experiences set in unique environments and time frames. Without reference to real-world experiences, readers would be unable to relate to science fiction.

Authors draw on their personal experiences when they write fiction, and children need to understand this. For example, Beverly Cleary drew on experiences with her own children in her Henry Huggins books as she wrote about children's struggles for acceptance. In *Soup,* Robert Newton Peck (1974) draws heavily on his own childhood experiences. The two main characters, Rob and Soup, are Peck and his best friend, so the author tells us. Children can find countless other examples by reading about authors in the *Something About the Author* series (Gale Research Company, 1988) or *Twentieth Century Children's Writers* (St. James Press, 1989). When children understand the connection between real-life experience and fiction, they can draw on their own experiences for their fiction, as Kristen did.

Vincent loves dinosaurs. He's reading a book on dinosaurs in preparation for writing his own dinosaur story.

Kristen, a fifth grader, began using her own experiences to enrich her fiction after her teacher showed her how authors did the same. When Kristen's parents separated and divorce was a possibility, she wrote a story about two children whose parents were getting a divorce. Kristen's story contained elements of personal experience, but it also differed from her real-life experience. For example, Kristen is an only child, but her story's character had a younger brother whose actions were central to the plot. Writing this story gave Kristen an understanding of the power of personal experience in fiction.

Teach Children to Research Fiction

Children may not realize that many fiction writers do research for their books. Help them see how facts and fiction are related and how writers handle the interplay between factual information and imagination. Give examples to children of how authors obtain accurate and realistic information for their fiction. Writers must be knowledgeable about the times and places they are writing about. A story set in London, for example, must not have its characters strolling down the Champs Elysees in Paris.

Author Jean Craighead George conducted field research in Alaska to obtain information on Eskimo culture and on wolves for her book *Julie of the Wolves*. In their science fiction adventure story *Norby and the Invaders,* Janet and Isaac Asimov based many of their ideas on documented scientific facts. Tom Clancy's *The Hunt for Red October* was so astonishingly accurate that the FBI investigated to find out how and where he got his information. He got it through research: public documents, interviews, and on-site investigations. Elizabeth Speare carefully researched details about pre-revolutionay New England for her book, *The Witch of Blackbird Pond,* including the houses, clothes, even what people talked about. *Cold Mountain,* a first novel by Charles Frazier, chronicles the life and times of a soldier who has deserted the Confederate Army and makes his way back home. The author is meticulous about every detail, going so far as to use the language that would have been used in the 1860s. Good fiction requires accurate information. Show young writers that they can obtain the information they need for their fiction through on-site investigation, reading, interviews, and their own experiences, as Kim and John did.

Fifth graders, Kim and John, collaborated on a story about an octopus that contained information found in an encyclopedia and library books. This information added realistic details to their story. They learned that octopi lurk among rocks and caves, have suckers on their eight tentacles, can paralyze and poison their prey, that *octo* means eight and *pus* means feet. Like all authors, Kim and John learned more about octopi than they included in their story. They even exercised poetic license and called tentacles "legs." Young writers, like Kim and John, can create superior stories by combining imagination with factual knowledge gained from diligent research, as excerpts and illustrations from their book *Hector the Octopus* illustrate. In *Hector the Octopus,* Hector feels ashamed because he has only seven legs. Throughout the story, Hector encounters sharks, sea horses, and other sea creatures as he lurks about in dark spots on the ocean floor. The young authors resolve Hector's problem by having a shark help Hector determine that he actually does have eight legs; he just forgot to count the one with which he counted. An illustration and part of their story appear on the following pages.

Page 1:

Hector was an octopus
who lived deep down on the
bottom of the ocean.
Hector was a very sad octopus

because he had only seven legs . . . poor Hector.
He never wanted anyone to know
his embarrassing position.

Page 2:

One day when he was lurking
under some rocks,
he heard a funny sound.
He was very curious to see what it was.
Hector approached the queer sound.
When he looked around, he saw
a little fish caught between two rocks.
Hector helped get the little fish free.
The fish asked if he could help
Hector in any way.

Page 3:

Hector said, "Yes, you can.
You can help me hide."
The little fish said, "Why do you
want to hide?"
Hector said in a sad voice,
"Because I have only seven legs."
"You do? Let me count them:
one, two, three, four, five, six,
seven, eight. I counted eight,"
said the little fish.
"That's because you counted wrong," said Hector.
"Let's drop the subject: but I know
where you can hide," said the little fish.

(Hector hides and the other sea creatures
worry about him. There are additional encounters
with other sea creatures. Eventually Hector
accepts his handicap, even becomes proud
of his uniqueness. As the book concludes
Hector encounters a school of sharks. They
convince him that he has miscounted. The final
page of *Hector the Octopus* follows.)

Last Page:

"Look, everyone! Look! I have
eight legs! I forgot to count the
one I counted with.
See! I'll count them for you . . .

Figure 7.1 **Hector the Octopus** Kim and John, fifth graders, collaborated on the story and illustrations and read their book at the Young Authors' Conference at Oakland University.

one, two, three, four, five, six,
seven, eight.
I'm the happiest octopus in the whole
world!"
And indeed, Hector was.

Engage Children in Literary Dialogue

I've always loved the term Nancie Atwell (1987) coined to describe talk about literature between and among herself and her students. She called it "Literary Gossip."

> I've learned the value and necessity of allowing kids to read as real readers do, choosing, skimming, skipping, and abandoning. Maybe the hardest lesson of all, I've learned how to respond authoritatively to what readers are trying to do without coming across like a teacher's guide or a test. Instead, I can affirm, challenge, gossip, joke, argue, recommend and provide information to reader needs. I can also offer some well-placed "nudges." (p. 170)

The fiction children write will be timid and anemic unless they understand what writers do, how they do it, and why. "Gossip" with your kids about the books they have heard or read. Talk about fictional characters. Get children's views on what makes a good story. Use selected fiction to show students that stories can be partially based on real people, their problems and feelings, and events that actually took place. This can be done through informal discussions. It can also be done through response journals, as Atwell did so effectively. Once you expose children to outstanding fiction, they recognize the interest real people can generate and the fertile ground they provide for stories. The possibilities are legion. For example, children will enjoy discussing *Nettie's Trip South* by Ann Turner, *Walk Two Moons* by Sharon Creech (1995 Newbery Medal Winner), *Dicey's Song* by Cynthia Voigt (1983 Newbery Award Winner), *Dear Mr. Henshaw* by Beverly Cleary (1984 Newbery Award Winner), *Nobody Listens to Andrew* by Elizabeth Guilfoile, *Tom and the Two Handles* by Russell Hoban, Tomie DePaola's semiautobiographical book, *The Art Lesson,* and Steven Kellogg's book about friendship and imagination, *Best Friends.*

It is amazing how quickly and easily children understand the connection between literature and writing. Mrs. Stanley (1988) discovered this while conducting a revision study with her third grade children. Early in the study she made this observation: "My students, particularly the more fluent writers, began fictionalizing their pieces early in the study. I could not discover why, I could only guess and wonder if it had to do with the fiction I was reading to them" (p. 26). As time went on, however, Mrs. Stanley discovered that her children were linking literature with writing. The more she engaged them in conversations about literature, writers, and writing, the more the children applied this knowledge to their writing. For instance, one day she noticed a few children rather furtively reading books during the writing period. She wanted them to know this was all right. So she asked the children a few questions: Would it be all right to read a book once in a while during writing time? Could this help you with your writing? How might it help? she asked. Here are a few of their responses:

I could get an idea for a topic.

I could check out how to write quotes.

If I'm publishing, I could see how the author puts the dedication down.

I might get ideas on how long to make my chapters.

I could see how the characters act.

Mrs. Stanley discovered that her third graders were capable of writing fiction. She never underestimated what they could do. The more you "gossip" with children about literature, writers, and writing the more they will apply this knowledge to their writing. As you discuss literature with your students, and as they retell stories they've read, engage them in discussions about the components of a story: characters, settings, conflicts, events, resolutions. Familiarity with these components enables children to anticipate the problems, events, and resolutions of stories they are reading, and it will help them create their own stories. Books that may prove useful are: *The Sign in Mendel's Window* by Mildred Phillips, *Sarah, Plain and Tall* by Patricia MacLachlan, *Are You There, God? It's Me, Margaret* by Judy Blume, and *A Gathering of Days: A New England Girls' Journal* by Joan W. Blos.

SUMMARY OF USING LITERATURE FOR WRITING FICTION

1. The best fiction is about real people, problems, and events set in a fictional mode.

2. Fiction is not simply thinking up imaginary events and people that never existed anywhere in the world before. Once children understand this, they can see that their own experiences are a resource for their own fiction.

3. Teach children the value and use of research in writing fiction.

4. Engage children in literary dialogue about the fiction they are reading so that they will understand what writers do, how they do it, and why.

IDEAS FOR WRITING

1. Imaging: Think of images evoked by certain words. Then write or draw pictures of the ideas that come to mind. Here are some words that make for interesting images: terror, meteor, storm, mountains, sea, pirate, crash. Add your own words. After creating images for one or more words, use your ideas to start a poem or story.

2. Create a mood: Write a description of a scene which creates a mood. Start with a teacher-written model. Here is an example:

As we entered the room an oppressive smell assailed our nostrils. The scent was pungent, sweet, and faintly unpleasant. It seemed to be a mixture of decaying flowers and room freshener. The room itself had a light and airy appearance, yet, strangely, it lacked cheerfulness and warmth. Someone had tried but failed to turn an unpleasant atmosphere into an inviting one.

3. Describing: Write a description of the physical appearance of a person which gives clues to mood. Start with a teacher-written model. Here is an example:

   John strode into the room, holding himself rigidly erect. Each step seemed deliberately rehearsed. As he moved from one place to another, he focused his eyes in the direction of his destination, and then, almost as if he were controlled by a machine, he marched toward the door, never veering from his chosen path.

4. Observing: Observe a stranger and write a fictional account about that person's life. Here are some common events to consider: (1) an elderly person waiting nervously on a park bench, (2) a couple jogging through the park, (3) a well-dressed man strolling slowly down the street, (4) a young girl skipping down the street holding her mother's hand.

5. Painting word pictures: Writers paint pictures with words. Paint a word picture of something or someone you see every day. Here are some scenes you could paint with words: (1) an ancient oak tree, (2) traffic on a rainy day, (3) the school hallway during recess, (4) school busses lined up after school.

6. Nudging nursery rhymes: Use a nursery rhyme, such as "Mary Had a Little Lamb" to write a short-short story. Add a surprise ending, as in this example:

   A little girl named Mary had a pet lamb. One day when she got to school she discovered, to her surprise, that the lamb had followed her. All the children laughed because they had never seen a lamb in school before. Mary was embarrassed, but she quickly recovered. She turned to her teacher, Ms. Nathan, and said, "I have brought a surprise for show and tell."

7. Writing leads: Opening sentences in novels and stories are sometimes filled with implied information. For example, this is the opening sentence in Chekhov's "The Lady With the Dog." "It was reported that a new face had been seen on the quay; a lady with a little dog." The following information is implicit in this opening sentence: (1) scene is a port, (2) seaside resort, (3) gossip circulated, (4) some find this new face newsworthy, (5) the lady is an animal fancier. Discuss the importance of opening sentences in writing. Give another example or two from books available in your room. Talk about opening sentences, sometimes called leads. Have children write opening sentences for possible stories. Actual stories may be written later.

REFLECTION AND SUMMARY

Reflection

The pleasure of literature is doubled when one shares it with another. Share literature and your literary experiences with your children. You will enrich yourself as well as your children. Literature is the life's blood of writing. Reading to children is the literary equivalent of a blood transfusion.

Modeling gives structure to writing. Modeling literature transforms poems and stories from abstractions into concrete realities. For example, some children may not know the difference between a folk tale and a Volkswagen. But when children are given models of folk tales, a different perspective emerges. Discuss what folk tales are and how they work. This will convey an understanding of their characteristic content and structure. After children have heard, read, and discussed folk tales, they will have the literary background needed to write their own, and they can do it.

There isn't anything mysterious about the influence of literature on writing. It is a sensible adjunct to teaching writing, though it is by no means sufficient. Many other strategies and procedures are likewise essential. Literature is a delightful world. The stories, information, and ideas they contain speak to the soul as well as the mind. Literature whispers a welcome, an invitation to share secret worlds. It is our privilege, as teachers, to usher children into the wondrous world of literature.

Summary

This chapter has presented the following main ideas.

1. Literature has great value in preparing children for writing. It accomplishes at least seven things:
   - Provides models for writing
   - Develops a love for reading, which feeds writing
   - Extends knowledge of and appreciation for language
   - Enlightens and entertains the minds of children
   - Enriches cultural literacy
   - Depicts the human condition
   - Develops children's sense of story.

2. Reading aloud supports learning to read and write. A comprehensive program of reading aloud includes:
   - Creating a receptive atmosphere for reading aloud
   - Selecting readings appropriate to children's ages and interests
   - Read selections in ways that enhance enjoyment and appreciation.

3. Strategies, procedures, and examples for modeling poetry and stories were presented.

4. Four guidelines for using literature in the writing of fiction were given:
   - Guide children to understand that the best fiction is about real people, problems, and events.
   - Help children understand that fiction writers incorporate real-life experiences, as well as imagination, into their stories.

- Show children the necessity of conducting research to enrich their fiction with accurate information.
- Engage children in oral and written dialogue about writers and writing so they will understand the art and craft of fiction writing.

QUESTIONS FOR REFLECTIVE THINKING

1. What is the value of tying literature into the writing program?
2. Why read literature aloud to children?
3. What types of literature should be read aloud to children?
4. How might you go about modeling the writing of a story or poem?
5. Suppose your children are having difficulty writing dialogue. How might you use literature to teach dialogue writing?
6. How can research be useful in writing fiction?
7. What is "literary gossip"? How can it be used to help children understand writing and writers?
8. What have you learned from this chapter that you didn't know before you read it?
9. What significant disagreements do you have with ideas and information described in this chapter? Explain why you disagree.
10. What ideas or information would you add to or delete from this chapter if you were the author? Explain.
11. Mini case study: You teach fourth grade in an urban school, and the majority of your children are members of minority groups. One of your goals is to help your children write fiction stories. Outline an instructional plan that will help you accomplish this goal.

REFERENCES

Adams, M. J. (1990). *Beginning to read: Thinking and learning about print.* Cambridge, MA: MIT Press.

Altsheler, J. (1910). *The riflemen of the Ohio.* New York: Appleton, Century, Croft.

Anderson, R., Hiebert, E., Scott, J., and Wilkinson, I. (1985). *Becoming a nation of readers.* Bloomington, IN: The Center for the Study of Reading.

Applebee A. (1978). *The child's concept of story.* Chicago, IL: University of Chicago Press.

Atwell, N. (1987). *In the middle.* Upper Montclair, NJ: Boynton/Cook.

Bandura, A. (1967). "Behavioral psychotherapy." *Scientific American,* 216, 78–86.

Bettelheim, B. (1976). *The uses of enchantment: The meaning and importance of fairy tales.* New York: Vintage Books.

Calkins, L. M. (1994). *The art of teaching writing.* Portsmouth, NH: Heinemann.

Charlip, R. (1964). *Fortunately.* New York: Scholastic.

Charlton, J. (1986). *The writer's quotation book: A literary companion.* New York: Penguin.

Chomsky, C. (1972). "Stages in language development and reading achievement." *Harvard Educational Review,* 42, 1–33.

Cleary, B. (1983). *Dear Mr. Henshaw.* New York: William Morrow & Co.

Coody, B. and Nelson, D. (1982). *Teaching elementary language arts.* Belmont, CA: Wadsworth.

Cramer, B. B. (1984). "Bequest of wings: Three readers and special books." *Language Arts,* 61, 253–260.

Cramer, R. L. (1976). "Providing models for good writing." *Learning: The magazine for creative teaching,* August/September.

Creech, S. (1994). *Walk two moons.* New York: HarperCollins.

Davies, R. (1990). *The Deptford trilogy.* New York: Penguin Books.

DePaola, T. (1989). *The art lesson.* New York: Putnam Publishing.

Elley, W. B. (1992). *How in the world do students read?* Newark, DE: International Reading Association.

Flood, J. (1986). "The text, the student and the teacher. Learning exposition in the middle school." *The Reading Teacher,* 39, 784–791.

Frazier, C. (1997). *Cold mountain.* New York: The Atlantic Monthly Press.

Gilbar, S. (1989). *The open door: When writers first learned to read.* Boston: David R. Godine.

Gillespie, J. T. and Naden, C. J. (1990). *Best books for children: Preschool through grade 6,* 4th ed. New York: R. R. Bowker.

Hennings, D. G. (1994). *Communication in action: Teaching the language arts,* 5th ed. Boston: Houghton Mifflin.

Hirsch, E. D. Jr., Kett, J. F., and Trefil, J. (1988). *The dictionary of cultural literacy.* Boston: Houghton Mifflin.

Kellogg, S. (1986). *Best friends.* New York: Dutton.

Koestler, A. (1941). *Darkness at noon.* New York: Macmillan.

Langer, J. A. (1995). *Envisioning literature: Literary understanding and literature instruction.* New York: Teachers College Press.

Light, S. (1991). *Parents reading aloud to their third grade children and its influence on vocabulary, comprehension, and attitudes.* Unpublished Dissertation, Oakland University: Rochester, MI.

Mailer, Norman. (1991). *Harlot's ghost.* New York: Random House.

Mandler, J. and Johnson, N. (1987). "Remembrance of things parsed: Story structure and recall." *Cognitive Psychology,* 9, 111–151.

Martin, B. Jr. (1971). *David was mad.* New York: Holt, Rinehart and Winston.

Martin, B. Jr. (1966). "A maker of boxes." In *Sounds of laughter,* New York: Holt, Rinehart and Winston.

Martin, D., James, G., and Corbin, M. (1998). *Style! Mumford's Literary Magazine, Volume 6.* Mumford High School, Detroit, MI: InsideOut Writing Project.

Numeroff, L. J. and Bond, F. (1985). *If you give a mouse a cookie.* New York: HarperCollins.

Numeroff, L. J. and Bond, F. (1991). *If you give a moose a muffin.* New York: HarperCollins.

Numeroff, L. J. and Bond, F. (1998). *If you give a pig a pancake.* New York: HarperCollins.

Palmer, G. M. and Coon, G. E. (1985). "Writing excellence through the literature connection." *The Advocate,* Vol. 5, No. 1.

Paulsen, G. (1995). *The rifle.* New York: Harcourt Brace.

Peck, R. N. (1974). *Soup.* New York: Knopf.

Rampersad, A., and Roessel, D. (Eds.) (1994). *The collected poems of Langston Hughes.* New York: Knopf.

Silverstein, S. (1974). *Where the sidewalk ends.* New York: Harper and Row.

Silverstein, S. (1981). *A light in the attic.* New York: Harper and Row.

Stanley, A. G. (1988). *Revision in third grade.* Unpublished Master's Project, Oakland University, Rochester, MI.

Stein, N. L. (1979). "How children understand stories: A developmental analysis." In *current topics in early childhood education*, L. Katz, Ed., Norwood, NJ: Ablex.

Steinbeck, J. (1939). *The grapes of wrath.* New York: Viking Penguin.

Stewig, J. W. (1975). *Read to write.* New York: Hawthorn Books.

Trelease, J. (1995). *The read-aloud handbook,* 4th ed. New York: Viking Penguin.

Viorst, J. (1982). *If I were in charge of the world and other worries: Poems for children and their parents.* New York: Atheneum.

Voigt, C. (1983). *Dicey's song.* New York: Atheneum.

Walters, T., Webster, P., and Cramer, A. (1998). *A never ending, never done bibliography of multicultural literature for younger and older children.* ERIC document ED 407-388, Rochester, MI: Oakland University.

Wing, H. R. (1966). "What is big?" *In Sounds of numbers,* Bill Martin, Jr., Ed, New York: Holt, Rinehart and Winston.

Williams, W. C. (1966). *The collected earlier poems of William Carlos Williams.* New York: A New Directions Book.

CHAPTER **8**
Evaluating Writing

Fortunately, both my wife and my mother-in-law seem
to love digging up mistakes in spelling, punctuation, etc. I can
hear them in the next room laughing at me.

Sherwood Anderson

A WRITER'S STORY

Evaluation can be good or bad, helpful or destructive. It can stimulate growth, or it can be a subtle poison. Arthur Gordon (1974) tells a story of two kinds of evaluation, frank and brutal versus gentle and encouraging. Years ago, at the University of Wisconsin, a group of aspiring young writers met regularly to criticize each other's writing. Their frank and often brutal criticism resulted in a name for the group, The Stranglers. Women were not welcome in this all-male bastion of brutality, so they initiated their own club called The Wranglers. They, too, shared their manuscripts with one another, but with a difference; their criticism was gentle and encouraging. Years later, an alumnus analyzed the careers of the members of each club. Among The Stranglers, not one aspiring writer had made a literary reputation of any sort. The Wranglers, on the other hand, had produced half a dozen successful writers, a few of national prominence. Was this a coincidence? Or did the kind of criticism given predetermine the outcome? A coincidence is possible, of course, but I do not believe the different success rates are a mere coincidence. On the contrary, I suspect that the nature of the evaluation writers receive influences, for good or ill, future writing success.

Knowledgeable, encouraging assessment is valuable. Not only must evaluation have a positive tone, it must achieve positive results. It can play a crucial role in writing growth, if judiciously and gently administered. If writers are to grow, there must be a little fall of rain, a gentle splash of encouraging words to sustain them as they struggle toward mature writing accomplishment. The purpose of evaluation is to improve writing. When wisely applied it does.

INTRODUCTION

A few basic premises inform the evaluation of writing. The concepts discussed in this chapter are not exhaustive, rather they represent the salient principles that ought to guide evaluation. Evaluation is controversial, more so than most writing issues. Research has given us some guidance, but research findings are filtered through personal experience and perspective. What follows represents my experience and perspective. As you read, bring your own experience and perspective to bear on the issues presented. Argue with me; accept, reject, or refine what I have to say; then come to your own conclusions, as a good reader must.

THREE PURPOSES FOR EVALUATING WRITING

Evaluation has three purposes. The first is instructional and is called formative evaluation. The second is administrative and is called summative evaluation. The third is research and is called research evaluation, or sometimes called "inquiry" research. While these three purposes overlap, each has a specific focus.

Formative Evaluation

Evaluation aimed at improving instruction is called formative evaluation. Its purpose is to improve an educational enterprise in a specific and direct sense. Accurate and timely assessment enables teachers and students to make informed decisions regarding the design of writing programs and projects, the delivery of instruction, the diagnosis of writing achievement, and the environment needed to support writing growth. If formative evaluation does not inform and improve writing instruction, it is useless.

Summative Evaluation

Evaluation designed to assess the state or quality of an enterprise or institution, or to report on its progress to an outside audience, is called summative evaluation. Its purpose is not aimed directly at improving instruction, yet it may indirectly bring about such a result. Summative evaluation guides administrative decision making. A school district, state, and even a nation needs to know whether its children are receiving effective writing instruction. Local, state, and national agencies need to know how writing is progressing so that goals can be set, programs evaluated, and resources provided. Teachers and administrators need to know how children are progressing so that they can report progress to parents and community. Such reports take many forms, the most common of which is the traditional report card.

Research Evaluation

Evaluation aimed at inquiring into the procedures, products, and processes of writing is research oriented. Its purpose is to inform and reform instruction in valid and reliable ways and to understand the conditions under which writing instruction works best. It leads to new or improved ways of delivering writing instruction. Research can tell us how well our students are writing, how writing influences reading, what strengths and weaknesses students exhibit, which schools are doing well or poorly, what strategies and processes are most productive, and whether our resources are spent wisely or foolishly. Writing research need not be limited in its methodology. No promising research paradigm need be excluded.

Quantitative and qualitative procedures can and should be used. Excellent research has been conducted through case studies, as Graves (1973) has shown, or through experimental studies, as Shanahan (1980) has shown.

FOUR PREMISES FOR EVALUATING WRITING

No Ideal Form of Evaluation

There are many kinds of writing evaluation. Portfolio, holistic, analytic, and primary trait are four kinds of evaluation used in schools today. Each has its advantages and disadvantages, each works well for certain purposes, less well for others. Evaluation must fit the purpose that a teacher, school, district, state, or nation has in mind. A specific form of evaluation may work well in a given situation but might be a poor choice in another. As we examine the forms and uses of writing evaluation, we will see why, for example, portfolio assessment works well in classrooms and school environments, but would be an impractical choice for conducting a national assessment of writing.

No Universally Accepted Standard of Good Writing

Agreement on what constitutes good writing is hard to come by. Purves (1991) found that what is considered good writing in one country is quite different from what is regarded as good writing in another. American raters focus on quality of content, Swedish, on quality of style. Raters produced high failure rates in some countries: the Dutch were severe, Americans lenient.

What Purves found at the international level is also true in America. Good writing, like beauty, exists in the eye of the beholder. One teacher emphasizes the mechanics of writing, another content; one school emphasizes narrative writing, another expository; one district emphasizes product, another process. It is not surprising, therefore, that there is no common definition. Surely it would be far more surprising if there were precise agreement. The assessment of writing is complex and so are those of us who are the producers and consumers of writing. A consensus on what constitutes good writing will always be elusive, but it is possible to develop a consistent set of standards for judging writing which are suitable for the needs of a given community of teachers and schools. Writing standards should reflect children's developmental needs and teachers' instructional goals. The evaluation standard for first graders, for instance, must be different from the standard for sixth graders; the standard for sixth graders must be different still from the standards for high school students.

It is easy to understand why different standards must apply when we consider an example. Marjorie, a first grade writer, made numerous attempts to use quotation marks in an early piece of writing. Twice she used quotation marks correctly, three times incorrectly. In all five instances, she used quotation marks in the context of conversation. Therefore, Marjorie's use of quotation marks, even though incorrectly applied in three instances, should be taken as evidence of superior writing mechanics. Now, if a sixth grader displayed this same pattern, the performance could not be rated as superior. If a high school senior displayed this pattern, the performance could rightly be judged inadequate. Of course, this example deals with mechanics, a writing issue on which we can usually agree. More complex issues, such as content and organization, are far more challenging.

Good writing is difficult to define, but this should not be taken to mean that writing cannot be assessed. When teachers work together, they can reach an acceptable accommodation of one another's perspectives. They can usually agree on standards that are flexible enough to account for developmental characteristics, writing experience, and individual capabilities. And, children can be expected to meet these standards in a learning environment that values writers in an intelligent and caring way.

Evaluate Writing, Writers, and Writing Process

Evaluating writing requires experience at three levels: writing, writers, and writing process. While these three levels of experience are connected, each requires a different knowledge base. For instance, a teacher might be familiar with good writing of many kinds yet make hash out of working with writers. One might understand the psychology of working with writers, but be uninformed about what constitutes good writing. In either instance, effective evaluation is unlikely to occur in the absence of knowledge and experience with all three levels on which evaluation is based: understanding writing, writers, and writing process.

Understanding writing: Read what good writers produce. This will give you a benchmark against which judgments can be calibrated. There is no other way to discover the dimensions of good writing. The teacher who has read many poems, novels, essays, good literature in short, has a storehouse of implicit knowledge that is necessary for evaluating writing. Yet, this knowledge can be put to destructive as well as constructive uses. For example, having read many fine poems could lead one to impose standards and expectations that inexperienced writers are unable to reach. I know of a teacher who called a young girl's romantic poem "trash." He may have known something about good poetry, but his harsh judgment exceeded fair expectations from an inexperienced writer. One's knowledge of good literature should draw others to it, not repel them. He caused a child to withdraw from writing, precisely what is not wanted.

Understanding writers: You must know writers if you expect to influence them. Maxwell Perkins, Ernest Hemingway's editor, possessed enormous knowledge of writing. Yet, his brilliance laid in knowing how to influence writers as much as in his knowledge of editing. Every writer is unique, and this must be honored. Perkins understood this, and thus his influence with writers was enormous. He knew his writers, as well as their writing. He was, therefore, in a position to make judgments and pass on suggestions to renowned writers with egos as large as their reputations.

Writers, even young ones, have egos. Insult writing, and you insult the writer. Children have wonderful ideas, and the thoughtful teacher learns when to say, "What a wonderful idea, Ellie, tell me more about it." She will also know when to say, "That's a good start Billy, but what's happening here at the end? What were

Lindsey loves writing stories and poems, and she does it very well. Lindsey is reading her latest story to her teacher, Ms. Ronketto.

you trying to do here?" After listening to Billy's response she may say, "Oh, I see. Why don't you try that part again, and see how it comes out?"

Understanding the writing process: You must know the process by which writing comes about. Understanding the writing process derives from experience as a writer, reader, and teacher. It is not enough to know the generalities of the writing process. The writing process is far more complex than planning, drafting, and revising. The stages are not linear, a straight line series of steps traversed in lock-step fashion. Writers plan, draft, and revise, but how they do this depends on purpose, audience, and the personal proclivities of the writer. For example, when I write a hot memo to my dean, separate stages are not discernible. On the other hand, this chapter went through clearly discernible stages: planning, drafting, and revising. Planning took weeks of reading, thinking, collecting. The first draft consisted of many pieces drafted and revised in sundry ways. Early drafts were replanned and revised many times. Stages of the process were discernible, but not linear. My writing process consists of habits and procedures suited to the style I have evolved over time. Your writing process may be different from mine, yet we may have elements in common. As teachers, we must recognize and accept the likenesses and differences of each student's writing process, and we must instruct them in the steps of the process that are often used among adult writers.

Errors Signal New Learning

Maurice Sendak's *Where the Wild Things Are* is a classic children's book that many of us have read. Max wasn't afraid of the Wild Things; he was pretty wild himself. Most writers are much more timid than Max. Writing terrifies many children and adults. And what is it that terrifies them? It's the expectation of error, uncertainties about punctuation, grammar, sentence structure, ideas for writing—all the Wild Things about writing that, "roar their terrible roars and gnash their terrible teeth and roll their terrible eyes and show their terrible claws." The successful writing teacher learns how to tame the Wild Things, so that children can do as Max did when he stepped into his boat and waved good-bye to the Wild Things.

Errors, the Wild Things of writing, litter the writing landscape of experienced writers as well as novices. But under the right conditions writers learn the conventions of written language and move on to much more challenging writing problems. They do this best when they are encouraged to explore at their own self-governing pace. If risk taking is rewarded, children explore writing and learn to handle its challenges. Shaughnessy (1977), in her classic book *Errors and Expectations*, explored the inhibiting and facilitating influence of errors in learning to write. Speaking to teachers, she reaches this thoughtful conclusion:

> For unless he can assume that his students are capable of learning what *he* has learned, and what he now teaches, the teacher is not likely to turn to himself as a possible source of his students' failures. He will slip, rather, into the facile explanations of student failure that have long protected teachers from their own mistakes and inadequacies. But once he grants the students the intelligence and will they need to master what is being taught, the teacher begins to look at his students' difficulties in a more fruitful way: he begins to search in what students write and say for clues to their reasoning and their purposes, and in what *he* does for gaps and misjudgments. He begins teaching anew and must be prepared to be taxed beyond the limits he may have originally set for himself as a teacher of writing. (p. 292)

It is the teacher's job to understand that young or inexperienced writers freeze in an atmosphere where errors are the moral equivalent of the death penalty. Writing teachers must know why errors occur, deal with them in an instructive and humane fashion, and appreciate their vital role in learning what is correct.

Writers do not make errors intentionally, yet errors are inevitable. Making errors is not harmful. Faulkner's advice to writers is, "Teach yourself by your own mistakes; people learn only by error" (Cowley, 1958, p. 129). Indeed, errors are the common bond among all successful experimenters. When children attempt to extend their knowledge to new levels, errors inevitably result. Our reaction to students' errors determines what happens next. If we react positively, new vistas for learning are opened; if we react negatively, the door to new learning is closed. Children must be encouraged to risk extending their knowledge to new horizons. If we do not accept the role of error in the extension of knowledge, new learning will be delayed or never accomplished.

Good things happen when children explore new knowledge in an open, approving atmosphere. Every teacher has seen children use what they know to grapple with the unknown. For example, if we accept early phonetic misspellings, children will expand their knowledge of the spelling system. When my children first began to ask, "Dad, how do you spell . . ." I seldom gave them the correct spelling. Instead, I explored what I suspected they already knew about the word they wanted to spell: "Listen, how do you think *rabbit* starts? What comes next? How do you think it ends?" I knew my children were not empty vessels. They knew books, words, letters, sounds. I felt they needed opportunities to use what they knew, connect what they knew with what they sought to know, and make their own errors. Usually this worked, though not perfectly, and not always. You have to sense when it is best to provide the answer to a child's question and when it is best to encourage them to explore the limits of their own knowledge.

STUDENT INVOLVEMENT IN EVALUATION

Students must learn to evaluate their own writing, and they need to evaluate the writing of their peers in collaborative writing settings. There are three ways to involve children in evaluating writing: portfolio assessment, self-evaluation, and peer evaluation. *Portfolio assessment* is a collection of writing that documents achievement and progress. While it is a relatively recent transplant into classroom assessment, portfolios have long been used in assessing the work of artists, architects, and other professionals. *Self-evaluation* is learning to reflect upon your own writing. It is closely allied with reflection and revision. *Peer evaluation* is students working together in collaborative settings to evaluate each other's writing. Writing knowledge is enhanced by considering others' writing as well as one's own.

Portfolio Assessment

A portfolio is a selection of representative works. The portfolio concept has taken root in classrooms and schools, particularly among advocates of process writing. Portfolios have deep roots in the commercial world. A photographer, for example, creates a portfolio so that interested parties can assess her work and range of experience. Potential employers examine the portfolio and, if pleased with the credentials, may offer a commission.

Literacy instruction has changed dramatically in the past decade. As new instructional strategies are developed, better assessment tools are needed. Teachers need assessment tools that reflect their practices and values. Traditional standardized tests will not do, as they seldom reflect modern teaching practices and are often based on flawed premises. Assessment procedures that reflect real world performance and achievement are needed. Portfolio assessment enables teachers to document real world reading and writing tasks.

Portfolios are organized collections of the written products and processes of reading and writing chosen to be representative of the owner's best work. Portfolios document achievement, growth, effort, and interests over time. This collection of works provides source material for teacher assessment and self-assessment. Portfolios are usually a collaborative effort between teacher and child. It is crucial for children to have a stake in selecting and reflecting on the contents of their portfolios. A portfolio belongs to the person who creates it. Ownership creates a willingness to participate, independent work habits, and healthy attitudes toward learning. The more children participate in creating their portfolios, the more likely they are to use them as a meaningful tool for self-assessment.

Purpose determines the kind of portfolio created and the work products that go into it. There are several models of portfolio assessment. The simplest model is a collection of best pieces of writing chosen by the student and teacher. These pieces are used for sharing, assessing, and grading. A more complex portfolio model includes not only finished pieces of writing but the related pieces that preceded the final product such as drafts, notes, and outlines. This type of portfolio enables the teacher to assess both writing process and written product. A third model of portfolio assessment emphasizes the connection between reading and writing (Tierney, Carter, and Desai, 1991). In this model, portfolio items related to reading and writing are included. The idea is to broaden portfolio assessment so that it reflects the language arts and content subjects. While this model adds complexity to the task, it reflects the thrust of recent educational reform efforts. One need not start with the most complex model, but it is a goal that teachers may wish to work toward.

Teachers who wish to incorporate portfolio assessment into their classroom routine should ask themselves which portfolio model best suits their instructional values and practices, yet still provides a suitable level of instructional comfort. You may prefer to start with the simpler portfolio model. As you become adept at managing portfolios, you may decide to broaden the scope of the portfolio concept.

Portfolio assessment, with its emphasis on self-assessment and student involvement, can be messy. Wiggins (1990) suggests that, "Teachers need to rethink their relationship with students and consider their roles as coaches or enablers of student performance. Some teachers may need to do some soul searching about whether students are too dependent on them for direction, standards, or judgment" (p. 51). Any teaching approach that emphasizes self-responsibility and independent participation in learning requires serious thinking. Portfolio assessment, for example, may require a reordering of instructional time. It may bring about a different way of looking at student involvement in learning. Linda Rief (1990) described her baptism into the challenges of portfolio assessment. She tells how she changed as she put self-assessment into practice in her middle school classroom:

> I used to make all the decisions about what the students read and wrote and what they learned from that reading and writing. Then I would test them on all the information. But times have changed. I've been turning the responsibility for learning over to them—they choose what they write, what they read, and what they need to work on in order to get better at both. I invite them to try different genres of writing, and I share a variety of literature that I love with them. They used to keep writing folders and were judged on all their writing. Now they select the best pieces to revise and rework. The portfolio of best pieces is separate from the working folders. My students, however, aren't the only ones who keep portfolios. I also keep a portfolio. My reasoning is that if I don't value what I ask my students to do, then they probably won't value it either. (Rief, 1990, pp. 24–25)

Ms. Rief has described the issues well. She realized it was time to change, and so she set out to meet the challenge. The following guidelines are designed to get you started on a portfolio assessment plan. Modify these ideas to suit your circumstances and your children's needs.

Models of portfolios: Introduce the portfolio concept by showing children how and why a professional photographer, model, or journalist might create a portfolio. If possible, invite a local professional person who has a portfolio to your classroom. Have her explain why the portfolio was created and how it is used to assess her work. Alternatively, it may be an even better idea to create your own portfolio and use it as a model. Teachers' portfolios might include personal writing, children's writing, and lesson plans.

Beginnings: Lead a discussion centered on creating portfolios for everyone. Ask students to contribute their ideas, and share your ideas for getting started. Discussion could center around these questions: (1) How can we get started? (2) How will a portfolio help me improve my writing? (3) What items should go into our portfolios? (4) Where do we keep our portfolios?

Portfolio container: Establish a secure place where portfolios may be kept. The portfolio container can be a large cardboard folder with dividers, a large manila folder, or a plastic basket. Find a convenient place where portfolios may be stored and where easy access is possible.

Portfolio contents: Children should have a primary role in selecting the pieces that go into their portfolios, and they should be responsible for creating and maintaining their portfolios. Initially, they may have difficulty knowing what items to select. Show them that portfolio contents derive from all manner of ordinary classroom activities: writing assignments, projects, independent writing, subject matter assignments, and other ongoing classroom work. Make a chart listing possible items for portfolios, and display it prominently. From time to time, add new items to the list or subtract from it, as experience dictates. The list below suggests items that have gone into portfolios, but it is best to develop your own list. It also pays to talk about what not to put into a portfolio. Traditional workbook assignments, dittos, and other similar materials are best left out of portfolios.

POSSIBLE PORTFOLIO ITEMS

Product Items	Process Items
Poems	Notes
Stories	Drafts
Personal narratives	Outlines
Essays	Webs
Books	Charts
Letters	Literature logs

Reports	Lists
Play scripts	Writing plans
Songs	Reading logs
News reports	Checklists
Self-assessments	Working journals
Videotapes	

Portfolios versus writing folders: Make a distinction between writing folders and portfolios. Both folders and portfolios are useful adjuncts to a writing program. A writing folder, however, should contain most of what a child has written, including incomplete pieces, drafts of completed pieces, and completed pieces that didn't work well. The writing folder is not selective but broadly inclusive. A portfolio, on the other hand, contains a *selected sample* of work. An illustrator doesn't put everything he has painted into his portfolio, but selects the pieces that give a sense of the range and quality of his work.

Learning self-assessment: Model ways in which children can assess their writing. For example, have them compare pieces of writing completed ten weeks apart. Examining changes that occur over a span of time can help children document progress and recognize changes in goals and interests. Teach them to ask and answer assessment questions when examining items in their portfolios: How have I changed from then to now? What do I learn about myself as a writer from this piece? What can I do now that I couldn't do before? What have I learned about writing that I didn't know before?

Reviewing portfolios: Review student portfolios periodically. Your personal schedule and school calendar should guide the frequency of review. This review should paint a picture of the student's efforts, achievement, and progress. Make note of strengths and weaknesses. Since it takes considerable time to review a portfolio, work with children to guide their selection of a limited number of items appropriate for your review. A table of contents will facilitate your review and help students keep track of their portfolio contents.

Captioning: Give children time to review the contents of their portfolios and write a brief description of each item. They should tell why any item was chosen, what they learned. Captioning provides a good review and helps teachers evaluate what students deem important.

Portfolio conferences: From time to time, a portfolio conference will be necessary. Use the conference to convey compliments and considerate criticism. Help children recognize the progress they have made. Ask students about the items they have included in their portfolios. Each item should be there for a reason.

Sharing portfolios: Schedule times when students share their portfolios with one another. Sharing portfolios works well with the author's chair and it fits naturally into peer evaluation sessions. Sharing is a good way to help children recognize which pieces to include or exclude from their portfolios.

Involving parents: Invite parents to help. Explain the portfolio concept, tell how it will be used and how it will benefit children. Suggest ways in which they can participate. At parental conferences, use the portfolio to document achievement and progress.

Grading and portfolios: If you are required to grade children's writing, have them select from their portfolios pieces that you will grade. Portfolio items can be shared with parents as examples of progress in writing from one grading period to the next. Portfolios certainly provide a sounder instructional foundation for determining grades than grading workbook pages, dittos, and grammar exercises.

Ms. Carol Sievert teaches third grade. She has recently started using writing portfolios to assist her in evaluating her children's writing. She describes her experience with portfolios in the "Voices" piece.

VOICES FROM THE CLASSROOM: Carol Sievert

Portfolios

It is important to me to develop my students' writing and writing style in a positive and yet critiquing way. At the beginning of the year we set up our "Writing Portfolios." In these writing folders, students keep the pieces they are working on organized. Ultimately, they select the pieces they consider to be their best work for evaluation. This gives them the freedom, after careful consideration, to select those pieces they believe to be their best.

I give my students a rubric for each assigned piece of writing. The rubric gives guidelines for the evaluation system I use. At the beginning of the year, I am more concerned with the students finding their writing style and working specific skills into their writing, for example, story elements for narrative writing.

As the year progresses, I give more assigned writing, such as informational or content–research-based writing. I have the students keep rubrics in their writing folders for all the writing they do. This is to remind them of my expectations. Of course, not all writing has a rubric. Students in my class are encouraged to write at all times. All of their writing is read and responded to. They can also place one non-assigned writing sample in their portfolio to be graded.

When my students are ready to revise their writing, I suggest they focus on one specific element of the revision process. I do this to give the students a focus point in their revision as well as to help them master a specific skill. When we do peer conferencing, this also helps the students focus on a particular problem and communicate with each other ways to improve their writing in a specific area.

I have found there is no simple way to evaluate writing. I encourage creativity, try to keep their ideas flowing, and focus on specific skills from time to time. The evaluation system I use helps the students see how they are progressing.

Self-Evaluation

Self-evaluation is the ability to improve one's own writing through self-directed thinking, revising, and editing. It is the ultimate writing skill. A writer must become her own best critic. It is said that the fox knows many small things, but the hedgehog knows one big thing. A writer needs to be both fox and hedgehog. A writer needs to know what details need refining, but must also know if the piece works as a whole. A writing teacher has no greater challenge than to start young writers on the road to self-assessment. This means helping children to become thinkers, revisers, and editors of their own work.

Revising and editing knowledge grows as children internalize a sense of what they are trying to accomplish. Writers must develop their own internal standards that center around the meaning they hope to convey. If young writers ask themselves the right questions, their writing will echo back an answer. Graves (1983) suggests teaching children to ask themselves two questions after they have drafted a piece:

What is this piece about? We want children to comprehend what they have already composed. Certainly, if writers cannot answer this question, an audience will have similar difficulties. As children become more skillful at understanding what they have already said in a draft, they are in a position to change their writing so that it will match what they intended to say.

What am I trying to do? Writers must become their own best critic. Writers may ask, "Is this a good ending to my story? I wonder what others might think?" As children develop skill in asking and answering Graves' questions, they talk themselves into making changes in their writing. Revision, or revisioning, is central to self-evaluation. It becomes the instrument through which writers learn to talk to themselves in constructive ways that lead to self-criticism and eventually to improving their writing.

It is more difficult to teach children to evaluate their own writing than it is to evaluate their writing for them. Teachers who have accepted the challenge, however, have found that self-evaluation offers the best prospect for substantial writing growth. Of course, teacher evaluation is still necessary, but teachers must not waver from the ultimate goal: help children become their own best critics. See suggestions below for implementing self-evaluation in your classroom.

IMPLEMENTING SELF-EVALUATION

1. Good questions help students evaluate their writing. During conferences, ask questions that lead students to think about their ideas, organization, and style as well as any mechanical skills you are stressing.

2. Encourage students to listen to their own writing before revising it. This can be done with a partner, reading one's writing aloud, or recording writing and playing it back.

3. Have students wait a day or two before revising early drafts. Then have them reread their compositions and imagine themselves as the audience. For example, ask students to imagine the piece they wrote was not their work but a piece found in a magazine.

4. Show students contrasting sets of words that illustrate exact vs. inexact word choice: horse vs. animal; pillows, blankets, and sheets vs. stuff. Then have students underline words in their writing that need to be changed from inexact to exact.

5. Have children write questions about the important ideas in their writing. A partner reads the account and listens to the questions. The writer and the partner discuss problems they encountered. The discussion should lead to decisions about rewriting.

6. After children have gained experience in self-evaluation and peer evaluation, have them help younger children with their writing.

7. Teach revision and editing skills in revision workshops. The workshop procedures are described under peer evaluation.

8. Place composition charts in key places around the room. The charts should cover composing strategies and writing mechanics. These charts remind children of the goals they are striving to meet.

Peer Evaluation

Peer evaluation has children working on writing in collaborative settings. It has many advantages. It helps children learn how their writing affects others; it helps children see how other writers approach writing; it confronts children with the need to revise and edit their drafts; it gives children a sympathetic audience. Most importantly, it helps children see how different individuals perceive the same piece of writing.

Peer evaluation can be conducted in whole class settings, small groups or one-on-one. It works well where students have developed trusting, collaborative relationships with one another. Initial peer evaluation sessions should be short and well planned. It helps to start with a whole class activity. The first sessions should establish standards of respect and tact, develop guidelines for constructive feedback, and stress the importance of avoiding destructive criticism. Small groups and one-on-one sessions can be planned after basic concepts have been learned in whole class settings.

Why peer evaluation works: Peer evaluation benefits writing in three ways. First, as students help others, they help themselves become better writers. Peer evaluation improves organization, sentence revision, theme writing, and critical thinking (Lagna, 1972). Second, peer evaluation helps children develop standards for judging the quality of their own writing. Peer evaluators look for the presence or absence of specific writing features in the writing of their peers. As they do so, they gain greater understanding of what makes their own writing comprehensible to others. Third, peer evaluation broadens the audience for writing. Since children relate well with their peers, it is reasonable that some writing be evaluated by this sympathetic audience. Broadening the audience for writing may also stimulate children to select a wider range of writing topics.

Implementing peer evaluation in writing workshops: Peer evaluation works well when the conditions for implementing are well planned. Children must be familiar with procedures for evaluating writing before they work in peer evaluation groups. One way to do this is to direct writing workshops designed to teach children how to evaluate their own writing. Following are procedures for directing writing workshops on evaluation:

1. Have children choose a piece of first-draft writing from their writing folders or portfolios or give them a day or two to write a first draft on a topic of their own choosing.

2. Take a piece of your own first-draft writing and make a transparency, and project it onto a screen. Have children read your draft, then ask, "What do you like about this piece of writing?" List responses briefly on the board. If children tend to single out only mechanics ask, "What do you think about the ideas in my piece?"

3. Then have children read the draft again but with a different focus. This time ask, "What would you change in my draft if you were writing it?" Make changes directly on the transparency.

4. Make comments as suggestions are given. Take every contribution seriously and acknowledge it with appreciation. Comments can include information related to good writing, praise for thoughtful suggestions, and ideas about authorship. For example, you might say, "Yes, Geraldine, writers do sometimes get their ideas out of order, especially in first drafts. I'm pleased that you noticed the difficulty I had getting the events in logical order. If you were rewriting this, how would you order the sentences?"

5. After the discussion, choose only one or two student suggestions you have recorded on the board. Then give them a writing task to consider in their own first drafts. For example, you might say, "Look for the best sentence in your draft. Talk about why you choose that sentence. Share your reasons with each other."

6. As the children work singly or in groups of two or three, circulate among them offering advice and praise. For example, listen to their reasons for choosing a best sentence. Share your own comments on that sentence in a positive way: "I love the way you started your story, 'It's funny how little things can take you by surprise.' That sentence makes me want to read on and see what this piece is about." Children often discover other strengths in each other's writing that they were not asked to find. When this occurs, praise this extra effort. Other children will imitate this responsible behavior.

Peer evaluation teaches children to draft, revise, and produce written work in group settings. Harmonious group settings are crucial to successful peer evaluation. As children experience peer evaluation, they become more sensitive to the feelings of their fellow writers. Much of this can be learned from the model teachers present in their own assessment of children's writing. While peer evaluation requires skill and dedication to implement, the rewards often exceed your expectations.

TEACHER INVOLVEMENT IN EVALUATION

We have examined three student-centered procedures for assessing writing: port-folio assessment, self-evaluation, and peer evaluation. We turn now to teacher-centered procedures for assessing writing: holistic, analytic, and primary trait. Each type serves a different purpose. It cannot be said that one procedure is better or worse than another. Rather, an evaluation procedure should be compatible with purpose and philosophy. Before choosing an evaluation procedure, there-fore, it is good to ask two questions: (1) Will this procedure provide useful sum-mative, formative, or research information? (2) Does this procedure fairly assess what I've been teaching?

Holistic Evaluation

Infrequent writing guarantees mediocre writing. On the other hand, frequent writing generates an endless stream of writing to evaluate. Is there a way to keep children writing steadily and yet not create an impossible paper load? There are a number of solutions to this dilemma. Portfolio assessment, self-evaluation, and peer evaluation are three options discussed earlier in this chapter. Holistic evalua-tion offers yet another way to lighten the paper load.

The term *holistic* derives from the word *whole.* In holistic evaluation, writing is assessed as a whole rather than in detail. The details regarding writing strengths and weaknesses are not counted, corrected, or commented upon, though notice may be taken to guide future decisions. Usually no more than three or four min-utes are devoted to each piece of writing. The goal is to reach an overall impression as rapidly as is consistent with reliable and valid assessment. Holistic evaluation operates on the premise that the whole adds up to more than the sum of its parts.

Writing has many components: content, organization, sentence and paragraph structure, word selection, mechanics, among others. In holistic evaluation, a rater may recognize strengths or weaknesses among these components, but does not comment on them separately, since the goal is to evaluate the composition holisti-cally. Holistic scoring assumes that counting errors is, by itself, an insufficient means of judging writing competence. The holistic scorer ranks compositions on a three, four, or five point scale. Evaluators are aided by a checklist or guide adapted to fit their standards of writing and their students' levels of writing achievement. The best compositions receive the highest score and the weakest the lowest.

A holistic scoring guide starts with prototype compositions and a description of writing features to guide evaluation. Prototype examples of children's writing, ranging from the lowest to the highest competency level, are assembled. In addition to proto-type compositions, a description of writing features is constructed to guide the rater in making decisions. A rater reads a composition and matches it with an approximately equivalent piece of writing in the graded series of prototype compositions, keeping in mind the writing features that describe different levels of writing achievement.

Following are holistic scoring guides for grades 1–2, 3–4, and 5–8 that de-scribe writing features. Scoring guides must be suitable for the students whose writing will be rated and compatible with teachers' philosophy of writing. The value of a scoring guide can go beyond the guide itself. Constructing or revising a guide can become a catalyst for agreeing on standards and writing philosophy.

HOLISTIC SCORING GUIDE: NARRATIVE GRADES 1–2

Score Low	Characteristics of Grade One Writing
1	Story shown through pictures, scribbles, or letter strings Does not make letter-sound connections May copy some words correctly
2	Exhibits some story characteristics Makes letter-sound connections using invented spelling Can spell a few words correctly May use punctuation occasionally
3	Contains a clear story line Uses invented spelling Many common words correctly spelled Uses punctuation correctly and incorrectly
4	Writes a well-developed story, may contain conversation Ideas clearly understandable, sometimes imaginative Invents spelling of more difficult words Common words spelled correctly Often uses punctuation correctly

High

HOLISTIC SCORING GUIDE: NARRATIVE GRADES 3–4

Score Low	Characteristics of Grade Three Writing
1	Lacks fluency, writes little or nothing What is written is incoherent Uses mostly invented spellings, can spell a few words Does not use punctuation
2	Story contains one or two coherent sentences Ideas can be understood Uses invented spelling, can spell some words correctly Uses some punctuation, usually incorrectly

3	Writes a simple story; some sense of sequence
	Writes clear simple sentences
	Some interesting word choices
	Exhibits some mechanical errors
	Spells common words correctly, invents more difficult words
4	Writes a clearly coherent story, uses story characteristics
	Story may include some conversation
	Sentences interesting and varied
	Demonstrates some originality of expression
	Word choice interesting and varied
	Uses capitals and ending punctuation consistently
	Spells many words correctly

High

HOLISTIC SCORING GUIDE: NARRATIVE GRADES 5–8

Score	**Characteristics of Grade Five Writing**
Low	
1	Lacks writing fluency, writes little or nothing
	What is written is incoherent
	Shows no use of writing mechanics
	Spells most words incorrectly
2	Writes story but it lacks development
	Uses simple brief sentences
	Ideas can be understood
	Many mechanical errors
	Spells some words correctly
3	Writes story with some story characteristics
	Uses simple and compound sentences
	Contains some interesting word choices
	Exhibits some mechanical errors
	Spells many common words correctly, invents more difficult words

4   Clearly coherent story, uses story characteristics

                Sentences varied in length and type

                Includes details, good word choice, some figurative language

                Some dialogue, may use quotation marks

                Some creative ideas and expressions

                Few mechanical errors

                Spells many words correctly

High

Teachers can prepare their own holistic guide and select prototype compositions from writing produced by their children. A scoring guide should represent the standards and instructional practices used in your school or classroom, and it must be appropriate for the children whose writing will be assessed. Through discussion and practice, consistency can be achieved by rating compositions together, discussing differences, and developing a consensus about assessing writing. Working cooperatively with other teachers enables you to learn from each other and to come closer together in implementing your writing program.

Making your own holistic guide increases familiarity with the problems and pitfalls of evaluation. But it is not necessary to start from scratch. You can use a ready-made holistic scale, such as the ones shown below, as a starting point. Relying on prepared guides may be less useful than making your own, even if there are minor imperfections in your guide. Whatever scale you use should represent the thinking and experience of the teachers who use it. The prototype compositions, of course, must be drawn from the population of children being evaluated.

STANDARDS FOR EVALUATING NARRATIVE OR STORY WRITING

Structure	**Does the story hang together?**
Low:	No identifiable beginning, middle, or end. Action and characters undeveloped. Details confusing. Story problem unresolved.
Middle:	Beginning, middle, end present but may be unclear. Some details given. Story problem present, resolution may be fuzzy.
High:	Clear beginning, middle, end. Action and characters well developed. Story problem clearly and appropriately resolved.

Ideas	**Is the story interesting, and does it have a plot?**
Low:	Story idea uninteresting, trite, or unclear. No plot or plot unclear. Ends abruptly in confusion.
Middle:	Story idea interesting and has a plot. May be inconsistencies or difficulties at various points. May have interesting ending.
High:	Story idea fresh and/or imaginative. Plot well developed and consistent. Has satisfying ending.

Setting	**Where and when does the story take place?**
Low:	No time or place identifiable. Details inappropriate or missing.
Middle:	Time and/or place suggested, but uncertain. May be inconsistencies.
High:	Time and place clearly identified. Specific details given. Stays internally consistent throughout.

Character	**Are the characters interesting and believable?**
Low:	Character development weak or absent. Details missing. Action and conversation related to character development inappropriate or missing.
Middle:	Some character development. Details not always consistent or appropriate. Action and conversation present but inconsistent.
High:	Characters believable. Details used to develop characters' personality. Action and conversation related appropriately to character development.

Conversation	**Does the conversation move the story forward?**
Low:	Conversation, if any, is muddled. Does not develop personality, story action, or story outcome.
Middle:	Conversation present. Works in some story elements, but not fully and consistently.
High:	Conversation appropriate and effective. Helps develop personality and interaction among characters. Related to story action and outcome.

STANDARDS FOR EVALUATING EXPOSITORY WRITING

Content

What is the quality of the ideas and information?

Low: Ideas vague, incoherent. Details may be irrelevant, inaccurate, or undeveloped. Not imaginative or original in any way.

Middle: Ideas are sound but not imaginative. Presentation of ideas is uneven in accuracy, completeness, logic, or relevance.

High: Ideas are clearly presented, complete, relevant, accurate, logical, rich in thought and imagination.

Organization

Are ideas and information arranged in an orderly way?

Low: Information incoherent, not well sequenced. Connections between ideas absent or mishandled.

Middle: Information usually coherent and sequential. Connections between ideas used but not consistently.

High: Information coherent and sequential. Connections signaled by transition words, phrases, or sentences.

Words

Is word selection interesting, accurate, and appropriate?

Low: Word selection inexact, limited, or immature. Figurative language used sparingly or inappropriately, if at all.

Middle: Word selection usually suitable and accurate. Overuses some words. Uses some figurative language, may lack freshness.

High: Shows flair for word choice. Uses words precisely. Figurative language used interestingly and accurately.

Sentences

Are there a variety of well-formed sentences?

Low: Sentences poorly formed, often awkward or puzzling. Run-ons and fragments common.

Middle: Some well-formed sentences. A few awkward or puzzling sentences. Some run-ons and fragments, but not frequent.

High: Well-formed sentences of varied length and structure. Smooth flow from sentence to sentence. Few run-ons and fragments.

Paragraphs

Are paragraphs ordered in an appropriate, interesting fashion?

Low: Topic difficult to discern; few, if any, topic sentences. Details incomplete. Orders ideas incoherently.

Middle: Usually sticks to topic. Uses topic sentences but inconsistently. Some awareness of paragraph types. Usually orders details well.

High: Shows good control of paragraph topic, uses topic sentences. Shows awareness of paragraph types—narrative, explanatory, persuasive, descriptive. Orders details well.

STANDARDS FOR EVALUATING MECHANICAL SKILLS

Grammar Usage

Low: Grammatical conventions for inflections, modifiers, verbs, pronouns, and nouns seldom observed. Frequent miscues.

Middle: Grammatical conventions for inflections, modifiers, verbs, pronouns, and nouns usually observed. Some miscues.

High: Grammatical conventions for inflections, modifiers, verbs, pronouns, and nouns observed. Miscues infrequent.

Punctuation

Low: Ending punctuation often missing. Internal punctuation used infrequently and often incorrectly. Unusual punctuation seldom used. When used, usually incorrect.

Middle: Ending punctuation often correct. Internal punctuation used, but with some inconsistency. Unusual punctuation present but with some miscues.

High: Ending punctuation nearly always correct. Internal punctuation and unusual punctuation often used correctly.

Capitalization

Low: Seldom capitalizes first word in sentence. Proper nouns and other conventions seldom observed. Capitals used inappropriately.

Middle: Usually capitalizes first word in sentences. Well-known proper nouns usually correct. Knows some other conventions, but inconsistently observes them.

High: Always capitalizes first word in sentences. Well-known proper nouns nearly always correct. Good command of other conventions.

Handwriting

Low:	Handwriting difficult to read. Letter formation and spacing make handwriting nearly illegible.
Middle:	Handwriting is readable. Letters usually clearly formed. Spacing may be crowded occasionally.
High:	Handwriting easy to read. Letters clearly formed, spacing appropriate.

Analytic Evaluation

Holistic evaluation does not eliminate the need for more detailed evaluation. Analytic scoring provides an evaluation option that looks at writing from a more detailed perspective. Still, holistic and analytic scoring have similarities. For example, both holistic and analytic scoring consider similar writing features, and both recognize that the whole is greater than the parts. On the other hand, holistic evaluation is rapid and impressionistic whereas analytic evaluation is deliberate and detailed. When teachers wish to focus closely on specific writing features, deliberate and detailed evaluation is appropriate. Analytic evaluation describes specific writing features as they might appear in actual compositions. Writing features are analyzed in terms of their absence or presence, strength or weakness, high or low quality.

The writing features assessed differ according to the type of writing evaluated. For example, a narrative guide will use different writing features than an expository guide. The number of features examined in analytic scoring varies with purpose, nature of the composition, and level of the student. Features examined in expository writing normally include content, organization, sentence and paragraph features, word selection, and mechanics. Features examined in narrative writing normally include story idea, setting, development, characters, conversation, and mechanics. Features can be added or deleted according to your purpose and writing philosophy. Writing features are rated on a scale of 1 to 5 on the analytic scales shown on pages 217–218. An evaluation scale of 1 to 3, 1 to 4, or 1 to 6 is sometimes used. Analytic evaluation enables teachers to give more detailed information to the writer than holistic evaluation permits. On the other hand, it is more laborious and time consuming. Even so, analytic evaluation is similar to the kind of assessment teachers have traditionally provided young writers. When analytic evaluation is used, it is crucial to give children positive information about their writing. Bleeding red ink all over a child's writing is more than simply useless; it is destructive. Analytic evaluation is formative and may be best used for diagnostic purposes.

An example of a narrative writing guide is shown on page 217. Each writing feature is rated on a scale of 1 to 5, adding up to a total score of 20. A place is provided for teacher comments at the bottom of the scale. The comments are suggestive of what one might say about a composition. Interpretative comments should be given to supplement the rating. An example of an analytic scoring guide for expository writing is shown on page 217–218. Each writing feature is rated on a scale of 1 to 5, fair to excellent.

ANALYTIC SCORING GUIDE FOR NARRATIVE WRITING

Student Name _____

Composition _____

WRITING FEATURES	RATING SCALE				
	Fair		Good		Excellent
Story idea	1	2	3	<u>4</u>	5
Story setting	1	2	<u>3</u>	4	5
Story development	1	<u>2</u>	3	4	5
Story characters	1	2	3	<u>4</u>	5
Story conversation	1	2	3	4	<u>5</u>
Mechanics (spelling, punctuation, etc.)	1	<u>2</u>	3	4	5
Points Scored	0	4	3	8	5

Total Score: <u>20</u>

Comments: Your lead caught my interest at once! You set the scene for the story well, but I had trouble figuring out the order of events. When you revise, think about working on this. The conversations between Ellie and Terry helped me understand what was happening in your story. Ellie comes across as smart and funny. Terry seems shy and uncertain. Is that what you tried for? After you've revised your story, edit it for correct punctuation and spelling. Harvey, this is going to be a lively story when you're finished.

ANALYTIC SCORING GUIDE FOR EXPOSITORY WRITING

Student Name _____

Composition _____

Content	Fair		Good		Excellent
Theme or controlling idea	1	2	3	4	5
Details	1	2	3	4	5
Originality	1	2	3	4	5
Examples and reasons	1	2	3	4	5

Content	Fair		Good		Excellent
Organization					
Plan of organization	1	2	3	4	5
Introduction	1	2	3	4	5
Development	1	2	3	4	5
Conclusion	1	2	3	4	5
Information in sequence	1	2	3	4	5
Transitions	1	2	3	4	5
Wording					
Precise word choice	1	2	3	4	5
Concrete, specific language	1	2	3	4	5
Figurative language	1	2	3	4	5
Sentences					
Sentence variety	1	2	3	4	5
Well-formed sentences	1	2	3	4	5
Avoids fragments, run-ons	1	2	3	4	5
Paragraphs					
Main or controlling idea	1	2	3	4	5
Relevant supporting details	1	2	3	4	5
Appropriate sentence order	1	2	3	4	5
Mechanics					
Spelling	1	2	3	4	5
Punctuation	1	2	3	4	5
Capitalization	1	2	3	4	5
Form	1	2	3	4	5

COMMENTS:

Primary Trait Scoring

As its name implies, primary trait scoring focuses on the assessment of a single writing feature rather than on the whole. Since it focuses on a specific trait or feature, the guide can be much simpler than scoring guides for analytic or holistic scoring. In primary trait scoring, for example, you might decide to evaluate a piece of writing on the trait of persuasiveness. If this were the case, all other writing features not relevant to persuasiveness would, in theory, be ignored. But, it is difficult to ignore all writing features but one, and therein lays one of the problems of primary trait scoring.

Nevertheless, primary trait scoring is useful for specific purposes. A teacher can, for instance, focus on a specific trait to see how effective instruction on that trait might have been. Suppose you have been teaching persuasive writing and you want to know whether your instruction is working. Using primary trait scoring, you could evaluate a set of compositions for the trait of persuasiveness. Valuable diagnostic information may result. You might discover how well your children have learned what you taught; or you might find they are not doing as well as expected. If they have done well, you might conclude that your instruction worked. If not, you can adjust instruction and try again. Primary trait scoring is sometimes used in district and state assessment protocols where the purpose is to discover how students measure up on a specific writing criterion.

Assessing one trait at a time has inherent problems. Raters have difficulty ignoring other important writing features while trying to focus exclusively on one. Furthermore, it is difficult to isolate certain writing traits. Punctuation, for instance, is easy to isolate as a primary trait; persuasiveness is more difficult because it is a more global trait. How persuasive a piece of writing is depends on a complex of factors: relevance and power of reasons cited, strategic order in which reasons are presented, subtle language clues, style, appeal to prejudice. Even grammar and spelling can have a negative or positive impact on persuasiveness. Thus, while focusing on one writing trait may seem simple enough, in practice primary trait scoring turns out to be more subtle than it appears on the surface. Nevertheless, it can be useful when used in an appropriate context and for a specific purpose.

GRADING CHILDREN'S WRITTEN WORK

Teachers are sometimes required to grade children's writing, even though they would rather not. They fear that grading writing will inhibit creativity and drive a wedge between teacher and child. Indeed, there is reason for concern, since it is well known that insensitive or inappropriate grading can inhibit writing and do serious damage to a writer's morale. Nevertheless, we cannot put our heads in the sand and hope the problem will go away. This discussion is for those teachers who face the uncomfortable necessity of posting grades for writing whether they like it or not.

When grades must be assigned, guidelines for establishing fair grading procedures are needed. Three issues must be considered if fair grading procedures are to be established: (1) What is the purpose? (2) What is good writing? (3) What guidelines are appropriate?

The Purpose of Grading

Parents' rights to know how their children are doing obligate educators to devise fair and sensible ways of reporting to parents. Grading is one way of conveying to parents a sense of how their children are achieving and progressing. Students also need to know how they are doing. Fortunately, there are many ways of showing students how they are progressing in writing; grading is only one among many options. Indeed, writing conferences and portfolio assessment are superior to grades at informing students of their achievement and progress in writing.

However, when grading is perceived as fair, accurate, and informative, it serves a useful purpose. When it fails in any of these aims, it can be destructive. Grading practices often deserve the terrible reputation they have acquired. I think it is fair to say that grading can unfairly compare children with one another, stifle creativity, and advance questionable values. While such complaints are sometimes justified, they paint a picture in broad strokes; missing are the subtleties that round out the finished portrait. Grading need not stifle creativity or unfairly compare children with one another. The values that grading implies are open to debate. Unfortunately, these values stimulate arguments that can never be satisfactorily settled, as they depend on premises that cannot be reconciled. A teacher then asks, "How can I make the best use of the grading system, even if it does represent values I question?" There are answers to this question, and they are considered below.

Recognizing Good Writing

Unfortunately, assessing children's writing often rests on overvaluing the mechanics of writing while undervaluing the content. Mechanics are the handmaidens of good writing, and they must not be ignored or demeaned. But they do not, by themselves, constitute good writing. Writers can and do achieve mechanical and grammatical excellence and still produce dull, lifeless writing. Writers can also violate mechanical and grammatical norms and still produce good writing. The two stories that follow illustrate this point.

Spring

I love Spring. I love Spring because the flowers bloom and the trees blossom. I love Spring because the birds sing. In Spring the leaves come out and everything turns green. The flowers are pretty in Spring. I love Spring.

Anonymous, Age 8

The lityl moyse

Once upon a time thar was a lityl moyse who livd in a lityl howl in a lityl hose The moyse had two lityl baby mice   one day one of the babys had a birthda He had a kac and four kandls. He had presnts and swets. He had a ptend gun and a ptend roket He had a toy indyin and he had one more thing   It was a lityl wind up moyse   He was vere hape.

Jennifer, Age 6

Clearly, *The lityl moyse* is a better piece of writing than *Spring*, even though it is far less "correct." *The lityl moyse* arises from a child's imagination and is patterned on her favorite mouse stories heard over the course of years. Jennifer is six years old and in first grade. *The lityl moyse* is her first lengthy independently written story. Consider the mechanics of *The lityl moyse*. Only three punctuation marks, a period, is used, and that appears at the end of the story. The convention of capitalizing the first word in a sentence occurs eight times, evidence of something known about sentence conventions but not yet fully understood. The story contains 81 words, 56 are correctly spelled, 25 are misspelled.

Spring is a mechanically excellent piece of writing. No words are misspelled, no punctuation mark misplaced. The conventions are observed. Even so, *Spring* lacks the fundamental qualities of good writing. There is no voice, no originality, no excitement in the language. The narrative is banal and the sentiment trite. Don't misunderstand. It is not that the young writer of *Spring* hasn't any good ideas. Nor is the case that the writer lacks the language to convey an interesting story. Rather, I suspect, circumstances have conspired to create a climate in which stilted writing is accepted, indeed praised, as good writing when it is merely "correct" writing. The failure here is not the writer's but the educational circumstances in which the young writer is trapped.

A fundamental criterion of good writing is the quality of the thinking that underlies the ideas. Children have language, curiosity, and creative instincts. They have a voice that is often unique. But you have to believe in children's capabilities if you wish to entice the good ideas out of the crevices of their fertile minds. An effective teacher needs a sound conception of what constitutes good writing, which will always be difficult to define, and there will always be legitimate disagreement in our understanding of what constitutes good writing. However, it is clear that correct writing is not synonymous with good writing. Post grades, if you are required or inclined to do so, but you must have a clear conception of what constitutes good writing if you want to assess children's writing fairly.

Ms. DeWard now must grade her fourth graders' writing, whereas in the recent past she only had to indicate "satisfactory" or "unsatisfactory." She talks about her current strategies for evaluating writing in the "Voices" piece below.

VOICES FROM THE CLASSROOM: Jennifer DeWard

Evaluating Writing

For the past four years that I have been teaching writing, the most challenging aspect has been evaluating my fourth grade students' writing. It is much easier to evaluate my students in math and social studies, perhaps because writing is so personal for my kids, and so subjective for me to grade. I have, however, come up with some strategies for evaluating writing

My students participate in writers' workshop four days a week. It is only fitting that I evaluate their writing according to the teaching that I do. For example, when I teach mini-lessons on skills such as dialogue, leads, and choosing exact words, I evaluate my students' progress in these areas.

As I conference with individuals and small groups, I am aware of which students are trying revision strategies I have taught. I make notes of these attempts, so that I will remember them when it comes time for evaluation. While one student's level of success may differ from another student's, what matters to me is that the students are making progress.

I also take effort into account. I know my students well. I know where each child started as a writer in my classroom, and I know how far each child has progressed. When I sit down to grade a piece of writing, I am aware of just how hard the child worked on that piece. I am always impressed with the quality of published pieces that I receive.

I do not grade every piece of writing that is produced in my classroom. I feel that children need time to explore and try different techniques and styles. Therefore, I only grade published pieces. Since I do a final proofread with my students before publishing, I look at the published piece to see if the student made changes we discussed. Most students are careful when it comes time to publish and this is seldom an issue. However, if a student published carelessly and improvements were not made, I ask them to make the changes before I will look at their writing again. If a student has published a number of pieces in a given period of time, I ask the student to pick a few of his "best" pieces for me to evaluate.

My kids write with enthusiasm during writers' workshop. They try different revision strategies, conference with their peers, and have a proofreading conference with me before they publish. So, it is not surprising that my students mostly receive A's or B's in writing. Their published writing is polished, and their effort along the way has usually been tremendous.

Guidelines for Grading Writing

Grading need not be punitive, degrading, or destructive of student creativity and morale. There are ways to mitigate, if not entirely remove, negative factors from grading. The guidelines below are presented in the hope that they will be helpful, even though they do not finally resolve the philosophical issues involved in grading children's writing.

GRADING WRITING

1. Have students select a few of their best pieces of writing from their writing portfolios or folders to be graded.

2. Make sure that writing selected for grading has traversed the cycle of the writing process—from planning to proofreading. Drafts and notes should be included so that you can evaluate the process as well as the product.

3. Assess only the student's best work. Professional writers are never judged on their drafts or their unpublished failures but only on their finished and refined writing.

4. Encourage children to help you establish criteria for grading. Collaborative decisions engender greater acceptance than unilateral ones.

5. Grading philosophy should be consistent with instructional philosophy. If you teach the writing process and self-evaluation, for example, do not neglect these factors in arriving at a grade.

6. Use holistic, analytic, primary trait, or portfolio assessment evaluation methods to aid your grading decisions where appropriate. Adapt assessment procedures to suit your needs and the needs of your children.

7. Take improvement into consideration in devising a grading scheme. Base some part of a grade on individual progress. On the other hand, a grading scheme weighted too heavily on personal progress creates its own inequities.

8. Delay grading children's writing as long as feasible. The younger the child the less necessary it is to assign writing grades. My own preference would be to delay assigning grades until middle school, and later if possible.

9. Grade as few pieces of writing as necessary in order to meet your grading objectives. A large number of grades is simply not necessary in order to make fair judgments.

10. Remember the famous dictum of computer buffs: GIGO—*garbage in, garbage out.* Assessment methods are, in the end, no better or worse than the criteria used and the judgments made.

Teachers often get frustrated, with good reason, at the evaluation procedures established in their schools. This happens most often when teachers have little input into the evaluation schemes they are required to use. In her diary entry, Ms. DeWard describes her frustration at a new writing evaluation scheme recently inaugurated in her school district.

DIARY OF A TEACHER: Jennifer DeWard

I am frustrated right now. For the past two years I have had to decide whether my students are "Satisfactory" or "Need Improvement" in writing. I felt that this was a good way of communicating with parents about their children's abilities. However, we have a new report card, and now I will have to give each student a letter grade in writing. How am I supposed to do this? What makes an A as opposed to a B writer? Is the ability to write a sentence taken into account when giving a grade, or does content matter the most? I know that I will have to work out a fair system, but right now it seems impossible.

For the past two years I have praised every student for the efforts they make. How in the world am I going to say to Anne or Toby, "Well, you're doing a good job, and I know you are trying your hardest, but this piece gets a C." I suppose I'll calm down in a few days, but right now I'm frustrated.

IDEAS FOR WRITING

1. Personalizing a scoring guide: Take one of the scoring guides (e.g., Holistic Scoring Guide) described in this chapter and share it with your students. Tell them this is the guide you use when evaluating their writing. Have the children help you rewrite the scoring guide in their own words. Then let them use the guide when they prepare pieces of writing that you intend to evaluate. Over time, rewrite any scoring guide you intend to use for evaluating writing. This is a good writing experience in itself, but, more importantly, it will familiarize you and your students with standards for judging writing.

2. Evaluating mistakes: Next time you evaluate a student's writing, choose one of the more obvious mistakes that appear in the piece. Take a sheet of paper and make three columns with the following headings:

Mistake	**Example**	**Analysis**
Quote marks	He "said, go away."	Has concept but not the details

   This example suggests both a strength and weakness in the student's knowledge about the use of quotation marks. The writer knows that dialogue requires quotes and that they often appear in conjunction with *said* or its many alternatives—thus a strength on which you can build. The writer does not know the proper placement of quotation marks—thus a weakness which you can correct. Mistakes children make usually suggest an asset as well as a deficit. If you work with children from this perspective, teaching and learning can proceed on a more optimistic premise.

3. Observing: There may be a near-perfect correlation between strong powers of observation and good writing, strong powers of observation and good detective work. The same is true for good teaching. Work to develop your powers of observation. For further details, read *Authentic Literacy Assessment: An Ecological Approach* by Lauren Leslie and Mary Jett-Simpson. Below are a brief set of guidelines for observing writing behavior.

   • Develop a plan for observing writing.
   • Keep a notebook in which to record observations.
   • Focus on student writing strengths.
   • Observe performance over a variety of writing tasks.
   • Compare your observations with actual student writing.

4. Evaluating Paul's writing: Read the following story written by Paul, a 10-year-old lad from England. After you have read the piece, answer the questions that follow, applying what you have learned from this chapter.

   You glide and swoop through the air performing endless feats of acrobatics. You are a graceful creature who has the whole world at your feet. Out of the forest you fly, your feathers, some smooth some fluffy hold your body in the air. You are the earths eyewitness to the everyday events. You perch on the wires like a human would wait at a railway station, waiting for the right time to take off—four,

three, two, one and a cloud of feathered creatures lifts in the sky like a cloud of locusts swarming to the crop of warmth. Over the sea, over the ocean your body
flys. A ship sounds a warning as the cotton wool fog closes in. You see an ice berg
the ship does not and the sea is the scene of death again. The fog clears and you
see land a magnetic impulse tells you that this is your destination. You can feel
the warmth of the friendliness of your new home.

Is this "good" writing? Why or why not?

What writing strengths or weaknesses do you detect?

What might you say to Paul about his piece?

REFLECTION AND SUMMARY

Reflection

Peter DeVries said, "I love being a writer. What I can't stand is the paperwork."
Haven't you sometimes said to yourself, "I love teaching writing, but I can't stand
the paperwork." Few tasks are more daunting or delicate than evaluating another
person's writing. There is the sheer tedium of it, especially late at night when
you've read yourself nearly to sleep. Then too, you worry about hurting feelings,
stifling creativity, or impeding growth. Indeed, there is reason for concern. Insensitive comments can cause irreparable harm, turn children away from writing,
and sow seeds of doubt that may linger for years, or even a lifetime. I have spoken
earlier of my student, a teacher, whose romantic poem was harshly criticized.
Years later, I helped uncover a writer huddled beneath the shell of indifference
she had constructed to protect herself. She has written many poems and stories
since, but, oh, the wasted years. Insensitive comments represent the evil spirit of
evaluation; but there is a humane spirit, for I have seen it in the words and deeds
of many considerate teachers.

Summary

This chapter has presented the following main ideas:

1. Five concepts guide the assessment of writing. Each concept deals with a
    significant aspect of writing evaluation.

    - Evaluation has three primary uses. It guides instruction, informs ad-
      ministrative decisions, and facilitates research.
    - There is no ideal form of evaluation. Purpose determines which proce-
      dures are best for a given situation.
    - There is no universally accepted standard of good writing; sensitivity
      for what constitutes good writing can be developed.
    - Effective evaluation is based on a thorough knowledge of writers,
      writing, and the writing process.
    - Errors should be examined for signs of progress and as possible indi-
      cators of movement toward new levels of achievement.

2. Students must be involved in the evaluation of writing. Three procedures for involving children in evaluating their own writing were suggested.
   - Portfolios are representative collections of students' work documenting achievement, progress, and effort.
   - Self-evaluation is helping children to become editors of their own writing through self-criticism and revising knowledge.
   - Peer evaluation is children working collaboratively to improve writing in whole class, groups, or one-on-one settings.

3. Teachers need ways to evaluate writing. Three procedures for evaluating writing were suggested: holistic, analytic, and primary trait.
   - Holistic evaluation assesses writing rapidly and impressionistically, usually within three or four minutes. Holistic evaluation is especially useful for evaluating writing in broad contexts.
   - Analytic evaluation looks at writing from a deliberate and detailed perspective. Writing features are evaluated in terms of strengths and weaknesses, presence or absence, high or low quality.
   - Primary trait evaluation focuses on assessing a single writing feature rather than on the whole. It is a highly focused form of evaluation, and is useful in special situations.

QUESTIONS FOR REFLECTIVE THINKING

1. What is the purpose of formative evaluation? How does it differ from summative evaluation?
2. What is one of the best ways for a teacher to gain an understanding of good writing? Why is such an understanding essential to evaluation of writing?
3. What is the role of error in teaching writing and learning to write?
4. What is a writing portfolio? How can portfolios be useful in teaching writing?
5. Why is it crucial to teach children to evaluate their own work?
6. In what ways are holistic and analytic evaluation similar? In what ways are they different?
7. How can holistic evaluation help lighten the teacher's paper load?
8. How is primary trait scoring different from holistic and analytic evaluation?
9. What guidelines would you suggest for grading writing in addition to or in place of the guidelines suggested in this chapter?
10. What have you learned in this chapter that you didn't know before you read it?
11. Mini case study: You teach third grade in a suburban community. Up to now, you didn't give grades in writing, but your school district is considering changing this policy. The new policy would require giving grades in writing. You have asked to appear before the school board to oppose the new policy. What will you say in defense of the old policy? What arguments will you make against the proposed new policy?

REFERENCES

Clegg, A. B. (1972). *The excitement of writing.* New York: Shocken Books.

Cowley, M. (1958). *Writers at work: The Paris Review interviews.* Middlesex, England: Penguin Books.

Gordon, Arthur. (1974). *A touch of wonder.* New York: Fleming H. Revell Co.

Graves, D. H. (1973). *Children's writing: Research directions and hypotheses based upon an examination of the writing processes of seven year old children.* Unpublished Doctoral Dissertation, State University of New York at Buffalo.

Graves, D. H. (1983). *Writing: Teachers and children at work.* Exeter, NH: Heinemann.

Lagna, J. R. (1972). *The development, implementation and evaluation of a model for teaching composition which utilizes individualized learning and peer grouping.* Unpublished Doctoral Dissertation, University of Pittsburgh.

Leslie, L. and Jett-Simpson, M. (1997). *Authentic literacy assessment: An ecological approach.* New York: Longman.

Purves, A. (1991). "The school subject literature." In *Handbook of research on teaching the English language arts.* Flood, J., Jensen, J. M., Lapp, D., Squire, J. R. (ed) New York: MacMillan Publishing Co.

Rief, L. (1990). "Finding the value in evaluation: Self-assessment in a middle school classroom." *Educational Leadership,* March, 24–29.

Sendak, M. (1961). *Where the wild things are.* New York: HarperCollins.

Shanahan, T. (1980). *A canonical correlational analysis of learning to read and learning to write: An exploratory analysis.* Unpublished Doctoral Dissertation, University of Delaware, Newark, DE.

Shaughnessy, M. (1977). *Errors and expectations.* New York: Oxford University Press.

Tierney, R., Carter, M. A., and Desai, L. E. (1991). *Portfolio assessment in the reading-writing classroom.* Norwood, MA: Christopher-Gordon.

Wiggins, G. (1990). "A conversation with Grant Wiggins." *Instructor,* August, 51.

CHAPTER 9
Writing as Therapy

Writing is a form of therapy; sometimes I wonder how all those who
do not write, compose or paint can manage to escape the madness,
the melancholia, panic, fear which is inherent in a human situation.

Graham Green

A WRITER'S STORY

*Amy came into my study and asked, "Can I use your typewriter, Dad?" I was tempted to
say, "I'm busy, honey. Some other time." Fortunately, I resisted the "busy father" temptation and asked, "What do you need it for, Amy?" "I have a poem I want to write," she
replied. A serendipity presented itself, and I relinquished the typewriter. When I returned,
Amy had pecked out this poem:*

The Beechnuts

Beechnuts, Beechnuts,
Flying away,
Drift to the river
And float away,
Past the cows,
Past the sheep,
And past the boughs.
Hello sea!

*The poem reflects Amy's experiences in a lovely English village, Nether Poppleton,
with its stately Beech trees, swiftly flowing river, and the picturesque farms that bordered
it. Her poem marked the beginning of an intense creative interlude. Amy was delighted
with the enthusiastic reception I had given her poem, "What a wonderful poem, Amy. I
love it." The next morning, well before my customary rising time, Amy came into my bed-
room, shook me awake, and asked, "Dad, would you like to hear another poem?" She knew
her first poem had pleased me, and she hoped her second poem would elicit a similar response. It did, and she soared for weeks on the wings of a serendipity.*

Writing can arise out of a serendipity. Like the three princes of Serendip, cultivate your readiness to respond to unplanned opportunities. Respond when opportunity knocks, and lovely surprises await you. Every teacher can be a prince or princess in the land of Serendip.

INTRODUCTION

Psychologists and psychiatrists use expressive writing as a therapeutic medium. This is sometimes called confessional writing, a genre of writing that dates to the Renaissance. In recent years, expressive writing has come into much wider use among therapists. But this chapter is not about psychiatric or psychological therapy. Teachers are not trained to engage in psychological psychiatric counseling. Therefore, they ought not to engage in it. When serious issues arise in the course of teaching, professionals with appropriate credentials should be consulted. What teachers do know is children. And teachers need to be aware of the special opportunities that writing provides for helping children get in touch with their inner life. Writing provides access to the inner world of thought and feeling that is part of children's interior existence. We discover children's inner worlds by observing them at work and play, talking with them and listening, and analyzing and appreciating their creative work. The issues children raise and the problems they reveal range from the trivial to the tragic, from the mundane to the monstrous. Writing gives writers and their audiences access to the concerns and burdens that children might otherwise bear alone. Blom (1974) said, "Writing seems to offer special opportunities that are qualitatively and quantitatively different from other forms of language expression. One of these is a strong contact with one's own inner life" (p 16). Writing is therapeutic, and awareness of this facet of writing can help teachers understand the needs of their children better than any other medium.

EXPRESSING FEELINGS THROUGH WRITING

Language serves the emotional needs of the developing personality. Usually these needs are expressed through oral language. Oral language serves the immediate need for emotional release, but it does not serve long-range emotional needs as well as writing. Oral language is temporal. Once words are spoken, they cannot be retracted, revised, or even remembered for very long. But written language is permanent; it can be examined, extended, and revisited. This characteristic makes it an ideal medium for expressing thought and feeling. The poems and stories that follow illustrate the range and richness of feeling that children express when they write.

Sorrow

Joel visited his father in the hospital and left knowing he might not see his father alive again. As he left, he looked up and saw his father waving good-by from his hospital window. That night Joel wrote a poem expressing his hopes and fears. Joel's beautifully expressed feelings sail bright red across the pages of my mind every time I read his poem.

Daddy, Buddy

Daddy, do you remember the kite we flew,
That sailed bright red across the sky until it
was no more than a speck
on the end of a taut string?
The string broke,
and we hugged and laughed in our buddy way,
as the kite flew into oblivion.
Remember that please,
as you stand there now in the hospital
window waving good-by.
Soon we will be a speck,
disappearing into distant awayness.
You will have to hold on to our string
very tightly,
and pray it doesn't break.
Daddy,
Buddy.

Joel

Teachers, too, have sorrows. Writing about them can be a therapeutic experience. Teri Pangori discovered that writing can be painful and, at the same time, cathartic, even when a tragic event strikes close to home. She talks about it in "Voices from the Classroom."

VOICES FROM THE CLASSROOM: Teri Pangori

A Visit Home

I hadn't thought about Montoursville for a long time. Whenever May rolled around, I would begin to plan an annual journey to my Pennsylvania hometown. My visits home always rekindled my love for small town peace and a slower pace. May came and went and I reluctantly decided to forego my yearly trip. I'd go another time, perhaps. That time arrived sooner than I had expected.

On a Wednesday evening in July, my husband and I, like millions of others, watched the news of a tragic plane crash. I remember telling my husband that I felt sorry for the victims' families and fell asleep, thankful that this horror had occurred so far from home. When my mother called the next morning, the tragedy of Flight 800 became more personal than I could have imagined. With a strange tremor in her voice, she told me that my cousin, Michelle, and several children of family friends had perished in the crash. My response was one of disbelief. Michelle was fifteen, not nearly old enough to die. International tragedies don't involve Montoursville. The thought was absurd.

Leaving my family behind, I flew into Montoursville, wondering how difficult this visit would be. I wasn't prepared for what I saw over the following days. Blue, gold, and black ribbons adorned nearly every tree and every fence post on

Main Street. Flowers and wreaths decorated buildings everywhere. At the high school, where my classmates and I had celebrated football victories and had danced a dozen dances, students sat in clusters talking, staring, crying. It was a mourning grounds. Hundreds of teddy bears wearing the names of lost friends sat on the floors.

Everyone was touched by this tragedy in some way, and without words the townspeople acknowledged each other's pain. Volunteers opened the volume of mail that was displayed at the school. They helped deliver the continual flow of floral arrangements. People attended funeral after funeral. It was a powerfully moving experience to see these kids saying goodbye to so many classmates.

I stayed in Montoursville for three very long, very difficult days. When my husband and my children greeted me at the airport, I held them for a long, long time. Even though months have passed since my visit home, I still think about the students, the families, and the friends who lost someone in the crash. I hope that they are coping and beginning to heal. I hope that those teenagers are doing silly adolescent things again. I hope that Main Street is bustling, that football games and dances have replaced grief sessions at the high school, that the churches hold more weddings than funerals again, and that Montoursville is dressed not in black, but instead in the beautiful colors of the Pennsylvania hills.

Loneliness

The poem "Tears" gives fresh meaning to the statement, "The heart is a lonely hunter." The writer momentarily draws aside the curtain that veils his inner world. He speaks of tears and travails, heartaches and hopes—in short, the loneliness of the human heart. Writing does not, in itself, solve the problems life presents. But articulating a problem is sometimes impetus enough to start an interior solution. Also, there is now the possibility that someone in the outer world may help banish interior terrors. A teacher or a friend may be the one who reaches out and starts the healing process.

Tears

The depth of my heart needs to be clean.
Lord, wash it with tears of joy.
Put the joy in the cup, make it easy to drink.

Because I'm weak, flowers never grow in my garden,
the sun never shone on me.
Darkness marinated in my presence; grief was a lost sound.

The moon hides from me,
my heart already at the crossroads,
never to enter the light.

Defeated with every turn, going the wrong way
struggling for hope, for victory,
protecting what's left,

my dripping spirit begs for one more chance.
There are no wings to save me,
no one to fly me away from trouble.
Solomon

Anxiety

The literary merit of fairy tales is well known. Less well known is their therapeutic value. Bettelheim's (1977) research supports the therapeutic value of fairy tales. Fairy tales are ". . . therapeutic because the patient finds his own solutions, through contemplating what the story seems to imply about him and his inner conflicts at this moment in his life" (p. 25). Fairy tales simplify situations, and this makes them an ideal literature for dealing with conflict.

Jennifer's story illustrates how the fairy tale genre provides a vehicle for dealing with anxiety. On the surface, her story seems imaginary, but the characters and events stem from real-life experiences. Jennifer wrote her story shortly after we had moved from America to England. Everything was new: friends, school, village, customs, language. She didn't like it, and her story seeks to resolve her anxiety.

Lisa and Griselda

Once upon a time there was a witch called Griselda. She was a nasty witch. She was always telling Lisa, her servant, to clean up her room. One day Griselda said go to the store and buy some eggs. Lisa was in a hurry and she dropped all the eggs. The witch was mad at her. One day the witch was going to her friend's house and took Lisa with her. They stayed too long because the witch was talking to her friend and it was getting dark and Lisa was getting afraid. Lisa did not know they were staying all night.

One day Griselda told Lisa to go to the store to buy some bread. There was a box of bread and she did not know how to get the bread out so she asked the man in the store. One day the witch took Lisa to a witches' party. First the witch opened the presents. Then they played chasing games.

Jennifer, Age 6

Jennifer's story illustrates how internal processes are externalized through writing. Characters and events in Jennifer's fairy tale represent real-life people and events. The witch-archetype in Jennifer's fairy tale represents the "bad" parents who make unreasonable demands and treat children unfairly. Lisa and Griselda symbolically express Jennifer's own real-life anxieties. For instance, Lisa is told to clean her room by Griselda. In real life, father and mother make Jennifer clean her room. Other story events can be traced directly to recent real-life experiences—the eggs, bread box, witches' party. The story ends with the statement, "Then they played chasing games," suggesting, perhaps, a resolution—anxieties can be resolved. Writing gave Jennifer a mechanism for reflecting on her concerns and an outlet for feelings that might otherwise be repressed. Children's writing can have symbolic meaning and can, as a consequence, serve a therapeutic purpose.

Love

Children are incredibly observant. Mary's poem is an example of profound ideas almost literally, "out of the mouth of a babe." Her poem expresses sadness and puzzlement that the white world has rejected her offer of love. In five simple lines, she expresses her love, asking only that it be reciprocated. "And a little child shall lead them," is the thought that comes to mind.

We Love

We can love
If white love
Can't you love?
Some want to love
Some do not

Mary, Age 6

Wonder

I have seen clerks ignore a child waiting patiently in line to serve a recently arrived adult. I have heard adults idealize childhood, describing it as care-free. I have known adults who think children incapable of deep thought. Yet, we see that Jennifer is concerned about racism, poverty, crime, pollution, justice, and death. The thoughts and feelings stirring in Jennifer's mind are not unusual among children. Children reflect adult concerns in their talk and in their writing.

I Wonder Why

I wonder why there is not a black Santa Claus
I wonder why Christmas only comes once a year
I wonder why I don't have a pair of new shoes
I wonder why it can't be a good Halloween
I wonder why someone stole our car
I wonder why the sky is full of pollution
I wonder why my grandmother is dead
I wonder why my daddy won't take us to dinner.

Jennifer, Age 6

Friendship

Grief is a powerful emotion, one not easily resolved. Janet's story celebrates friendship, even as she grieves. Writing this story helped her displace the sorrow she felt over the loss of her friend, David.

I Have a Friend in Heaven

"Look at this," mom said, pointing to an article in the newspaper. "The poor boy. Isn't it so very sad." She showed me the article. I read about one paragraph, and I couldn't bear to read another word. Staring out at me from the paper was a picture of a small boy, perhaps five years old. He was peering through the bars of a crib in the isolation ward of a hospital. His hair was bright red and his smiling little face was sprinkled with hundreds of freckles. David Gregory, a victim of a fatal disease, Leukemia, was playing with a toy airplane and grinning, possibly one of the last smiles he would ever show. In less than a month, David would celebrate his sixth birthday, maybe.

We called this little boy's parents and made arrangements to meet him. He came from a family of seven children, and his parents were very poor. So you can see that even though they wanted to, his mother and father couldn't get him all that David wanted and needed.

Almost every Sunday we took him somewhere, usually the zoo, which was his favorite place. We tried to show him a good time, but it ended up with him showing us a good time. We stopped at a store one day and had him pick out something he wanted. He chose a farm set, and almost cried when he got it because he was so happy.

I had been taking dance lessons ever since I was four, and was almost eight when I met David. We had a dance recital every year in which I had a few solos. This year we invited David to attend. We got front row seats for him and his family, and after I had performed, David came backstage and gave me a dozen beautiful, red roses.

We exchanged letters and phone calls for about another month or two. At Easter, David didn't forget me nor I him. It was soon after Easter that we received a call from his mother telling us that David had passed away, and inviting us to his funeral. Well, of course we went, still in shock, even though we had expected it. Ever since we had known David, we prayed every day.

On the sad day of the funeral, we said our good-byes to the tiny child, whom we had come to love so much. In his hand he held a rose from the spray I had sent.

This is a tragic story in many ways, but not entirely. David showed me what real courage is. He also taught me that there is joy and reward in giving. What began as pity changed to admiration, for I got as much, or more from knowing David, than I gave to him. I truly have a friend in heaven.

Janet

Self-Confidence

Writing is uniquely suited to enhance self-confidence (Denman, 1981; Kean, 1983; Clay, 1983; Graves, 1994; Dyson, 1989, 1993). Literacy not only broadens the mind, it strengthens personality as well. When literacy is impaired, personality suffers. Society stigmatizes children who cannot read or write. When they are treated as failures, they sometimes behave in unacceptable ways. It is no coincidence that most juvenile delinquents and prison inmates have impaired literacy skills. Children who have difficulty learning to read and write lose confidence in themselves and begin to think they are stupid or abnormal. Such children often seek help, directly or indirectly, from teachers. "Something Concerning a Matter in School" was written by a high school student whose self-confidence was shaky, largely due to impaired reading and writing skill.

Something Concerning a Matter in School

I need some help in trying to do good in school if I can try and stop playing around like a little kid. Maybe I could get something done and get down to work because I don't want to fail and go back instead of forward. If I do, my friends and my mother are going to tell me that I play too much, or I don't do enough of this or that. The reason I am talking about this is because I think it is a problem for me to try to solve with a little help. I know a teacher that is trying to help me and so far I am doing good as far as she is concerned, but she said I could do better.

    Keith

Keith seldom wrote, and he read poorly. He was failing in school and felt the pressure of this failure from parents, teachers, and friends. His parents enrolled him at Oakland University's Reading-Writing Clinic where a fine teacher began mending his shattered self-confidence by successfully tutoring him in reading and writing. His behavior changed as literacy grew.

Keith wrote his piece at the clinic for his English teacher. His account is not remarkable, though the human element of his story is compelling. Keith makes a number of revelations and requests. He apologizes for past mistakes, promises to improve his behavior, hopes to improve his academic performance, and asks for help.

His plea for aid went unanswered. Grammatical and mechanical errors were red-penciled and in the margin his English teacher commented, "All teachers can help you," but offered no help. Correcting writing has a time and place, but this was neither the time nor place. One does not red-pencil a plea for help. Keith reached out, but no helping hand was extended. Keith's story had a happy ending due to his success in the clinic, but stories often have unhappy endings.

Reading gives children access to literature, and literature gives children insight into their inner resources. Writing enables children to explore the dimensions of their inner worlds and reflect on their relationship with the outer world.

Self-Esteem

Tommy's experience illustrates how a sensitive teacher used writing to strengthen his self-esteem. I overheard the following conversation between Tommy, a fourth grade reluctant writer, and his teacher.

"Miss Keense, there's a story I want to show you." After a brief pause Tommy said, without much conviction, "You might not like it." As Ms. Keense read, Tommy watched. He soon discerned approval in Ms. Keense's face. A smile lit his face, as he pointed to a passage in his story, "This next part is going to be funny."

As I witnessed this exchange, I realized that an important emotional transaction had occurred. Ms. Keense did think the story was funny. She commented thoughtfully on his story and urged him to continue his good work. As Tommy rushed off from his brief conference he said, "I'm going to write another story, *even better this time.*"

Successful writing enhances self-esteem (Brand, 1977; Cramer, 1978, 1998; Romano, 1987). Self-esteem is further strengthened when children find that their teacher, parents, and classmates approve of their efforts. Mearns (1929) was seldom more insightful than when he said, "It is not enough to discern a native gift; it must be enticed out again and again. It needs exercise in an atmosphere of approval. Above all it must be protected against the annihilating effect of social condemnation" (p. 268).

Conflicts and Concerns

Children often reveal personal conflicts and concerns in their writing. Revelation is the first step toward resolution. Writing is the ideal medium for revealing personal problems because we can communicate intimate information without directly facing those to whom our message is addressed. Written messages are mediated by impersonal symbols that provide distance between the sender and receiver. It is the need to communicate intimate messages that makes writing an ideal medium for conveying and resolving conflicts and concerns.

The following vignettes illustrate a range of concerns children first disclosed to their teachers in the course of everyday writing. Most of these matters were resolved, at least to some degree. While not all problems have a ready resolution, nevertheless, it is therapeutic to write about them.

1. An eighth grade girl writes that she takes drugs and drinks a lot. She trusts and admires her teacher and hopes that her teacher can help her. Her teacher helped.

2. A high school girl writes that she is pregnant and doesn't know what to do. She is afraid to tell her parents or her boyfriend. She hopes her teacher can help her. Her teacher found someone who could help.

3. A fifth grade boy writes a poem describing the hurt of not knowing who his father is. He writes stories featuring happy family relationships. No solution here, but writing brought the issue to the surface where it could be examined.

4. A sixth grade girl writes that she is ashamed of her shabby clothing. She describes her embarrassment in a note to her teacher. Her teacher helped.

5. An eighth grade girl writes a story in which the main character is a teenage girl who writes poetry and wants to share her poems but fears rejection. The teacher suspected that the character in the story represented the fears and desires of its author, and quietly suggested a resolution.

6. A seventh grade boy explains that he sometimes misses school because a classmate is extorting his lunch money. He wonders where he can get help. His teacher knew where to get help.

7. A first grade boy writes that he does not eat breakfast because there is no one at home in the morning to make it. His school provided breakfast.

Worries and Fears

Ms. Brown, a second grade teacher, noticed that her children told her things in writing that they seldom mentioned orally. One day she suggested writing about things that worried them. Their responses revealed much that she knew about and some worries she had not anticipated. Here are five examples of what her children wrote.

> I often worre about my friends moving away. I often worre about rain in the nite. I often worre about cars in the nite.

> I often worry about my Gramma because she lives all alone and I go over to her house sometimes.

> I often worry about trying to do work in schol. Kids have trouble doing work. Kids get hurt in schol.

> I am worry about my little Brothr becase my lettle Brothr be at home Bi hes self and I am saad Becas smbide can brake in my house.

> I worre going to bed in the dark I worre to be alone at nite.

Their writing helped Ms. Brown understand her children's physical, social, and psychological needs. Loneliness and fear of the dark were mentioned. One youngster mentioned his concern for his little brother's safety. She responded in the following ways:

1. She led discussions on the most common concerns her children's writing revealed. These discussions were informal and often impromptu.

2. She located stories and poems that dealt with loneliness, fear of the dark, and other worries revealed in the stories her children wrote.

3. She read aloud books and stories she had selected and encouraged children to read related literature independently.

4. She used drawing, painting, and drama to help children express their concerns.

5. She responded directly to individual needs when more specific intervention seemed warranted, as in the case of the little brother home alone.

Writing is not a panacea for solving problems, but it does give children and teachers an additional way of coping. In the instances described, school or community resources were sometimes available to help resolve or ameliorate the problems children revealed. Problems children reveal cannot, and sometimes should not, be resolved by a teacher. But intervention in the form of an act of kindness, praise, approval, and human sympathy are invaluable and cost nothing.

It is often said that childhood is a glorious time—no responsibilities, no worries, no problems. This is certainly not the case today and probably never was. Ms. Susan Martin, a middle school teacher, describes how she used writing to deal with an incident involving a racial epithet.

VOICES FROM THE CLASSROOM: Susan Martin

Therapeutic Journal Writing

Once of the most valuable uses of our daily journal writing was dealing with friction among the diverse groups of kids in our school. Often fights erupted on the playground, usually stemming from a racial epithet. After one disturbing fight, I assembled my eighth graders and had them take out their journals. I said we would have a longer writing time than normal, and that I would be reading their entries. Usually I did not, so as to preserve their privacy. I asked them to write about their feelings: why they thought it happened, what they could have done to prevent it, and how we could learn from it. After they wrote, I collected their journals and read them.

I found that most of them shared the same thoughts. They wanted to get along, resented the pettiness that was causing friction, and wanted to grow together as a group. I responded to each child personally. In almost every response, I had asked questions or solicited comments in return. I was pleasantly surprised by how many responses I received. By taking the time to acknowledge their feelings and respond to them, I validated what they had written. With permission, I read selected passages aloud that were particularly meaningful.

This experience was repeated several times throughout that year, and it helped the class grow together and mature in their attitudes toward each other and toward me. I believe in the healing power of writing, and I'm glad that I had the chance to use writing in such a positive way.

Under the right conditions, writing breaks down barriers that keep children from sharing their deepest thoughts. Writing enables children to deal with the emotions that living generates. Writing integrates the inner world with the outward circumstances of life. Writing about loneliness, for example, informs the outside world. Perhaps someone will help fill the void and provide a solution. On the other hand, it may be that no one can or does respond. Even so, the act of writing itself may help. Writing is therapeutic.

CREATING A THERAPEUTIC WRITING ENVIRONMENT

In the movie, *Field of Dreams*, a farmer builds a ballpark in a cornfield. The farm is in the country, and there seems little likelihood of attracting anyone to play on it. The farmer's statement of faith is, "If I build it, they will come." It turns out "they" do come—a magical ending to the film makes it a delightful experience. The underlying premise of the film is, "You've gotta believe." I believe this is also the underlying premise of teaching. You can build a "field of dreams" in your classroom—a place where "they" will come. What is the "they" I refer to? All the good things that faith in children generates.

Trust and Respect Children

Writing requires mutual trust and respect. Children have a world of their own into which they sometimes invite trusted adults. Of course, by dint of superior

Mrs. Wilson knows what it takes to create a secure, stimulating writing environment in her classroom. Here she discusses a word study activity with Jonella.

authority, teachers may enter without invitation, but when they do they are ministers without portfolio—present without credentials. Successful work with children requires reciprocated trust and respect. Sara's poem evokes the strong feelings and marvelous analogies that children's writing often exemplifies.

One Face

I want hazel eyes that split
atoms and dimensions,
causing a time warp between worlds.

I want a smile that when my teeth show
the earth shakes and trembles,
knocking the Richter Scale off the charts.

I want a perfect almond skin tone
so that when I walk past trees,
squirrels follow me home.
Sara

The common traits of successful writing teachers are that they believe in the capabilities of children, and they trust and respect children as individuals. Of course, other factors are important: acquaintance with the writing process, teaching experience, and a solid educational background, whether formal or self-acquired. While knowledge is required, character is even more important. Succeeding with children begins and ends with character, and in the restaurant of writing instruction, no substitutes for character are accepted.

Ms. Debbie Clark knows the importance of building trust and respect among her students. She found that sharing a very personal writing assignment with her middle graders brought her closer to her students. She describes her experience in the "Voices" piece.

VOICES FROM THE CLASSROOM: Debbie Clark

Building Trust and Respect

Building trust is essential in a Writer's Workshop classroom. I know that for my students to trust me with their writing, they have to know that I value their writing and look at them as writers, not just my students. I build this trust in a number of ways, but the one method I find most successful is sharing my own life with my students through my writing.

Last year one of my writing assignments was writing a biography of a grandparent or someone close to their grandparent's age. I decided to use my own father as a model for my interview, since he was about the same age as their grandparents would be. When I interviewed my father, I was amazed at what I learned about his childhood and early life that I had never known. The experience was delightful for both of us. I completed my biography and shared it as a model with my classes. Two months later my father passed away.

As I began planning my biography unit this year, I wasn't sure if I felt strong enough to pull out my father's biography to use as a model. I didn't know if I could get through presenting his words to my classes without breaking down in front of them. But the more I thought about it, the more I realized how important it was that they see how the biographies they authored could become valuable to them later in life. I decided to give it a try.

The day I presented my father's biography, I began by telling my students the story of writing it. I explained how special my father was, and how grateful I am that I had the chance to sit down and talk to him about his life before he passed away. I then read his biography, shedding a few tears in the process.

I feel that sharing my life and my feelings allowed students to see how important writing is. Sharing my personal feelings helped my students make a vital connection between the words written on paper and their own lives.

Receive Writing Graciously

An effective way to increase the therapeutic quotient of a classroom is to improve the climate for receiving it. Writing is a gift and must be graciously received. How writing is received determines its quality and quantity. When a gift is given, the giver expects the recipient to appreciate and acknowledge it. When a gift is graciously received, the giver experiences the joy of giving. On the other hand, an indifferent reception implies rejection. In such cases, the giver may decide that further gifts are unwarranted. Teachers who receive children's writing with respect have discovered the first premise for stimulating more and better writing.

Private writing requires special handling. It may be for the teacher's eyes only. Designate a place where children can deposit private writing, a designated desk drawer, for example. Mearns (1929) discovered the value of this practice, for he understood that fear of adverse judgment or fear of failure hindered trust. Children are reluctant to trust their writing into the hands of someone who might not receive it graciously. Of course, once a trusting relationship is established reluctance gives way to eagerness.

Ms. Carol Sievert teaches third grade. She knows the importance of receiving writing graciously. Her students soon learn that personal writing is treated with the dignity that such writing deserves. In her "Voices" piece, Ms. Sievert tells how one of her children constantly wrote about the death of her mother. Writing was this child's preferred therapeutic medium.

VOICES FROM THE CLASSROOM: Carol Sievert

Writing with Feeling

Chelsey lost her mother to cancer as a first grader. As a third grader, Chelsey was still trying to manage her loss. One of the ways she did this was through writing. Chelsey constantly wrote stories, poems, and letters about and to her mother. One story especially gave me insight into Chelsey's inner pain.

Chelsey wrote a story about a dying mother's last conversation with her daughter. Chelsey's story evoked such a loving scene between a mother and a child it was almost painful to hear it. Chelsey used writing to express her inner most thoughts and feelings about the love she felt for her mother and the love her mother felt for her. Writing was the way she dealt with her pain. I remember looking into the faces of my students and seeing how Chelsey's story had tapped into their lives. I will never forget this courageous little girl. She used writing as a way to deal with and survive a great sorrow in her life.

Practice Empathetic Teaching

Empathetic teaching is prerequisite to therapeutic success. An empathetic teacher is sensitive to children's feelings, responsive to their needs, involved in their concerns. The empathetic teacher projects a genuine interest in what children write, how they write, and what they think about their writing. Empathetic teaching enhances communication between the teacher and her children.

Empathetic teaching cultivates a positive emotional posture. An empathetic teacher accepts strengths as well as weaknesses, successes as well as failures. She takes responsibility for herself and teaches responsibility to her children. An empathetic stance does not require you to wear mental blinders. Criticism can be given, but it must be given in ways that young writers can accept, and it must never be harmful.

Empathetic teaching seeks harmony between our responsibilities as teachers and our behavior as human beings. Teachers have to operate on a double track. On the one hand, they are the leaders responsible for guiding and directing learning. On the other hand, they are ordinary human beings with thoughts and feelings akin to those of their charges. Children need to see teachers as normal, everyday people. I recall the surprise my daughter expressed when she saw her third grade teacher in a grocery store—*wearing jeans*. What surprised her, I suppose, was the realization that Ms. O'Shagnessey had a real life outside of the classroom, just like mom and dad. Children need to see the teacher as the person in charge, the leader of the group, but also as someone who projects the humanness that places them within the context of their own lives.

Replenish Creative Energy

Creative activity is draining. Writers need periods of rest and refreshment lest they grow stale and bored. Three activities renew the creative energy needed for writing. First, read aloud to children. Reading aloud recharges creative energy and gives children new ideas and information. Second, encourage children to read independently. The wider and deeper they read, the richer the mix of ideas and information available for writing. Third, sometimes it is okay to choose not to write. Even professional writers must escape from their writing from time to time, and occasionally, so must children. A stimulating writing program, with its attendant rewards and values, recalls children to the pleasures, charms and challenges of writing.

Include Everybody In

A gracious hostess welcomes every guest and treats every guest with dignity. Writing teachers have similar obligations. Writing talent is not parceled out according to intelligence quotients, attitude measures, or behavioral patterns. Andy, class clown and troublemaker, turned out to be Ms. Anderson's best sixth grade poet. Sheila, a quiet fifth grader, wrote the best stories Ms. Brean had received in years of successful teaching of writing. Teach long enough, and you discover that your best writers are not always the ones you expected.

Invite special education students to the writing forum. Writing is just as important for children whose development proceeds at a measured pace as for those who proceed rapidly. Elly, a mentally retarded fifth grade child shed tears of happiness when her teacher read her haiku to a classroom visitor. Warren, a third grade special education student, literally jumped up and down with excitement on seeing his published book displayed at his school's Young Authors' Conference. Elly and Warren were perfectly capable of writing, and doing so enriched their academic and emotional well-being. Children thought to have little writing talent often surprise us with their sensitive writing. Good writing often comes from unanticipated sources.

Uncover and Enlarge Talent

Mark Medoff, author of *Children of a Lesser God,* visited his high school many years after achieving success and fame as a writer. There he met his former English teacher, who had faithfully taught her students all the thousands of days since Mark Medoff had graced her classroom. He looked at her and wanted to say something special, but all he could manage was, "Ms. Roberts, I want you to know you were very important to me." Ms. Roberts, tears in her eyes, had her reward. Not much perhaps, but Medoff's words, spoken from the heart, are what every real teacher longs to hear and deeply appreciates. Ms. Roberts was the first to uncover and enlarge Medoff's talent.

Writing teachers are diamond miners, sifting tons of ore in search of an occasional gem. They are diamond cutters polishing the facets that make talent sparkle. Good writing teachers think of potential when they work with young writers. Uncovering and enlarging writing talent is challenging, and it requires persistence, patience, and caring. Ann's writing showed insight that surprised Ms. Elson, a sophisticated writing teacher. Ann's spelling and mechanics were weak, but these skills came along under patient tutelage. Ann may become a successful and famous writer someday, as Mark Medoff did. Ms. Elson may or may not experience the joy of a return visit from a prize pupil, nevertheless, she uncovered and enlarged Ann's writing talent.

SUMMARY OF IDEAS FOR CREATING A THERAPEUTIC WRITING ENVIRONMENT

1. Children invite into their world teachers who they trust and respect.
2. You can increase the therapeutic quotient of a classroom by improving the climate for receiving writing.
3. Empathetic teaching is prerequisite to therapeutic success.
4. Writers sometimes need rest and refreshment from writing lest they grow stale and bored.
5. Writing talent is not parceled out according to IQ. Often the unlikely prospect possesses the greatest potential writing talent.
6. Uncovering and enlarging writing talent is a writing teacher's main therapeutic mission.

IDEAS FOR WRITING

1. Faces: Look for pictures of faces showing different emotions. Identify the emotions and describe them. Emotions to look for include: sadness, joy, excitement, fright, love, hate, envy, jealousy, grief, anger, disappointment, anxiety.

2. Feelings: Write an account of a time when you experienced strong emotions. Recall the events that led to your feelings. For example, you may have been disappointed in the behavior of a friend or angry because you had been unfairly criticized.

3. Decision: You are on a one-person life raft and are the only survivor of a shipwreck. After a day on the raft, your food and water supply are running low. Then you see another survivor clinging to a tiny piece of driftwood. What will you do?

4. Poem: Think of all the words you associate with the idea of *loneliness.* Write these words in a box in the corner of a paper. Then write a poem or story. You will find that some of the words you wrote work well in your story or poem.

5. Story: Write a story or poem based on a disappointment such as: a present you hoped for but did not get, a game you wanted to win but lost, a broken promise, a trip you did not get to take, a friend who let you down. Perhaps you have your own keen disappointment you'd prefer to write about.

6. Colors: Cut different colors of paper into shapes. Write how you feel about these questions: What does this color mean to you? What do you associate with this color? How do colors affect your moods? A good book to read before doing this activity is *Hailstones and Halibut Bones* by Mary O'Neill.

7. If I Were in Charge: Judith Viorst wrote a poem called, "If I Were in Charge of the World." Suppose you were in charge of the world. What would you change? What would stay the same? First, write some statements telling what wouldn't be: "If I were in charge of the world there wouldn't be homework." Then write statements telling what would be: "If I were in charge of the world, Saturday would come four times a week."

8. The future: Everybody has dreams and wishes for the future. Sometimes our dreams are about ourselves and sometimes they are about others. What are your dreams and wishes for the future? Tell about your dreams and wishes for yourself, your friends, your family, the world.

9. Sayings: Everyone knows a few sayings: For example, you have probably heard these sayings: *Children should be seen and not heard; Don't criticize your neighbor until you've walked a mile in his or her shoes; Waste not want not.* Some sayings are interesting, others boring or foolish. What kind of sayings can you write? Write your own sayings about: adults, peace, war, poverty, hunger, poetry, friends, school, work.

10. Giving advice: Most of us like to give advice to others. Of course, it's easier to give advice than take it. What advice would you give to: Americans, teachers, best friends, zoo keepers, story writers, textbook authors, politicians, parents. Maybe you have a better idea of who you'd like to give advice to.

REFLECTION AND SUMMARY

Reflection

A teacher once said to me, "Thank you for letting me write. My daughter was killed in a car accident just months before I enrolled in this course. Writing has helped me deal with the loss of my little girl." She handed me a sheaf of papers and said, "Would you like to read these poems and stories? I feel like I can trust them into your hands." Then she hurried from the room in tears. I've seldom felt so privileged and seldom so bereft of words of consolation. Yet it wasn't merely consolation she sought; she needed someone to share her grief, and perhaps someone to celebrate victory over it. I did not take on the role of grief counselor; I have no training in it. I did not say, "I know how you feel." I cannot even imagine the pain of such a loss. But I could be a sympathetic reader. And I could say to her, "Your daughter must have been a lovely person. I'm so sorry." Writing can be therapeutic. It can reach the inner world of the writer and commence an interior solution. It can reach the outer world and commence an exterior solution as well.

Summary

This chapter has presented the following main ideas:

1. Writing is therapeutic. It is an outlet for expressing the strong emotions children experience. Children learn to channel their thoughts and feelings in positive and creative ways through writing. Illustrative examples of feelings expressed through writing include sorrow, loneliness, anxiety, love, wonder, friendship, self-confidence, self-esteem, conflicts and concerns, and worries and fears.

2. Teachers can cultivate a therapeutic writing environment. The following steps were suggested;

   • Establish a healthy classroom environment where writers can blossom.
   • Trust and respect children.
   • Receive writing graciously, as you would receive a gift from a friend.
   • Practice empathetic teaching.
   • Creative efforts are draining, and rest and refreshment are essential.
   • Invite everyone into the writing circle.
   • Work to uncover and enlarge children's natural talents.
   • Designate a special place where children may deposit private writing.

QUESTIONS FOR REFLECTIVE THINKING

1. What distinction does the author make between psychiatric counseling and the therapeutic value of writing in classrooms?

2. What are some of the ways in which the emotional needs of children can be expressed through writing?

3. What distinctions may be drawn between oral language and written language as a medium of emotional release?

4. Reread the poem "Tears". How would you respond to this poem assuming you had received it from one of your students?

5. How can successful writing enhance self-confidence?

6. Suppose several of your students have had a verbal dispute centering around racial issues. How might you use writing to ameliorate this problem?

7. You have taken a new teaching position and wish to enlist the trust of your students. How might you use writing to accomplish this goal?

8. What experiences have you had in using writing as a therapeutic medium? Describe one such experience and tell what you learned from it.

9. Do you agree or disagree with the idea of writing as a therapeutic medium? Make a case by citing experiences or research that supports your view.

10. What have you found to be the most interesting or useful idea about writing as a therapeutic medium?

11. Mini case study: Kenny is one of your eighth grade students. He seems uninterested in writing, but you have noticed that his "doodles" are quite sophisticated. How might you use Kenny's artistic inclinations to interest him in writing?

REFERENCES

Bettelheim, B. (1977). *The uses of enchantment: The meaning and importance of fairy tales.* New York: Vintage Books.

Blom, G. E. (1974). "Psychological growth through various forms of language use." Mimeographed: Paper Delivered at the International Reading Association Annual Meeting, New Orleans, LA.

Brand, A. G. (1977). "The therapeutic benefits of free or informal writing among selected eighth graders." Research Paper Prepared at Rutgers University, New Jersey. ED 884–891.

Clay, M. (1983). "Getting a theory of writing." In *Explorations in the development of writing,* Barry Kroll and Gordon Wells, Eds. New York: John Wiley and Sons.

Cramer, R. L. (1978). *Reading, writing, and language growth: An introduction to the language arts.* Columbus, OH: Merrill Publishing Company.

Cramer, R. L. (1998). *The spelling connection: Integrating reading, writing, and spelling instruction.* New York: Guilford Publishing Inc.

Denman, M. (1981). "Personality changes concomitant with learning writing." *Research in the Teaching of English,* 15 (2).

Dyson, A. H. (1989). *Multiple worlds of child writers: Friends learning to write.* New York: Teachers College Press.

Dyson, A. H. (1993). *Social worlds of children learning to write in an urban primary school.* New York: Teachers College Press.

Graves, D. H. (1994). *A fresh look at writing.* Portsmouth, NH: Heinemann Educational Books.

Kean, J. (1983). "Building self-esteem through writing." Wisconsin Writing Project, School of Education, University of Wisconsin-Madison, ED 249 511.

Mearns, H. (1929). *Creative power: The education of youth in the creative arts.* New York: Dover Publications.

Romano, T. (1987). Clearing the way: Working with teenage writers. Portsmouth, NH: Heinemann.

O'Neill, M. L. (1961). *Hailstones and halibut bones: adventures in color.* New York: Doubleday.

CHAPTER 10

Teachers as Writers

It is time to set the record straight. High-school writing teachers should not write.

Karen Jost, Teacher

I need to know I am a learning, feeling, thinking, growing individual along with my students. Reading, writing, and speaking tell me I am. They are what make me human. They make me literate. They empower me.

Linda Rief, Teacher

A WRITER'S STORY

It was her first assignment as a high school writing teacher, and she was beginning to love helping kids discover their voices on the page. That spring, at a staff meeting, plans were announced for a literary magazine which would include students' work as well as teachers'. A tentative show of hands revealed that some colleagues had pieces to submit. So why didn't she? She had written pretty steadily through childhood, even into college. But for almost twenty years she hadn't put pen to paper. Except . . . there was a poem, scribbled on a Smithsonian wrapper one sunny morning after a surprise spring snowfall. That evening she searched the dresser drawer where she was sure she had stashed it. No poem. She sat down, began writing and soon found herself weeping.

What began as a poem about looking for a poem suddenly became a piece about her grandmother who had died the year before. Tears of grief, certainly, but also tears of gratitude. She was writing! For months after she was afraid the experience had been a fluke. Each time she started a poem, there was a sense of fear or awe. Ten years later she had become familiar with the uncertainty, but she will never forget the power and joy of that first poem.

She spent over twenty years teaching in a Detroit public school system. Along the way she discovered her own voice as a poet. She has won prizes and awards for her poetry and for her work as a teacher of writing; she publishes regularly in literary magazines. Her first book of poems, Trio: Voices from the Myths, *was published in 1998, and her second book is now in press.*

Upon retirement from teaching, she established InsideOut, a private, nonprofit literary arts organization dedicated to inspiring the creativity of Detroit's youth and to publicizing and celebrating their work. She was recently featured in People *magazine for her work with*

InsideOut, her writing, and her exemplary life as a teacher of writing. Her return to writing started with a misplaced poem, the surprise that writing often brings, and the tearful discovery that she was writing again. Terry Blackhawk, a writer and teacher of writing.

INTRODUCTION

Should teachers write? Terry Blackhawk's experience as a teacher says *yes*; my inclination is a definite *yes*. But many classroom teachers say *no*. Who's right? Who's wrong? Or, perhaps there is no right or wrong involved in the question: Should teachers write?

I am a university professor, and writing is a vital part of my job description. Fact is, if I didn't write, chances are I wouldn't be a university professor. Furthermore, my teaching schedule accommodates stretches of time that make writing possible. Even so, some university professors manage to do precious little writing. So where do I get off urging classroom teachers to write? After all, classroom teachers' schedules allow little time for writing, except perhaps over the summer. But summers are often reserved for other professional activities, to say nothing of having a life.

So, from the Ivory Tower heights of academia, am I perpetrating another piece of academic nonsense when I plead the cause for teachers as writers? Do teachers out there occupying the trenches have the better of the argument when they say, "No way." Or, is there a middle way?

A REBEL'S SIDE OF THE ISSUE: TEACHERS SHOULD NOT WRITE

Some years ago, Karen Jost (1990), a high school English teacher, wrote an excellent piece in the *English Journal* titled, "Why High-School Writing Teachers Should Not Write." Her article was passionate and persuasive—a rebel's yell, "Hell no, we won't write!" Jost's article generated a heavy response from English teachers, most of them saying, "Right on, Karen." After a lively presentation of her thesis, *English teachers should not write,* Jost concludes with this statement:

> In short, it is impossible to imagine committing to serious writing without sacrificing either our school extracurricular involvement or our personal time. In either case, I suggest the sacrifice is not worth the benefits. Professionally we are committed to the development of students as whole people, not just as writers. As such, any scraps of free time we can salvage might be more fruitfully spent stomping the bleachers at half time than in the solitary pursuit of an elusive metaphor. For the full-time high school English teacher, writing is neither a realistic nor a professionally advantageous avocation. (p. 66)

I found Jost's article refreshing, and if I were to accept her premises, I would abandon my quest to interest teachers in writing. She makes a number of arguments for why teachers should not write: (1) Writing is not professionally advantageous; (2) Realistically, teachers' schedules do not permit writing; (3) Teachers already do lots of "technical" writing; (4) "Serious" writing requires commitment, discipline, and time. Consider each of Jost's arguments with me.

Writing Is Not Professionally Advantageous

It is undeniably true that while university professors are rewarded for writing classroom teachers are not. At prestigious universities, research and scholarly writing are rewarded—promotion, prestige, money. On the other hand, writing poetry or fiction is often regarded with skepticism, if not hostility. This is especially so if you make money doing it. There is nothing so deconstructing to an English professor's tenure and promotion prospects as a best seller. Better to publish an opaque essay in an obscure journal. Even excellent teaching, while commendable, is seldom rewarded on a par with scholarly writing. Not withstanding these minor quibbles, there is no question about it, writing is professionally advantageous in universities and is not in elementary and high schools.

So, Jost's point is a good one if you accept her premise that professional advantage is a necessary condition to induce teachers to write. But I reject this premise. There are reasons for teachers to write, but securing professional advantage is not one of them. Schools are organized on different premises than universities. The rewards and duties are different, and this is unlikely to change, though change might be desirable. Schools are unlikely to reward teachers for writing, even if they are successful writers. So, the case for teachers as writers must be made on different grounds, and I will do so.

Realistically, Teachers' Schedules Do Not Permit Writing

Jost says that a teacher's daily schedule and responsibilities leave little time for writing, whereas a university professor's schedule does. There is merit in Jost's claim, though not as much as she might imagine. Teachers are with their charges continuously from 8:00 to 4:00 with little, if any, free time to pursue anything other than basic teaching responsibilities. University professors, on the other hand, have a less burdensome teaching load, though few are aware of the heavy advising and administrative responsibilities most university professors bear—but that's another story.

It is true that teachers have many responsibilities and little time or support to accomplish them, and this diminishes the opportunities available for writing. But does this mean that writing is out of the question? While agreeing that teachers have limited time to devote to writing, I do not agree that writing is out of the question. Much depends on how extensive a commitment is envisioned, and the role that writing might have in instruction. I envision a moderate commitment to write that is directly connected to writing instruction. For example, Lisa Montpas, a junior high school English teacher, wrote a poem she called "The Ark," and used her poem as a means of motivating her students to write poems.

The Ark

The Giraffe gave a laugh, well into the night
Just a giggle with a wiggle and a bump to her right . . .

Where the Zebra was "zzzzing," and snoring out loud.
He jumped with the nudge and cried, "Hey! Settle down."

"What's the fuss?" asked the Parrot, stretching his wings,
Which started the Ferret, who started to sing.
This caused the Camel to give quite a shout.
He took two steps back and stepped on the
Snout of one VERY LARGE Wart hog,
Who cried, "What's this all about?"

The Panda was napping, just after her snack.
She raised her large head to complain of the lack
Of the peace and the quiet she thought she deserved.

When the nosy young Fox shouted, "Who had the nerve?"
To awaken his slumber, which was really not much,
Since he slept very little, due to carousing and such.

"I beg to admonish all those who are squawking.
I really just want to stop all this talking."

However, this plea, it never was heard.
Too much noise for the voice of a small Baby Bird.
So she flew through the yelling and throwing of things,
To knock on the door of the Queen and the King.

Oh, how she shook when the door gave a creak.
And when it did open, she barely could speak,
"I'd just like to tell you, I'm not getting much sleep."

The King and the Queen gave a nod of their heads,
And everyone crept to their very own beds.

The stars were all shining; the night was so dark,
But in one quiet corner of that little Ark,
The spotted Giraffe,
Gave one little laugh,
Then the King yelled, "BE QUIET OR YOU'LL SLEEP ON THE RAFT."
Lisa Montpas

Teachers Already Do Lots of "Technical" Writing

Jost argues that teachers already write. She lists letters, notes, lists, work-sheets, tests, and handouts as forms of writing that teachers regularly produce. True. But this begs the question, since advocates of teachers as writers have in mind the kinds of writing teachers routinely ask their students to do—poetry, fiction, and essays. And Jost understands that this is the intent of those who advocate that teachers write: "But it is clear that the academics do not have just any type of writing in mind—rather a very specialized form of writing, namely, essays and fiction and poetry, the kinds of writing we assign our students. . ." (Jost, 1990, p. 66).

Jost is right. I am encouraging teachers to try their hand at writing poetry, fiction, and essays because these forms are most often associated with creative endeavor, though not exclusively so. Also, these are the forms of writing that teachers routinely expect students to produce, and students receive significant instructional benefits when teachers model these forms. The routine "technical" writing teachers produce is important, indeed often crucial, to teaching success. But these are seldom the forms we expect our students to produce.

"Serious" Writing Requires Commitment, Discipline, and Time

Jost argues that writing requires serious commitment, steady discipline, significant time. This is certainly true. Professional writers pursue writing with the same commitment that good teachers pursue teaching. Indeed, if they are to succeed, they must do so. But teachers already have full-time jobs. If these things are so, how can anyone expect teachers to write? They cannot unless there is a flaw in Jost's argument. And there is.

The flaw lies in her spurious use of the word *serious*. *Serious* means grave, weighty, or complex. Writing is so *serious, so weighty, so complex,* Jost implies, as to preclude the possibility of teachers' writing worthwhile poetry, fiction, and essays. Takes too much time, commitment, and discipline. But is this so? Absolutely not. Jost further suggests that those who advocate for teachers as writers intend that writing must be for publication. Not true either. Jost implies that it is frivolous to pursue writing unless extensive time, energy, and commitment are devoted to its pursuit. Jost is mistaken. How seriously writing is pursued is a matter of choice, and most teachers who write choose a modest commitment. Not only is this an appropriate option, but a modest commitment is what is needed, what is realistic, and what is sufficient.

Teachers do not need to pursue writing with anything like the commitment and discipline that professional writers or university professors pursue writing. Teachers *must* reserve their most serious commitment to their primary job—teaching. Writing can be pursued in a fashion similar to how one might pursue an interest—take tennis or golf, for instance. One need not become a "serious" player simply because one enjoys the challenge of the game or benefits from the exercise. Writing, if it is to work for teachers, must be voluntary. It must be pursued as an adjunct to instruction, a pleasurable pastime, or a personal interest.

Jost has made four arguments for why teachers should not write, and I have considered each in turn. Her arguments present a challenge to the notion that teachers ought to write. On the other side of the ledger, there are reasons that might persuade teachers to consider adding writing to their instructional arsenal. I recognize the limitations of the arguments for teachers as writers. I understand that obstacles stand in the way. Still, I ask you to consider the alternative to Jost's proposition: "teachers should not write."

SUMMARY OF JOST'S ARGUMENTS CONCERNING
WHY TEACHERS SHOULD NOT WRITE

1. Writing is not professionally rewarding as is the case, for example, for university professors.
2. Teaching schedules and other teaching responsibilities do not provide time for writing.
3. Teachers already do lots of writing of a technical sort such as letters, worksheets, tests, and handouts.
4. Writing requires too much commitment, discipline, and time for teachers to engage in it in a "serious" way.

THE OTHER SIDE OF THE ISSUE: TEACHERS SHOULD WRITE

There are four issues from the alternative side of the issue to consider. They are not just reasons why teachers should write, rather they are a duke's mixture of matters relevant to the proposition "teachers should write" (1) What's in it for teachers personally and professionally? (2) Why write poetry, fiction, and essays? (3) How much time, energy, and commitment will writing require? (4) What instructional purposes does writing serve?

What's In It for Teachers?

A sound investment earns a satisfactory return. The more risk you take, the more you can expect to gain or lose. This is true whether one is talking finance or personal fulfillment. Teachers have chosen a profession where financial rewards are scarce, but where psychic rewards can be great. Writing is one way to maximize the psychic rewards of the profession we have chosen. What's in writing for teachers is satisfaction, increased credibility, and personal and professional empowerment.

The satisfaction of writing: I teach a course on "Teaching Writing." It would be more accurate if I called this course, "Writing and Teaching Writing," because that is what I do. My students, teachers all, take pleasure in the poems, stories, and essays they write. I do not expect extraordinary writing, though I sometimes get it; I do not anticipate formal publication, though I occasionally recommend it when exceptional pieces are written. I publish my students' best work as an end-of-class project. Every teacher chooses one or two pieces for this class publication. No copies are sold, no royalties earned. Yet, teachers get enormous satisfaction from seeing their work published in our end-of-class books.

Most teachers relish writing once they have exorcised their anxieties. Teachers are talented and creative. They are often surprised to discover they enjoy writing or at least enjoy "having written," as Eudora Welty put it. Often, enjoyment is associated with sharing writing with others. Enjoyment of writing, however, may not arrive quickly. It will take time to develop your potential, and it will require an atmosphere of approval for your efforts. Kids are a great audience for teachers because they are nearly always generous with their approval and appreciative of a teacher's efforts. Teacher-writers generally have no intention of becoming professional writers, though many have. Most write for personal satisfaction, the intellectual challenge, or as an aid to teaching. These are all satisfactory outcomes, and if something more happens, all the better. When Terry Blackhawk first started writing poetry, she did not write for publication. But as her interest grew, she began submitting her poems to journals—and something more happened.

Shop Closed
(due to the death of the shoemaker)

I didn't even know his name, yet when I heard he'd died
I hoped he'd gone fishing and when he first felt the final jolt
he thought it some great walleye racing his line through the deep
before he knew it was really God reeling him in at last.

I don't know where I'll take my shoes now. Oh, something
will turn up, but I'll miss that clutter: the sheer adventure
of matching ticket to tag; the smell of leather and solvent,
his stuffed pheasant, a cat's paw on a sign.

Authentic, rustic—muttering, unshaven—I see him pawing
through piles of shoes, flesh hanging loose from arms once
strong—frames of a former self fixed to the wall. A summer day, the trout
held high. Mounted, too, the trophy fish, firmly preserved.

Terry Blackhawk

Terry Blackhawk's poem is a lovely evocation of the spirit of a working man's life. She sees in the shoemaker's shop a metaphor for life that likely escaped the notice of the shoemaker's regular patrons. But it was all there for anyone with an eye to see and an intent to record. It is just such everyday themes that are available for any writer. Whether our poems or stories are published is not what finally matters. Publication may be an occasional serendipity for the interested teacher, but it is not the goal. The goals include exploring possibilities, discovering capabilities, gaining satisfaction, and using writing as an instructional strategy.

Increased credibility: Credibility is a necessary, though insufficient, condition for effective teaching of writing. Writing does not, in itself, make an effective writing teacher. Effective teaching requires more than writing credentials, but writing can enhance credibility. Admittedly, credibility may be acquired in other ways. It may be rooted in personality, knowledge, empathy, talent, commitment—many things. But often credibility resides in students' awareness that you are a participant, not just a spectator. When you write with your students, you become a participant in their experience. Every poem, story, or essay a teacher writes and shares establishes credibility. Writing with your students says,

"I know what it is to write. I've experienced the problems and challenges you face. I, too, am a writer."

Personal and professional empowerment: There is nothing to writing. All you do is sit down at the typewriter and open a vein." So said the great sports writer, Red Smith. How long has it been since you "bled" over a piece of writing, reaching for the right word, noodling for an apt metaphor, untangling a sick sentence? Good writing is hard, and excellent writing is a miracle, and nothing makes you tingle like knowing you've chosen the exact word or written a sentence that sings. Puts you on top of the world—briefly. Of course, you plunge right back down again three sentences later, but that is part of the exhilaration. Writing is a roller coaster of emotions, a back and forth journey from the Valley of Despond to the top of Mt. Everest. It's empowering.

Whatever empowers us personally, empowers us professionally. When you write, you feel what your students feel as they face the frustrations and challenges of writing. It is not sufficient to have had these experiences years ago, too much has disappeared down the memory hole, too many miles have rumbled past. Writing with your students renews your belief in what you are doing, strengthens your conviction that you are on top of your profession. You realize that teaching kids to write is wondrous and impossible. Then something special happens; a kid you had just about given up on surprises you with an exceptional poem or story and you say to yourself, "I'm a great writing teacher." Powerful.

Why Write Poetry, Fiction, and Essays?

Teachers do technical writing almost daily: exams, quizzes, handouts, assignments. As necessary and useful as these forms are, they are only part of a teacher's writing repertoire. There are reasons for writing poetry, fiction, and essays. I discuss three of the reasons here: (1) familiarizes you with the forms your students write, (2) stimulates the creative impulse, and (3) banishes fear of writing.

Familiarizes you with the forms your students write: Wilderness guides would hesitate to lead followers down paths not recently trod. Guides must recognize land marks, wild life, topography, and botanical features. Writing teachers are like wilderness guides. They lead students down paths recently explored, take them to places they have been, introduce them to experiences they have had, share knowledge they have acquired, discuss composing problems they have encountered. In short, teachers who write are better prepared to lead students along writing pathways they want their students to explore.

When teachers write they experience the same problems their students face. Suppose, for instance, you want your students to write free verse. Having written a free verse poem, you have wrestled with issues your students will encounter: What will I write about? Where do I begin? How do I punctuate free verse? Are there traditional topics for free verse? What are the rules, if any, for free verse? Is what I've written any good? Will others like what I wrote? You cannot experience these issues vicariously; you have to experience them directly.

There is no substitute for direct, recent experience with the forms you want your students to learn. It is one thing to say, "Write a poem" and quite another to say, "Before we begin writing poetry, I want to share a poem that I wrote"; or "I have a first draft of a poem I've started. I'd like your ideas on how I might improve it." In her diary entry, Ms. DeWard tells how her own writing efforts put her through the same struggles, roadblocks, and triumphs that her students face when they write.

DIARY OF A TEACHER: Jennifer DeWard

Over the past four years that I have been teaching, I have learned how important it is for me to write and share my writing with my students. I believe that when I write, I encounter the same struggles, roadblocks, and triumphs that my students experience in my classroom.

Of course, teachers have enough responsibilities with grading papers, lesson planning, and attending PTA meetings. I am just like you. Some evenings I am so overwhelmed with teaching related tasks that it seems I will never make it to the weekend. However, I usually find some time to write a short piece to share with my students. The benefits are well worth it.

Sit down one evening and brainstorm ideas for a story about your family. Don't worry about making your paper neat and tidy—students need to see that brainstorming can take many forms. Then, spend fifteen minutes writing a one page "sloppy copy" to share with your class. Make overhead transparencies so that your writing can be easily viewed. Ask your students for their suggestions. If you feel uneasy about children critiquing your writing, imagine how nervous your students become when you critique their writing. Over the next week, share successive drafts of your writing. As your drafts steadily improve, your students will realize that revision makes writing better. They will love to look at your sloppy copies, so be sure to display them in the room. You will be amazed at how many students model interesting things that you have done without even realizing where their brilliant ideas came from. I bet that your class will eagerly anticipate the next draft of your story, and you will be pleasantly surprised at how easy it is to write when you have a receptive audience.

Awakens the creative impulse: While not everyone is equally creative, there is creative potential in everyone. Writing is an art form, and under the right conditions writing stimulates the emergence of creativity. Children are influenced by the examples of creative endeavor that surround them. This is especially so when students and teachers are members of a creative community. The writing class can be a creative community. When teachers write with their students, the community of writers has a wholeness, a completeness that is missing when they do not participate. Ms. Dalmage created a writing community in her first grade classroom. She believed that writing could be a catalyst for creative endeavor. She believed that if she wrote, her children would participate more robustly. She wrote a story for her children, told them she had written it just for them. Melissa's response illustrates the influence Ms. Dalmage's story had on one child's imagination, "Ms. Dalmage, did you *really* write that story for *us?*" Ms. Dalmage's answer confirmed what Melissa already suspected: "Yes, Melissa, I wrote that story just for you." Melissa returned to her seat with a gratified look on her face. This bit of intelligence impressed Melissa and her classmates mightily. Ms. Dalmage was part of the writing community she had created in her classroom. Melissa and her classmates wrote well and often throughout the year. The creative spirit rarely slumbers in Ms. Dalmage's first grade classroom.

Banishes fear of writing: Fear erects barriers. It keeps us from exploring our creative potential. But fear can be overcome. Most of my students fear writing. They think writing is for those who have "special talents," and they seldom count themselves among the specially talented. They think writing is a gift, given or withheld at birth, rather than a craft to be learned. Teachers express these concerns, and I take them seriously; their concerns are genuine, they are not flimsy excuses.

Fear of writing sometimes has roots in unpleasant, even devastating, experiences in school. Someone has stomped upon a child's efforts, or more benignly, neglected a child's potential. Chloe, an imaginative second grader, got stomped on. She handed a story about "imaginary" people to her teacher who read it and ripped it up in front of Chloe and the class. She sent Chloe to her seat to write a "better" story. The story Chloe had written "had too much imagination." Chloe stopped writing, and for the remainder of the school year pleaded with her mother to stay home from school. As school ended, Chloe's mother sought help, and enrolled Chloe in Oakland University's Summer Reading Clinic. Soon Chloe was writing imaginative stories again, and her teacher, Ms. DeJong, noticed a distinct "Chloe voice." As the clinic ended, Ms. DeJong asked, "Chloe what did you learn in the clinic?" Chloe responded, "I learned that I have an imagination." Only then, on the last day of the clinic, did Ms. DeJong learn from Chloe's mother of Chloe's devastating experience. But wait a minute! There are two teaching stories here. One teacher stomped on a child; another teacher, Ms. DeJong, unaware of Chloe's terrible experience, restored Chloe's confidence and gave Chloe back her imagination.

Some folks have uncritically accepted the canard, "Writers are born, not made." Perhaps some are, though a writing gene has yet to be identified, and even if one were identified there must still be environmental influences. I believe everyone has some writing potential; I believe there is creative power within every individual. Creative potential can be exploited by environmental influences, and in this context I am speaking of the influence of a good teacher. Risks must be taken if potential is to be realized, and many are reluctant to take risks. Reluctance, however, can be overcome when the writing environment is safe, where a community of writers has been established by a good teacher. The safer the writing environment the more likely one is to take risks.

Ms. Hough feared writing poetry and feared sharing her poetry even more. Her poem, "Road Block," tells of her struggle to write her first poem. It is a remarkable success for a first effort and a thoughtful description of her struggle to write her first poem. Her fellow students received her poem generously; an atmosphere of acceptance and appreciation made the risk acceptable. She was delighted and surprised. Later, she shared her poem with her students. Subsequently she wrote other poems and stories. She overcame her fear and learned to trust her own potential.

Road Block

Road block, mental block.
Traffic stopped, thoughts stopped.
Casting concern for my pride to the roadside,
I frantically put pen to paper,
Searching for an alternate route.

Can I summon the courage to
Expose my vulnerability,
Breaking through the block
In what seems to be a suicidal attempt
To express my thoughts?

But as I write, I find the block
Is merely an illusion.
Like a mirage, it fades as I draw closer,
Vanishing in the glow of
Unexpected discoveries.

Susan Hough

If you hesitate to write, consider the action that Ms. Hough took. Throw off the shackles of fear that keep you from exploring your writing potential. You may find, as Ms. Hough did, that your fears will vanish, ". . . in the glow of unexpected discoveries." Break out of the protective cocoon you may have woven around yourself. It will not be easy, but it will be rewarding. Take risks. Expose your vulnerability, and you will discover your inner writing voice.

How Much Time, Energy, and Commitment Will Writing Require?

How long does it take to drive from New York to Los Angeles? You can't answer that question in the abstract. You need data. What vehicle will be driven? How many drivers? Must speed limits be obeyed? What route will be taken? What will the weather be like? Answers to questions depend on variables, some of which may be difficult to calculate. Just so, with the question, "How much time, energy, and commitment does writing require?" This question can only be answered authoritatively by each individual who chooses to consider the issues, calculate the cost, and arrive at a decision.

Michael Steinberg (1994), a high school teacher, made a commitment to write with his students. He had spent a summer in a writing program, and found pleasure in doing so. Here he could write without the burden of teaching all day. But summers end, and when he returned to teaching he struggled to find the time and energy to write:

Before I returned to the classroom last fall I was worried that I'd lost my passion for teaching. Once I got back into teaching I was afraid my duties and obligations would diminish my writing time. At first that's exactly what happened. I couldn't focus on writing the way I could when I had all day to write. But I've since learned to write for the joys and surprise, and for the sheer love of putting words on the page. Now when teaching and committee meetings and paper grading become a burden, the writing is my therapy. (pp. 17–18)

No use pretending otherwise, a decision to write takes time, energy, and commitment. How much is required? Is it worth the candle? No one can answer for you; you have to find out for yourself. Here are some questions that may arise as you begin the journey:

How often should I write?

What kinds of writing interest me?

What will I write about?

Where will I find the time and energy to write?

Should I share my writing with my students?

What instructional uses can I make of my writing?

Will I stick with writing long enough to give it a fair trial?

I cannot give you an answer to the question, "How much time, energy and commitment does writing require?" It is a constant struggle to write, no matter the amount of time, energy, and commitment one possesses. Maybe you can only write once a week for an hour. If so, start with the one hour. I have found my writing is never simply an upward curve. My writing dips into valleys more often than it rises to mountain peaks. I suspect this is normal. You will experience similar valleys and mountain peaks. If you have written in the past and now find that years have gone by without much writing, take up your pen again. You have not forgotten how to write, though your technique may be rusty. It's like riding a bike. You never forget how to push the pedals, though you may wobble around the first time you remount. Same way with writing. You don't forget, but you may wobble.

Carmeneta is one of those writing teachers who doesn't wobble. She loves writing, and she constantly strives to improve her writing. Carmeneta Jones teaches in Jamaica, and has spent the past year at Oakland University studying for her Master's degree in Reading and Language Arts. Carmeneta teaches in classrooms with few of the amenities common in American schools. And while she may not enjoy the amenities of American classrooms, she has something even more valuable—a wise philosophy of instruction. In her poem, "Education in Crisis I," Carmeneta writes about teaching practices she deplores.

Education in Crisis I

Education in crisis!
I can't believe this.
Things of the past
Still today exist.
"Think what I say.
Do as I tell you.

Do this my child.
Abide. It's a rule.

We still have cows jumping over the moon.
A spoon can only be defined as a "spoon,"
You dare not call it a ladle.
Stick to the meaning in your dictionary
Cause context clues are deemed unnecessary.
Recall the black and white,
Retrieve it from your memory."

There are many questions you may wish to ask,
Dare you to interrupt "School Master's" class?
And all you zealous learners
With your multiplicity of interpretations,
You dare not question the teacher's elucidation!
There is only one politically right answer
Flowing from **THE** exclusive source,
The repertoire of the wiseacre. . .
"Open your receptacles, I'll replenish them.
Education today is our greatest mayhem."

I sit firmly at the top
In this competitive
Intellectual workshop.
This ladder you see
Accommodates only a few
Selectively hand-picked
By the who knows who.
So your talent is dungled and mired,
Cause **I AM** the Chosen One
Authority has hired.

You knock at my door
With your new thinking,
But to my anachronistic ways,
I'll die clinging. You see,
A seasoned pedagogue am I
Pedantic is the style.
"It keeps my faculties alive."

In this technologically advanced era
Electronic devices fashion the future
But withheld from minds wishing to put them to use.
Prettifying the "four walls" is unforgivable misuse.
The more things change, they remain the very same
Denying masters of the future is a nation's shame.
And this education ministry!

Is it a source of society's misery?
Lisa Delpit acclaims it is a God-given right

OUR CHILDREN CAN ALL
LEARN TO READ AND WRITE!
So teacher, only expert in the classroom,
Disregarding student's knowledge
Will "Dis" em power.

Can pupils forever play the role, Little Miss Muffet
Sitting comfortably on prescribed tuffet?
Evaluate their status to Literate Jack Honors?

Education today does not need a crisis.
Some things of the past we must resist.
The dawning of the millennium
Bids a debugging of the system.
Children learn according to their rhythm.
Literacy advances economic progress.
Bells are chiming, "Enrich the process!"
New ideas can improve the old tradition.
Au! We need balanced literacy instruction.
Teachers all, send your voices a echoing,
It's time you part take in the policy making.
Your collegial effort can only be good.
A demonstration of professional brotherhood.

Carmenta Jones

What Instructional Purposes Does Writing Serve?

Robbins (1996) conducted a year-long study of twelve English teachers to investigate relationships between teachers' personal writing and their approaches to writing instruction. He found that most did not believe that writing made them writers. Neither did they see much connection between their writing and their teaching. They believed that to be a writer is to be exceptional. If you hold these views, I hope to persuade you that there is a tight connection between yourself as a writer and your work as a teacher of writing. I hope to persuade you that writing is not the exclusive preserve of the gifted. On the contrary, writing is a democratic art form; everyone can do it, albeit at different levels of capability.

Does writing have any instructional benefits? Yes, and they are very practical. First, writing enables you to serve as a credible model for your students, a powerful teaching tool. Second, writing aligns teaching with practice—it enables you to practice what you preach. Ms. Kristin Wilson found that becoming a writer helped her eighth graders overcome their reluctance to write. In her "Voices" piece, Ms. Wilson tells how writing for her students helped make her a better teacher of writing.

VOICES FROM THE CLASSROOM: Kristin Wilson

Teachers as Writers

I have 24 eighth grade students, and I had been having a difficult time getting them to write. Then I discovered a simple way to break through the barrier. I became a writer for them. This is how I started. We read a story about bravery and discussed it. I told them I was going to work on a piece about my brother who had triumphed over his learning disability. I modeled on the overhead, listing ideas I might include in my story. They were touched.

For the next week we worked with partners drafting and revising our stories. I had a partner just like they did. Each day I showed them the progress I had made. This got them really involved in helping me tell my story. Each time I shared my draft, I felt nervous. I couldn't believe it! I, their teacher, felt nervous when students read my piece. Then I realized how nervous they must feel when I read their pieces—and graded them. That's when I knew how important it was for me to remain a writer and make myself vulnerable. There are two reasons why I write.

The first reason is to make myself a better teacher. I felt like one of the students working on my rough drafts. I knew they would be shared with my partner and eventually the entire class. I had the same feelings they had; I went through the same work; I got stuck like they did; I felt proud when I finished just like they did. It is hard to share your writing because you expose yourself in so many ways. You're not only sharing your thoughts and experiences, but you're inviting criticism.

The second reason is to let my students know me better. This allows me to know them better. I couldn't believe how much sharing this one story opened their hearts and minds to me. The "simple" idea of becoming a writer in front of my students no longer felt simple. Although it was difficult, the payoff was unbelievable.

Models writing for students: Much of learning is based on modeling, a form of imitation. Writers, at least the candid ones, describe their early writing efforts as imitative. Garrison Keillor (1995) tried to write like E. B. White and A. J. Liebling, excellent role models, indeed. Keillor said, "I tried awfully hard to imitate them, and that helps you to get through a lot of your own dreadful early writing and get into something else" (p. 121). Woody Allen (1995) said, "But I found myself able to write in a comic mode, at first directly imitative of Shulman or sometimes Perelman. In my brief abortive year in college I'd hand in my papers, all of them written in a bad (or good) derivation of Shulman. I had no sense of myself at all" (p. 204). Keillor and Allen eventually acquired their own writing voice and without damaging their creativity and originality. As a practical matter, you cannot stifle personality. *Personality will win out.* There is ample evidence that modeling is nothing more than a normal way of acquiring writing technique. And that is why modeling, imitation if you prefer, is beneficial rather than harmful to writing growth.

Nearly every craft or profession sponsors some form of modeling, though it is not usually so identified. For instance, art students copy paintings of the masters. Their copies are critiqued by an experienced artist. They discuss progress and the

Renee is involved in a writing project in which she and her classmates have talked, read, discussed, and researched dinosaurs. Renee and her classmates have written poems, stories, and reports about dinosaurs.

students return to the museum and copy some more. Surgical residents observe experienced surgeons. Initially, they are given minor responsibilities: "Sew this patient back up." Gradually, residents are initiated into more complex elements of surgery. All the while, experienced surgeons model the procedures and talk about what is happening and why. Think of your work with young writers as the experienced writer gradually initiating your "residents" into the craft of writing. You model the procedures; you talk about what you're doing; you explain why you do it this way or that. You hold a sacred position in the lives of your students. No one else can match the influence you have over your students.

There are many ways to model writing. Usually they are accompanied by think-aloud procedures, talking about what you are doing as you do it. Four examples for modeling writing with children are shown below.

MODELING WRITING WITH CHILDREN

1. Write as your students write. For instance, if you have scheduled a 40-minute writing session, tell students that you intend to write for 10 minutes while they are writing. Then share your writing. This makes it easier for students to share their writing.

2. Write initial drafts of poems, essays, stories, or reports on an overhead projector. As you write, talk about writing. For instance, write two leads to an essay, explaining, as you write, the value of more than one lead.

3. Revise a draft of your own writing, using an overhead projector. Talk about ideas you have for improving it, illustrating changes as you go. Ask students to suggest changes, and talk about their suggestions as you implement them.

4. Bring a finished piece of your writing to class, and use it to introduce the writing of stories, poems, or essays. As you read your piece, tell how you went about writing it, how you arrived at a topic, how you got started, the drafts you went through, problems you encountered.

Many teachers want to be writing models, but they wonder if they can do it; they wonder if writing is necessary or useful. Don't feel you are alone in this struggle. Sharon Miller (1994) wanted to be a model for her students, yet she struggled against the idea. There must be some other way, she thought. Eventually she decided she had to write. You may fight a similar battle when you confront the question, "Should I write?"

> In my heart I sincerely wanted to change as a teacher of reading and writing and believed that I could teach reading and writing in this new way without being a writer myself. Surely I could change everything else, follow every prescribed detail but that one minor one and still succeed. What I'd failed to realize was that I had to know what I was doing to be able to help my students. (p. 32)

Aligns teaching with practice: Rief (1994) quotes a remark made by a student to her teacher: "You know what I like about this class? You're not like the gym teacher. Like when she coaches swimming, she never gets in the pool. She never gets wet. She just stands on the side yelling, 'Go faster! Go faster!' " (p. 92). Perhaps the writing teacher who never writes is like the swimming coach who never gets wet. If we never write with our students, aren't we standing poolside yelling, "Write better! Write better!"—all the while refusing to get wet? Might not our credibility as a writing teacher be enhanced if we plunged into the pool now and then and did a little writing with our students?

Students know what we value by what we do, not by what we say. The writing teacher is a living example of aligning teaching with practice. Its opposite is expressed in the saying, "Don't do what I do, do what I say." But this maxim doesn't work because it is based on a flawed premise. Children are inclined to do what their mentors, heroes, and teachers do and less inclined to do what they say. Teachers can usually require compliance with their words, but forced compliance is not effective. When we combine what we say with what we do, we have a powerful teaching environment, a melding of word and deed. This combination creates the most credible teaching-learning context.

Writing can have a beneficial influence on teaching, but it will not eradicate other teaching shortcomings. Undoubtedly, there are excellent teachers of writing who do little writing of the sort I am advocating. It is also likely that there are teachers who write but are, nevertheless, ineffective teachers of writing. The teacher who writes does not acquire a magic elixir that transforms mediocre teaching into excellent teaching. Teaching is too complex to yield to simplistic formulas. Good teaching is a marvelously textured concatenation of capabilities. Writing will not catapult you into the teaching hall of fame, if there were such a place, but it might advance your chances of getting into this mythical kingdom.

SUMMARY OF REASONS WHY TEACHERS SHOULD WRITE

1. Teachers who write are rewarded in three ways: personal satisfaction is derived from exercising one's creative talents, credibility is enhanced among one's students, and personal and professional empowerment results from facing the challenge of writing.

2. There are three reasons for teachers to write poetry, fiction, and essays: it familiarizes teachers with the forms their students write, it awakens the creative impulse within teachers, and it helps banish the fear of writing.

3. A decision to write does take time, energy, and commitment; how much time, energy, and commitment can only be determined by each individual teacher.

4. Writing provides at least two important instructional benefits: it enhances credibility as a writing teacher, and it aligns teaching with practice.

IDEAS FOR WRITING

1. **Make a commitment:** The journey into writing begins the day you make a commitment to write. Writers learn to write by writing. Like any skill, time must be invested in what you are learning. You're not trying to become a Steinbeck or a Thurber, you're only becoming better than you are.

2. **Choose writing models:** Identify a few writers and read their works. Whether you emulate a columnist, novelist, poet, or journalist doesn't matter. Take Faulkner's advice and see if it works for you: Read. Read everything. Serve your apprenticeship with the masters. Then write.

3. **Don't be afraid:** If you let fear predominate, you will never write. Your first writings won't be your best, but they will start you toward your goal of writing for pleasure and as a role model for your students. Your journey into writing can be an adventure. It may be difficult to start, but jump right in and write. Your journey will have its peaks and valleys, every journey does. If you get sidetracked, let your students and writing colleagues help you get back on track.

4. **Enroll in a writing course:** Many universities and colleges offer writing courses at the graduate and undergraduate level. Belonging to a commu-

nity of writers will give you the support you need to develop the habit of writing regularly. Your life is full of stories waiting to be told. These stories can be shared with your students. Your experience as a writer will help you develop a writing community in your classroom.

5. Enroll in a summer writing project: Writing seminars may be offered through your local university or school district. These projects typically run five days a week for three to six weeks and may offer university credit. A writing project setting will give you the opportunity to be part of a writing community where you will receive constructive feedback from members of your writing community. Participants share writing techniques. They read their pieces to one another. Friendships develop as you share the pain and pleasure of writing, and these friendships often continue long after the summer is over. It is an opportunity to discover the writer within you.

6. Start a journal: Purchase a journal and carry it with you everywhere you go. Jot notes about interesting or unexpected events. Write about feelings of delight and days clouded with sorrow. Take a trip to a park, pause and write about all that you see, hear, smell, or feel. Some writers keep journals for specific purposes, such as a travel journal, in which they record their experiences in new places. Find time every day to write, if only briefly, in your journal. After a while, you may find yourself thinking about what you want to write in your journal and how you're going to write it. This is a good sign because it means writing is becoming a habit and you're rehearsing what you might say. Another benefit of journal writing is that you are your own audience. For novice writers, a journal is a nonthreatening, productive way to build fluency, confidence, and the realization that you have something worth saying.

7. Start a writing group: Readers get together to discuss books they've read, so why not a group where writers meet to share their writing? Invite your colleagues to meet after school to share their writings. Talk about how the writing is going and how to keep writing. Writers need an audience. A writing group provides the support needed, and it is a wonderful way to build relationships with colleagues. If there aren't enough interested colleagues in your building, extend the invitation to a neighboring school or people in the community.

8. Read: Locate books on writing and teaching writing. There are many excellent resources that will enrich your teaching and writing life.

   - Strunk W. and E. B. White. (1959). *The elements of style*. New York: Macmillan Publishing Co. Paperback of fewer than 100 pages. Perhaps the most popular book on writing ever published.
   - Zinsser, W. (1980). *On writing well*. New York: Harper and Row. Excellent advice for any writer, and especially beginning writers.
   - *Paris Review:* Poems, essays, stories, and interviews with top writers; first published in 1953; many editions have been published since.
   - National Public Radio Audiotapes: Writers talking about their writing and their writing process.

- Murray, D. (1985). *A writer teaches writing.* Boston: Houghton Mifflin. Excellent advice on writing and teaching writing.
- Murray, D. (1989). *Expecting the unexpected.* Portsmouth, NH: Boynton/Cook. Collection of 24 of Murray's articles on teaching writing.
- Atwell, N. (1998). *In the middle: New understandings about writing, reading, and learning,* 2nd ed. Portsmouth, NH: Boynton/Cook. Best book on writing for middle, junior high, and high school teachers.
- Calkins, L. (1994). *The art of teaching writing,* 2nd ed. Portsmouth, NH: Heinemann. Many ideas for writing and teaching writing.
- Graves, D. (1994). *A fresh look at writing.* Portsmouth, NH: Heinemann. Writing activities and actions which encourage the reader-writer to write and reflect.

REFLECTION AND SUMMARY

Reflection

Priorities are an issue in the lives of busy people. Teachers are busy with so many tasks that it is difficult to know how to prioritize. Instruction must be planned, papers read, parents kept informed, committee assignments completed, family responsibilities tended. In the midst of these responsibilities, is it just too much to consider writing an additional priority? I cannot answer this question for you; you have to answer it yourself. Still, I make this simple case for including writing on your list of priorities, *writing aids instruction.* If writing is to have a place on your list of priorities, it must have a niche in the time you spend preparing for instruction. If you cannot justify placing writing in this category, perhaps it is because I have failed to make a persuasive case. Or, perhaps you are persuaded, but hesitate to take that existential leap into the dark. My advice—leap. Chances are you won't hit bottom, but if you do at least you had the guts to take the leap.

Summary

1. Four reasons were given that presented the negative side of the question, "Should teachers write?"
   - Writing is not professionally advantageous.
   - Realistically, teachers' schedules and responsibilities do not permit writing.
   - Teachers already do lots of "technical" writing.
   - "Serious" writing requires too much commitment, discipline, and time.

2. Four reasons were given that presented the positive side of the question, "Should teachers write?"
   - Writing provides satisfaction, increased credibility, and personal and professional empowerment.
   - Writing poetry, fiction, and essays familiarizes you with the forms your students write, stimulates the creative impulse, and banishes fear of writing.

- Teacher-writers must set their own priorities and answer their own questions regarding how much time, energy, and commitment they can devote to writing.
- Writing helps you model the writing process and aligns teaching with practice.

QUESTIONS FOR REFLECTIVE THINKING

1. Jost says that writing is not professionally advantageous for teachers. Do you agree or disagree? Make a case for or against Jost's position.

2. Given that teachers are busy with the many important routines of teaching, should they be expected to write with their students? Defend your position.

3. Do you agree or disagree that the "technical" writing teachers routinely do (e.g., tests and handouts) is sufficient exposure to writing? Make a case for your position.

4. The author claims that an investment in writing provides teachers with "a satisfactory return." What "returns" does the author envision?

5. The author states that, "there is creative potential in everyone." Do you agree or disagree with this position? Make a case for your position.

6. Make your own best case for or against the proposition, "Teachers should write and be a writing model for their children."

7. In what area or areas do you have significant agreements or disagreements with the author? Choose one or two areas and explain.

8. What did you learn in this chapter that you didn't know before you read it?

9. Mini case study: Your high school principal has called you to her office. It seems your principal, in visiting your classroom recently, found you writing poems at your desk while your students were also writing poems. You anticipate a possible reprimand for writing poems when you should have been teaching. What will you say to your principal in defense of what you were doing when she visited?

REFERENCES

Allen, W. (1995). "The art of humor I." *The Paris Review,* Vol. 37, No. 136.

Blackhawk, T. (1998). *Trio: Voices from the myths.* Roseville, MI: Ridgeway Press.

Jost, K. (1990). "Why high-school writing teachers should not write." *English Journal,* March, 1990, pp. 65–66.

Keillor, G. (1995). "The art of humor II." *The Paris Review,* Vol. 37, No. 136.

Miller, S. L. (1994). "A teacher writes to find her way." *Workshop: The teacher as writer,* Maureen Barbieri and Linda Rief, Eds. Heinemann: Portsmouth, ME, pp. 31–38.

Rief, L. (1994). "Writing for life: Teacher and students." *Workshop: The teacher as writer,* Maureen Barbieri and Linda Rief, Eds. Heinemann: Portsmouth, ME, pp. 84–101.

Robbins, B. W. (1996). "Teachers as writers: Tensions between theory and practice." *Journal of Teaching Writing,* Vol. 15, No. 1, pp. 107–128.

Steinberg, M. (1994). "Teachers writing, writers teaching: Serving two passions." *Workshop: The teacher as writer,* Maureen Barbieri and Linda Rief, Eds. Heinemann: Portsmouth, ME, pp. 10–17.

CHAPTER 11

Writing Poetry with Children

Alas for those who never sing, but die with all their music in them.

Oliver Wendell Holmes

It is the supreme art of teachers to awaken the joy in creative expression and knowledge.

Albert Einstein

A WRITER'S STORY

I had lived in England for three months, and knew no one, or so I thought. Sipping tea and reading The Herald Tribune *in Betty's, a quaint restaurant in downtown York, I looked up and saw an old friend, Geoffrey Summerfield. We had been colleagues at the University of Nebraska a decade earlier. After tea, Geoffrey invited me to a poetry reading. Ted Hughes, an eminent English poet, was to read his poetry. I had never heard poetry read aloud by a poet, and I had little interest in hearing one, either, but I wanted to be with my friend, so I went. That evening changed my view of poetry forever. It changed my perception of the value of poetry for children; it changed my opinion about who could write poetry. For the first time, it occurred to me that I could write poetry. The next day I wrote my first poem. I've written many poems since, but I have never submitted a poem for publication. I do not know if they are publishable, but that doesn't matter. I have an audience for my poems—my children, students, friends. They seem to like them, and that is pleasure enough.*

I learned to value the creative side of my nature, to cherish my personal experiences for they are the substance of any poetry that is in me. Writing poems, such as they are, has put me at ease with the poetry of others. I now enjoy inviting children and teachers to poetry. I know some of them will discover their own poetic voice, listen to the music of their own words, create their own poetry. If you pick up this book in the belief that you have no poetry in you, I hope that when you put it down you will see how seriously you have underestimated yourself.

INTRODUCTION

"Poetry is when you talk to yourself," Mearns (1929) told his fourth grade kids. He illustrated his definition by reading excerpts of children "talking to themselves" on the playground and in the classroom. He showed them how forcefully and eloquently they expressed themselves in natural settings that seemingly had nothing to do with poetry. While Mearns knew his definition of poetry was incomplete, he wanted a starting point that would appeal to his fourth graders. He knew there were hidden treasures in their everyday language. He sought to honor the language power they possessed, but dismissed as mere talk. He succeeded because he understood that reluctance to use language is not the same thing as the inability to use it. "Talking to yourself poetry" illustrated his point and started his fourth graders down the road that leads to poetic writing. It takes time and effort to create a poetry writing program, and you need practical ideas and guiding principles that will sustain poetic writing. The following ideas and principles will help you develop the poetic instincts of your children.

IDEAS AND PRINCIPLES FOR DEVELOPING CHILDREN'S POETIC INSTINCTS

Nurture Children's Creative Spirit

Creative power must be nurtured. Eddie, a seventh grader, read like a second grader. His teachers considered him hostile, a juvenile delinquent in the making. He dressed and groomed himself to cultivate the image of a rebel. Outwardly, he appeared sullen and uncommunicative. Fortunately, one teacher, Ms. Morgan, saw beneath his facade. She discovered he had a remarkable talent for drawing, and a curiously gentle side that belied his outward demeanor. Ms. Morgan, imitating the Little Engine that Could, taught Eddie to read and write. She described her strategy this way: "I used art as an entry to Eddie's mind and kindness to restore his damaged self-image." There is no simple formula for awakening the creative spirit within children, but there is always a place to start. Success is never assured, but the only true failure is not to try. The suggestions below will nurture the creative spirit slumbering beneath the surface of youthful insecurity.

NURTURING CHILDREN'S CREATIVE INSTINCTS

1. The early stages of creative endeavor are sometimes chaotic and uncertain. During these times particularly, children need approval from individuals they respect—parents, teachers, peers. When they get it, they will work hard to continue meriting approval.

2. Cultivate an openness of mind and spirit. Openness is not flabby and vacuous, and it does not require the uncritical acceptance of poor ideas as the equal of good ones. Openness is a vigorous state of mind charac-

terized by the presence of one's own ideas and opinions but, neverthe-less, receptive to children's ideas and opinions.

3. Place your highest value on ideas, and allow the mechanics of writing to take their rightful place as the handmaiden of good writing. Grammar and mechanics must be taught, should be taught, but they are best acquired within the context of meaningful writing. No amount of grammatical or mechanical sophistication can turn a poor idea into a good one.

4. Steadfastly maintain faith in the creativity of your children; remain calm and self-assured when your faith is tested. Patience is needed to receive the uninspired products that inevitably precede the inspired. Patience is also needed to wait through the long periods when little is produced to reward your faith in the creativity of children.

Present Poems and Poets

Experiencing poems: Enjoying poetry may be an acquired taste, like learning to like spinach. Children may love humorous poetry on first exposure, other types may require cultivating taste. Most children enjoy rhyme, but they can come to enjoy free verse. Most children enjoy nonsense poems, and they can come to appreciate serious poems. Children's experience with poetry can be broadened and certainly should be. Seek out poetic anthologies that have a broad range of uses: poems to be read aloud, children's favorite poems, humorous poems, tragic poems, poems suitable for modeling, poems about death and loss. The following list contains most, if not all, of these categories. The teacher who is interested in acquiring her own library of such books can do so readily enough at bookstores, book sales, flea markets, and local libraries. Eight anthologies of poems for children are:

1. John Ciardi. (1963). *You read to me, I'll read to you.* New York: Lippencott.

2. Hana Volavkova, Ed. (1993). *I never saw another butterfly: Children's drawings and poems from Terezin Concentration Camp 1942–1944.* New York: Shocken Books.

3. Carol Ann Duffy, Ed. (1996). *Stopping for death: Poems of death and loss.* New York: Henry Holt and Co., Inc.

4. David Booth, Ed. (1989). *'Til all the stars have fallen: A collection of poems for children.* New York: Viking Penguin

5. Javaka Steptoe, Ed. (1997). *In daddy's arms I am tall: African Americans celebrating fathers.* New York: Lee and Low Books.

6. X. J. Kennedy and Dorothy M. Kennedy, Eds. (1982). *Knock at a star: A child's introduction to poetry.* Boston: Little, Brown and Co.

7. Eloise Greenfield. (1978). *Honey I love and other love poems.* New York: HarperCollins Publishers.

8. X. J. Kennedy and Dorothy M. Kennedy, Eds. (1992). *Talking like the rain: A read to me book of poems.* Canada: Little, Brown and Co.

Experiencing poets: The value of poetry is enhanced when we consider the poet and poetry in close proximity. Like adults, children know little about poets. We have all heard of the starving artist, mostly as a metaphor. But the idea of the starving artist is not entirely a joke. Even America's finest poets seldom make a living from their published poems. Most poets make a living teaching, editing, driving a truck. Whatever it takes. They live next door, teach down the hall, check out your library books. There is a pool of poetic talent in every community. They may not be professional poets, few people are; they may not be widely published, even fewer attain this distinction. Nevertheless, they are a resource for stimulating interest in poetry among children.

Most children have never seen or heard poets recite their poems. Children need to know about poets; personal stories that show the human dimension; professional experiences that illustrate the poet at work. A modicum of information about poets is useful and often fascinating to those who are engaged in reading, writing, and listening to poetry. The first time I heard a poet tell why he had written a certain poem, I understood the connection between his words and the experience that led to his poems. If you can locate a local poet, invite him or her into your classroom to read poems and talk about writing poetry. If you can't find a poet, perhaps the next best thing is to find brief biographical sketches and read them to your children.

Bernice Cullinan edited a book of poems, *A Jar of Tiny Stars,* which contains a selection of poems by ten award-winning poets and brief biographical sketches of each poet. The poems were selected by children as their favorites from among the works of Arnold Adoff, John Ciardi, Barbara Esbensen, Aileen Fisher, Karla Kuskin, Myra Cohn Livingston, David McCord, Eve Merriam, Lilian Moore, and Valerie Worth.

Develop an Appreciation for Poetry

Poetry is rooted in the emotional side of our natures rather than the intellectual. Walter (1962) said, "When we read poetry with real understanding, we seek to share the poet's emotional experiences or to find in his experiences a reflection of our own" (p. 57). Poetry emerged among our ancestors as an expression of their emotions not their intellects.

English majors may experience only the intellectual side of poetry if they are taught to dissect poetry piece-by-piece, much as a medical student might dissect a cadaver. But dissection does not often lead to a deeper understanding of a poem's personal meaning, does not purchase appreciation of a poem's beauty, does not arouse an emotional response in our inner spirit.

An emotional response to poetry does not require an emotional outburst. Children recognize and will reject unwarranted gushing over poetry. What is needed is a favorable response, and this begins with the teacher's response to poetry. If you must honestly confess to indifference to poetry, then the right place to start is with yourself. In that case, some of the suggestions listed on page 275 for generating an appreciation for poetry apply to you as well as to your children.

DEVELOPING APPRECIATION FOR POETRY

1. Start with the known. Most children have heard some poetry, though they might not have thought of it as poetry. Share the familiar, then introduce the unfamiliar. Mother Goose rhymes, poetic songs, jump rope rhymes are familiar and may serve as an introduction. Young children are especially attracted to humorous and nonsense poetry. Read aloud examples such as: (1) Song: "Blowing in the Wind," Bob Dylan; (2) Song: "Puff the Magic Dragon," Shel Silverstein; (3) Humor: "Little Abigail and the Beautiful Pony," Shel Silverstein.

2. Associate poetry with pleasurable activity. Choose your favorite poems and read them aloud. Invite children to recite poems in chorus. Encourage children to choose a poem and illustrate it. Urge children to bring poems from home that they have clipped from newspapers, books, or magazines. Offer opportunities to memorize and recite a poem or verse of a poem. Have children copy favorite poems into their personal poetic journal.

3. Start where children are and broaden their poetic horizons gradually. Even silly verse can serve a purpose. A colleague of mine remembers his father's favorite verse which became his favorite, as a boy:
   The boy stood on the burning deck
   His feet were full of blisters.
   He looked aloft, his pants fell off
   And now he wears his sister's.

The silly poem that grabbed my friend's attention is delightfully nonsensical and mildly risque. I suspect nonsense and mildly risque subject matter may account for the extraordinary popularity of Shel Silverstein's poems. Some will argue that such poems are unsuitable for young children. Others may insist that such poems are not poetry at all, merely verse. But whether verse or poetry the idea is to get kids interested. Taste can be elevated, but first you have to get children to the table.

Stimulate Observation and Imagination

Observation is essential to good writing. It gives writers the raw material on which imagination is imposed. There is value in keenly observing the world that surrounds us, *not merely seeing, but observing.* Writing poetry requires a marriage between imagination and observation. Imagination gives poetry its wings, its special distinctiveness. It is perhaps poetry's most remarkable quality. Imagination is not a magic carpet, an ethereal other worldly concept. It, too, is grounded in reality. Robertson Davies said imagination is, "A good horse to carry you over the ground—not a flying carpet to set you free from probability" (Brussell, 1988, p. 277). Walter distinguishes between imagination and observation in the following example.

Suppose you look out the window and say, "Oh, I see a butterfly!" Have you used imagination? Not if the butterfly is really there. Suppose you say, "I see a pretty yellow butterfly on the purple flowers." Have you used imagination? Not yet. The butterfly is there and the flowers are there, and they really are a butterfly and flowers. But suppose you think about the butterfly for a while and then say, "The butterfly is a fairy's golden airplane sailing over the purple flowers." Have you used imagination? Yes, because you have been able to see how an ordinary object is like something very different. Your statement has gone through three stages. The first stage is obviously not poetry. The second stage makes the picture come alive by the addition of color words and is often mistaken for poetry. But it is still just a picture. The third stage satisfies the first qualification for poetry—imagination—and is therefore a little poem. You might write it like this:

The butterfly
Is a fairy's golden airplane
Sailing over the purple flowers. (Walter, 1962, p. 29)

While I believe Walter makes useful distinctions between imagination and observation, I do not agree that the "second stage" has none of the elements of poetry. What is poetic need not be so restrictive, unless one believes that poetry is reserved only for the elite. Children move through stages of maturity in their poetic writing. They do not start as sophisticated poets; it is hoped that this is where some are headed and may someday land. But if not, their efforts need not be classified as nonpoetic or "merely" verse.

Read Poetry Aloud

Poetry is rooted in an oral tradition. It is important, therefore, for children to hear poetry read aloud. Select poetry that matches children's capacity to respond. The relevant factors in matching poetry to children include language, length, theme, interest, and relevance. When selecting poems to read aloud, choose poetry you enjoy; choose poetry that touches on life in some special way; choose poetry that incorporates the many moods and tones of children's lives. There are many important issues to consider when selecting poetry for children; the four described in the following paragraphs are particularly pertinent.

First, keep in mind that children enjoy humorous and nonsense poetry. Read poems from Shel Silverstein's books *Where the Sidewalk Ends* and *A Light in the Attic*. Jack Prelutsky has written several books of poetry which children enjoy. *The New Kid on the Block* is one of my favorites. And, of course, sprinkled in among the humorous and nonsense verse of Silverstein and Prelutsky are more serious poems.

Second, children need poems that deal with both the tender and ragged edge of life. Read poetry that deals with death and disaster, sorrow and suffering, triumph and tragedy, love and loneliness. Read poems selected from among the best classic poets and children's poets. In no particular order, these include but are not limited to: Edgar Allen Poe, Robert Frost, William Shakespeare, John Ciardi, Elizabeth Barrett Browning, Mother Goose, William Wordsworth, Lewis Carroll,

Robert Browning, Arnold Adoff, Emily Dickinson, A. A. Milne, Barbara Esbensen, William Carlos Williams, Nikki Giovanni, Mary O'Neill, Langston Hughes, Theodore Seuss Geisel, Maurice Sendak, Margaret Wise Brown, David McCord, Karla Kuskin, Henry Dumas, Eve Merriam, Myra Cohn Livingston, Valerie Worth, Lillian Moore, and Aileen Fisher.

Third, children appreciate poetry that other children have written. I enjoy reading poetry to children written by children. One comment I recall is quite revealing: "Did someone my age write that poem?" Hearing poems other children have written generates confidence that, "I can do that, too." Collect copies of the poems your children write for use with future classes. Some schools publish collections of poems written for Young Authors' Conferences. Newspapers sometimes publish collections of children's poetry. Two marvelous collections of children's poems and drawings are:

Richard Lewis, Ed. (1966). *Miracles: Poems by children of the English-speaking world.* New York: Simon and Schuster.

Hana Volavkova, Ed. (1993). *I never saw another butterfly: Children's drawings and poems from Terezin Concentration Camp, 1942–1944,* 2nd ed. New York: Schocken Books.

Fourth, children enjoy and respect the poems their teachers write. When I teach poetry to teachers, I ask them to share their poems with their kids. I encourage teachers to talk about course requirements, homework, assignments. Teachers discover that their children are fascinated. They offer advice and encouragement; they ask questions:

Did your teacher like your poems?

What did he say to you?

Were you scared when you read your poems in class?

What did the other teachers say?

Do you like writing poems for your teacher?

Children's interest in their teachers' writing experience provides a multitude of opportunities for teaching poetry to children. Write an occasional poem for your kids. It need not be wonderful. You will rarely be disappointed in their response.

DIARY OF A TEACHER: Jennifer DeWard

I love reading poems with my students. I introduce a new poem each Monday. Students keep these poems in their poetry folder throughout the year, and we practice reading them between subjects or whenever we need a pick-me-up. At first, I usually chose humorous or rhyming poems. My kids enjoy them and it seems to hook them on poetry. Recently, I have been reading other types of poetry—free verse, haiku, poems with a more serious tone. My fourth graders seem to enjoy these poems as well as the humorous and the rhyming poems.

Listening to poetry read aloud anchors the sounds and meaning of poetic language in children's minds. Marissa is a budding young poet who shares her poetry with her teacher, parents, and classmates.

Write Poetry and Share It

Children need sources of inspiration for writing, and teachers are in a best position to provide it. Teachers are the burr under the young writer's saddle; teachers can inspire children by example. If teachers want to awaken the slumbering imaginations of children, they must first awaken their own imaginations; if teachers want children to appreciate beauty, they must convey to children their own feeling for the beautiful; if teachers want children to write poetry, they must first write their own poetry.

You may sincerely believe that you cannot write poetry. You may have heard that writing poetry requires special talent. Well, yes and no; partly true, partly false. Indeed some writers are highly gifted, and great poets are certainly rare. But most writers have mastered their craft in much the same way that fine stone cutters master their craft. Work as a poet apprentice; learn the craft to the level that interests you. Perhaps you will never publish your poems. On the other hand, you may find that your poems are publishable. There is no need to rule out this possibility in advance, nor any reason for disappointment should it not occur.

Praise and Criticize with Care

Gertrude Stein said, "No artist needs criticism, he only needs praise." The validity of this remark depends of what Stein means by *criticism*. Criticism has two distinct meanings: (1) to find fault and (2) to render judgment regarding quality or worth. Writers need the latter type of criticism, thoughtful analysis regarding the quality or worth of their ideas. Writers do not need the former, finding fault with their work. The one is positive and useful, the other negative and useless. Criticism is an academic guidance system for improving writing when it is thoughtfully presented.

Praise is also needed because it motivates when judiciously applied. Intellectual and psychological insights are needed to use praise and criticism well. If they are used well, the intellectual, social, and emotional growth of children will follow. If they are used insensitively, growth will be hindered. Since everyone reacts differently to praise and criticism, no single approach, no single piece of advice, is likely to work for all children.

Writing is like the geography of a mountain range—a succession of valleys and peaks. When good work is produced, recognition must be forthcoming regardless of whether it meets the usual conventions. Extravagant praise is seldom warranted or even wanted. But recognition and appreciation are always warranted and desperately wanted. Reserve your highest praise for work which shows a personal touch, bears the mark of original invention, or delights in a particular way. Of course, not everything children write can reach the highest standard. It is important, therefore, to also encourage those writers whose work is not going well. Criticism combines evaluation with instruction. Its purpose is to promote progress. It is a delicate yet essential part of writing instruction. Do not avoid criticism, for praise alone will not enable students to reach their potential. Praise is essential, but it should be combined with supportive criticism if students are to understand how to improve their writing. Criticism can be conveyed directly and indirectly.

An indirect way of conveying criticism is through questions. Questions can bring useful information to the surface. The right questions can help writers discover what they know but didn't know they knew; the right questions can stimulate writers to rethink their work; the right questions can help writers assume a new perspective. But just as important as the right question is the right manner. An instructional conference is as delicate as a rose. The slightest inflection of voice or touch of hand sends subtle signals that add or detract from the question itself. The following list of questions may guide your thinking. However, only you can determine the right questions for your students, only you can sense the right tone and time that will summon the young writer to further reflection:

What were you trying to say in your poem?

Are you satisfied with the way your poem ends?

Walt, what's the main thing you're getting at in your poem?

How's your work going? Tell me about it.

What do you like best about your poem? Why?

Did anything you wrote surprise you? What?

Ann, what did you learn about your writing this time?

What idea do you like best in your poem?

Do you like your poem? Talk to me about it.

As you read your poem aloud listen for the sounds you like best.

Have you listened to your poem read aloud? May I read it for you?

Instructional criticism can also take the form of praise. Praise a specific writing skill, and you reinforce that skill. For example, I can imagine a teacher saying: "I love the first line of your poem, ' Wispy cobwebs strung the fences.' The words *wispy* and *strung* give me a vivid picture of how the cobwebs must have looked that day." Praise for precise word choice will lodge in the writer's mind.

Sometimes instructional criticism requires more direct help than a question or an approving comment can provide. In such cases, give direct instructional suggestions such as the following:

You seem to be having difficulty with the rhyme in the first stanza, Eleanor. First, think of what you want to say. Get your ideas on paper. *Then* work on the rhyme. Later you can use the rhyming dictionary to help you make lists of rhyming words.

or

Dorsey, the first stanza of your poem is wonderful. Every line is compact and beautifully written. However, I'm not sure the last stanza works as well as the first. What do you think?

These two scenarios are examples of direct criticism, although the first is more direct than the second. There is a school of thought which shuns direct instruction, relying instead on discovery learning. I question the idea that all learning must be through self-discovery. Of course, discovery learning is valuable, but by itself it is insufficient. Some knowledge is best communicated directly, some indirectly. As many channels of communication as possible should be used.

Write Group Poetry

When introducing a new writing task, it is sometimes fruitful to start with group composition. Group composition has many benefits, one of which is that it enables teachers to model writing. It also gives children experience in cooperative learning and builds confidence for independent composition. When initiating group composition, keep the guidelines below in mind.

GROUP COMPOSITION

1. Choose a topic and discuss it. Make notes or a web on the board when ideas are suggested.

2. Ask for lines to initiate the poem. If none are forthcoming, suggest a line of your own to get things started. Record suggestions on the board or on large chart paper.

3. Encourage everyone to contribute to the poem. When suggestions slow down, add a line of your own.

4. Help children feel the rhythm of the lines by clapping, tapping, or chanting. This gives children a feeling for the rhythm or meter in their contributions.

5. Make one or more poems from the suggested lines. Have children select the lines they want for the first draft of the poem.

6. When the first draft is finished, revise the poem together. Take suggestions for improvements, and contribute some suggestions of your own.

7. Make a final copy of the poem. Send home copies, display the poems in the classroom, share them with the principal and students from other classes. Always seek a suitable audience for children's best writing efforts.

Ms. DeClerck writes group poetry with her first grade children. In her "Voices" piece she tells how she does it.

VOICES FROM THE CLASSROOM: Melissa DeClerck

Writing Group Poetry

Poetry is the first type of writing I do with my first graders. Poetry is something that my students can do successfully, and it is a wonderful way to boost their confidence. I begin by choosing a simplified cinquain format or a patterned poem. Then, I collect as many poems as I can that use that format, which may include poems of my own or those of my former students.

Over the course of a week, I read poems aloud. I ask for comments and I give my own as well. On the last day, I choose one good example and put it on the overhead, and we read it together. I ask my students to look for any patterns they see in the poem. They hardly ever have any trouble doing this. By writing a group poem first, my students become familiar with the format. Then we write individual poems.

After deciding on a topic, we brainstorm words and phrases for our group poem. We eliminate words and phrases till we get down to the words and phrases we want in our poem. I praise my students for any input they give. I make suggestions when they get stuck. We revise and edit during and after writing the poem.

THE LANGUAGE OF POETRY

Music and poetry have much in common. Like music, poetry must be heard to be fully appreciated. No other use of language can match poetry for beauty, power, and technical brilliance. Poetry is unrivaled as a medium for verbal expression. Poetry is the music of language.

Children are natural poets. They are closer to the nuances of language than adults. Adults take language for granted; children do not. When children write poetry, they speak quietly of the joy that poetry brings them. The following discussion concerns the language of poetry. It covers eight technical devices used in poetry: rhyme, rhythm, line, stanza, onomatopoeia, alliteration, repetition, and imagery. Some poetic devices, such as rhyme and rhythm, are a natural part of language learning. Others, such as line and stanza, need only be discussed as children have a specific need for them. Still others, such as onomatopoeia, alliteration, repetition, and imagery, should be discussed from time to time to help children understand more fully the sounds and sense of poetic language.

Rhyme

Rhyme is the most universally recognized poetic device. Rhyme adds a pleasant rhythmic quality to poetry. Three types of rhyme are used in poetry: near, internal, and ending. Near rhyme occurs when related sounds and words are repeated although the full elements of rhyme may be missing. For example, *toast* and *fist* are near rhyming words, whereas *toast* and *roast* are full rhyming words. Internal rhyme occurs when words are rhymed within the same line or in different lines of a poem but before the end of a line of poetry. It gives a pleasing sound to poetry. In "Halloween," David used internal rhyme in line 3: All the *night* they had a *fight*. Read David's poem and look for the lines that use ending rhyme.

Halloween

Line 1: A big black cat began to yowl
Line 2: A little brown dog began to howl
Line 3: And all that night they had a fight
Line 4: They fought and they fought

Line 5: They started to bite
Line 6: Until their mothers and fathers saw them.
Line 7: They were very alarmed
Line 8: Until they found they were unharmed.

David, Age 8

Ending rhyme is the most familiar rhyme scheme. It relates one part of a poem to another through sound. Rhyme adds to the pleasant sound of the poem and should do so without detracting from meaning. The first two lines and the last two lines of David's poem exemplifies this principle. The rhyme is natural and there is no straining to achieve rhyme for the sake of rhyme. David wisely avoids rhyme in lines 3 and 4 and 5 and 6. Perhaps he could not come up with a rhyme that did not destroy the meaning of what he had to say. Wisely, he did not sacrifice meaning to rhyme. When meaning is sacrificed to rhyme, the natural voice and rhythm of children's language are not fully reflected in their poetry.

Rhythm

Rhythm in poetry is like the beat in music. The rhythmic beat of poetry means that certain words receive more emphasis than others or are held for a longer duration. Words and their sounds are arranged in poetry in such a way that they constitute an ordered, recurrent flow of sound and silence. The rhythm of poetry is the music of the words. Watch a two-year-old child sway to the music of a song, and you cannot doubt that a sense of rhythm is as natural as breathing. Swaying to the beat of music, following the flow of words, the rhythmic tapping of a foot all come without effort to children and adults. Poetry is simply a more ordered and deliberate realization of the rhythmic use of words.

There is no need, indeed no profit, in trying to force rhythm into children's early poetic writing. One does not carry coals to Newcastle; coals they have aplenty. One does not force rhythm into children's poetry; it is a natural outcome of exposure to reading, writing, and listening to poetry. The goal in writing poetry with children is to help them create their own music, their own rhythms, in their own words.

Lining

The most obvious visual distinction between prose and poetry is the look of the line. Prose extends from margin to margin. Lines of poetry do not—with the exception of prose poetry. Poetry simply looks different than prose. Not only is the look of the line distinct, but there are also differences in capitalization and punctuation.

How is line length determined in poetry? In free verse, the poet's personal inclination dictates line length. Of course, the rhythm of the language guides the poet's decisions, but no formal rules tell the poet what constitutes an appropriate line of free verse poetry. Poets sometimes rely on traditional accent or numerical measure to determine line length, depending on the verse form and the poet's personal inclinations. Some verse forms specify the number of syllables or words per line. The length of a cinquain or haiku line, for example, is determined by syllable or word counts. Other verse forms present similar constraints on line length. Three steps are recommended for illustrating to children how to line a piece of natural poetry.

1. Identify a piece of natural poetry written by one of your students. If you prefer, use your own writing.
2. Read the piece aloud. Make slash marks at each point where there is a natural pause for breath or emphasis. These pauses signal the rhythmic pattern of the language. Do not worry about getting the slash marks in exactly the right place. Close is good enough.
3. Add double slash marks at points where a new subtopic is introduced. The double slash marks indicate the stanza breaks in the poem.

Punctuating and Capitalizing Poetry

Punctuation and capitalization of poetry varies widely. For instance, Nikki Giovanni usually does not use punctuation nor does she capitalize words in her poems. Her style is reminiscent of e. e. cummings. On the other hand, Langston Hughes and Robert Frost typically punctuate their poems in the traditional way—much like punctuation marks are used in prose. They also capitalize words in the traditional way. The Hughes and Frost approach is still the dominant mode of punctuating and capitalizing poetry. Still, there are exceptions, and these exceptions simply illustrate another instance of poetic license. The two poems that follow illustrate the traditional and nontraditional way of punctuating and capitalizing poetry.

true love

i was so in love
with his icy blue eyes
that one night
i ventured to his house
and found him sleeping
i lifted his eyelids
staring into the
infinite pools
that chilled me
in a satisfying way
and before he awakened

i plucked them out of his head
and ran home with them in my palm
and
framed them
Heidi

Where?

Where do you get an idea for a story?
Does it come from the heart?
Does it come part by part?
Or is it just happily there from the start?

Where do you get an idea for a song?
Do you dream it at night?
Is it a sudden insight?
Or does it come as you struggle and fight?

Where do you get an idea for a poem?
Do you say a short prayer?
Do you just sit and stare?
Or is it just suddenly, wondrously there?

Ron

Stanza

A stanza is a group of lines in a poem separated from other lines by space. Like the lines of a poem, there are traditional stanza arrangements, such as quatrains and tercets, for example. Writers of free verse determine their own stanzas, depending on the way they wish to shape their poem and the emphasis they wish to give it. Making stanzas for poems is similar to paragraphing in prose. Stanzas are essentially subtopic breaks in the poem. Stanzas are an example of the historical connection between music and poetry, as Padgett's (1987) account indicates:

> Back when poems were set to music, the stanza conformed to the tune. To coincide with the musical line, the stanzas were of equal length and hewed closely in measure and beat. They followed strict patterns. As now, the song often had a stanza that served as refrain (a stanza that would be repeated at intervals throughout the song).
>
> Even after poets no longer wrote for music, they continued to write poems that looked like those their predecessors set to music. Some poets didn't realize that the earlier poems had been written for music. And habit has its own force. But others just liked the way those songs looked. Since most people meet a poem first on the page, poets are very concerned with the way the poems look. For some poets, strict stanzaic patterns represent a challenge, for others the

stanza is just an instruction to readers to pause. Some poets even use stanza breaks so the reader won't get confused or bored. (Padgett, 1987, p. 194)

Onomatopoeia

The lovely Greek word, *onomatopoeia*, describes words that imitate their natural sounds. Words such as *buzz, growl, sizzle, hiss,* and *hum* are onomatopoeic. When they are pronounced, they sound like the natural sounds they represent. *Hum,* for example, sounds like someone *humming.* Onomatopoeia can enhance the sound of a poem, an effect that is beautifully achieved in Bacmeister's (1968) poem, "Galoshes."

Children like exotic words like *onomatopoeia,* and they enjoy working with onomatopoeic words. After reading poems such as "Galoshes" and other onomatopoeic poems, encourage children to invent their own onomatopoeic words. Give them a few examples such as:

zitt: the sound of a mosquito taking a bite

zott: the sound of a mosquito being swatted

sqit: the sound of a mosquito being squashed

Then have them work in pairs to create lists of real onomatopoeic words as in the following words:

sizzle	purr	whine
pop	whoosh	screech
roar	ding-dong	jingle
bang	clang	growl
crack	bong	chug

Alliteration

Alliteration is the repetition of stressed, initial sounds of words in one or more closely following words. Usually alliterative sounds are made by consonants. Alliteration requires the repetition of only one sound, normally one or two letters. Alliteration is used to good effect in Craig's poem.

Rabbits

Fuzzy, furry
Flipping, flapping, wiggling
Happy, gay, glad, funny
Bunnies
Craig, Age 9

Children can use alliteration in their writing and will enjoy doing so. The ideas on page 287 are useful for helping children use alliteration in their poems.

USING ALLITERATION IN POETRY

1. Read several poems containing examples of alliteration. Point out alliterative phrases. Then have children listen for alliterative phrases in the poems you read to them.

2. Write alliterative phrases on the board such as: *big bony bunnies, friendly freckled frogs, slithery slippery snakes.* Then have children write similar phrases of their own.

3. Choose a topic and write a group poem. Ask children to contribute their own lines to the poem. Some of the phrases recorded on the board may become lines for the poem.

4. Have children write their own poems in which they use alliteration. Then have them read their poems from the author's chair.

Repetition

Few things sound quite so lovely as the perfect achievement of repetition in poetry. Repetition of words, phrases, and sentences helps the poet achieve a desired effect in sound, meaning, or mood. Poe, for example, used repetition to create an ominous mood in "The Raven." The repetition of, "Quoth the Raven, 'Nevermore' " establishes the poem's foreboding mood. Repetition reaches its zenith in the last two lines of Robert Frost's "Stopping by Woods on a Snowy Evening." The repetition of "And miles to go before I sleep, And miles to go before I sleep" is a classic in the annals of poetry. Children, too, can use repetition well.

Elizabeth tells what was on her mind when she wrote "Drifting": "Are you familiar with the time in the day when your mind lies there drifting? Time seems to stand still. A peaceful, heavenly time. Early in the morning when the sun peeks out from behind the trees and I smell that smell—that fresh smell. I feel like I'm floating on a soft, fluffy cloud. That time of the day means a lot to me. That's why I wrote this poem." Read "Drifting" aloud and you will sense the rhythm and beauty that repetition adds to Elizabeth's poem.

Drifting

My shadow lay low and silent. The sun at the bottom
of the sky. The fresh morning air, a lovely scent sweeter
than apple pie.
A time where there's
nothing to do, or say.
A time where my
mind just lay,
drifting,
drifting.

The lilac fields and daffodils, all dancing fancy free.
These beautiful lilacs and daffodils are where they want to be.
A time where there's
nothing to do, or say.
A time where my
mind just lay,
drifting,
drifting.

My legs carry me to the river banks, I splash around in
the cool, quiet stream. Something peeks out from behind the
trees, the sun's precious light beams.
A time where there's
nothing to do, or say.
A time where my
mind just lay,
drifting,
drifting.
Elizabeth

Teach children to use repetition in their poetry. See the guidelines below to direct your efforts.

USING REPETITION IN POETRY

1. Read "Stopping by Woods on a Snowy Evening" by Robert Frost. Comment on the soothing effect the repetition of a specific line has on the reader. Then ask, "Why do you think Frost repeated the last line instead of some other line?"

2. Read "Drifting" aloud. Have children identify the repeated lines. Point out that this poem is a good example of effective repetition, and that it was written by a ten-year-old child.

3. Ask children to look for repeated words, phrases, and sentences in poems and songs they encounter. Comment informally on the examples they bring to you.

4. Have your children try repetition in their own poetry. Their first efforts may prove clumsy. But continue to encourage their experiments and gradually your children's use of repetition will improve.

Imagery

Good poetry is filled with fresh images. An image is a vivid mental picture which appeals to the senses and to the imagination. Imagery achieves the unique, picture-like quality which distinguishes poetry from ordinary language. The raw material for images enters the bloodstream of the writer through the senses: taste, sight, smell, touch, hearing. Writers transform their experiences into images which capture the uniqueness of the person, place, or thing described. This requires thought, imagination, and hard work.

Even though our senses are constantly at work, it is possible to block out what our senses tell us. The closer writers are to their senses the better chance they have of describing their experiences in strong, vivid images. We can become insensitive to the message of our senses, though this is more likely to happen to adults than to children. Creating images is important in writing poetry, and it is especially important to create fresh images. The guidelines below may help children create stronger, fresher images.

CREATING IMAGES FOR POETRY

1. Pose a question such as: What is fog? Urge children to "think wild." Tell them you want their most unusual, colorful, and even zany ways of describing how they feel, smell, taste, touch, or see fog.

2. Set a time limit, say five minutes. Record their words, phrases, and sentences on the board. Accept all contributions. Comment on those contributions that are most unique and apt.

3. Put small groups of children together to organize the words, phrases, and sentences into a poem. Move about the class assisting and encouraging each group in their work.

4. When the poems are complete, have each group present their composition. Lead a discussion centering on the images they have created.

Simile and metaphor are figurative expressions and are especially useful for creating poetic images. A simile is a figure of speech comparing two unlike things. *Like* and *as* often signal simile: *funny as a broken leg.* Metaphor is also a figure of speech in which a word or phrase denoting one object or idea is used in place of another to suggest a likeness between them: *bridges of iron lace.* Children are quite good at creating similes and metaphors. They occur naturally in everyday language, although if you tell children to make a list of five similes and five metaphors, they might ponder over the assignment all day with little success. Following are examples of similes and metaphors taken from children's ordinary conversations. You can gather examples of figurative language by listening to children's conversations and by searching their writings.

Simile

his eyes were like two half moons

smelly as a sow's foot

soft looking as a deer's face

a face as soft as a bowl of whipped cream

savage as a starved dog

Metaphor

twisted tongue of death

the wasp of an essay kept stinging me

the trees held

their breath in quietness

the feathery fingers of the highest trees

that dog's breath of a boy

Language as it exists in its natural context is often the language of poetry. Some of the technical devices used in poetry exist in the natural language of children and some do not. Children can rhyme, for example, but they do not speak in rhymes. On the other hand, children's natural language is rich in imagery. One could easily demonstrate the use of imagery, alliteration, and repetition using Mearns' technique of recording informal language on the playground. Line and stanza, on the other hand, could not be so demonstrated. Consequently, a variety of techniques should be used to teach the technical devices of poetry. The right context is essential, and frequently that context is poetry itself.

Poetry is for everyone, and Ms. Marinelli reminds us of this in her "Voices" piece. Ms. Marinelli tells how she taught poetry to her special education children and how enthusiastically they responded to it.

VOICES FROM THE CLASSROOM: Gail Marinelli

Poetry for Special Education Students

I teach special education. My caseload is twenty students. This is my sixth year teaching. My students range in age from five to thirteen, many of whom are reluctant writers. I wanted to begin a poetry unit in a fun, nonthreatening way. I typed, in poetic form, words to songs they knew and read them aloud. The first was not a song all my kids knew. It was, "Shower the People You Love With Love," by James Taylor. A few kids recognized the poem as a song. We then read the poem "Bong" together. Then we listened to the CD to hear the poem sung with music. Next, I read "Habitat," by Walkin' Jim Stoltz. Most of the kids recognized this poem as a song as soon as I reached the chorus because Jim Stoltz did a concert at our school.

After reading the poems and talking about them as songs, my students wanted to hear more poetry. They liked the idea that a poem can be put to music. We then read the poem, "The Unicorn," by Shel Silverstein. Most had never heard this as a song. After reading the poem to the kids, and reading it as a group, I sang "The Unicorn" song. My students wanted to hear more poetry and wanted to try writing poems.

I was concerned about the transition from reading to writing poetry and then a serendipity—one morning a thick fog descended on the neighborhood. The kids were amazed by it and talked about it all morning. I wrote *fog* on the board and we listed words associated with fog. At first their ideas were predictable: *white, clouds, smoke, cold light dust.* After I suggested fog made me think of *fairy breath* the kids added: *takes you to another world, another dimension.* Once all the words were listed, we grouped them, adding other words as we needed them. There was no risk. All they had to do was use what we came up with together. My kids wrote some amazing poems. And the best part, *there was no groaning!*

My students changed from kids who were not thrilled to talk about poetry, to poets begging for more. Not only do they love to hear poems, but they now are willing to write poems, either free verse or rhyming.

FORMS OF POETRY

A poetic form is a structure for creating a poem. Poetic forms have guidelines which describe such things as number of lines, line length, rhyme scheme, and traditional subject matter. Traditional Japanese haiku, for example, is a poetic form with the following guidelines: (1) Haiku has three lines with five syllables in line one, seven in line two, and five in line three. (2) Haiku is free of opinion, alludes to a specific moment in time, and links nature and human nature.

There are many poetic forms and each has its traditional guidelines. Padgett (1987) lists 74 entries in his book on poetic forms and claims not to have exhausted the subject. The guidelines for poetic forms are seldom slavishly observed. Poets are an independent lot. They take liberties with poetic forms, and write poetry in ways that satisfy their own creative instincts. Poets, chafing under the restrictions of traditional forms, have sometimes invented new forms. The very expression, *poetic license,* suggests independence. Children, likewise, are entitled to some poetic license when working with a new form. Introduce children to a variety of poetic forms. New forms will add to children's poetic repertoire, challenge their imaginations, and expand their writing experience. Guidelines for introducing a new poetic form are listed below.

INTRODUCING NEW POETIC FORMS

1. Familiarity should first come through the ear and then the eye. Therefore, read aloud poems which exemplify the form. This will help children discover the structure of the new form.

2. Write a poem of your own in the new form, and share it with your children. Writing will familiarize you with the form and give you confidence as you teach it. Children will identify more readily with the new poetic form if you start with one of your own poems.

3. Pass out copies of poems which exemplify the new form. Then discuss the new form, emphasizing its suitability for conveying feelings and ideas. Talk about its technical guidelines: number of lines, line length, and related details. Encourage children's questions and observations.

4. Help children learn the purpose and structure of each new form.

Guidelines for poetic forms can be bent or even ignored, but children should be aware of the guidelines. The springboard of creativity has more bounce when children are first fortified with knowledge of the new poetic form. Each form has its advantages, limitations, and challenges. Poetic forms ranging from acrostics to tanka are described in alphabetic order.

Acrostic

An acrostic poem is one in which the first letter of each line forms a word, phrase, or sentence when read downwards. For example, in Amy's acrostic poem the vertical word is *dad.*

> **D**o I love you?
> **A**re you kidding?
> **D**oes water run down hill?
> **Amy, Age 11**

There are also double and triple acrostic poems. A double acrostic has a word or phrase at the beginning and end. A triple acrostic has a word or phrase at the beginning, middle, and end. These forms are quite challenging, but some children may want to try them.

Simple acrostic poems are easy to write. First, choose a word or phrase for your acrostic poem. Second, write the word or phrase vertically down the page. Third, write the lines that complete the poem. The acrostic form is well suited to writing valentine poems. The poem below spells out the name, Ben.

> **B**eam me up, Scotty.
> **E**arth is no place for me.
> **N**eed rest in eternity.
> **Ben, Age 16**

Alphabet

Letters of the alphabet are an excellent point of departure for creating poems. Alphabet poems can be written in many different ways. For example, an *a* to *z* poem starts with a word beginning with *a* and proceeds through the alphabet to *z*. Or the alphabet poem can be reversed and written from *z* to *a*. Another alphabet poem uses only words beginning with a single letter, such as *p* (Peter Piper picked a peck of pickled peppers). Of course, a few departures from the chosen letter are permitted. A simple alphabet poem is the LMNO poem. Instead of using the entire alphabet, have children choose three, four, or five letters, such as *l, m, n,* and *o,* to write their alphabet poems. "Always Bantering Couple" is an example of an alphabet poem in which all letters of the alphabet are used in order, starting with *a* and ending with *z*.

Always Bantering Couple

Alexandra bantered coolly,
Discussing epiphanies, fielding gossip,
Honing idle jabberwocky.
Kenneth listened, momentarily noticing
Other people quixotically responding;
Speculating together, unleashing vacuous words.
Xeroxing yesterday's zenith.
Peggy Elson

Cinquain

Cinquains are five-line poems with two, four, six, eight, and two syllables in lines one through five, respectively. Adelaide Crapsey, an American poet, invented the cinquain. A modified cinquain is frequently used in place of the syllabic structure Crapsey originated. In this modified form, the five-line cinquain has one, two, three, four, and one word(s) per line, respectively. Below are cinquains written by children.

Number of Words

1 Seagull
2 Speckled, motion
3 Graceful wings dipping
4 Distance in your heart
1 Fisherman
   Anonymous

1 Mountains
2 White heaven
3 Purple in summer
4 Peaks reaching to God
1 Purity
   Angela

Clerihew

Clerihew consists of two couplets of unequal length. They are usually humorous or satirical in nature and often take the form of a biographical sketch. Clerihew is an interesting form to use with the study of historical figures, as the example below illustrates.

Abraham Lincoln
Started thinking
I'll free the slaves
From southern knaves
Colin, Age 13

Diamante

The diamante is a seven-line contrast poem originated by Iris Tiedt. It takes its name from the arrangement of its lines and words into the shape of a diamond. The diamante is called a *contrast poem* because the first three lines contrast with the last three. This contrasting feature is well illustrated in "War." The contrasting feature of diamante and its unusual shape snags children's interest. Diamante is especially suitable for children in intermediate grades and above. A diamante poem is arranged in the following way:

Line Structure

1   One subject noun
2   Two adjectives
3   Three participles (*ed* or *ing* words)
4   Four-word sentence summing up the poem
5   Three participles (*ed, ing* words opposites of line three)
6   Two adjectives (opposites of line two)
7   One noun (opposite of the subject noun of line one)

War

death, sorrow

fighting, killing, hating

Nightmare of all nations

helping, healing, loving

life, joy

Peace

David, Age 13

Free Verse

Free verse is unrhymed poetry, unrestricted in length or rhythmic pattern. Writers are free to determine their own rhythm or meter; *free* to decide where one line or stanza ends and another begins; *free* to decide content and imagery without restriction; *free* to decide when the poem is finished without reference to a predetermined poetic structure.

Free verse is a natural form of poetry for children. Many children write poetically, even though they have little, if any, formal knowledge of poetry. Children should write free verse before attempting rhyming poetry. Encourage them to write free verse poetry around the common stock of daily experience. Initiate free verse by having children select a topic and discuss it. Write the ideas and images on the board. Mapping ideas in diagrammatic form may help children organize and visualize their ideas. Then the teacher and children can work together to shape their ideas and images into a poem. The following poems are examples of a free verse poem.

Idea-Less

Pen poised
Mind empty
Paper blank
Ideas wanted
Situation desperate
Case hopeless.
Jennifer

The Crystal Night

I closed my eyes as I walked through the town,
People hated for one solitary reason;
Not their faces, or their clothes,
But for the Star of David dangling over
Their left breast
It was meant to make them feel worthless,
A Scarlet letter.
For the Jewish shone pride,
Nurenberg laws only soaked up one solitary tear,
When their freedom disintegrated,
Down with the war.

As I walk, I hear the crunch of glass,
That littered the street from the night's events.
Each time I step, the crunch of glass
Feels like needles stabbing me in the heart.
Tears may blur my vision,
When I think of families beaten,
And synagogues burned,
On that crystal night,
That has shattered not only souls,
But also my hope
That this war has just begun.
Germany has just started its path,
Across the great wide open.
It has many more goals,
Until this war has finished
Vanessa

Haiku

Writing haiku is a national pastime in Japan. Japanese poetry, of which haiku is
the best known, emphasizes the wonders and beauty of nature. Since it is strongly
influenced by Buddhism, it also stresses the oneness of all creatures with the uni-

Free verse is a natural form of poetry for children. Adam and his classmates try different forms of poetry, including haiku, free verse, and various rhyming forms.

verse. The individual who understands one thing at one moment in time is better prepared to understand all moments and all things.

Content and language style are important characteristics of haiku. Traditionally, there are three criteria for haiku. They are free of opinion; they allude to a specific moment in time; they link nature and human nature. The language of haiku is uncomplicated and often free of metaphor or simile. The Japanese haiku is a three-line, seventeen-syllable poem. The first line has five syllables; the second, seven; and the third, five (5-7-5).

An English adaptation of haiku consists of three lines in which the first and third lines are slightly shorter than the middle line. This simpler form avoids the syllable count, a challenging discipline. Padgett (1987) maintains that there is no point in counting syllables in writing English haiku, since the English and Japanese languages do not share the same language rhythms. While Padgett makes an interesting point, the traditional syllable count can produce good poetry. Teach children the traditional guidelines for writing haiku. If your children find this too restrictive or too difficult, another form of Japanese poetry, senryu, provides a less-demanding alternative. Naturally, children's haiku will sometimes depart from the traditional criteria. Nevertheless, their efforts should be recognized and appreciated. Nick, who enjoys writing haiku, wrote the following poem.

Snow drifts helplessly
Not knowing which way to go
Then joining the rest
Nick, Age 10

Prose

Prose poetry is a cross between traditional poetic verse and prose. Prose poetry does not use rhyme, nor does it have a specified rhythm. It does make use of strong imagery and the freshness of language associated with traditional poetry. Padgett (1987) has given this description of prose poetry:

> You may find yourself writing a poem whose lines don't seem to have any natural breaking points; try recopying it as prose. Or you might find yourself trying to write a short story, when all you really want to do is to capture a moment or series of moments; try leaving out the characterization and plot. In both these cases, you can rework your piece a little and perhaps turn it into a prose poem, which might be the form it ought to have been in all along. (Padgett, 1987, p. 152)

Jeni's poem fits Padgett's description of prose poetry well. "My Chariot" has strong images but no plot or characterization. Originally, Jeni lined this poem in the traditional manner. Later, she experimented with the idea of writing it as a prose poem.

My Chariot

Sometimes I sit alone at night. Loneliness paws at me, asking for my virginity. I feel God at the windowsill, knocking, asking, ready— waiting to take me there. I waited for my chariot at the river of unforgotten dreams. I hear a tinkling of bells and down Eternity Road comes my chariot. It is white and pillowed with cushions. Three others are seated there. One, a red brilliant light enclosed his head. This man is on his way to hell. Another, a woman, is on her way to her second life—reincarnation. And someone else, on his way to eternity. When I reached heaven, I lived again, happy, loved, and cared for once again.
Jeni, Age 13

Quatrain

The quatrain is a four-line poem or stanza. It is the most common of all verse forms. Most often the quatrain is part of a longer poem organized into four-line stanzas. Songs and ballads are often written in four-line stanzas or quatrains. Quatrains have numerous rhyme schemes. In George Coon's delightfully humorous "Homophones," each quatrain or stanza has an aabb rhyme scheme—the first line rhymes with the second (aa) and the third line rhymes with the fourth (bb). There are other rhyme schemes as well: abab, abba, abcd. A quatrain may be combined with a couplet to produce a six-line poem and, of course, there may be any number of four-line stanzas. Ben's "Three Sides of a Square" illustrates a duke's mixture. The first two stanzas are quatrains with an aabb rhyme scheme. The last stanza is a combination of a tercet and a couplet.

Homophones

Wood you believe that I didn't no
About homophones until too daze ago?
That day in hour class in groups of for,
We had to come up with won or more.

Mary new six; enough to pass.
But my ate homophones lead the class.
Then a thought ran threw my head.
"Urn a living from homophones," it said.

I guess I just sat and staired into space.
My hole life seamed to fall into place.
Our school's principle happened to come buy,
And asked about the look in my I.

"Sir," said I as bowled as could bee,
"My future rode I clearly sea,"
"Sun," said he, "move write ahead.
Set sale on your coarse. Don't be misled."

I herd that gnus with grate delight.
I will study homophones both day and knight.
For weaks and months, through thick oar thin.
I'll pursue my goal, Eye no aisle win.
George Coon

Three Sides of a Square

Mulling around inside of me,
There are my selves, we number three.
They are not animate for eyes to see,
Meet emotional, physical, and rational me.

Emotional expresses my love or hate,
And conveys my opinion when someone's late.
Physical watches my body's well being,
And assures me of what I'm seeing.
When rational appears there will be no fight.
This side of me has true insight.
On matters concerning wrong or right,
Which of these appeals most to me?
The question's been answered; the number's three.
Benjamin, Age 16

Senryu

When children write haiku, they may unintentionally produce a poem more accurately called senryu. Senryu is a three-line Japanese poetic form. Unlike haiku, it is not restricted to seventeen syllables, does not require the capturing of one moment, and need not refer to a specific time or season. Senryu can be introduced before haiku since it is easier for young children to manage. Group composition is a good way to start writing senryu. Here are some examples of children's senryu.

I have a big dog
As big as a pony
I ride him to school.
Tony, Age 8

Fog is so strange
It swirls through the trees
And sleeps on the river.
Harold, Age 10

Tanka

This ancient Japanese poetic form resembles an extended haiku. Tanka adds two lines of seven syllables to the basic haiku pattern of 5-7-5, giving a thirty-one syllable, five-line composition structure of 5-7-5-7-7. This elaborate syllabic pattern makes writing tanka a challenge. An alternative form of tanka ignores the syllable count. Padgett (1987) suggests making the first and third lines short and the second, fourth, and fifth slightly longer. Either form may be used. The traditional form is more challenging, but Padgett's alternative may prove more manageable for some children. Tanka is not restricted by the traditional criteria which guide haiku. Tanka can more easily accommodate a continuing theme or a progression of ideas and events. Here are two examples of tanka.

Icicles on the eaves
Dripping slowly in the sun
Losing their life's blood
Waiting to be saved by night
Knowing their end is in sight.
Pat, Age 13

Fog drifts in patches
Seeking to blanket the earth
With its wet greyness
The wind whimpers its sadness
Waiting to reclaim glory.
Jimmy, Age 12

As you introduce new poetic forms to children, make enjoyment the primary objective. It is easy enough to make poetry dull. When introducing a poetic form, therefore, do not concentrate on its technical components. Rather, stress its purpose, pleasure, and challenge. Fill children's minds with the sounds and sense of a poetic form by reading poems which illustrate it. Then engage them in writing with pleasure as the primary goal. Along the way, present the technical components, but do not allow them to dominate.

IDEAS FOR WRITING POETRY

1. Memorize and illustrate: Read poems by authors such as Shel Silverstein, Karla Kustin, Jack Prelutsky. Choose a few favorites for students to memorize. Illustrate your favorite poem, and make a copy of it to display on a bulletin board of "Favorite Poems."

2. I wish: Write an "I wish . . ." poem. Let your imagination carry you into the magic land of dreams and fantasy. Here is an example:

   I wish
   I had a mansion in the sky
   And a chariot pulled by winged horses
   Driven by angels.

3. Quiet: Write a *quiet* poem. Feel free to choose an alternate theme such as: noisy, loud, sweet, soft, green, love, old, kind. Here is a *quiet* poem:

   Quiet
   Is my breath on a frosty morning and the dew settling softly on the morning grass
   Is my father reading the evening paper
   and my cat purring in my lap.

4. Everywhere: Poetry is all around us. On the way home you may notice a leaf falling gracefully to the ground or a shadow creeping slowly across the lawn. Keen observation of such small events are topics for poetry.

5. Wind: Write a poem about a windy day. Pretend you are the wind, and you have magic powers. Wherever you go, you can do good. Write a poem about what you would do if you were the wind with magic powers. Try the same poem with a raindrop on a rainy day.

6. Sounds of poetry: Read a poem with lovely sounds such as Rhoda Bacmeister's "Galoshes." Many of the words in her poem sound like the things they are describing: *splishes, sploshes, slooshes,* and *sloshes*. There is a special name for words that imitate their natural sounds. It is called onomatopoeia. Read "Galoshes" out loud. Then write a poem using onomatopoeic words.

7. Couplet: There are many kinds of poems and many ways to rhyme lines within a poem. Think of an idea for a poem. Make a list of rhyming words for your poem. Then write a couplet—two rhyming lines.

   As I was walking in the park,
   I thought I heard an otter bark.

8. Triplets and tercets: Now that you know what a couplet is, take the next logical step and write a triplet or tercet—three rhyming lines.

   Trees are lovely in the day
   But nighttime brings a ghostly sway
   That steals the loveliness away.

9. Epitaph: An epitaph is an inscription on a tomb or gravestone in memory of the person buried there. Often epitaphs are serious, but sometimes they are humorous. In Boot Hill, a graveyard for outlaws and cowboys, one epitaph reads simply, "He Called Bill Jones a Liar." Write an epitaph for these people:
   - A cowboy who died in a gunfight
   - A person who loved animals
   - A young soldier who died in battle
   - A well-loved pet

10. Patterns in poems: Read the following poem. Look for the pattern, then write a similar poem with a different theme.

    a bird died
    because
       it couldn't fly
    because
       its feathers were covered with oil
    because
       oil spilled into the sea
    because
       people neglected their duty.

11. Irony and satire: Write a poem about the way things are, but ought not to be. A poem like this says things one way but means them another way. This is called irony or satire, as in this poem:

    Acrid, billowing factory smoke
    Hides the unsightly snowcapped mountains
    Trucks quietly paint picturesque sooty designs
    On corroded city buildings
    Children chatter happily on their way to school
    Coughing, laughing, rubbing their eyes in delight
    As the city gasps gaily to life.

REFLECTION AND SUMMARY

Reflection

One thing you have not found in this chapter is a satisfactory definition of poetry. How do you define love? Or life? Or poetry? Many have tried, and all have failed. And so I shall also add my failure to those noble efforts. Poetry is the use of words that soar above the cadence of everyday prose. Poetry is a way of life. Of living.

Of knowing. Poetry splashes the page in a rainbow of words and images. Poetry is a mystery of moods and tones, of thoughts and feelings. In the end, it cannot be satisfactorily explained; it must be felt. Perhaps Dylan Thomas, the Welsh poet, had feelings uppermost in his mind when he said, "Poetry. I like to think of it as statements made on the way to the grave." Of course, my definition of poetry, or anyone's definition, will only get you halfway there—halfway to an understanding of what poetry is; halfway to an understanding of why children need poetry in their lives.

Poetry is a bridge between the inner and outer worlds of childhood. Writing poetry helps children know themselves and their world better. Writing poetry enables children to transmit their internal experiences to the outer world—to symbolize their experiences in words. Writing is a natural way for children to deal with the reality of their inner world and to come to terms with the reality of their outer world. Much that children write reveals the nature of the struggle waged between these two worlds. Therefore, read poetry to children. Allow children to write poetry. Show children how to share poetry with you and with each other. Help them to reach inside themselves so they may express their inner world to the world outside of themselves. Encourage them to spin daydreams and notice spiderwebs on a foggy day. Share sources of inspiration with children. Help them to discover that many of the exciting landscapes in life are internal.

Summary

This chapter has presented the following main ideas:

1. Children need encouragement and good models when they first begin writing poetry.
   - Nurture the children's creative spirit.
   - Present poets and poems.
   - Poetry must have personal importance before it can be fully appreciated.
   - Stimulate observation and imagination.
   - Read poetry aloud.
   - Inspire poetry by personal example.
   - Praise and criticize with discrimination.
   - Write group poetry.

2. Poetry is the music of language. The language of poetry covers eight technical devices:
   - There are three kinds of rhyme: near, internal, and ending.
   - Rhythm in poetry is analogous to the beat in music.
   - Lining is the most obvious visual distinction between prose and poetry.
   - Stanzas are groups of lines in a poem separated from other lines by space.
   - Onomatopoeia describes words that imitate their natural sounds: *buzz, sizzle, hiss.*
   - Alliteration is the repetition of stressed, initial sounds of words in one or more closely following words: *Fuzzy, furry ferrets.*

- Repetition of words, phrases, or sentences in a poem achieves an effect in sound, meaning, or mood.
- Imagery is a vivid mental picture which appeals to the senses and to the imagination.

3. A poetic form is a structure for creating a poem, including such details as number of lines, line length, rhyme scheme, and subject matter.

QUESTIONS FOR REFLECTIVE THINKING

1. What are some ways to help nurture children's creative spirit?
2. How might children benefit by exposure to poems and poets?
3. How might you go about developing an appreciation of poetry among children who have had little exposure to it?
4. What is onomatopoeia? How can it be used to enhance the sound of poetry?
5. Cinquain has a specified form, whereas free verse does not. How might you introduce each of these poetic forms to children?
6. How is leaning about line and stanza different from learning about rhyme and rhythm in poetry?
7. Gertrude Stein said, "No artist needs criticism, he only needs praise." Do you agree or disagree? Explain.
8. Mini case study: Walter (1962, p. 374) suggests that the following statement is an observation but is not imaginative: "I see a pretty yellow butterfly on the purple flowers." On the other hand, she says this statement is imaginative: "The butterfly is a fairy's golden airplane sailing over the purple flowers." Tell why you agree or disagree with the distinction Walter has made. Then write a poem that has the elements of imagination that Walter speaks about.

REFERENCES

Adoff, A. (Ed.). (1968). *I am the darker brother: An anthology of modern poems by Negro Americans.* New York: MacMillan Publishing Co., Inc.

Bacmeister, R. (1968). "Galoshes" from *Another here and now story book* by Lucy Sprague Mitchell. Copyright, 1940, by E. P. Dutton and Co., Inc.: (renewal Copyright 1968 by Lucy Sprague Mitchell).

Booth, D. (Ed.). (1989). *'Til all the stars have fallen: A collection of poems for children.* New York: Viking Penguin.

Brussell, E. E. (1988). *Webster's new world dictionary of quotable definitions.* Englewood Cliffs, NJ: Prentice Hall.

Ciardi, J. (1963). *You read to me, I'll read to you.* New York: Lippencott.

Coon, G. E. (1976). "Homophones." *The Reading Teacher.*

Cullinan, B. E. (Ed.). (1996). *A jar of tiny stars: Poems by NCTE award-winning poets, children select their favorite poems.* Honesdale, PA: Boyds Mills Press, Inc.

Duffy, C. A. (Ed.). (1996). *Stopping for death: Poems of death and loss.* New York: Henry Holt and Co., Inc.

Giovanni, N. (1987). *Spin a soft black song.* New York: A Sunburst Book, Farrar, Straus and Giroux.

Greenfield, E. (1978). *Honey I love and other love poems.* New York: HarperCollins Publishers.

Hopkins, L. B. (Ed). (1967). *Don't you turn back: Poems by Langston Hughes.* New York: Alfred A. Knopf, Inc.

Kennedy, X. J. and Kennedy, D. M. (Eds.). (1982). *Knock at a star: A child's introduction to poetry.* Boston: Little, Brown and Co.

Kennedy, X. J. and Kennedy, D. M. (Eds.). (1992). *Talking like the rain: A read to me book of poems.* Canada: Little, Brown and Co.

Lewis, R. (Ed.). (1966). *Miracles: Poems by children of the English-speaking world.* New York: Simon and Schuster.

Mearns, H. (1929). *Creative power: The education of youth in the creative arts.* New York: Dover Publications.

Padgett, R. (Ed.). (1987). *The teachers and writers handbook of poetic forms.* New York: Teachers and Writers Collaborative.

Prelutsky, J. (1984). *The new kid on the block.* New York: Greenwillow Books.

Silverstein, S. (1974). *Where the sidewalk ends.* New York: Harper and Row Publishers.

Silverstein, S. (1981). *A light in the attic.* New York: Harper and Row Publishers.

Steptoe, J. (Ed.). (1997). *In daddy's arms I am tall: African Americans celebrating fathers.* New York: Lee and Low Books.

Volavkova, H. (Ed.). (1993). *I never saw another butterfly: Children's drawings and poems from Terezin concentration camp, 1942–1944.* New York: Shocken Books.

Walter, N. W. (1962). *Let them write poetry.* New York: Holt, Rinehart and Winston.

CHAPTER 12
Spelling and Writing

My spelling is wobbly. It's good spelling but it wobbles
and letters get in the wrong places.

Pooh Bear

It's a damn poor mind that can only think of one way to spell a word.

Andrew Jackson

A WRITER'S STORY

A young boy stands in the schoolmaster's office about to receive a strapping: "You know it's coming to you?" "Yes sir," the boy replied. The boy took his licks, as the schoolmaster insisted, ". . . like a man." Then, a serendipity. The schoolmaster took the boy to his home, invited him into his study lined with more books than the boy had ever imagined existed and said, "You do not behave yourself very well in school, but I do not know that it matters. It is possible that you have a mind . . . It may be there are books here that will be of help. You are to come and go as you please. You are to take what books you want to read." The boy became a passionate reader.

The boy grew up, had a family, abandoned his conventional life as a manager of a paint factory and headed for Chicago, a place of literary ferment in the early 1900s. He wanted to experience the literary renaissance of mid-western America; he wanted Paris on Lakeshore Drive; he wanted to write. Over the next few decades, he wrote short stories, novels, memoirs. His first collection of short stories, Winesburg, Ohio, *became his most important work. His stories departed from the traditional emphasis of plot and action and blazed a new path—one of psychological insight into the thoughts and feelings of story characters.*

He became friends with William Faulkner, not yet a successful writer, but seeking a place in the literary world. Faulkner drew inspiration from his friend, and wrote his first novel, Soldier's Pay. *The friend recommended Faulkner's book to his publisher in return for the promise that he wouldn't ". . . have to read the manuscript."*

The boy from a small town in Ohio grew into a highly respected writer. He influenced the work of Hemingway and Faulkner—Nobel prize-winning authors. Do you know his name? Probably not, for even avid readers may not have heard the name much less read the writings of Sherwood Anderson, *the boy who took his whipping "like a man."*

Sherwood Anderson is an important writer; yet perhaps his greatest contribution was the influence he had on other writers. Teachers, too, can exert influence—in the best sense of that word. You don't have to win a Nobel prize to have a hand in shaping those who do.

INTRODUCTION

Sherwood Anderson once said, "Fortunately, both my wife and my mother-in-law seem to love digging up mistakes in spelling, punctuation, etc. I can hear them in the next room laughing at me." He knew his reputation as a writer didn't rest on accuracy in spelling, grammar, and punctuation. He did know, however, that his published work had to be correct, and so he depended on his wife, mother-in-law, and editors. In other words, he kept the mechanics of writing in appropriate perspective. As we examine issues in spelling, and later grammar and punctuation, it is well to keep in mind that the mechanics of writing represent the "good manners" of writing, not the essence of what writing is all about.

Spelling symbolizes literacy for many people. This is not surprising considering the historical connection between spelling and reading. Colonial Americans learned to read, more often than not, from Noah Webster's *Blue Back Speller.* Of course, there is an important connection between spelling and reading, but spelling must not be mistaken for literacy itself. Spelling has a role in literacy but it occupies a supportive, not a primary role. Spelling is highly visible, more so than reading, and this explains why it is often assigned a more prominent role in judging literacy than it can reasonably sustain.

This chapter will discuss the following topics: stages of spelling, approaches to teaching spelling, influences on spelling growth, strategies for teaching and learning spelling, instructional issues in spelling, choosing spelling words, invented spelling, and assessing spelling growth and achievement.

STAGES OF SPELLING DEVELOPMENT

Researchers have found that learning to spell is developmental and that it proceeds in stages (Beers and Henderson, 1977; Temple, 1978; Gentry, 1981). Researchers have used different names to describe the stages of spelling growth, but the content remains the same despite differences in nomenclature. Except for the first stage, I have used the nomenclature proposed by Henderson (1989) to describe the stages: prephonetic, phonetic, patterns within words, syllable juncture, and meaning-derivation.

Prephonetic Stage

Prephonetic means before phonics or before children have acquired an understanding of the association between letters and sounds. This stage is also called *preliterate*—before literacy—an unfortunate term in my view. I do not believe the years preceding the phonetic stage can be described as nonliterate as the term preliterate implies. Children scribble, draw, make wavy lines, and write letters. While they do not write in a formal sense, they do convey messages through drawings and mock writing. Activities for the prephonetic stage include phonemic aware-

Word sorts are especially useful for developing spelling knowledge. Here Eric works on a sorting activity while his teacher, Ms. Wagner, keeps an eye on Eric's progress.

ness, writing the alphabet, listening to books read aloud, writing and drawing, invented spelling when children are ready, rhyming activities, and word sorts with pictures, letters, sounds. Expect to see "writing" such as appears in Figure 12.1 or variations on this theme.

Phonetic Stage

The phonetic stage of spelling is the beginning of true alphabetic writing. In the beginning, children write mostly with consonants and a few vowels. They may write *wn ap nth* for *went up north*, or *i cn wr* for *I can write*. Children progress from spelling that is hard to read to spelling that is easy to read. During this stage, spelling is influenced by two factors: (1) the letter-name spelling strategy and (2) surrounding speech sounds (Henderson, 1989).

Letter-name strategy: Children use the sound of a letter's name to represent words. Most consonant letters and all long vowels, when pronounced distinctly, say their names closely enough for children to discern their approximate spelling. The letter-name strategy does not always result in correct spelling. Long vowel sounds, for instance, are often represented by two letters, as in *feel*. So when Carla wrote *i fel hpe* (I feel happy) she spelled the double vowel in *feel* with one vowel, an incorrect spelling but easy enough to read.

Figure 12.1 Prephonetic Stage Prephonetic writers do not yet connect letters with sounds, but their "writing" may include their names, copied words, letters, numbers, scribbles, cursive-like lines, letter-like forms, and drawings. This piece by Shamirah contains her name, numbers, letters, and her drawing.

Children correctly represent most single consonants. The most predictable consonants are: *b, p, f, v, m, n, t, d, s, k, j, z, l, r.* The consonants *c, g, h, w,* and *y* are less predictable, yet are soon learned. Consonant blends and digraphs are more difficult than single consonants. Early spellers tend to represent them with one letter, but soon progress beyond this stage. Vowel letters are often missing or incorrect early in this stage. Toward the middle and end of the phonetic stage, however, progress in representing vowel spellings is evident.

Surrounding speech sounds: The context in which certain letters and sounds appear within words determines whether they will be included or omitted when a word is spelled. For example, the letters *m* and *n* are often omitted before a final consonant. Thus, *band* may be spelled *bad* with the *n* omitted and *camp* may be spelled *cap* with the *m* omitted.

Activities for the phonetic stage include sorting words and pictures by beginning and ending sounds, working with word families, sorting rhyming patterns, listening to rhyming poems and verse, sorting words from language experience stories, starting systematic spelling instruction, choosing personal words from writing for spelling, and writing every day. Figure 12.2 shows that Ben can make systematic connections between letters and sounds. Examples of phonetic stage spelling are listed on page 309.

PHONETIC SPELLING

4 for four	pl for play	ts for toys
sd for said	fd for found	hg for hug
ct for kept	pb for people	rmb for remember
tat for that	gv for gave	y for why
wz for was	u for you	rop for rope
bne for bunny	tgr for tiger	cad for could
hrd for heard	a rad for around	haim for him
nan for none	halp for help	wat for went
uv for of	wt for went	wth for with
trn for turn	wan for when	wt for what

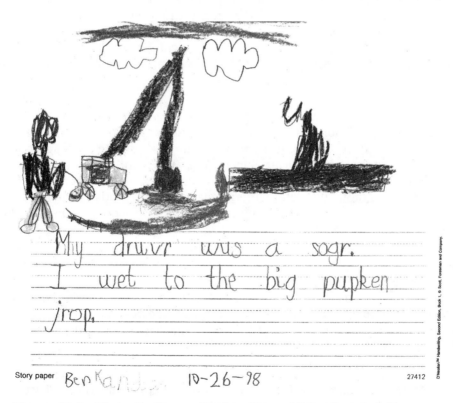

My druvr wus a sogr.
I wet to the big pupken
jrop.

Story paper Ben Ka… 10-26-98   27412

Figure 12.2 Phonetic Stage   Ben's writing exhibits characteristics typical of the phonetic stage of spelling. His story translates as follows: *My brother was a soldier. I went to the big pumpkin drop.*

Patterns within Words Stage

English spelling is not based on one-to-one letter-sound correspondence, and that is the major concept learned when children discover three principles during the patterns within words stage: (1) silent vowel markers appear in children's spellings, (2) certain short vowel patterns are spelled correctly, and (3) progress is made in correctly spelling consonant blends and digraphs.

Silent vowel marker: Long vowel sounds are signaled by the presence of a silent vowel or "marker," as it is called. The silent *e* in *cake,* for instance, signals a long vowel sound for the first vowel in *cake.* Thus, a misspelling, such as *caik* for *cake,* shows that the writer has understood a spelling principle though has not yet gained the correct spelling. Other examples of understanding the principle of the silent vowel marker without getting the word correct are: *boet* for *boat, cain* for *cane, rane* for *rain.*

Short vowel patterns spelled correctly: We begin to see single vowel patterns in one-syllable words spelled correctly. Children start to replace the one-to-one matching of letters to sound that dominated the phonetic stage; a more sophisticated understanding of spelling is now evident. For example, mismatches in short vowel spellings begin to disappear. Now we are less likely to see *bed* spelled *bad,* or *up* spelled *ap.*

Consonant blends and digraphs: Another sign of progress is correctly spelled consonant blends and digraphs. Words such as *ship, thin, brat, spin, trip* are likely to be spelled correctly. The instructional emphasis during this stage is single syllable long vowels, short vowels, blends, digraphs, *r* influenced spellings. Activities for phonetic stage include: sorting words by long and short vowel patterns, sorting digraph and blend patterns, starting word study journals, playing spelling games, and continuing systematic spelling instruction. Figure 12.3 illustrates patterns within words spelling.

Dear Rebecca,

How are you? I lrnd how to make frens with other people one Tanya Dods But I'm not her frend any more. I love you The peopl here do not have any more snow. I hrd all abowt the snow you got there I saw a fotugraf of peopl diging the snow at your house.

Jennifer

Jennifer shows progress in spelling blends and digraphs but still has difficulty with certain vowel spellings and doubled consonant spellings.

Figure 12.3 Patterns Within Words Stage

Syllable Juncture Stage

At the syllable juncture stage, children have a basic spelling vocabulary and command of many long and short vowel patterns. A syllable juncture is the place within a word where syllables meet. Where syllables meet, errors arise because letters are often dropped, doubled, or changed at the juncture of syllables. Errors occur where inflected endings or suffixes are joined to base words: *careing* for *caring, stoped* for *stopped, trys* for *tries.* Errors also occur in the internal structure of a word where syllables meet: *buble* for *bubble, litle* for *little.* Three syllable juncture spelling patterns are dropping, doubling, and changing. Examples of the types of errors that often occur at syllable junctures are shown below.

SYLLABLE JUNCTURE ERRORS

Dropped	Doubled	Changed
hate, hatd	bagged, baged	cried, cryd
file, fild	boring, borring	galleries, gallerys
	ceiling, ceilling	easiest, easyest
lying, lyeing	necessary, neccesary	mysteries, mysterys
taking, takeing	chimney, chimmney	parties, partys
tapes, taps	always, allways	juries, jurys
minutes, minuits	almost, allmost	injuries, injerers
named, namd	beginning, begining	bunnies, bunnyes
claimed, claimd	planned, planed	earlier, earlyer

During this stage, progress is made in applying rules governing doubling, dropping, and changing letters, but for some spellers problems with doubling, dropping, and changing letters persist. Errors found in junior high school writing, for example, are often associated with doubling, dropping, and changing letters at juncture points. Activities include word sorts dealing with dropping, doubling, and changing, systematic spelling instruction, frequent writing, and creating a spelling dictionary for troublesome words. Figure 12.4 shows the type of spelling errors often found during the syllable juncture stage: *hopeing* for *hoping* and *wantted* for *wanted.*

Meaning-Derivation Stage

Spelling derived forms: Many words have a spelling-meaning connection. Words related in meaning are often related in spelling even though there are changes in sound within the related form. Say these words out loud: *sign, signal,*

Dear Matthew,

I hope you are well. I heard you have been on TV. I am hopeing to come home soon. I cried today because I wantted to see you. I miss you very much. My I will be glad to come home.

Amy

Amy has a core of known words and makes a credible attempt at spelling *hoping* and *wanted* but misses due to dropping and doubling errors.

Figure 12.4   Syllable Juncture Stage

signature. The sound of *sign* has changed in the two related words, but the spelling of *sign* remains constant. The /g/ is silent in *sign* but sounded in *signal* and *signature.* The *i* is long in *sign* but reduced in *signal* and *signature.* The meaning connection between these three words holds the spelling of *sign* constant in the two derived forms. Imagine how difficult it would be to spell multisyllabic words if the derived forms were spelled according to letter-sound relationships rather than retaining the stability that meaning-derivation provides.

Children who have progressed through the earlier spelling stages are now ready to examine meaning related words derived from French, Greek, Latin, and other languages. Words illustrating the spelling-meaning principle are shown below.

SPELLING-MEANING CONNECTION

Base Word	Derived Form
policy	political
memory	memorial
sign	signature
resign	resignation
compose	composition
combine	combination
obey	obedient

Spelling homophones: Homophones illustrate another spelling-meaning connection. Cramer and Cipielewski (1995) found that homophones were the most common error category in grades 7 and 8 and the second most common in grades 4 to 6. The most prominent issue in homophone errors is incorrect usage—a meaning problem. Children write *tail* when they mean *tale* or *your* when they mean *you're*, while getting the letters correct. Homophone usage errors are typically regarded as spelling errors. Homophone errors would be substantially reduced if just ten of the most common homophones were used correctly. But it

> *The Army is where men and women go to train for war. In the Army they help each other, they work, they listen to one another's problems, and they try to help. But someday the war will begin. More and more troubles will form. Graves get thick, bullets are made, and guns cleaned.*
>
> *As soon as the terrifying war begins, dreams fade away, laughter faints, songs are drowned out by the sound of gunfire. It is impossible to live with. It's unreasonable, unimagunable, unreal.*
>
> *As soon as the war starts nightmares and death begin. The most terrible war was World War II. Thousands of men were killed or injured. Horrible noises are heard: men screaming in pain, generals shouting orders, rifles firing, cannons blasting, bombs exploding. Be glad you weren't there.*
>
> *Jennifer*
>
> Jennifer spells well and has no spelling problems until she miscues on *unimaginable*, a minor problem easily correctible during editing.

Figure 12.5   **Meaning-Derivation Stage**

takes a long time, much repetition, and effective instruction to teach correct homophone usage. This is true for all homophones, but it is especially true for the ten homophones shown below, which are the most common homophone misspellings (Marine, 1995).

TEN MOST COMMONLY MISSPELLED HOMOPHONES

to	there	its	your
too	their	it's	you're
two	they're		

Meaning-derivation is the final stage of spelling growth. While most words are spelled correctly during this stage, errors still occur with homophones, doubling, and derived forms. For example, *suppose* may be spelled correctly but *supposition* may be spelled *suppasition*. Activities include working on meaning related spelling sorts, studying Greek and Latin forms, continuing systematic spelling instruction, reading widely to extend meaning vocabulary, and sorting homophones for meaning and spelling. Figure 12.5 shows typical spelling seen during this stage.

APPROACHES TO TEACHING SPELLING

Teachers need to know the problems and issues that accompany any approach to spelling instruction. This section describes two options which teachers often use in directing spelling instruction. Sometimes teachers have no choice; they must use whatever approach has been forced upon them. This is unfortunate because it is difficult to work with an approach you do not know or do not think is best for your children. The only option I would deny teachers is the option not to teach spelling at all.

Spelling Textbook Approach

Spelling textbooks are the most common approach to teaching spelling. They've been around for a long time. Noah Webster started it back in 1783 when he published *A Grammatical Institute of the English Language;* later he renamed his work *The American Spelling Book* and later still they were commonly referred to as Webster's "Blue Back Spellers" (Unger, 1998). They were used for half a century or more to teach spelling, reading, and grammar.

Teachers, if they teach spelling at all, often chose spelling textbooks because of convenience. Preparing spelling lists and activities is time consuming, and many teachers haven't the time to add another big chore to their list of things to do. Others choose spelling textbooks because they have found them as good or better than other available alternatives. Whatever the reason, most children who are taught spelling at all get their instruction from textbooks.

Modern spelling textbooks have common features. These features include: (1) student textbook with thirty-six spelling lessons; (2) teacher's edition with lesson plans; (3) spelling lists based on criteria; (4) a weekly lesson plan; (5) word study activities focused on phonics, structure, and meaning; (6) testing and evaluation procedures; (7) writing, handwriting, dictionary, editing, and proofreading features; (8) systematic review; (9) ancillary materials and provisions for adjusted instruction; (10) spelling strategies instruction; and (11) diagnostic placement tests.

Spelling textbooks often seem much alike, yet significant differences exist. Textbooks are chosen by teacher committees and/or administrators. Usually a checklist of criteria is used to guide selection. Checklists should contain criteria developed by teachers that are relevant to the children who will use the books. Checklists should consider a school or district's curricular goals and standards and usually do.

Cooperative Approach

The Cooperative Spelling Approach requires teachers and children to establish spelling lists and activities jointly. The major task in this approach is selecting relevant words and preparing suitable spelling activities. The hardest task in this approach is coordinating instruction across grade levels. If this challenge can be met, the approach will work well. The following tasks must be accomplished since, by the nature of the approach, there are no ready-made materials available for use.

Selecting Words: Students and teachers jointly select spelling words. Words are selected from written work, reading material, and other sources. The intent is to use words chosen by students from their writing, an excellent concept. But it is also necessary for teachers to provide supplemental words. These supplemental words should be coordinated across grade levels for maximum effectiveness. If they are not, serious deficiencies in spelling instruction are likely to result.

Management: This approach works best when management of important instructional issues is well organized. The approach requires cooperation between student and teacher as well as among teachers and administrators. The approach works best when these three matters are attended to: (1) an effective reading and writing program is in place, (2) procedures for selecting personal and supplemental spelling lists have been established, and (3) activities and procedures for studying words are developed and followed. These are major tasks, and often they are neglected at the school or district level, leaving the teacher to carry the burden alone.

Spelling instruction must be managed well regardless of the approach chosen. Seemingly simple questions arise and must be answered: How many words should a given child study per week? How should spelling words be practiced? Such questions have more than one answer, and the answers may depend on factors that only the classroom teacher can provide.

THREE SPELLING INFLUENCES

Spelling is influenced by reading, writing, and instruction. Each contributes to success, and when any one of the three are neglected, ineffective spelling instruction is the likely result. The reason each influence is crucial is elementary, as Holmes might say to Watson. Reading provides background information about the written language—letters, sounds, words, structure, and meaning. Writing is the forum in which the game is played. You wouldn't expect baseball to be learned without opportunities to throw, catch, and hit. You can't expect spelling to be learned as a theoretical exercise. Kids must practice producing language in a meaningful writing context. Finally, there must be instruction. Some kids learn to spell without benefit of formal instruction, but most do not. They need organized instruction focused on words, strategies, and principles of English spelling.

The Influence of Reading

Spelling serves as a gateway to reading; reading serves as a gateway to spelling. In either instance, there is mutual advantage. Information about letters and sounds derived from spelling can aid reading and it works the other way around. This reciprocal relationship serves both reading and spelling well. Gates (l937) found that a strong reciprocal relationship exists between reading and spelling. Henderson's (1989) research supports Gates' conclusion: "Children's first major source of information about correctly spelled words is the sight vocabulary of their beginning reading material, dictated stories, poems, trade books, and basal texts" (p. 91).

Research on phonological awareness shows an overlapping knowledge base between reading and spelling. Ball and Blachman (1991) investigated the effects of training in phonemic segmentation and instruction in letter names and letter sounds. They found that phonemic awareness instruction combined with instruction connecting the phonemic segments to alphabet letters significantly improved early reading and spelling skills. The connection between reading and spelling is most pronounced in the primary grades (Blachman, 1984; Stanovich, Cunningham, and Cramer, 1984; Juel, Griffith, and Gough, 1986; Mann and Liberman, 1984; Cramer, 1985).

Word study helps children discover the rules and patterns which determine spelling and contributes to a better understanding of English orthography (Templeton and Morris, 1999). Recognizing spelling patterns helps children predict the spelling of related words. While reading and spelling share common components, they are not mirror images. Spelling requires greater precision and more control over letter-sound relationships than reading.

The Influence of Writing

Early writing adds power to beginning reading and spelling instruction. First-draft writing should emphasize fluent expression of ideas while temporarily deemphasizing the mechanics of writing. This is necessary because the amount of attention available for performing any task is limited. Two strategies help children focus their attention on the message rather than on the mechanics of writing. The first is a short-term solution, the second is long term. First, invented spelling relieves the immediate pressure for correct spelling while drafting. Second, the acquisition of a spelling vocabulary gradually provides the automaticity needed for fluent writing. Writing with invented spelling is the best way to increase children's practical knowledge of letters and sounds because it enables children to use their oral and written language knowledge to approximate words they have not yet learned to correctly spell. It frees writers from devoting too much attention to encoding, enabling them to concentrate on the message.

The Influence of Spelling Instruction

Children need consistent spelling instruction starting in first or second grade and continuing through grade eight. Many students would benefit from continued instruction throughout high school. At the elementary school level, 60 to 90 minutes of instruction per week is needed to teach spelling adequately. Consistent instruction requires that meaningful activities for learning words be part of the spelling routine; it requires learning a well-chosen set of words; it requires connections between reading, writing, and spelling.

Spelling instruction should concentrate on developing a serviceable spelling vocabulary, crucial spelling principles, and spelling strategies. If a core spelling vocabulary is not established early, children will not have a sufficient base upon which to build new spelling knowledge. By grade eight, children should be able to automatically spell the vast majority of the words most likely to be used in writing or encountered in reading. Whether this instruction takes place in spelling textbooks or through an individualized approach is less important than that it take place.

STRATEGIES FOR TEACHING AND LEARNING SPELLING

A strategy is a plan designed to achieve a particular outcome. All children, whether good or poor spellers, need strategies to learn unknown words. Getting new words into long-term memory is the purpose of a spelling strategy. In the earliest stages of spelling, children tend to rely on sound, and in the beginning sound cues are the major strategy used to spell unknown words. As children move through the stages of spelling growth, they acquire additional, more sophisticated, spelling strategies. It is the good spellers who are most likely to add spelling strategies to their spelling knowledge base; poor spellers, unfortunately, are more likely to have a much smaller strategy pool. Good spellers learn many strategies on their own; poor spellers are less likely to do so, yet they are most in need. Seven strategies students need to know are described.

Pronunciation Strategy

Some words are misspelled because they are mispronounced or underarticulated (Templeton and Morris, 1999; Cramer and Cipielewski, 1995; Carrell and Pendergast, 1954). For example, failure to fully articulate a word like *probably* may result in this spelling—*probly.* Fully articulated pronunciation is helpful on certain words but not on others. Words such as *favorite, February,* and *chocolate* may benefit from clear articulation of the unarticulated or underarticulated troublesome part. The list below contains words to which this strategy applies, and it is helpful in many other words as well.

PRONUNCIATION STRATEGY

Common Misspelling	Target spot	Fully Articulated
midle	middle	mid dle
Febuary	February	Feb ru ary
favrite, favernt	favorite	fav o rite
difrent, diferent	different	diff er ent
choclate	chocolate	choc o late

Problem Parts Strategy

Gates' (1937) study of spelling difficulties located the troublesome features within words. He demonstrated that words have "problem parts" which generate a significant percentage of the errors children make in spelling. It makes sense, therefore, to teach children to locate the place within a word which gives them difficulty and to study that part in particular. If a child misspells *laughing* as *lafing,* as they do 57 percent of the time, then *ugh* is the problem, not the rest of the word. Locating troublesome parts in a misspelling is best done after pretesting. Children should be taught to locate their own problem parts. Teacher modeling of the process is helpful. The list below gives a few examples of "hard parts" in words and the percentage of errors these parts generated in Gates' (1937) study.

GATES' LOCATION OF SPECIFIC SPELLING PROBLEMS IN WORDS

Correct Spelling	Common Misspelling	Percentage of Errors
big*g*est	bigest	67
ch*ief*	cheif	56
fr*ie*nd	frend	28
fr*ie*nds	freinds	25
*im*prove	inprove	58
move*m*ent	movment	48
omi*tt*ed	omited	80
sen*s*e	sence	79

Visualization Strategy

Radebaugh (1985) reported that good spellers used visualization far more often than poor spellers. Poor spellers' overwhelming strategy was "sounding out." This strategy is useful but limited because it won't take a speller far beyond the phonemic stage of spelling. Visualizing is the creation of a mental picture to help spell a word. Visualization in spelling has two dimensions: (1) visualizing the target word or a related word in its written form and (2) visualizing a setting in which images are pictured. For example, children may be urged to visualize the word *can,* which they know, to help them spell *man,* which is unknown. Visualizing may also involve creating a mental picture in which images of people, animals, objects, and actions play a role in remembering or imagining the spelling of a word. For example, one might visualize a *ghost* as a *host* serving goodies: g + host = ghost or a *mosquito* who has *quit* his job of biting people: mos *quit* o. Three strategies can be used to teach visualization: (1) ask questions, (2) make suggestions and (3) give examples. Visualizing may come naturally to some children; others need to be coached. Suggestions for coaching visualization are given on page 319.

VISUALIZATION STRATEGIES

1. **Ask questions**

   What part of the word gives you trouble?

   What part is hardest for you to remember?

   Can you picture the troubling part?

   How does the word look in print?

2. **Make suggestions**

   Picture the word in your imagination.

   Your idea has to work for you, not for someone else.

   Your picture may apply to all or part of the word.

   Think of your picture when you write the word.

3. **Give examples**

   separate: picture *a rat* with a tail curled like an *e* as in:

   sep A RAT e

Mnemonic Strategy

A mnemonic strategy is intended to help recall a difficult word or word part. Mnemonics are mostly useful for a small number of difficult to remember words. Mnemonics are sometimes most effective when they are silly rather than serious. Kids can have fun with them. A few examples of mnemonics are illustrated below.

MEMORY STRATEGY

Spelling Problem	Memory Clue
whole word: attendance	*at ten* the *dance* starts
whole word: define	pay *de fine*
whole word: misspell	*Miss Pell* will never *misspell*

Divide and Conquer Strategy

The more letters in a word the more chances there are to misspell it. Teach kids to divide long words into structurally correct parts and conquer the word one piece at a time. Divide words in ways that maintain their structural integrity. Most long words can be divided into their affixed parts and their root word or broken into syllables. Compounds can be broken at their meaning units. Examples are shown below.

DIVIDE AND CONQUER STRATEGY

Compound Words *Divide between meaning units*	Affixed Words *Divide between affix and base word*	Syllables *Divide between syllables*
snow/flake	un/want/ed	dis/a/point
fire/fly	need/ed	com/man/der
ring/worm	im/ma/ture	hol/o/caust
pony/tail	in/cal/cu/la/ble	por/cu/pine
ham/burger	re/ad/just/ment	re/a/li/za/tion

Rhyming Helper Strategy

A word often shares a linguistic feature that is similar to a feature in another word. Rhyming words often share similar ending features. Such features are sometimes called word families because they share a common phonogram, usually a vowel-consonant combination, as in *rat, fat, cat* or *cart, dart, smart*. Rhyming words usually have a similar spelling pattern, but not always, so it is good to make kids aware of this. Show them patterns like *caught, taught, shot* where the examples sound alike, but one deviates from the spelling of the other two. Awareness of the inconsistencies is just as important as awareness of the consistencies.

Words share similar features other than rhyming. For instance, words share similar beginnings and endings: starting blends: *star, stick, stop;* ending blends: *blend, send, sand;* digraph beginnings: *ship, shape, shop;* digraph endings: *slush, mush, hush.* Three books are helpful in dealing with word matters.

Bear, D. Templeton, S., Invernizzi, M. S., and Johnston, F. (1996). *Words Their Way.* Englewood Cliffs, NJ: Prentice-Hall.

Cunningham, P. (1995). *Phonics They Use.* New York: HarperCollins.

Pinnell, G. S. and Fountas, I. C. (1998). *Word Matters.* Portsmouth, NH: Heinemann.

Spelling Consciousness Strategy

Good spellers are aware of their spelling knowledge, poor spellers are not. The challenge is to help children develop a stance of self-monitoring. This is a difficult challenge, but one that, if successful, will help children become better spellers. Three ideas may help: (1) strategy awareness, (2) proofreading for spelling errors, and (3) searching for misspellings in the print environment. Some tips on developing spelling consciousness are listed on page 321.

DEVELOPING SPELLING CONSCIOUSNESS

1. Teach these spelling strategies:

pronunciation	problem parts	visualization
mnemonic devices	divide and conquer	rhyming helpers
spelling consciousness		

2. Teach these editing and proofreading strategies:

editor's trick: reading backwards	paired editing with peers
teacher's intentional misspelling	editing personal writing
editing writing of others	class editing

3. Practice searching environment print looking for:

misspelled signs	intentionally misspelled ads
newspaper spelling errors	other environmental print

Command of a reasonable number of spelling strategies can help children improve their spelling knowledge. The seven spelling strategies presented in this section are summarized below.

SUMMARY OF SEVEN SPELLING STRATEGIES

1.	Pronunciation	Fully articulate and pronounce the word.
2.	Problem parts	Identify the part that gives you trouble. Then practice it, spelling the whole word.
3.	Visualization	Visualize a similar word or picture the word in an unusual context.
4.	Mnemonic device	Think of a memory trick to help recall the word.
5.	Divide and conquer	Divide the word in smaller structural parts and conquer it.
6.	Rhyming helpers	Link the target word with a rhyming word spelled the same.
7.	Spelling consciousness	Learn spelling strategies, practice proofreading, and look for errors in print.

INSTRUCTIONAL ISSUES IN A SPELLING PROGRAM

There are a number of day-to-day issues that teachers need to consider when planning a spelling program. This section deals with day-to-day problems encountered in teaching spelling: number of words assigned, studying spelling words, pretesting and testing, reviewing spelling words, principles and strategies, time on task, and a summary of spelling principles and conventions.

Number of Words Assigned

There is little research to guide decisions about how many words a given child should practice each week. There are some traditional notions about how many, but this is only a guide. Classroom teachers are best able to determine how many words a child can handle in a week. Trial and error may be necessary for a period of time. Thereafter, monitor progress and adjust the number accordingly. Kids who progress well may have more words than those who are having difficulty. Good readers can handle more words than average or slowly progressing readers. The guidelines below are useful as a starting point.

DETERMINING NUMBER OF SPELLING WORDS

1. Have the child read her spelling list aloud. If she cannot read it fluently, the list must be adjusted. A child is not likely to retain spelling words that she cannot fluently decode, though she may remember them temporarily.

2. Spot check to see if the child knows the meanings of the spelling words. Unknown words can be learned by rote, but there is a high likelihood that they will soon be forgotten, since they are unlikely to be used in writing.

3. Monitor spelling achievement. Children who are progressing well should get 80 percent or higher on a spelling test at the end of a study period. If a child consistently falls below this level over a five- or six-week period, reduce the number of words assigned.

4. Adjust the level of word complexity. A child may not be developmentally ready to handle complex spelling patterns until simpler patterns have been learned.

The guidelines on page 323 can help you make an estimate of the right number of spelling words for each child. It may be necessary to adjust either the number of words assigned or the word patterns and principles studied or both.

NUMBER OF SPELLING WORDS ASSIGNED PER WEEK

Grade Level	Below Average Reader-Speller	Average Reader-Speller	Good Reader-Speller
1	4–6	8–10	10–12
2	6–8	10–12	12–15
3	8–10	12–15	15–20
4	10–12	15–20	20–25
5	10–12	20–23	20–25
6	10–12	20–23	20–25
7	10–12	20–23	20–25
8	10–12	20–23	20–25

Studying Troublesome Words

Research has shown that certain words continue to be misspelled across grade levels. Cramer and Cipielewski (1995) conducted a study in which they collected 18,599 compositions from children in grades 1–8. The sample included children from all states, as well as urban and suburban areas. Analysis of these first-draft compositions yielded lists of words particularly troublesome at each grade level and across all eight grade levels. A method of studying troublesome words is suggested below. It is neither necessary nor wise to use this procedure on words that children can learn in simpler ways.

WORD STUDY PROCEDURES FOR DIFFICULT WORDS

STEP 1: Prepare: Fold a piece of paper into three columns.

STEP 2: Study: Study your word until you think you can spell it.

STEP 3: First writing: Write the word in the first column. Check it. If correct go to the next step.

STEP 4: Second writing: Fold under the first column and write the word in the second column. Check it. If correct, go to step 5.

STEP 5: Third writing: Fold under the second column and write the word in the third column. Check it. If correct, stop for now.

STEP 6: Error: If you make an error at any point, start again at step 2.

STEP 7: Practice: Practice again another time.

Taking Spelling Tests

It is common practice to administer a pretest, midweek test, and final test. A pretest is essential because it tells children what they need to learn. A final test is useful because it helps you monitor progress. A midweek test is optional. If you use a pretest and midweek test, it is best to have children work with a buddy to self-correct their tests. Self-correction, if established and monitored effectively, works well (Horn, 1947; Horn, 1960; Hodges, 1981). The final test should be administered by the teacher. Teachers can administer pretests but this discourages self-monitoring and adds to the difficulty of managing spelling instruction. Have students work as partners to administer the pretest to each other. Teach them to follow the procedures outlined below before they correct their pretests.

PROCEDURES FOR SELF-MONITORING BEFORE AND AFTER CORRECTING THE PRETEST

1. **Known words:** If you think you've spelled a word correctly, put a check mark beside it.
2. **Unknown words:** If you think you've probably misspelled a word, put an X beside it.
3. **Uncertain words:** If you don't know whether a word is correct or not, put a question mark beside it.
4. **Assessment:** How often were you right in your best-guesses about words you thought were correct, incorrect, or uncertain?
5. **Correct your pretest:** Compare your pretest words with a correct copy.
6. **Study:** Practice words you missed. Use the procedures outlined on page 324.

Reviewing Words

Spelling words must be recycled within grade levels. Choose a period of time, say four to six weeks, and spend a week reviewing words previously taught. Continue this pattern throughout the year. Two procedures are helpful: (1) give review tests at regular intervals and (2) monitor writing for frequently misspelled words and review them regularly.

Research shows that certain words are misspelled across grades 1–8. Every teacher knows that words like *again, there, their, a lot* continue to be misspelled even into high school and college. These words may look easy, but they are not. Therefore, they must be taught and retaught across grade levels. Cramer and Cipielewski (1995) identified 100 words that continue to be troublesome regardless of grade level. These words are shown on page 325.

100 MOST FREQUENTLY MISSPELLED WORDS GRADES 1–8

1. too
2. a lot
3. because
4. there
5. their
6. that's
7. they
8. it's
9. when
10. favorite
11. went
12. Christmas
13. were
14. our
15. they're
16. said
17. know
18. you're
19. friend
20. friends
21. really
22. finally
23. where
24. again
25. then
26. didn't
27. people
28. until
29. with
30. different
31. outside
32. we're
33. through
34. upon
35. probably
36. don't
37. sometimes
38. off
39. everybody
40. heard
41. always
42. I
43. something
44. would
45. want
46. and
47. Halloween
48. house
49. once
50. to
51. like
52. whole
53. another
54. believe
55. I'm
56. thought
57. let's
58. before
59. beautiful
60. everything
61. very
62. into
63. caught
64. one
65. Easter
66. what
67. there's
68. little
69. doesn't
70. usually
71. clothes
72. scared
73. everyone
74. have
75. swimming
76. about
77. first
78. happened
79. Mom
80. especially
81. school
82. getting
83. started
84. was
85. which
86. stopped
87. two
88. Dad
89. took
90. friend's
91. presents
92. are
93. morning
94. could
95. around
96. buy
97. maybe
98. family
99. pretty
100. tried

Notice that most of the 100 most frequently misspelled words are not long words. Most are six letters long or shorter. So the problem is not simply orthographic. Many of these words are homophones, and the big problem is usage. Others are contractions, a common spelling difficulty. Others have easily reversible letters such as *ei* or *ie*. In any case, if these words are not taught and retaught across grade levels, some children will never learn them.

Reviewing Spelling Principles, Conventions, and Strategies

There are spelling principles, conventions, and strategies that all children need to know. Often we assume that they should be learned after one or two exposures. But for many children this does not work. Homophones, contractions, and possessives require continued emphasis.

Spelling strategies must also be taught and retaught. A strategy can be applied to a single word or to a class of words. Poor spellers need time to learn spelling strategies, even good spellers cannot learn them in a single exposure. Strategies must be applied at different levels, within different contexts, using different example words. Students who have a grasp of spelling principles, strategies, and conventions are likely to succeed in spelling.

Time on Task

How much time should to devoted to formal spelling instruction? No one can answer this question for every classroom teacher, but I think it is clear that practice time is essential. I recommend about 60 to 90 minutes per week, but this can vary depending on how much writing, revising, and reading is done in a classroom and the approach to spelling that is used. Spelling instruction should be scheduled three to five times a week, depending on the instructional approach and the activities used. Three possible plans based on 90 minutes per week are suggested below.

TIME ALLOTTED FOR SPELLING INSTRUCTION

	Day 1	Day 2	Day 3	Day 4	Day 5
5-Day Plan	20	15	20	15	20
4-Day Plan	25	0	25	20	20
3-Day Plan	35	0	35	0	20

Principles and Conventions of Spelling

There are a small number of important principles and conventions of spelling, and all are implicated in the spelling errors children make. Good spellers learn them, poor spellers do not. Children acquire principles and conventions as a by-product of reading and writing and direct instruction. The nine basic conventions of spelling are summarized and illustrated on page 327.

NINE SPELLING PRINCIPLES AND CONVENTIONS

1. Alphabetic nature of English: The extent to which each speech sound is represented by a specific letter.

2. Position within word: The position of a letter(s) within a word can influence the sound or spelling of another letter(s) within words—silent *e* influences the long sound in *make*. The *gh* *(ghost)* never has a /f/ sound at the beginning of a word but can have /f/ sound in a middle or ending position *(laughing, laugh)*.

3. Meaning-spelling: Words related in meaning are closely related in spelling in spite of changes in sound in the derived form: *heal—health*.

4. Homophones: A word with the same pronunciation as another but with a different meaning, origin, and spelling: *bore, boar*.

5. Apostrophe: A mark (') used to show omission of one or more letters and to show possessive forms: *don't, do not; Bill's place*.

6. Compounds: Two or more words combined into a single meaning unit. There are three types: closed, open, hyphenated: *railroad, ice cream, vice-president*.

7. Capitalization: Proper nouns start with a capital letter: *Tom, New York*.

8. Abbreviation: A period follows most abbreviated words: *Sept.* for *September*.

9. One word not two; two words not one: Words such as *away* and *around* are one word not two; words such as *a lot* are two words not one.

CHOOSING WORDS FOR SPELLING

There may be as many as one million American-English words, far too many to learn to spell them all. Fortunately, no one need learn anywhere near one million words or even one-tenth that many. Here's why a smaller core vocabulary will suffice. If children can spell the 2,000 words most often used in writing, they will have enough words to correctly spell about 95 percent of the words normally used in writing (Folger, 1941). This is a good start, but insufficient. Add to the 2,000 an additional 12,000 well-selected words, and a satisfactory spelling vocabulary would be in place. Making progress toward 100 percent becomes increasingly difficult since every percentage point beyond 95 percent adds thousands upon thousands of additional words. The goal of a spelling curriculum is to establish a core writing vocabulary and an understanding of basic spelling principles and strategies. Once a core spelling vocabulary has been acquired and crucial spelling principles and strategies have been learned, additional thousands of derived and analogous words can be spelled that have never been taught.

What criteria will produce spelling lists from which basic spelling principles and strategies can be illustrated and practiced. Six criteria should be considered:

(1) developmentally appropriate words, (2) high frequency words, (3) frequently misspelled words, (4) linguistically patterned words, (5) content related words, and (6) personally selected words. A brief description of each criteria follows.

Developmentally Appropriate Words

Children should learn spelling words that match their stages of growth in reading, writing, and oral language as closely as possible. Researchers, principally under the leadership of Edmund Henderson, have identified five stages of spelling development: prephonetic, phonetic, patterns within words, syllable juncture, and meaning-derivation. Each stage implicitly suggests the need for the introduction of certain orthographic concepts and the avoidance of others. Word lists should be constrained by the boundaries of knowledge children have acquired as they proceed through the stages of spelling growth.

High Frequency Words

A core spelling vocabulary of 2,000 or so of the most common words used in writing and reading is crucial to selecting and sequencing spelling lists. Frequency lists abound, but each list was developed for different reasons and drawn from different sources. No single list will suffice. The best advice is to consult at least three such lists. Important frequency lists include:

1. Carroll, John et al. *The American Heritage Word Frequency Book.* Boston: Houghton-Mifflin, 1971. Contains 86,741 different words sampled from textbooks, novels, encyclopedias, magazines, and other grade 3–9 sources.

2. Dolch, Edward. "A Basic Sight Vocabulary." *Elementary School Journal,* 1936. Contains 220 high frequency words.

3. Dolch, Edward. "The 2,000 Commonest Words for Spelling." *Better Spelling.* Champaign, IL: The Garrard Press, 1942. Lists the 2,000 most common spelling words.

4. Harris, Albert and Jacobson, Milton. *Basic Reading Vocabularies.* New York: Macmillan, 1982. Contains 10,000 high frequency words from running text in eight basal reading series.

5. Thorndike, Edward and Lorge, Irving. *The Teachers Word Book of 30,000 Words.* New York: Columbia University, 1944. Contains 30,000 words arranged alphabetically. Frequency of occurrence for the word in general is given as well as its frequency in four different sets of reading matter.

If it were only a matter of selecting high frequency words, the task would be easy. A major problem in constructing spelling lists is how to integrate words of the highest frequency with other word selection criteria such as linguistic patterns, developmental appropriateness, frequently misspelled words, and personal words. It is a herculean task to compile a list of 10- to 15,000 words and honor all relevant criteria.

Frequently Misspelled Words

From a practical perspective, it is clear that children should learn to spell words that are most commonly used in spoken and written language. Up to a certain point, frequency in oral and written language gives important direction in selecting spelling words. But frequency cannot be the only consideration. This is where error analysis research can aid selection. Some words are difficult to learn and hang on as troublesome across many grade levels. Generally, frequently misspelled words are also high frequency words, so working them into spelling lists is not especially difficult.

Teachers know that words such as *because, know,* and *our, too, two, to* cause spelling problems. Not only is there a question of when to first teach them, but when and how they should be retaught. The idea that a word or spelling concept should be taught only once or twice over the course of grades 1–8 is unwise because it ignores a body of research demonstrating that certain words are unlikely to be learned permanently in one or two exposures. The following studies can help you determine which words have proven difficult for children to learn.

1. Cramer, Ronald, Beers, James, Hammond, Dorsey, and Cipielewski, James. *The Scott-Foresman Research in Action Project: A Study of Spelling Errors in 18,599 Written Compositions of Children in Grades 1–8.* Scott, Foresman Addison Wesley, Glenview, IL: 1995. Screens 1,584,758 words to determine most frequently misspelled words across and within grade levels 1–8 and categorizes 55 different types of spelling error patterns across eight grade levels.

2. Farr, Roger et al. *An Analysis of the Spelling Patterns of Children in Grades Two through Eight.* Center for Reading and Language Studies: Indiana State University, 1989. Identifies words children often misspell and reports patterns of spelling errors.

3. Gates, Arthur. *A List of Spelling Difficulties in 3,876 Words, Showing the "Hard-Spots," Common Misspellings, Average Spelling-Grade Placement, and Comprehension Grade Ratings for Each Word.* New York: Bureau of Publications, Teachers College, Columbia University, 1937. Early study of spelling difficulties that locates the features within words which are most likely to generate spelling errors.

Linguistically Patterned Words

Linguistic patterns are the organizing principle around which the other criteria revolve. Linguistic features, such as meaning, sound, structure, and etymology, provide insight into how words are spelled. For example, there is an important link between meaning and spelling, vowel patterns and spelling, word structure and spelling, and etymology and spelling. Good spelling lists consider all of these linguistic features. This makes list making challenging, but in the end provides the best way to organize learning. Furthermore, organizing lists by linguistic features does not preclude considering other criteria for word selection, though it adds to the complexity of list construction.

Content Words

Math, science, history, English, reading, and other subjects have a key vocabulary which changes as children move from grade to grade. It is important for kids to learn this vocabulary. Consequently, content words should be included on spelling lists. There are two options for dealing with content words. They can be worked into weekly lists, or they can be taught separately. If incorporated into weekly lists, they must fit a linguistic pattern. While this is not difficult to do, it does scatter content words across many lessons. If incorporated into separate spelling lessons, they can be taught at the time teachers want them taught.

Since there is a dearth of useful studies to guide selection of content words, one has to rely on subject matter textbooks, content lists in spelling textbooks, and other such sources.

Personal Words

Personal words are selected from writing or reading *by children*. Each list is personal and specific to the child who selects them. Personal words should constitute a portion of the words children study each week. Which words to choose and how many can become a problem. Two criteria should apply: (1) personal words should be ones a child misspells in written work or encounters in reading, and (2) personal words should be within a child's meaning and word recognition vocabulary. If these two criteria are followed, there is not likely to be a problem. It is important for kids to avoid selecting exotic words. An occasional exotic word can be a good choice, but it is a good idea to keep an eye out for this potential problem.

How many personal words are chosen can also become a problem. If you are using spelling textbooks, most programs suggest three to five personal words per week. If you are following the cooperative spelling approach, establish a balance between the number of personal words selected and the number assigned by the teacher.

INVENTED SPELLING

"Invented spelling describes children's first efforts to spell words they have not yet mastered" (Cramer, 1998, p. 82). It is making an educated guess about the spelling of an unknown word you want to use so that you can continue writing without interrupting your flow of ideas as you draft. All writers do this at one time or another, or they choose another word in place of the one they intended to use. This latter option is unsatisfactory, but if invented spelling is forbidden children have no other choice.

Imagine a first grader, let's call her Anna. Anna has a 10,000 word oral vocabulary but can only spell 50 words. What kind of a story can Anna write with 50 words at her command? An impoverished one, of course. On the other hand, if Anna is encouraged to spell as best she can, her story can be as rich as her imagination and oral vocabulary will allow. I cannot imagine Mark Twain stopping every ten minutes to consult a dictionary as he wrote *Huckleberry Finn*. Time enough to consult a dictionary or other resource after drafting's done. Yet many would deny this sensible strategy to children who have not yet acquired a core spelling vocabulary. The fuss that has arisen over invented spelling has its roots in misunderstanding the purpose and contribution of invented spelling. This section considers the salient issues involved in invented spelling.

Spelling is an obstacle to writing, particularly for younger children who have not been in school long enough to learn a core spelling vocabulary. Invented spelling raises two instructional questions and we must choose one or the other: (1) Should writing be delayed until a core vocabulary has been learned? or (2) Should writing begin before a core spelling vocabulary has been learned? Advocates of invented spelling chose the latter alternative because research and experience have shown that invented spelling leads to better reading, writing, and spelling both in the short and long term.

First graders may have oral vocabularies ranging from 5- to 15,000 words, but they can spell perhaps 5 to 500 words, nowhere near the size of their oral language vocabularies. Children's wealth of oral language can hasten the long journey to literacy if we put it to use, and the sooner the better. Visit classrooms where writing is well taught and invented spelling is encouraged, and you will find children who write early and make rapid progress in reading, writing, and spelling, not in spite of invented spelling but because of it. Invented spelling advocates do not presume that spelling instruction is unnecessary. Rather, they believe spelling should be taught in tandem with learning to read and write. When consistent spelling instruction is provided, alongside of reading and writing, invented spelling will not confuse or delay growth in standard spelling. It is far more likely to improve spelling.

Research on Invented Spelling

Cramer (1968, 1970) conducted a study of invented spelling as part of a larger study comparing the Language Experience Approach to a Basal Reader Approach. He found that first grade children who used invented spelling became superior spellers, far better than their basal reader counterparts who did not use invented spelling. The invented spelling group spelled better on lists of regular words and irregular words, and most importantly, they spelled better in written composition. These children also performed better in reading and writing than their basal reader counterparts and they maintained their superior literacy achievement across six years (Stauffer and Hammond, 1969; Stauffer, Hammond, Oehlkers, and Houseman, 1972).

Read (1970, 1971, 1975) studied the invented spellings of preschool children. He showed that different children invented essentially the same system of spelling, and that their spellings were uniform from child to child. Clarke (1989) studied the effects of invented spelling versus traditional spelling among first grade children. She measured reading, writing, and spelling achievement. While achievement in reading was similar, children using invented spelling showed superior spelling and phonetic analysis skill. Low achieving children benefited most from invented spelling. Healy (1991) compared the effects of invented spelling and traditional spelling on growth in reading and writing among first graders. The invented spelling group produced better and more writing than children in the traditional spelling group. Garcia (1997) investigated the effects of invented spelling on first graders' reading, writing, and spelling growth. Results showed that invented spelling had a beneficial influence on word attack skills, vocabulary knowledge, and writing.

The evidence shows that children who use invented spelling spell, read, and write better than their counterparts in traditional programs. There is neither permanent nor temporary damage or delay in learning standard spelling. On the contrary, literacy achievement tends to be accelerated and superior.

When to Stop Using Invented Spelling

Invented spelling stops as correct spelling replaces it. No one needs to invent the spelling of a known word; we often need to invent the spelling of unknown words. We want children to spell correctly the words they know and invent those they do not know. It is always necessary to invent the spelling of unknown words *while we are drafting,* and it should always be acceptable. Ask yourself, "Do I use invented spelling when I am drafting?" You almost certainly do, but you correct your spelling when you revise and before presenting your writing in a public forum. This is what we want children to do.

Ms. Biz Smith Williamson believes that her kindergartners benefit from early writing, but before they can do conventional writing they must know how to use their phonetic knowledge to invent the spelling of words. She tells about her procedures in the "Voices" piece.

VOICES FROM THE CLASSROOM: Biz Smith Williamson

Early Invented Spelling

I teach kindergarten in Grosse Pointe, Michigan. I have 21 students in my class. Prior to this year, most of my teaching experience has taken place in the third and fourth grades. Teaching young children is rewarding. It pleases me to know that they will leave kindergarten as confident writers who will focus more on ideas rather than the mechanics of writing.

Two of our main academic centers are Language Arts based, Journal Center and Letter Center. The basic structure at these two centers remains the same every week. However, details such as the letter of the week and the thematic topic change. While the students are at these two centers, I am able to focus on their writing progress.

Most of my students have an understanding of letter-sound connections. This background knowledge is helpful when they begin combining letters to make words. When writing in their journals my students are encouraged to sound out words as they write. It is not acceptable to say, "I can't spell this word." They are always reminded that they can spell a word if they first think about the way the word sounds and then ask for assistance. It is not unusual to hear the children discuss the best way to spell a word when they are writing at one of the centers. Recently I introduced the letter *J* and *j*. One student wanted to write the word "jellyfish." I heard him ask the students in his group if they could help him. One said, "Well, we know it begins with the letter *j*, so you better make a *j*." Another child added, "Yes, start with a *j* then add *a* or *e*." A third said, "I hear *l* so write *l*." The first child said, "I hear *f*, does anyone else hear *f*?" They all agreed and together they spelled "JELF." For kindergartners in early November, I think they did a great job.

ASSESSING SPELLING GROWTH AND ACHIEVEMENT

Teachers need to know how children are progressing in spelling. First and second graders are beginning to read, and those who are making progress have acquired some spelling knowledge. What is the state of this progress? Children in grades 3 through 8 have also acquired spelling knowledge, and teachers need to know what level of spelling knowledge has been acquired so that accurate placement in textbooks or on personalized lists can be made. This section discusses assessment of early spelling growth and assessment of spelling achievement for instructional placement.

Early Spelling Growth

Assessment of early spelling growth should be checked at regular intervals to determine how children are progressing. A good way to assess early spelling growth, especially in K–3, is to administer the Morris Spelling Test. Asa, Jacob, and Linda's performance on the Morris Test in February of their first grade year is shown below.

PERFORMANCE ON MORRIS TEST IN FEBRUARY OF FIRST GRADE

Word	Asa	Jacob	Linda
back	b	bac	back
sink	c	sik	secek
mail	m	meal	mail
dress	j	jas	drees
table	t	tabl	table
side	c	sid	side
feet	f	fet	feet
stamp	c	sape	stamp
letter	l	latr	lettre
stick	c	sic	stik
bike	b	bik	bike
seed	s	sed	sede
monster	m	mistrt	monstr
elevator	ltv	livtr	elvattr

Assessing spelling performance should be easy enough so that a teacher without much training in spelling development can make one of three decisions about performance on the Morris Test: (1) Progress is rapid, (2) Progress is moderate, (3) Progress is slow. After deciding which of these three categories is appropriate, we must ask: *What does the information suggest for future instruction?* Testing is a waste of time unless this question is answered. It need not be answered perfectly. Diagnosis is always tentative and subject to follow-up observation of performance during instruction—"kid watching" as Yetta Goodman calls it. And it's good to remember Yogi Berra's advice as well, "You can observe a lot by just watching."

Look at Asa, Jacob, and Linda's spelling performance on the Morris Test in February, as shown on page 333. Each child exhibits a different pattern: Asa exhibits slow progress, Jacob moderate, and Linda rapid. I have analyzed each of these cases, made tentative conclusions about performance, and suggested how the information can be used to plan future instruction. As instruction continues, adjustments should be made based on observation of performance and continued administration of the Morris Test from time to time.

Case 1: Asa, slow progress: Asa is at the earliest level of the phonetic stage of spelling.

Tentative conclusions about Asa's performance:

- At the beginning of the phonetic stage of spelling
- Beginning to make letter-sound connections
- Makes letter-sound connections with beginning consonants only
- Spells elevator *lvt*. Does best here, but this exception suggests that he may have thought elevator was two or three words
- Does not have a fully established concept of word

Recommendations for instruction

- Instruction on letter-sound relationships, phonemic awareness
- Word sort activities focused on beginning and ending consonant sounds
- Writing with invented spelling every day
- Basic reading instruction, probably at a beginning level
- Dictate, read, and reread stories—group and individual
- Read shared books aloud in groups
- Read aloud to every day

Follow-up

- Observe daily performance and make adjustments as needed
- Administer Morris Test again in April or May

Case 2: Jacob, moderate progress: Jacob is at the phonetic stage of spelling, though he is further into this stage than Asa.

Tentative conclusions about Jacob's performance

- Middle to late phonetic stage
- Solid grasp of letter-sound connections

- Beginning and ending single consonant always present, usually correct
- Consonant blends not fully established, but may be close—*st* in *monster*
- Always honors vowel sounds; on the cusp of grasping marking principle
- Concept of word established
- Most likely making satisfactory progress in reading

Recommendations for instruction

- Word sorts focused on consonant blends, digraphs, short vowel patterns
- Writing with invented spelling every day
- Dictate, read, and reread personal stories
- Individualized reading from trade books
- Group comprehension instruction
- Read aloud to every day

Follow-up

- Observe daily performance and make adjustments as needed
- Administer Morris Test again in April or May

Case 3: Linda, rapid progress: Linda is at the late phonetic to early patterns within word stage of spelling.

Tentative conclusions about Linda's performance

- Excellent grasp of letter-sound connections
- Has a good start on a spelling vocabulary
- Consonant blends and digraphs solidly established
- Aware of silent vowel marker principle
- Concept of word fully established
- Most likely making excellent progress in reading and writing

Recommendations for instruction

- Word sorts focused on long vowels, contrasting vowels
- Writing with invented spelling every day; work on revision
- Individualized reading from trade books
- Group comprehension instruction
- Read aloud to every day

Follow-up

- Observe daily performance and make adjustments as needed
- Administer Morris Test again in April or May

Asa, Jacob, and Linda are typical of what one might expect of first graders. Each child exhibits a different pattern of growth in spelling knowledge. Administer the Morris Test three times a year, preferably in November, February, and May. Not only will you have information about spelling growth, you will also have information about reading performance, particularly phonics.

Placement for Instruction

Placing children at their correct spelling level accelerates growth; placing them at their independent level slows growth; placing them at their frustration level stops growth. You can determine placement levels by giving the Spelling Placement Inventory shown in Appendix C on page 337. A spelling placement inventory consists of a list of words from grades 1–8. Although placement inventories are reasonably accurate, misplacement happens even with a good placement test. It is necessary, therefore, to monitor spelling performance for four to six weeks following initial placement. Adjust placement up or down when children consistently perform above or below their placement level.

Giving the placement inventory: A spelling inventory is easy to administer (see Appendix C). Ideally, you want to start at an independent level and test until a frustration level is reached. Start the inventory at least two grade levels below current grade placement. Typically, a third grader would start with the first grade list, a fifth grader with a third grade list, an eighth grader with a sixth grade list. Severely handicapped readers may need to start at the easiest level. Administer an inventory in small groups so you can monitor how students are doing. Continue testing until each student is missing half or more of the words on a given list. Start with your strongest or weakest readers, then move up or down until you have tested the entire class. Administer the inventory over two or more sittings, depending on the age of your children.

Interpreting the scores: Each correctly spelled word is worth five points. Multiply the number of correct words on each list by five. Use this score to determine the independent, instructional, and frustration levels.

An independent level is reached when a child achieves a score of 85 to 100 percent. Not all children have an independent level, others will show independent scores across two or more grade levels. Do not place children at their independent level as it is not sufficiently challenging.

The instructional spelling level is reached when a child achieves a score of 50 to 84 percent. Some children achieve instructional level scores spanning two or more grades. Placement is normally at the highest instructional level achieved, but exceptions can be made. An instructional level should be challenging, but easy enough so that frustration is not continuously encountered. An instructional level implies the need for teacher support.

The frustration level is reached when a child scores 45 percent or less. Do not place children at this level since it is too difficult, and learning will almost certainly be impeded. Criteria for interpreting scores received on the Spelling Placement Inventory is explained on page 337. Keep in mind that placement is a tentative decision. It must be adjusted upward or downward if subsequent monitoring of performance indicates that the initial placement was too easy or too difficult.

CRITERIA FOR DETERMINING INDEPENDENT, INSTRUCTIONAL, AND FRUSTRATION SPELLING LEVELS USING A SPELLING PLACEMENT INVENTORY

Level	Criteria Scores	What It Means
Independent	85 to 100	Do not place at this level. Not challenging enough; does not need teacher support.
Instructional	50 to 84	Place at this level. Just right; growth can occur; needs teacher support.
Frustration	45 or Lower	Do not place at this level; too hard; growth will be slowed or stopped; even teacher support will not suffice.

IDEAS FOR TEACHING SPELLING

1. Pretesting with a buddy: Before studying a week's list of words take a pretest—test yourself before studying your words so you'll know which words you know how to spell and which you do not know. First, give the test to your buddy. Then have your buddy test you. Correct your test yourself; then have your buddy check your work.

2. Fruitflake words: Compound words are two words joined to make a word with a distinct meaning: *football, tennis court, vice-president.* But these are ordinary, sensible compounds. You can do better than that. What's a fruitflake word? Maybe you can think of what it might mean. Work with a buddy or a small team to make fruitflake compounds. Define each nutty fruitflake word your team makes.

3. Meaning schmeaning: Having trouble spelling big words? Knowing how to spell a smaller related word can help. For example, if you know how to spell *sign,* you can spell *signal* even though the sounds in *sign* change when you say *signal.* What longer, meaning related word goes in the "Missing Word" column?

Meaning of Missing Word	Missing Word
To write your name	has *sign* in it
Book of songs	has *hymn* in it
When you quit your job	has *resign* in it
Where animals live	has *habit* in it
More than 50 percent	has *major* in it

   Write five more puzzlers using these words: *minor, labor, combine, compete, memory.*

4. Concept of word: Work with a buddy. Take your dictated stories or a big book that your teacher has read to you. Read the stories aloud, pointing to each word as you read. Try to read as rapidly as you can while pointing to each word as you go.

5. Inventing mentoring: When your class is going to write a story about a holiday, such as Halloween, think of a list of words that might be needed. For Halloween, kids might want to spell words like: *ghost, scarecrow, haunted house, trick, treat, mask, costume.* Ask your kids to invent their own spelling of each list word. Then write one or two examples of kids' invented spellings on the board. Work through each invented spelling, showing how to make each invented spelling more complete.

6. Hinky pinkies: Hinky pinkies are rhyming words with two syllables— *honey bunny.* Hink pinks are rhyming words with one syllable—*fat cat.* Read the hinky pinkies and hink pinks below. Then write five of your own.

   What do you call a crazy house? A mad pad.

   What do you call a poor chicken? A penny henny.

   What do you call a fancy box of chocolates? A dandy candy.

   What do you call a lazy ant? A can't ant.

   What do you call an angry father? A mad dad.

7. Art smart: Make a collage of words that have something in common. For example, search for words that start with the same letter, end with the same two letters, rhyme, have three syllables, and so on. You can put whatever type of words you want in your collage. Oh yes, *collage* means to paste things on a piece of paper such as words cut out from magazines, newspapers, or old books. Make your collage beautiful!

8. Homophone sentences: Work with a partner. Make a list of ten homophones that you have recently studied. Write each homophone in a sentence, making sure you have used the homophone correctly. Now dictate your sentences to your partner. Then write your partner's sentences. Check each other's work.

REFLECTION AND SUMMARY

Reflection

Spelling is a symbol of literacy, but not a good one since it can lead to serious misjudgments about one's literacy and intelligence. A poor speller may be a capable individual or not, but one needs much more information than spelling provides to make fair judgments about literacy or intelligence. On the other hand, if your spelling is "wobbly," as Pooh Bear claimed his was, you need to do something about it. Individuals who spell poorly put themselves at risk of adverse judgments that may unfairly stigmatize their true capabilities.

Throughout the eighties and early nineties, many schools abandoned systematic spelling instruction and replaced it with, you guessed it, not much. Now there is a reversal of this trend. Spelling is being taught again, but I fear it is not being well integrated with reading and writing. If so, it will fail again. Spelling is part of a three legged literacy curriculum: one leg is spelling, another is reading, and the third is writing. Cut away any of the legs and you have an unbalanced literacy curriculum. Spelling deserves a place in the literacy curriculum because of its inherent value and because it contributes to early reading and writing success.

Summary

This chapter has presented the following main ideas:

1. Four spelling myths were shown to be false: English spelling is irrational and irregular; poor spellers are dumb, good spellers are smart; spelling is learned by rote memory; spelling doesn't count.

2. Spelling has its beginnings in acquiring a concept of word and by developing basic knowledge of letters, sounds, and phonemic awareness.

3. Spelling knowledge develops through five stages.
   - Prephonetic stage: children experiment with written language and gain an understanding of words as objects that represent spoken words.
   - Phonetic stage: children invent spellings and make connections between letters and sounds, showing they have discovered the alphabetic nature of writing.
   - Pattern within word stage: children discover orderly structures within words.
   - Syllable juncture stage: children discover the principles of spelling associated with affixing words—dropping, doubling, and changing.
   - Meaning-derivation stage: children learn that the spelling of derived forms is associated with meaning and structural principles.

4. Two approaches to teaching spelling were presented.
   - Spelling textbook approach: spelling words and activities are provided through textbook materials.
   - Cooperative spelling approach: spelling words and activities are prepared jointly by teachers and children.
   - Result: Either approach can work well or poorly depending on teachers' willingness to work within the limitations each approach offers.

5. The major influences needed to develop competent spellers are reading, writing, and systematic spelling instruction.
   - Reading is a necessary but insufficient source for learning to spell.
   - Writing provides the forum for practicing spelling.
   - Spelling must be taught systematically across grades 1–8 in an integrated reading, writing, spelling approach to literacy.

6. Good spellers do not simply memorize words, they acquire strategies for learning how to spell words. Strategies presented were: pronunciation, problem parts, visualization, mnemonic devices, divide and conquer, rhyming helpers, and spelling consciousness.

7. The number of words to be assigned, methods of studying words, and procedures for systematic review were presented.

8. Six criteria for selecting spelling words are: developmentally appropriate words, high frequency words, frequently misspelled words, linguistically patterned words, content words, and personally chosen words.

9. Invented spelling was described as a valuable, though misunderstood concept. Research has shown that it benefits reading, writing, and spelling growth.

10. Assessment of early spelling knowledge helps teachers understand how children are progressing; placing children at their instructional spelling level is essential in any approach to spelling instruction.

QUESTIONS FOR REFLECTIVE THINKING

1. What is the most significant distinction between the prephonetic and the phonetic stages of spelling?

2. How can applying the principle of *meaning-derivation* help one to spell more accurately?

3. What are three major influences on spelling proficiency? How does each contribute to spelling knowledge?

4. Why is it especially important for poor spellers to learn a set of spelling strategies?

5. What is the value of selecting spelling words based on appropriate selection criteria?

6. What is invented spelling? How can it be useful in learning to spell?

7. What is likely to happen when children are placed at spelling levels well above their instructional level?

8. Mini case study: Lynn is in kindergarten. She writes every day. Her most recent story contained 102 words. Lynn misspelled these words: *ivs* for *adventure*; *td* for *told*; *wn* for *weren't*; *rmb* for *remember*; *nx* for *next*; *ct* for *kept*; *nva* for *never*; *ft* for *forgot*; *lfe* for *life*. Lynn correctly spelled these words: like, as, day, my, big, your, mom, dad, I, cat, with. Answer these questions: (1) What strengths do you see in Lynn's spelling? (2) Is Lynn likely to become a good reader, writer, and speller? How do you know?

REFERENCES

Ball, E. W. and Blachman, B. A. (1991). "Does phoneme awareness training in kindergarten make a difference in early word recognition and spelling development?" *Reading Research Quarterly*, 26(1), 49–66.

Beers, J. W. and Henderson, E. H. (1977). "A study of developing orthographic concepts among first grade children," *Research in the Teaching of English*. 11, no. 2 p. 133–148.

Blachman, B. A. (1984). "Language analysis skills and early reading acquisition." In G. Wallach and K. Butler, Eds. *Language learning disabilities in school age children,* 271–287. Baltimore, MD: Williams and Wilkins.

Carrell, J. and Pendergast, K. (1954). "An experimental study of the possible relation between errors of speech and spelling." *Journal of Speech and Hearing Disorders,* 19, 335–339.

Clarke, L. K. (1989). "Encouraging invented spelling in first graders' writing: Effects on learning to spell and read." *Research in the Teaching of English,* 22(3), p. 281–309.

Cramer, B. B. (1985). *The effects of writing with invented spelling on general linguistic awareness and phonemic segmentation ability in kindergartners.* Unpublished Doctoral Dissertation, Oakland University, Rochester, MI.

Cramer, R. L. (1968). *An investigation of the spelling achievement of two groups of first grade classes on phonologically regular and irregular words and in written composition.* Unpublished Doctoral Dissertation, University of Delaware, Newark, DE.

Cramer, R. L. (1970). "An investigation of first-grade spelling achievement." *Elementary English,* 47(2), 230–237.

Cramer R. L. (1998). *The spelling connection: Integrating reading, writing, and spelling instruction.* New York: The Guilford Press.

Cramer, R. and Cipielewski, J. (1995). "A study of spelling errors in 18,599 written compositions of children in grades 1–8." In *Spelling research and information: An overview of current research and practices.* Glenview, IL: Scott Foresman Co.

Folger, S. (1941). "The case for a basic written vocabulary." *Elementary School Journal,* 103, 22–24.

Garcia, C. A. (1997). *The effect of two types of spelling instruction on first grade reading, writing, and spelling achievement.* Unpublished Doctoral Dissertation, Oakland University, Rochester, MI.

Gates. A. I. (1937). "Generalization and transfer in spelling." New York: Bureau of Publications, Teachers College, Columbia University.

Gentry, R. J. (1981). Learning to spell developmentally. *The Reading Teacher,* 34, 378–381.

Healy, N. A. (1991). *First-graders writing with invented or traditional spelling: Effects on the development of decoding ability and writing skill.* Unpublished Doctoral Dissertation, University of Minnesota, Duluth, Morris, and Twin Cities, MN.

Henderson, E. H. (1989). *Teaching spelling,* 2nd ed. Boston: Houghton Mifflin.

Hodges, R. E. (1981). *Learning to spell.* The ERIC Clearinghouse on Reading and Communication Skills and the NCTE, Urbana, IL.

Horn, E. (1960). "Spelling." *Encyclopedia of educational research,* 3rd ed. Edited by C. W. Harris, New York: The Macmillan Co., pp. 1337–1354.

Horn, T. D. (1947). "The effect of the corrected test on learning to spell." *Elementary School Journal.* 47, January, 277–285.

Juel, C., Griffith, P., and Gough, P. B. (1986). "Acquisition of literacy: A longitudinal study of children in first and second grade." *Journal of Educational Psychology,* 87, 243–255.

Mann, V. A. and Liberman, I. Y. (1984). "Phonological awareness and verbal short-term memory: Can they presage early reading problems?" *Journal of Learning Disabilities,* 17, 592–599.

Marine, K. (1995). "Using the research: Developing a spelling curriculum." *Spelling research and information: An overview of current research and practices.* Glenview, IL: ScottForesman.

Radebaugh, M. R. (1985). "Good spellers use more visual imagery than poor spellers." *The Reading Teacher,* 38, 6, 532–536.

Read, C. (1970). *Children's perceptions of the sounds of English: Phonology from three to six.* Unpublished Doctoral Dissertation, Harvard University.

Read, C. (1971). "Preschool children's knowledge of English phonology." *Harvard Educational Review*, 41, 1–34.

Read, C. (1975). *Children's categorization of speech sounds in English.* NCTE Research Reports No. 17, Urbana, IL: National Council of Teachers of English.

Stanovich, K. E., Cunningham, A. E., and Cramer, B. B. (1984). "Assessing phonological awareness in kindergarten children: Issues of task comparability." *Journal of Experimental Child Psychology*, 38, 175–190.

Stauffer, R., Hammond, D., Oehlkers, W., and Houseman, A. (1972). *Effectiveness of a language-arts and basic-reader approach to first grade reading instruction extended into sixth grade.* Cooperative Research Project 3276, University of Delaware, Newark, DE.

Stauffer, R. G. and Hammond, W. D. (1969). "The effectiveness of a language arts and basic reader approach to first grade reading instruction extended into third grade." *Reading Research Quarterly*, 4, 468–499.

Temple, C. (1987). *An analysis of spelling errors from Gates 1937 Study.* Unpublished Manuscript, University of Virginia, 1978.

Templeton, S. and Morris, D. (1999). "Questions teachers ask about spelling." *Reading Research Quarterly*, Vol. 34, No. 1, 102–112.

Unger, G. H. (1998). *Noah Webster: The life and times of an American patriot.* New York: John Wiley and Sons, Inc.

CHAPTER **13**

Grammar, Punctuation, and Writing

> Now, the sentence was not invented by grammarians—
> although they sometimes seem to think so.
>
> *David Lambuth*

> Today I worked very hard. This morning I put
> in a comma. This afternoon I took it out.
>
> *Oscar Wilde*

A WRITER'S STORY

Young Isaac set off for the public library. He worried about what might happen; would someone make fun of him, laugh at him? As he raced toward Nowolipski Street, a voice within him shouted, "I must learn the truth." Opening the heavy door, Isaac entered the library. A long hall-like room loomed ahead, stacked from floor to ceiling with books. He felt so dizzy he thought he might faint. Isaac never imagined so many books existed in the entire world. A corpulent, beardless man patching books greeted him amiably. Encouraged by the librarian's friendly greeting, Isaac reveals that he is returning a book checked out by his older brother. A fine has accumulated, and Isaac hasn't a "groshen," so to excuse his brother's delinquency and remain in the good graces of the librarian, Isaac lies. His brother, he says, has been drafted into the army and sent off to the war.

The librarian sympathizes, then asks, "What do you want to know?" Isaac replies, "I want to know the secret of life." Isaac is chagrin at his uncensored words, but the librarian listens quietly. After questioning Isaac about his interests and his family, the librarian climbs a ladder, brings down two books and says, "If a boy wants to know the secret of life, you have to accommodate him." Years later, Isaac warmly recalls the episode, "A great surge of affection swept over me toward this good person along with the desperate urge to read what was written in these books." The good librarian knew that the secret of life has never been encapsulated in a book, and I'm sure he also knew that books open doors to the intellect and to the soul—perhaps the "real" secret of life.

I hope that kind librarian lived long enough to learn that the young boy he "accom-modated," Isaac Bashevis Singer, went on to earn a Nobel prize for his novels and stories about Jewish folklore, legends, and mysticism.

INTRODUCTION

While Singer wrote mostly in Yiddish, I suppose he had to contend with the grammar of his native language just as those of us who speak and write English. Why is grammar so feared by students? Hughes Mearns faced this fearful question from one of his eighth grade students: "Are we going to have grammar in this class?" Mearns replied, "Grammar? I suppose it is like good manners, or friendliness, or unselfishness, or sportsmanship; it's something one lives and therefore cannot get satisfactorily out of a book" (Mearns, 1929, p. l7). Mearns' reply puts grammar into perspective. He implies that grammar has social and intellectual benefits, but it is acquired naturally, not by studying rules set out in a book.

The reason most often given for teaching grammar is that it makes better writers. Learn the rules of grammar, it is said, and you will make fewer grammatical errors in your writing. And fewer errors, of course, means better writing. But does research sustain this belief? If you study grammar diligently, will it make you a better writer? Or will you become a better writer by writing and learning grammar in the process of writing?

Technically, the mechanics of writing are not part of the grammar of language. Nevertheless, this chapter includes a discussion of that aspect of mechanics dealing with punctuation, since it is often included in a broader definition of grammar. The thesis of this chapter is that grammar and mechanics are best learned in the context of writing. You may disagree with this view, and you certainly need not take it on my say so. But consider the evidence presented, and come to your own reasoned conclusion.

GRAMMAR

Defining Grammar

There are many definitions of grammar (Hartwell, 1985). There are prescriptive grammars, the kind that appear in traditional grammar books. There are descriptive grammars, the kind linguists concoct. There are elitist grammars, the kind language mavens wish to impose on everyone. No single definition can be all inclusive. My favorite is this one: *grammar is a description of the language patterns which native speakers use automatically.*

Grammar, broadly defined, improves writing. It makes sentences clearer, and ideas more intelligible, though this says nothing about how it is acquired. The rules of grammar are derived through linguistic analysis, but convention plays a role as well, particularly in matters of usage and mechanics. Kane (1988) gives this explanation of what is grammatical:

The sentence *She dresses beautifully* is grammatical. These variations are not: *Her dresses beautifully. Dresses beautifully she.* The first breaks the rule that a

Jerome is a writer, and his teacher makes sure he revises his early drafts. She does most of her grammar and mechanics instruction during writing time.

pronoun must be in the subjective case when it is the subject of a verb. The second violates the conventional order of the English sentence: subject-verb-object. (That order is not invariable and may be altered, subject to other rules, but none of these permits the pattern: "Dresses beautifully she").

Grammatical rules are *not* the pronouncements of teachers, editors, or other authorities. They are simply the way people speak and write, and if enough people begin to speak and write differently, the rules change. (p. 11)

These definitions are sufficient, I think, to let us set forth on our journey to discover what the study of grammar and mechanics have to offer by way of helping or hindering children in their quest to write the language effectively.

Research on Grammar and Writing

I did not get much writing instruction in high school, but I did experience the usual instruction in grammar: subjects, predicates, parts of speech, and that marvelously named grammatical concept, *the dangling participle*. I understood little of it and cared even less. I see now that it didn't matter whether I understood it or not. I had my trouble with grammar as a youth, and as an adult grammar still mystifies me. I have a good grasp of the implicit structure of English, but even so I make my share of grammatical errors nearly every time I sit down to write. What in the world is wrong with me? Nothing. I do not live or die by grammar. Such grammar as I know, comes from my native oral language background and from experience as a writer. One thing seems certain, little of what I know about grammar came from the rules and descriptions set forth in traditional grammar lessons I studied in school.

After an extensive review of research, Braddock, Lloyd-Jones, and Schoer (1963) concluded that "The teaching of formal grammar has a negligible or, because it usually displaces some instruction and practice in actual composition, even a harmful effect on the improvement of writing" (pp. 37–38). Hillocks (1986) conducted a meta-analysis (study of studies) on grammar, usage, and mechanics to determine what influence they had on writing. He concluded that, "School boards, administrators, and teachers who impose the systematic study of traditional school grammar on their students over lengthy periods of time in the name of teaching writing do them a gross disservice which should not be tolerated by anyone concerned with the effective teaching of good writing" (p. 248). Hillocks and Smith (1991) reported that when three of the best studies in Hillocks' meta-analysis were examined separately, the case against grammar was even stronger: "Apparently any focus on instruction is more effective in improving the quality of writing than grammar and mechanics" (p. 597).

Elley, Barham, Lamb, and Wyllie (1976) directed a long-term study of grammar and mechanics on writing, and found they had no beneficial influence. Harris (1962) conducted a well-controlled two-year study where one group received grammar instruction and the other group spent an equal amount of time reading and writing. He found that the nongrammar group wrote more complex sentences with fewer errors and scored higher on a number of other criteria. Smith and Elley (1997) conclude that while some exposure to the rules of grammar may be useful, it is not a prerequisite for learning to write effectively.

It is beyond debate that writers must correctly use grammar and mechanics in their writing. But research gives us no reason to expect that traditional grammar instruction will improve writing quality. If we continue to teach grammar and mechanics outside of the context of writing, then we should not be surprised to find that the results are negligible, even counterproductive.

Reasons Given for Teaching Grammar

Grammar instruction has a long, unbroken tradition in American schools. It has never gone out of fashion, though its strength has waxed and waned. Various versions of grammar have been tried—traditional, structural, transformational. Arguments can be made for each type, but there is little evidence to recommend one over the other. Reasons for stressing grammar abound, and three reasons, in particular, are often cited: it makes a better writer, it enriches knowledge of the language, and it helps in learning foreign languages.

Makes a better writer: Do we learn to write by writing, or do we learn to write by learning grammatical rules? Research unambiguously shows that teaching grammar has no appreciable influence on learning to write. Research does not support the traditional belief that instruction in grammar improves writing. So if five hours a week are available for teaching English, "How do you get the most bang for your buck?" Do you spend five hours teaching writing, five hours teaching grammar, or divide the time equally between writing and grammar? If your objective is better writers, you spend five hours teaching writing, and you teach grammar when and as needed in the context of writing. Principally, this means teaching grammar through revision, modeling, and mini-lessons.

Maria, grade four, published a book she called *Peace is Black and Madness is Red: A Book of Pomes.* Her lovely "pomes" stemmed from a discussion of abstract nouns. Maria's teacher had discussed abstract nouns as words around which poems might be written. Maria quickly drafted nine poems in her journal. Later, she lined her poems with the help of her teacher, Ms. DeWard, hurried to the computer, typed them, and printed them out. Maria illustrated her poems and published them in a book. (See Figures 13.1, 13.2, 13.3, and 13.4.) I talked with Maria about her poems. She has a wonderful sense of what they mean, but she still has no idea of what an abstract noun is. I don't think this matters, and it is obvious that she has a wonderful sense of what a "pome" is.

Enriches knowledge of the language: There is the so-called "humanist" reason for teaching grammar. Language is a unique characteristic of humanity. Therefore, knowing and appreciating the structures, categories, and conventions of the English language is valuable in itself, it is said. Grammar is good because the study of it enhances one's knowledge and appreciation of language.

The "humanist" argument is not easily refuted, since its premise is aesthetic, not subject to empirical verification. Accepting the "humanist" argument requires balancing potential gains against probable losses. As it turns out, most students do not gain much knowledge of language as a result of studying traditional grammar. Oh, bits of grammatical information may be acquired as a result of traditional grammar lessons, but it floats around in a contextualess sea unless applied in writing. Traditional grammar instruction does not develop an appreciation of language in most students. It is far more likely to teach students that language study is uninteresting, perplexing, and boring. Literature can do much more to develop an appreciation of language than the study of grammar. The "humanist" argument is far more sensibly illustrated in the beauty of a poem or the enjoyment of a novel than in sorting out the parts of speech.

Helps in learning foreign languages: It is an article of faith among some advocates of foreign language learning that knowing the grammar of English will make it easier to learn French, Chinese, or Swahili. While there is no direct, reliable evidence to sustain this view, the argument has an appealing logic. If you know how nouns and verbs are modified in English, might not this grammatical awareness help you understand how similar or dissimilar categories work in a foreign language? Seems logical, but the evidence is that few students actually learn how verbs and nouns are modified through a study of traditional grammar. Further, might not relevant grammatical knowledge be more readily learned as a

Figure 13.1   **Title Page: Peace is Black and Madness is Red: A Book of Pomes**

foreign language is taught? Finally, most children do not acquire enough grammatical knowledge as a result of traditional grammar instruction to be useful in foreign language learning (Macauley, 1947).

Teaching Grammar and Mechanics in a Writing Context

I recently overheard part of an argumentative conversation in the Reading Clinic I direct. Jamie and Allie were reading drafts of their dinosaur stories to one another in a peer editing conference. Jamie claimed that quotation marks were needed if you used conversations in a story. Allie said, rather heatedly, that she knew that, but she wasn't sure where quotation marks started and ended, "So I left them

Peace
is Black
like frowning guns sitting in a dark closet
never being used
because there is no war so nobody needs a gun
because everybody has peace
and works out their problems like civilized people
not like monkeys and gorillas fighting for bananas and coconuts
not wanting what they already have

Figure 13.2   Peace is Black

out." Jamie showed her where he'd put them and then turned to his teacher and asked, "That's right, isn't it Ms. Morgan?" Ms. Morgan confirmed Jamie's assertion, and the two partners went on working. After peer editing ended, Ms. Morgan wrote two examples on the chalkboard of how quotation marks are used in conversation. Her mini-lesson took no more than three or four minutes and it arose spontaneously as a result of Allie and Jamie's conversation. This episode illustrates the idea of teaching at the point of need and in the context of writing. The combination of peer editing and a spontaneous mini-lesson provided appropriate instruction for a specific writing convention when it was needed.

Grammar and mechanics are important and it is precisely because they are important that it is unwise to teach them under conditions that almost guarantee they will not be learned. When grammar and mechanics are disliked, even feared, it becomes harder to teach them, even in appropriate contexts. The young girl

Imagination
is *Orange*
like the fireworks that explode
like new ideas that come to your head
when you read a fantasy book
about the most wonderful thing

Figure 13.3 **Imagination is Orange**

who asked Mearns, "Are we going to have grammar in this class?" was expressing her fear of the subject as well as her dislike of it. Her attitude had a history. English instruction, as she knew it, was loathsome. Yet she hoped that her new teacher, Hughes Mearns, might have something better to offer. He did—an opportunity to express her creative power through writing.

Earlier in this book (Chapter 4) I described revision as the single most powerful way of learning to write. Cox (1999) supports this concept: "Grammar and language conventions can be taught as part of the writing process. Doing so is most meaningful during the editing and revising stages of writing" (p. 394). If children have little opportunity to revise and edit their writing, then they will not, indeed cannot, discover and correct the grammatical and mechanical errors that are inevitable in early drafts. Finding and correcting miscues in early drafts takes place at several levels. Peer editing is one of the best ways to do this. When three or four children work together to read and discuss their work, they are likely to discover flaws they can readily correct. Children possess more grammatical and mechanical knowledge than they apply in their writing, particularly early drafts. This is not surprising since adult writers have the same problem. Even experienced writers need editorial support from peers and teachers.

Sadness
is *Blue*
like the tears
that trickle down your face
as you cry about what has happened
as the world cries
with nothing that will please it
so the oceans get larger
and deeper

Figure 13.4 Sadness Is Blue

Ms. DeWard, like all teachers, faces the question of how to teach the skills that she knows her students need. She describes, in her diary entry, how she uses individual conferences and students' writing to help them learn how to punctuate dialogue.

DIARY OF A TEACHER: Jennifer DeWard

This year I have used conferences to instruct many students on how to punctuate dialogue. I use examples from students' own writing to do this. Most students catch on quickly and understand the need for these skills. I have also shown a few students how to start a new paragraph every time a different character speaks. This is a tricky concept for fourth graders, and I have taught this mini-lesson to students who are ready for it.

Some of my students are at the beginning stage of their understanding of dialogue. They have difficulty understanding when and where to put quotation marks. During a conference with these students, I emphasize putting quotation marks around a person's exact words. If I tried to teach all of the other aspects of dialogue, I might confuse them. This is the beauty of the writers' conference. I can choose what skills to teach to each of my students. I know my students well and I know what lessons they need and when they need them.

Children do not automatically make use of grammatical concepts they have been taught. However, when grammatical concepts are taught in conjunction with writing, they are learned better. Weaver (1998), whose research on this issue is superb, summarizes the case for teaching grammar in a writing context: ". . . teaching *grammar* in the context of writing works better than teaching grammar as a formal system, if our aim is for students to *use* grammar more effectively and conventionally in their writing" (p. 33).

Basic Sentence Concepts

Grammar is mostly concerned with the structures and patterns of sentences. A sentence can be defined as a complete thought, yet a complete thought may also define a word, paragraph, or essay. Another definition of grammar says that a sentence is a group of words that includes a subject and predicate. Yet, successful writers violate this norm every day. Perhaps a sentence is a group of words that starts with a capital letter and ends with a punctuation mark. But this definition also lacks precision. Actually, there is no conclusive definition of a sentence. Even though defining a sentence is difficult, writers have been writing good and bad sentences since the Sumerians invented writing more than 5,000 years ago.

There are many ways to write a sentence, and often this is determined by purpose and style. Some writers develop a unique style to suit a specific purpose—humor for instance. Russell Baker, long-time humor columnist for the *New York Times*, often wrote sentences in the following style:

> Grammar funny stuff. Not make sense. Not good to write, 'She look good.' Why not? Rule say must write, 'She looks good.' Look good anyway you write it, no? Yes. Had grammar teacher in high school. Name, Sarah Fuller. Sarah never look good except at my essay. Look plenty good then. Take bucket red ink pour all over essay. Sarah say, 'Fix mistakes Russell!' How? Can't read paper—too much red ink. Grammar sure funny stuff, Sarah.

There are entire books about sentences, and the subject can become complicated. While children do not need to know all of this sentence arcana, there are a few sentence concepts that children need to understand and practice in a writing context. Children are not starting from scratch. They possess an enormous reservoir of sentence knowledge. The sentence concepts described below already exist in children's oral language.

Three basic sentence concepts are described in this section: (1) there are four sentence types, (2) there are three basic sentence patterns, and (3) combining sentences can improve writing.

Four sentence types: There are four sentence types: statement, question, command or request, and exclamatory. Knowing these sentences are punctuated, combined, and organized is useful for writers. Children already have oral command of each of these sentence types, so teaching them the nomenclature is less important than helping them understand how to punctuate and order their sentences into a coherent paragraph or longer piece of writing.

1. Statement sentences tell, declaim, or state something. They end with a period. *Example: Some children enjoy writing, others do not.*

2. Question sentences ask something. They end with a question mark. *Example: Do you like to write?*

3. Command or request sentences give commands or make requests. They end with a period. *Example: Finish your poem. (command) Please finish your poem. (request)*

4. Exclamatory sentences express strong feeling, surprise, or emphasis. They end with an exclamation mark. Even though an exclamatory sentence takes the form of a statement, question, or command, it still ends with an exclamation mark. *Example: Come here! (command) What's the big idea! (question) I'm mad! (statement)*

Three sentence structures: There are three common sentence structures: simple, compound, and complex. This terminology may confuse children, and they may think they know nothing about such sentences. One way to help overcome the confusion associated with formal descriptions of sentences is to show children they use simple, compound, and complex sentences when they talk. Record sentences children use in classroom conversation, and write examples on the board or on a handout. Then use their sentences to demonstrate the three sentence structures. For example, point out the independent and subordinate clauses that are a natural part of the complex sentences they speak. Keep in mind that it is less important for children to know sentence terminology than it is for them to write sentences. For example, it is not necessary for kids to identify and label sentence parts, because it is not labeling or identifying that makes a good writer. Writing requires transferring oral language knowledge into written language and then transforming and reshaping it through revision.

1. Simple sentences have a complete subject and predicate. *Example: Ernie mowed the lawn.*

2. Compound sentences join two or more independent clauses into one compound sentence. Each part of the sentence must have a complete subject and predicate. Conjunctions such as *and, but, or, so, yet* join the simple sentences in a compound sentence. A comma precedes the conjunction to mark the division of the independent clauses within the compound sentence. *Examples: The girls played basketball, and the boys watched. The game lasted two hours, but everyone stayed to the end.*

3. Complex sentences have one independent or main clause and one or more subordinate clauses. The independent clause can stand alone as a sentence, but the dependent clause cannot. Subordinate conjunctions such as *although, after, if, where, when, while* introduce a subordinate clause. A comma separates the subordinate from the independent clause.

Examples: Although it rained, everyone enjoyed the picnic. While sunshine would have been nice, we managed to have fun without it.

Ms. Clark is an experienced English teacher. Like all good teachers, she's always looking for better ways to teach sentence writing. In her "Voices" piece she describes how she discovered an effective way to teach her children how to write better topic sentences.

VOICES FROM THE CLASSROOM: Debbie Clark

Better Sentence Writing

My eighth graders begin the year with varied writing skills. Some years they need help with grammar and mechanics, other years they need less help. I never know where to begin until I assess their writing. This year as I read assessment papers, I was disappointed at the topic sentences. I was not sure how to tackle this problem without making my students feel inadequate. Then I found the solution.

The next writing session I explained topic sentences by showing them examples I had taken from their own writing. I wrote these examples on the overhead, then we did a "thumbs up or thumbs down" to vote for the topic sentences that we liked the best. Next, I asked students to write not one, but three topic sentences for their paper. I had them share these with their peers and choose the topic sentence they liked best.

What a difference! Their topic sentences were creative and exemplified voice and style. I was proud of my students, and they were proud of their creative ideas.

I learned that students can help each other. They can learn from each other's examples. I have always modeled writing assignments for students using my own writing, but I seldom used my students' own writing as models. My students were positive about this experience, and I know it will be a helpful teaching tool in other areas of writing as well.

Combining sentences: Combining sentences often conveys meaning more clearly and more economically. According to research, combining sentences usually results in better writing and more mature syntactic structures. O'Hare (1973) showed that combining sentences into increasing complex sentence structures increased syntactic fluency and improved overall growth in writing quality. Since that early study, many other studies have shown similar results for children and adults (Hillocks and Mavrogenes, 1986). Hillocks and Smith (1991) believe that the most important sentence combining finding is its influence on writing quality. While it is clear that sentence combining has a positive influence on writing, researchers do not know how or why it has this effect. Three possible reasons are: (1) it extends conceptual knowledge (Freeman, 1985), (2) it leads to increased attention to other aspects of writing (Crowhurst, 1983), and (3) it has a positive influence on revising and editing (Strong, 1986).

Six sentence combining procedures with accompanying examples are recommended in the guidelines on page 355.

SENTENCE COMBINING

1. Two sentences with the same subject but different predicates often make a more economical sentence.

   Example: Janet directed the band. She also played the drums. Janet directed the band and played the drums.

2. Two sentences with the same predicate but different subjects can also be combined.

   Example: Anthony is a fine writer. Jake is a fine writer. Anthony and Jake are fine writers.

3. An appositive is a noun or phrase that follows another noun and explains it further. Sentences can be combined using appositives.

   Example: Maria is a fast reader. She just finished reading War and Peace. *Maria, a fast reader, just finished reading* War and Peace.

4. A preposition and its object make up the prepositional phrase. Sentences can be combined by turning a descriptive sentence into a prepositional phrase.

   Example: That girl is a whiz at math. She has a calculator in her hand. That girl with the calculator is a whiz at math.

5. When two or more sentences have the same subject and predicate, their modifiers can often be combined.

   Example: That music is loud. But that music is fine. That music is loud but fine.

6. Combining sentences usually results in more economical writing. Even after combining, cutting unneeded words can improve your writing.

   Example: Taffy prefers friends who are on the intelligent side. She also likes her friends to be funny.

   Combined but not economical: Taffy prefers friends who are funny and on the intelligent side.

   Combined and economical: Taffy prefers funny, intelligent friends.

Basic Expository Paragraph Concepts

Defining a paragraph: A paragraph is a distinct subsection of a larger piece of writing. Paragraphs deal with a particular idea or belief. In expository writing, a paragraph normally contains a topic sentence, related sentences, connecting words, and a system for ordering sentences. Paragraph length varies with purpose, topic, audience, preference, and current writing fashion. An expository paragraph may range from one word to many hundreds, but usually they range from 75 to 200 words. Kane (1988) defines expository paragraphs this way: "They explain, analyze, define, compare, illustrate. They answer questions like What? Why? How? What was the cause? The effect? Like what? Unlike what? They are the kinds of paragraphs we write in reports or term papers or tests" (p. 67).

Paragraph types: There are various paragraph types. Four of the most common are explanatory, narrative, persuasive, and descriptive. Explanatory paragraphs tell how something is done. For example, a sequence of instructions may be required to assemble a bicycle or install an air conditioner. Narrative paragraphs tell a story or describe an event. The narrator is either taking part in the story or is an outside observer. For example, in Jack London's *White Fang*, the narrator is an outside observer. Persuasive paragraphs strive to convince readers to view the world as the writer sees it. A book reviewer, for example, may try to persuade the reader that a book is good, bad, or ugly. In persuasive paragraphs, reasons are stated in a convincing order, sometimes building from least to most convincing. Descriptive paragraphs tell how something or someone is viewed, striving for just the right word or image, and a perspective from which the word picture is understood or appreciated. Of course, paragraphs may be an amalgam of more than one type.

Paragraph structure: Paragraphs usually have a topic sentence and related sentences which develop the topic. Topic sentences convey the main idea of a paragraph; they usually come first in a sentence; they may also appear in the middle or end. A good topic sentence is concise, just long enough to convey the idea. Topic sentences are usually declarative; rhetorical questions can also make good topic sentences, but should not be overused. Occasionally, a paragraph may not have a topic sentence. All sentences in a paragraph must be related to the topic. If they are not, the paragraph will wander off the topic. Related sentences convey the content and are ordered in specific ways. If related sentences are relevant, linked, and effectively ordered, the flow of the paragraph is enhanced.

Sentences within paragraphs must be ordered effectively. There are various ways to do this. For example, related sentences can be presented as they occur in time, such as least to most recent. Scenes can be described according to the physical position of the viewer, for example, from where the viewer stands to the horizon. Steps in a process can be arranged in the logical order in which they occur—first, next, last. Sentences can be ordered so that they build toward a climax. Lawyers, for instance, often use climactic ordering in presenting closing arguments to juries.

Sentences within paragraphs must be connected with each other. Linking words and phrases signal the kind of relationship that exists between and among sentences. For example, there are: *time relationships*—after, before, during; *cause-effect relationships*—because, consequently, therefore; *spatial relationships*—above, behind, inside; *comparison or contrast relationships*—in spite of, on the one hand, similarly; *sequential relationships*—first, second, last. The links between and among sentences gives paragraphs the coherence needed to achieve the writer's purpose.

PUNCTUATION

The purpose of punctuation is clarity. Punctuation helps readers understand the writer's meaning by signaling the logic, rhythm, and structure of writing. When punctuation is used well, it compliments and clarifies the writer's message. When poorly used, it muddles meaning. It is important, therefore, for students to understand the purpose of punctuation and the rules which define its use. Punctuation operates on three levels: flexible conventions, inflexible rules, and personal style or preference.

1. Punctuation has flexible conventions. For example, the last comma in a series is optional. Recently, certain style manuals eliminate the last comma, but others still suggest its use.

2. Punctuation has inflexible rules. For example, a period at the end of a statement is not optional.

3. Punctuation may sometimes be determined by a writer's personal style or preference. For example, e. e. cummings used little or no punctuation in his poetry, but individual style or preference is the prerogative of the sophisticated writer, not the novice.

Pacing Punctuation Instruction

Children learn punctuation gradually. The speed with which children gain control of punctuation depends on how frequently they write and the effectiveness of direct and indirect instruction. When children first begin writing, punctuation may be scarce or even missing altogether. A slightly more advanced young writer may sprinkle punctuation here and there, sometimes correctly and sometimes incorrectly. Read the original and translated versions of the two pieces of first grade writing shown in Figures 13.5 and 13.6. Notice that the original version of "A Pothole Surprise" shows no conventions except the capitalization of the word *I*. No punctuation is used. On the other hand, the original version of

---

Original Piece
a Pothie Surprise
    now day I wos wageg doun a stret and I hrd a fune soun I loot doun the pothole I fel doun I had a rope and I throow it op thaa and eve bude climd op

Translation
A Pothole Surprise
    One day I was walking down a street and I heard a funny sound. I looked down the pothole. I fell down. I had a rope and I threw it up there and everybody climbed up.

Figure 13.5   Early Punctuation Effort of a First Grade Writer

---

Original Piece
The Fox and the Bird
A brid was in a tree. And a fox cam alog. And the fox said u ar sege is. Gob
I wot to here sam. More avoe sege. she did she brot. her shes and. The fox
got the shes and he ran away.

Translation
The Fox and the Bird
A bird was in a tree. And a fox came along. And the fox said you are
singing. Good I want to hear some. More of your singing. she did she
brought. her cheese and. The fox got the cheese and he ran away.

Figure 13.6   **Early Punctuation Effort of a First Grade Writer**

"The Fox and the Bird" shows a quite different circumstance. This writer uses periods correctly about half of the time and uses a capital letter to start most sentences. Each writer presents a different but potentially fruitful opportunity for instruction. The writer of "A Pothole Surprise" (Figure 13.5) may not be ready for instruction in punctuation. So, it may be best for this writer to gain additional fluency in writing before working on punctuation. On the other hand, the writer of "The Fox and the Bird" (Figure 13.6) is ready for a mini-lesson on using periods. It is also possible that both writers could benefit from a mini-lesson on periods, and the only way to know this is try and see what happens. But a good guess is that the second writer is the better candidate just now for a lesson on the mechanics of writing—specifically periods.

If children write three hours per week and if punctuation instruction is taught through modeling, revision, and mini-lessons within the context of writing, significant progress can be made. Punctuation clarifies writing, and this is an important concept for children to learn. Errors signal opportunities to teach the rules and conventions of punctuation. Therefore, errors should not be considered disasters, but signals for instructional planning.

Research on Punctuation

How, when, and under what circumstances punctuation skill is acquired has not been researched as exhaustively as other aspects of writing. A few studies give a general, though incomplete, picture of how children learn to punctuate their writing. Calkins (1980) compared two third grade classes to see how children in each class acquired punctuation under different teaching conditions. One teacher taught punctuation in the conventional manner using isolated drills. The other integrated punctuation instruction with writing. As one might expect, the children taught punctuation in the context of daily writing fared significantly better. This outcome should surprise no one. Skills learned outside of a context of meaningful application are unlikely to be learned readily or retained long. Cordeiro, Giacobbe, and Cazden (1983) found that first grade children appeared to form and test hypotheses about how to use punctuation in their writing. Another finding was that writing provided more opportunities to use punctuation than textbooks or worksheet exercises. Finally, they found that clear, accurate explanations facilitated learning, while abstract explanation caused confusion.

Guidelines for Teaching Punctuation

What are the best practices for teaching punctuation? Research provides some guidance, but it is not definitive. The experience of successful writing teachers is also helpful. Guidelines for teaching punctuation derived from research and teacher experience are listed below.

TEACHING PUNCTUATION

1. Write frequently, and teach punctuation within the context of the writing children are doing.
2. Start with the most common punctuation rules and conventions. Periods, question marks, and exclamation marks are among the most frequently needed for writing. So they are a good place to start.
3. Evaluate progress to determine when and what punctuation conventions should be taught or retaught.
4. Teach mini-lessons, and connect lessons with punctuation issues that arise as children write.
5. Model punctuation, using your own writing as an example.
6. Keep terminology and explanations simple, clear, and accurate.
7. Teach ending before internal punctuation.
8. Analyze punctuation errors; they are your best guide to future instruction.
9. Adjust instruction to suit differing rates of learning. For example, some writers are ready for quotation marks before others have mastered the period.

The most common punctuation marks and an example or two of their use in writing are shown below.

USES OF PUNCTUATION MARKS

Period: (.)

at the end of a declarative sentence or statement

after an indirect question

indicates an abbreviation or an initial

Question Mark: (?)

at the end of a direct or rhetorical question

Exclamation Mark: (!)

conveys strong emphasis at the end of a sentence

within a sentence to stress a word or construction

Colon: (:)

introduces quotations

introduces a specification, often a list

Semicolon: (;)

may be used between independent clauses

in lists in a series

Comma: (,)

separates words in a series and independent clauses

separates date from year and city from state

separates single word adverbs, phrases, and clauses (with exceptions)

after greeting in a friendly letter and after closing in a letter

before a quotation

Quotation Marks: (") and (')

sets off direct conversation

encloses certain titles and words given in a special sense

Apostrophe: (')

shows letters omitted from contractions

shows ownership

Dash: (—)

introduces a list

shows force or emphatic pause

precedes and follows coordinated elements

Parenthesis: ( )

encloses less important information within a text

A list of the most common capitalization concepts is shown below. The examples illustrate the major capitalization concepts.

CAPITALIZING CONCEPTS

First word in a sentence:

Our friends will visit in August.

Proper nouns:

I attended San Gabriel Elementary School in South Gate, California.

Proper adjectives:

We ate dinner at a wonderful Mexican restaurant.

Names of the days and months:

I'll see you on Sunday, January the 15th.

Initials:

R. L. Adams; M. A. Pobuda

In the greeting and closing of friendly letter:

Dear Alice, Sincerely yours

Abbreviations:

MI (Michigan), St. (Street), Sun. (Sunday), Dr. (Doctor)

Titles:

Mr. William Azar; Dr. Ann Porter; General McArthur

First word in a quotation:

Ashley said, "We refuse to go to bed this early."

IDEAS FOR WRITING

1. Combining sentences: Practice packing more information into a sentence by combining two or more sentences. Begin with two or more separate sentences and combine them into one. Start with simple sentences, like the ones below, and then work on more complex ones. Incidentally, there is usually more than one good way to combine sentences.

   Four Simple Sentences:

   Mary had a new dress.

   It was blue.

   She was going to Susie's party.

   She decided to wear the new dress.

2. Finding teacher's "mistakes": Write two or three sentences every day and put them on the chalkboard or bulletin board. Make a variety of grammatical or punctuation mistakes. You might say, "Find three punctuation errors in this sentence." Or, you could say, "How many punctuation errors can you find in this piece?" Don't neglect to inject a little humor into your notes. Here is an example:

   Last night I bought a horse and then after thinking it over I decided to take the horse back to the store and get a refund but the manager said we do not take back horses

3. Finding one another's mistakes: Exchange short notes with a partner in your classroom. Make a few mistakes in your note. See if you can find each other's mistakes. It's a good idea to make a correct copy of your

note first, and then write the same note again with whatever mistakes you want to make.

4. Proofreaders' marks: When you proofread a piece you have written or a piece that someone else has written, use proofreaders' marks. Below are six common proofreaders' marks you can practice using. Exchange papers with a friend and practice using these six proofreaders' marks.

Add a period⊙   Take something ou<del>i</del>t   make a capital. (cap)

Add som⁁thing. e   Transp<del>so</del>e. (tr)   ¶ New paragraph.

5. Editors' questions: Here are six questions to ask yourself when you proofread your writing or when you help a friend.

Does each sentence start with a capital letter?

Does each sentence end with the correct punctuation mark?

Are quotation marks used correctly?

Do I need to add a comma or take one out?

Is each word spelled correctly?

Can I combine two sentences into one briefer, clearer sentence?

6. Grammar jokes: Have you heard this one? *Question:* What is a pronoun? *Answer:* A noun that's lost its amateur status. What kind of language joke can you make? Here are a few questions and answers to get you started.
   - Why did the lady noun excuse herself after she sneezed? (Answer: Because she was a proper noun.)
   - Why didn't the two verbs leave the fort? (Answer: Because they were compound verbs.)
   - Why did the capital letter go to the end of the sentence? (Answer: To watch the exclamation point.)
   - Why did the infinitive split? (Answer: To go see the participle dangle.)
   - What is an adverb? (Answer: A verb with good math skills.)
   - Why is the future tense always worried? (Answer: Never knows what's going to happen.)

REFLECTION AND SUMMARY

Reflection

Research has raised serious doubts about the effectiveness of traditional grammar instruction, but classroom teachers often reject these findings. Why do teachers reject the idea that traditional grammar instruction doesn't work? Perhaps because of a failure to distinguish between two issues—*should* versus *how.* One issue is: *Should* grammar be taught? Most teachers believe it should be taught, and they are right. Few teachers, I think, would question that statement. Effective writing depends on applying grammatical rules and conventions correctly. The second issue is: *How* should grammar be taught? This is the crucial issue. The traditional approach does not work, and this has been demonstrated over and over again for the past 75 years. No matter how much one wants to believe otherwise, the evidence is simply not there. Such grammar as children possess and apply comes from their oral language and from genuine writing experience, not from traditional grammar lessons. Research that questions the value of traditional grammar does not mean that grammar has no role in writing. It means that we must teach grammar within the context of writing.

The mechanics of writing, particularly punctuation, present a slightly different issue. Children do not possess punctuation conventions as part of their oral language. Even though punctuation conventions are not acquired through oral language, reading written language aloud helps children understand the connection between spoken language and the marks we use to punctuate written language. While punctuation conventions are not acquired directly through oral language, as grammar is, they are best acquired in the context of writing.

Summary

This chapter has presented the following main ideas:

1. Grammar and mechanics are best learned in the context of writing.
   - There are several definitions of grammar. One of the better definitions is that grammar describes the language patterns which native speakers use automatically.
   - Research has shown that teaching traditional grammar does not improve writing.
   - Three reasons given for learning grammar are: it makes better writers, enriches knowledge and appreciation of language, and aids in learning a foreign language. None of these reasons have a substantial basis in research.
   - Learning grammar and mechanics is essential for effective writing, but they are best learned in the context of writing.
   - A practical knowledge of three sentence concepts facilitates writing: (1) awareness of the four types of sentences—statement, question, command or request, and exclamatory, (2) awareness of three common sentence patterns: simple, compound, and complex, and (3) practice in combining sentences.

2. Punctuation facilitates writing. Punctuation influences clarity and helps the writer signal the logic, rhythm, meaning, and structure of writing.
   - Children learn punctuation gradually. Instruction can be paced in harmony with signs of growth evident in children's writing.
   - While there is little reliable research on punctuation, what evidence exists suggests that punctuation skills develop best in a writing context.
   - Nine best practices guidelines for teaching punctuation were suggested.

QUESTIONS FOR REFLECTIVE THINKING

1. What does grammar contribute to writing? How might grammar be defined?
2. Hillocks, Braddock, and others cite studies showing that formal grammar instruction has a negligible influence on writing improvement. Why might this be so?
3. What instructional practices might have a positive influence on the growth of grammatical knowledge in writing?
4. Why teach grammar and punctuation within a writing context?
5. What are some effective ways to teach punctuation?
6. Some say that teaching grammar and punctuation is a waste of time. What arguments can you cite to support, refute, or clarify this claim?
7. What do you now know about grammar and punctuation that you did not know before you read this chapter?
8. Does the author believe that grammar and punctuation are necessary adjuncts to learning to write? Explain.
9. Mini case study: Tim just finished third grade. He reads like an advanced fifth grader. Even so, his third grade teacher describes him as a poor writer, and she says he did poorly on all punctuation and grammatical worksheets. Assume you will be Tim's fourth grade teacher. What might you do to improve Tim's performance in writing, grammar, and punctuation?

REFERENCES

Braddock, R., Lloyd-Jones, R., and Schoer, L. (1963). *Research in written composition*. Champaign, IL: National Council of Teachers of English.

Calkins, L. M. (1980). "Research update—when children want to punctuate: Basic skills belong in context." *Language Arts, 57*, 567–573.

Cordeiro, P., Giacobbe, M. E., and Cazden, C. (1983). "Apostrophes, quotation marks, and periods: Learning punctuation in the first grade." *Language Arts, 60*, 323–332.

Cox, C. (1999). *Teaching language arts*. Boston: Allyn and Bacon.

Crowhurst, M. (1983). "Sentence combining: Maintaining realistic expectations." *College Composition and Communication, 34*, 62–72.

Elley, W. B., Barham, I. H., Lamb, H., and Wyllie, M. (1976). The role of grammar in a secondary school English curriculum. *Research in the Teaching of English, 10*, 5–21.

Freeman, A. K. (1985). "Sentence combining: Some questions." In A. K. Freedman, Ed. *Carleton papers in applied language studies, volume II*, pp. 17–32. ERIC Document Reproduction Service No. ED 267 602.

Harris, R. (1962). *An experimental inquiry into the functions and value of formal grammar in the teaching of English*. Doctoral Dissertation, University of London.

Hartwell, P. (1985). "Grammar, grammars, and the teaching of grammar." *College English, 47*, 105–127.

Hillocks, L. G., Jr. and Mavrogenes, N. (1986). "Sentence combining." In *Research in written composition: New directions for teaching,* pp. 142–146. Urbana, IL: National Council of Teachers of English.

Hillocks, L. G., Jr. and Smith, M. W. (1991). "Grammar and usage." In *Handbook on teaching the English language arts.* J. Flood, J. M. Jensen, D. Lapp, and J. R. Squire, New York: Macmillan Publishing Co.

Kane, T. S. (1988). *The new Oxford guide to writing.* Oxford: Oxford University Press, Inc.

Macauley, W. J. (1947). The difficulty of grammar. *British: Journal of Educational Psychology,* 17, 153–162.

Mearns. H. (1929). Creative power: The education of youth in the creative arts. New York: Dover Publications Inc.

O'Hare, F. (1973). Sentence combining: Improving student writing without formal *grammar instruction.* Urbana, IL: National Council of Teachers of English.

Smith, J. W. A. and Elley, W. B. (1997). *How children learn to write.* Katonah, New York: Richard C. Owen Publishers, Inc.

Strong, W. (1986). *Creative approaches to sentence combining.* Urbana, IL: National Council of Teachers of English.

Weaver, C. (1998). "Teaching grammar in the context of writing," pp. 18–38. In *Lessons to share: On teaching grammar in context,* C. Weaver, Ed. Portsmouth, NH: Heinemann.

CHAPTER 14
Creating Writing Environments: Nurturing Creative Potential

It is of the utmost importance that we recognize and nurture all of the
varied human intelligences, and all of the combinations of intelligences.

Howard Gardner

A WRITER'S STORY

Eric, a first grader, wrote, illustrated, and published a book which he titled, Big Bear.

P. 1: *"Good morning Big Bear. Time for breakfast."*
  "Okay."
P. 2: *"Do you want K'S?"*
  "No. I want honey."
  "Okay."
P. 3: *"What did you do to the play room?"*
  "I did nothing."
  "No, you made a mess."
P. 4: *"Now you clean it up."*
  "Okay."
  "But I still love you."

*Asked about his story, Eric said, "This is my favorite book. It makes sense, and it has
better pictures. It's neat because all of it is talking. It's not like, 'He walked downstairs.' "
When asked what it takes to make a good writer, Eric said: "Mistakes are not always bad.
You can use your imagination and make something out of that mistake. Take your time.
Don't say, 'I have to get the most books done.' Don't just want to publish something.
Something else could also fit with it. Then you can have a table of contents. My next book
is about information—radios, movies, and what toys kids like to play with."*

Eric wrote his book in dialogue—an idea which grew out of a class discussion. He knows that dialogue can move a story along quite well. He's showing, not telling. He views "mistakes" as opportunities for creative thought. Where did he get this wonderful idea? Eric's teacher created a safe, well-managed writing environment and nurtured Eric's creative potential.

INTRODUCTION

This chapter describes the conditions needed for creating writing environments and nurturing creative potential. There are many ways to manage writing, but unless the writing environment is effective, it will be difficult to get the best writing from your children. Of course, a well-managed classroom is conducive to effective learning, but there is no one way or best way to manage writing instruction. The ideas presented in this chapter do not exhaust the possibilities for managing a writing environment. Instructional plans must compliment your personality and style and augment the experiences and practices that are part of your current instructional routine. Knowing what to teach and how to motivate writing is necessary, but it is insufficient. A well-managed writing environment is needed. Exemplary learning environments ignite interest and elicit the best that is in children. This chapter describes twelve factors that influence classroom environments and discusses issues relevant to nurturing creative potential.

CREATING ENVIRONMENTS FOR LEARNING

I use the term *environments* in its broadest sense: all the conditions, circumstances, and influences surrounding and affecting the development of children in schools and classrooms. Even more specifically, I refer to classroom environments created and maintained by teachers, in cooperation with children, as they endeavor to manage integrated literacy instruction. Institutions, whether schools or prisons, have environments that are either *cultivated* or *perpetrated* by those in charge of the institution; the institution's environments are established either in cooperation with or in opposition to the institution's inhabitants. A cultivated environment promotes the development of the individuals who inhabit a given institution. A perpetrated environment, on the other hand, is an imposed environment brought about by neglect or blundered into by the authorities in charge. Such an institution is at best offensive and at worst, evil. Prisons are typically institutions where the environments are perpetrated upon the inmates. Bad schools, like prisons, have environments that have been imposed upon the "inmates." Good schools have cultivated environments, thoughtfully developed, carefully nurtured, and dedicated to the growth of the children who inhabit such schools.

Schools are institutions and classrooms are subunits within the larger institutional framework. Teachers, to the degree that they have the freedom to do so, can cultivate good environments within bad institutions. But it is far easier to cultivate good classroom environments within a good institution. Unfortunately, teachers do not always have a choice or a voice in the larger institutional frame-

"What did you do to
the play room?"
"I did nothing"
"No, you made a mess."

3

Figure 14.1   A Page from Eric's book, *Big Bear*   When Eric published his book, *Big Bear,* he illustrated each page with a drawing of a bear. He said, "I like how I illustrated it. The cover—it's the best bear that I drew in this whole entire book. In most of them, the legs are wrong." He didn't bother to fix the legs that he says he got wrong. He thinks that some mistakes are inconsequential.

work. Fortunately, they nearly always have some choice and a voice within their own classrooms.

Physical Environment

Philosophy determines the choices one makes. The way you organize and arrange the physical environment illustrates your philosophy of teaching and learning. Teachers who take pride in the physical environment of their classrooms usually want their children to make their own investments in the classroom environment. The teacher establishes the model, and the children imitate and innovate off of the teacher's model.

Stimulating surroundings make for productive working conditions. Attractive and interesting classrooms feature places for quiet independent work as well as space for cooperative learning. Arrangement of furniture and displays of children's work create an interesting workplace. There should be display centers, interest centers, a science-math center, pictures, plants, and collections resulting from children's work. An informal center where children may go to read or write is especially desirable. If possible, it should have rugs, pillows, comfortable chairs, and a library with books for individualized reading and for research.

Intellectual Environment

Gandhi, a man who changed the world forever, said, "You must be the change you wish to see in the world." If you wish to shape your classroom's intellectual environment, you must be the change you wish to see in your classroom. You can create an intellectual environment where ideas are valued—no one else can do it for you. An intellectual environment means tolerance of one another and openness to ideas and opinions that may conflict with your own ideas and opinions. Respect children's ways without abandoning your own perspective and without relinquishing discipline. Acquire a working knowledge of your children's abilities and aspirations while remaining alert to their limitations and uncertainties. Respect individual initiative, recognize individual achievement, encourage self-expression, establish reasonable standards of conduct, and develop a spirit of community within your classroom. Model those intellectual traits you wish to influence, as Gandhi did.

An open intellectual environment values diversity of thought and behavior. You have, undoubtedly, walked into classrooms where everyone was quiet and everything orderly. Every child is at his or her seat. Desks are arranged in orderly rows. Questions are asked, hands raised, answers given quietly and politely. Such arrangements are unlikely to stimulate challenging intellectual give and take. A challenging intellectual environment generates noise and bustle, argument and counterargument. Most children can operate effectively in a busy, buzzing, workplace. After all, this is the normal condition of most working environments, and classrooms are, or ought to be, working environments.

Still, children and teachers differ in the amount of noise and bustle they can tolerate. There are times, therefore, when an escape into reflective quiet is needed. But fair analysis rejects the notion that quietness and orderliness are preconditions to learning. Classrooms where interaction among students is forbidden are unnatural, uncomfortable, and unhealthy. They do not promote learning or concentration. On the contrary, they produce a dislike for learning and a spirit of indifference.

Emotional-Social Environment

Children crave security and stability. A cooperative, hopeful atmosphere can be created. Children need the assurance of acceptance and sympathetic understanding. They need to know that they are not discounted. Teachers cannot hand out emotional security like they were handing out pencils, but they can eliminate unfavorable influences. The teacher's emotional demeanor will be reflected in the emotional tenor of the classroom. Kindness, courtesy, and respect for others are influences that can be modeled, but they cannot be coerced. A classroom cannot always be an emotionally tranquil place, nor should it be. But it can be a place where children know the security of acceptance and tranquility of humane consideration.

Risk Taking Environment

There are various kinds of risk taking. Jumping off of bridges into rivers of uncertain depth is the kind of risky business we hope our kids will avoid and usually don't. Parents and teachers often wish their kids wouldn't take dangerous chances, but generally we recognize that risky behavior is inevitable and perhaps a necessary part of growing up. For instance, I recently saw a twelve-month-old baby who was just learning to walk. In the space of five minutes, that child must have fallen twenty times. Undeterred, she returned again and again to the risky business of walking. It would be a disaster, of course, if that child gave up after a few falls. How would she ever learn to walk? Kids are inherently risk takers, and this characteristic can be used to advantage in teaching writing.

Unfortunately, academic risk taking often flies out the window, even among children whose behavior in the physical world is bold. Why is this so? I suspect that it has to do with such emotions as fear of failure, self-protection in case of failure, lack of confidence in one's academic potential. These emotional states are complex, but they can be overcome or ameliorated in classrooms that are safe for risk taking. Do risk taking and safety go together? Absolutely. An experienced stunt coordinator works relentlessly on safety precisely because he knows the extent of the risk involved. A safety net is essential if we wish to get kids to take academic risks. A safety net is what the InsideOut Writing Project, directed by Terry Blackhawk, provides for many Detroit students. The project places professional writers in schools and provides opportunities for students to publish their own writings. The poem below, by Maya Allen, was published in *The Dream Keepers* Volume 1 (1999) under the auspices of the InsideOut Writing Project.

Song As Far As The Eye Can See

I am strong
I cannot go wrong
I will not be singing any sad songs.

I live in Detroit, and I go
to Cody High. When I have business
to take care of, I don't act shy.

I have a lot of wonderful teachers
that are sending me
on my way. When I awake

In the morning, I feel I'm going
to have a great day. I'm hard
on myself about subjects and grades,

I won't be another low life
on the corner
playing spades. I am beautiful,

so is my spirit. I am intelligent,
wise. When you want
to find out about me, talk to me,

look into my big brown eyes.
They'll tell you the truth
about me, my soul, my spirit

as far as the eye can see.
Maya

Responsibility Environment

Teachers are facilitators of learning; they make learning possible in carefully crafted ways. Ultimately, they are responsible for means and ends. While teachers manage the overall learning environment, it is not their responsibility alone. There must be mutual responsibility, a community of learners building a responsible classroom environment together. For example, who cleans up the messes that inevitably occur in a working environment? It can't be the teacher alone; it shouldn't be the children alone. It should be a mutual responsibility. Who sets the rules of the working community? It can't be the teacher alone; it shouldn't be the children alone. It is a mutual responsibility. Who brings ideas to classroom discussions? It can't be the teacher alone; it shouldn't be the children alone. It is a mutual responsibility.

In a mutual responsibility classroom, children can be trusted; so can the teacher. In a mutual responsibility classroom, everyone has a role to play and a say in how the work is to be accomplished. In a mutual responsibility classroom, children are responsible for themselves and for each other and so is the teacher. I visited such a classroom recently, Ms. DeWard's fourth grade classroom. Students knew what their responsibilities were as the writing workshop proceeded over the course of an hour. While the teacher conferenced with individual children, the rest of the children leafed through their writing journals, then proceeded to work. They worked alone or with partners; they knew when to move from writing to the Author's Chair; they knew when it was time to put away their work and proceed to the next activity. It was a partnership of responsibility.

Cooperative Environment

Encourage cooperation among your students, and build cooperation into your daily activities. This means children will sometimes work in cooperative learning groups of two or three for some reading and writing projects. They may work in slightly larger teams to complete certain projects. The common threads that run throughout a cooperative environment are teamwork and pride. Teachers can model cooperative talk and tasks; they can reinforce and reward the successful efforts of groups and individuals.

Competition can coexist with cooperation, but it must be competition where kids strive to be their best within the larger framework of the whole. We want children to work cooperatively as a team. The best teams are those where the goals of the team supersede the goals of any individual on the team. In the end, this cooperative spirit works in behalf of the individual as well as the team.

In her "Voices from the Classroom" piece, Ms. Wilson describes how she directed a successful cooperative writing project among her eighth graders.

VOICES FROM THE CLASSROOM: Kristin Wilson

Classroom Research

I have 24 students in my reading class. I wanted to find a way for students to "want" to research a topic of interest. I found a way that couldn't fail: a talk show format was the answer.

I introduced the project by forming groups to put together a talk show of their own. This excited them. I suggested the following guidelines.

1. Select a debatable issue to be discussed on the show.
2. Choose "experts" to represent each side of the issue.
3. Create an active part for everyone in your script.
4. Only the talk show host may use cards to read from.
5. Research must be used in the script.
6. Find factual data for the script.
7. Use appropriate language and behavior on the show.
8. Follow due dates established.
9. Strive for creativity and organization.

It was as if I didn't even mention the dirty word—research. They didn't seem to mind that they would be spending days in the media center and evenings in the library. Each group selected its topic quickly.

I provided a "Timeline and Due Dates" sheet for them to follow. This information helped them pace themselves and helped me to organize and control the flow of work.

To stay organized, I listed each group on a clipboard and visited each group and recorded what each member was doing and what research they were using. I provided materials, advice and guidance. The class almost ran itself once I set up a schedule for the group and myself to follow.

I also passed out, in advance, the evaluation form I would be using. There were two areas of evaluation: (1) **Presentation:** knowledge of material and ability to answer questions from the audience, organization, creativity, effort and enthusiasm, and overall flow of the show; (2) **Criteria met:** host/hostess, experts representing each side, guests with clear understanding of roles, and choosing an issue that could be debated. Knowing evaluation guidelines in advance eliminated a lot of questions and directed students' attention to the appropriate aspects of the show.

Everyone got into character when they presented, and they used their research well. If I had given each student a test on their topic, all would have passed with flying colors. This was a fun way to use research and writing in my classroom, and it was meaningful to my students.

Self-Assessment Environment

A famous mayor had a standard question he often asked: "How am I doing?" He was asking citizens how they assessed his work as Mayor of New York. Evaluation from outside one's self is important, but more important still is self-assessment. Students need to ask themselves, "How am I doing?" Self-assessment helps students judge their progress toward achieving their goals. The better children are at self-assessment, the more able they are to take ownership of their learning.

Organize instruction so that students make progress toward more effective self-assessment. For instance, some teachers have students read their writing to each other. The partners exchange compliments and criticism, each striving toward understanding their own writing better as well as that of their partner. There are many opportunities to model self-assessment questions to students. For example, during writing conferences ask questions that require self-assessment:

1. Do you think your second draft is better than the first? In what way do you think it is better?
2. In looking over your writing folder, is your writing better now than it was last month? In what ways?
3. What is the best piece of writing you've done this month? Tell me why you think so.
4. How much better at writing do you think you can become?
5. Are you feeling better about yourself as a writer now than last year? Tell me about it.
6. What goals have you set for improving your writing next month?

Each of these questions requires reflection on past or future achievement in writing. The teacher provides the model for asking self-assessment questions with the intent that children will begin asking themselves similar questions. On the first sign that they have done so, give children a gracious compliment on their self-assessment progress. Make explicit how effective you think your children are becoming in monitoring their work habits, their behavior, their progress toward self-assessment.

Workshop Environment

A principal stepped into Ms. E's writing workshop as she was writing at her desk and said, "I'll come back when you're teaching." If it doesn't look like teaching, is it still teaching? If it's a workshop environment, it may not look like teaching to the uninitiated, but it may be the best teaching that occurs during the school day.

Workshop is a good term. It suggests a businesslike atmosphere where work is accomplished. Workshops often look messy, and it doesn't always look like teaching, at least not in the traditional sense. Visiting a writing workshop for the first time, one might suspect a lack of orderliness. A visitor might wonder why the teacher isn't teaching, since she is probably not lecturing. A visitor might be suspicious of the noise and bustle that accompanies a working environment. A visitor might fail to recognize the similarity between a working classroom environment and the workshops teachers and principals attend at professional conferences, even though the purposes and procedures have much in common.

Workshops are an informal and natural way of accomplishing academic tasks. A writing workshop generates an environment where individuals and groups go about their work cooperatively and informally. There may be meetings among workshop participants; some children may be publishing books; some may be working on drafts; the teacher may be conferencing with a student. All of this activity occurs within a loosely organized, informal environment where kids are working, where everyone has something to do, either alone or cooperatively. A principal out to evaluate effective teaching need not "come back when you're teaching." You're probably engaged in the most effective teaching you'll do all day.

In her diary entry, Ms. DeWard describes how she manages the workshop environment for her daily writing workshop.

DIARY OF A TEACHER: Jennifer DeWard

Recently a first-year teacher asked me how I organize and manage my classroom during writers' workshop. It was not an easy question to answer. It got me thinking. How in the world do I organize and manage my classroom?

If you visited my classroom during writers' workshop, you will see 24 students writing, talking, illustrating. Some students will be sitting at their own desks, others will be sprawled out on the floor writing. Some students will be revising with a friend, and inevitably one student is walking from table to table asking the other kids what title they like best for his story. It may sound chaotic, but exactly the opposite is true. My writers' workshop is productive. We worked hard early in the year to establish the right environment for writing, now things are running smoothly.

My students usually write in their author's notebooks. This is an ordinary spiral notebook designated at the beginning of the year as the "author's notebook." I tell my kids that when they write in this "special" notebook, they are no longer fourth graders but important authors. Students keep their notebooks in their desks. Each student also has a hanging file folder in the back of the room. Students store many different items in their folders: a scribbled idea list, half finished products, construction paper book covers. Many students like using their hanging file folder because they worry that important papers might otherwise get squashed in their desks.

My students know that there is one main rule during writers' workshop. They must actively participate in some stage of the writing process. I seldom have behavior problems. My students enjoy writing and choosing what they want to work on; there is really no time to fool around. I allow my students to talk during this writing time because I have come to realize that many students truly do get ideas and inspiration from their peers. I try to make sure that students are talking mostly about their writing. I do not think it is necessary to talk about video games during writing time. I admit that sometimes the noise level bothers me. At those times, I walk around the room and make sure that my students are on task. If they are, I do my best to ignore the conversational murmur. However, there are times when I designate the last ten or fifteen minutes of workshop as "quiet reflective time."

Literate Environment

Literary gossip: A visitor in Ms. Wilson's eighth grade English classroom encounters a highly literate environment. He sees students reading books, writing drafts, visiting the library. He hears students reading their writings to one another, planning their writing projects, working cooperatively. He watches Sarah illustrating her book, now in its third draft. The visitor reads some "literary gossip" exchanged between Ms. Wilson and her students. Ms. Wilson has recently discovered "literary gossip," a term coined by Nancie Atwell (1998). Her journal comments below show how "literary gossip" has added to the literate environment Ms. Wilson has established in her classroom.

> Literary gossip works like a charm. I'm so glad you told me about this idea. The kids absolutely love it. The idea is to drop me a "note" about the novel they are reading and "gossip" about it. This format of writing to me as a "person" rather than a formal entry in their journal for a "teacher" to read really opened some kids up. They were actually quite witty in their notes instead of being so dry. I got to know what they're thinking about the whole book. They weren't afraid to let me know if they didn't like it. They also weren't afraid to admit when they were confused. Their "gossip" prompted me to write back to them more often. It was a wonderful opportunity to communicate one-on-one. I'm spreading the word that this idea is a keeper.

The visitor in Ms. Wilson's classroom had entered the "literate zone," but unlike the Twilight Zone, there is no mystery here. Ms. Wilson, a fine young teacher, works hard to establish and maintain a literate environment in her classroom. Writing in Ms. Wilson's class has become as natural as grass on the Savannah.

Dialogue journals: You write to me, and I'll write back. That's dialogue journaling; that's literary gossip. A dialogue is a conversation between and among friends or acquaintances. Dialogue journaling is a conversation between teachers and their students using journals as the medium of written exchange. Like oral

Melissa is a "gossiper." When she reads a book, she likes to comment on it to her teacher, who returns the favor with a little gossip of her own.

conversations, literary gossip and dialogue journaling have rules of decorum, which are described below. Observing these best practices enriches the experience of "gossiping" and journaling.

LITERARY GOSSIP AND DIALOGUE JOURNALING

1. The dialogue must be mutual. Both parties have a responsibility to sustain the dialogue. When one party lets the other down, the conversation is over. First grader, Andy, put it like this: "Im not gona rit until you rit me bak."

2. Conversations flag when boredom sets in. Try to get journalers and gossipers focused on what's important or interesting to them. Then the conversation is likely to continue.

3. Don't correct grammatical and mechanical errors. Such matters, while important, are best attended to in other writing forums. A teacher should, however, note writing needs that can be handled later in mini-lessons or revising experiences.

4. Don't restrict gossip and dialogue journaling to written conversations between teacher and students. Encourage students to dialogue among themselves. This increases opportunities for students to write while easing the paper load.

5. Listen to entries with your head and your heart. Your head will tell you about instructional needs your students may have; your heart will tell you about their emotional needs. Reach out to satisfy both needs.

Learning logs: A learning log is a journal used for subject area learning. Learning logs have a natural connection with expository writing, but they can also stimulate expressive writing when a writing prompt lends itself more to expressive than expository writing. Learning logs are used to record notes, respond to teacher generated questions and requests, and pose or answer self-generated questions. Teachers can provide the prompts that motivate students to respond in their learning log, or they can guide students to develop their own prompts. Effective prompts, closely connected to subject matter interests, are the key to effective use of learning logs. Writing in a learning log can be a powerful tool for learning content related ideas and information. Possibilities for stimulating subject matter writing are enhanced when teachers elevate a basic idea beyond its obvious uses. Imaginative teachers, of which there are many, will undoubtedly do so with learning logs. Some learning log prompts are listed below.

LEARNING LOG PROMPTS FOR SUBJECT MATTER WRITING

Leading questions

1. What do I already know?
2. What do I want to know?
3. What did I learn today?
4. What new idea did I learn?
5. How can I apply what I learned?
6. What questions did you ask yourself?
7. What problems did you identify?
8. What might you say if you met . . .?

Direct requests

9. List five things you learned about . . .
10. List one thing that confused you.
11. Write a paragraph about . . .
12. Suppose you lived during the Ice Age . . .

13. Describe why you think . . .
14. Take notes in your learning log on . . .

Note taking: Note taking is often necessary for expository writing. Note taking not only supplements memory, but is also useful for organizing information into a coherent map or outline. One of the biggest problems in note taking is that students tend to copy directly from sources, usually word-for-word. This problem can only be overcome with focused instruction. Students need to know how to take notes, how to paraphrase, how to organize notes for writing, how and when to cite sources. Few students learn to do these things on their own. Most students use sources inappropriately because they have not learned how to do the right thing. Instruction designed to replace bad habits will solve the problem. The skills needed are complex and cannot be learned in a few brief exposures; however, patient instruction, paced over time, will work. Suggestions that will lead students in the right direction are listed below.

NOTE TAKING FOR EXPOSITORY WRITING

1. Decide where you want your students to record their notes. A learning log is a good place for certain projects. For more extensive research reports, it may be best to use note cards.

2. Show students that expository text is usually organized in outline form through the use of bold and italicized type along with the use of graphs, tables, and boxed material.

3. Model how bold and italicized headings can be turned into questions likely to be answered in the text that follows. For example, if the bold heading is **The Louisiana Purchase,** the question asked and likely to be answered in the text is: What was the Louisiana Purchase?

4. Select statements from texts and model how you would restate an author's words into your own words and meaning. This is called paraphrasing, and few students know how to do it. After modeling, provide practice exercises.

5. With large chunks of text, such as chapters, model how chapter titles and headings can be used to make predictions and set purposes for note taking.

6. Model how notes are used to create outlines or maps for writing. The task is to identify main ideas and place supporting details in subordinate relationship to the main ideas. Mapping, because of its visual characteristics, is ideal for helping students understand the relationships between and among elements of text structure.

7. Show students when and how to cite reference sources. A written guide with examples is useful.

Predictable Environment

Predictable has many meanings, but in this context I am thinking of a meaning centering around certainty. Reading and writing time must be predictable, certain, assured. Kids must have a reliable, uninterrupted, predictable period of time for reading and writing. For instance, children need to know that writing workshop is scheduled for sixty minutes three or four times a week. Once a predictable writing workshop schedule has been established, the time scheduled must be sacrosanct. Only unusual and unforeseen circumstances should replace or displace it. If scheduled time for writing workshop must be displaced, as circumstances sometimes require, reschedule even if it means stealing time from other curricular objectives. Predictable reading and writing time is essential since both require sustained stretches of time in order to be effective. Furthermore, a predictable writing schedule leads to "off-stage rehearsal" for writing, as Graves (1983) suggests.

Integrated Environment

Reading and writing are process activities, but they are also content accumulating experiences. Reading and writing provide countless opportunities to deal with content. Social studies and science are content subjects. But you cannot engage effectively with these subjects in a nonliteracy environment. Reading and writing must accompany them. Science, of course, works best when it deals with concepts in a hands-on fashion. But even hands-on science requires reading, though not necessarily from science textbooks. Science can provide significant opportunities for writing: writing up experiments, describing observations, preparing reports.

Literacy strategies are helpful in learning content material. For instance, KWL (What do you know, what do you want to know, what have you learned) and Directed Reading Thinking Activities (DRTA), and note taking are strategies that work extremely well in science and social studies. They provide a forum for recalling prior knowledge and using it to understand and retain content concepts and information. Writing about science or social studies makes it much easier to learn and retain scientific and historical information.

Expectation Environment

Years ago, researchers conducted an experiment where teachers were given false IQ information about their students. A student with an IQ of 95 might be identified to a teacher as a student with an IQ of 120. This false information created a subtle expectation among the teachers involved in the experiment. The researchers found that if a teacher thought she had a bright student, she tended to expect that student to achieve at the level appropriate for the student's presumed IQ. The students responded by living up to their teacher's expectations.

Like all studies, the study was criticized for one weakness or another, thus calling into question the validity of the findings. Nevertheless, the study stands as a metaphor for teacher expectation. Teachers tend to get what they expect from their students; students tend to achieve at the level of their teachers' expectations of them. It is a sound working premise for teachers to hold high expectations of their students. If you expect good writing from your students, and work hard to achieve what you expect, you are likely to get a better performance than general indicators of capability might predict.

NURTURING CREATIVE POTENTIAL: THE IMPOSSIBLE FLIGHT OF THE BUMBLE BEE

Teachers can nurture young writers much like a seed is nurtured in its early stages of development. The seed of an oak tree is inert until the right conditions of moisture, soil, and sunshine are present in its environment. Once the conditions are right, the oak seed grows and reaches its potential or fails to, depending on an incalculable number of conditions. If it is to reach its potential, it must endure storms as well as sunshine. Children are seeds. If they are to reach their potential, they must endure storms as well as sunshine. Parents and teachers can supply the sunshine. The vagaries of life will supply the storms. Teachers are an invaluable element in the environment needed to help children discover and achieve the creative potential they possess.

Can creative potential be realized? Some say that creativity cannot be taught, just as some say creative writing cannot be taught. Perhaps creativity cannot be taught directly, but I believe creative potential can be influenced by good teaching. Kurt Vonnegut, Jr., in discussing the success of the Iowa Writers' Workshop, makes the point that ". . . the best creative writing teachers, like the best editors, excel at teaching, not necessarily at writing" (Vonnegut, 1999). I think there is no doubt that the creative potential children possess can be nurtured, and nurturing is what good writing teachers do best. Teachers do not have to be great writers to turn out students who are great writers, though they must know something about writing if they wish to influence it.

The Mystery of Creativity

The world is full of mysteries. A physicist once claimed that, according to the laws of physics, a bumble bee should not be able to fly. Yet, bumble bees fly. A physicist once "proved" that a baseball cannot curve when thrown by a pitcher. Tell that to Cal Ripkin as he strikes out on a high-hard curve thrown by Nolan Ryan. Later, the mystery of flying bumble bees and curving baseballs was better understood, but here is a mystery not yet understood: three students of a professor at Cal Tech have won Nobel prizes. Could this simply be the fickle finger of fate, a random turn of the wheel of fortune? I don't think so; I think a good teacher influenced the Nobel prize winners.

Not enough is known about creativity, but its manifestations are everywhere observable in the artifacts and ideas that men and women have created over the centuries. While books and articles enough to fill a small library have been written about creativity, it remains, like the peak of Mount Everest, something of a mystery. Everyone knows Mount Everest is there; a few people have actually stood on its peak, but it is shrouded in mystery. Creativity has this same mysterious quality.

I cannot satisfactorily define creativity except to say the usual things known to all of us. Creativity is the exercise of artistic inclinations, imaginative ideas, and inventive capabilities. It is all of this, yet surely it is much more than this. I wish I could describe how one releases the creative potential children possess. I'd love to say do this or that; avoid this or that; presto, you've got a creative environment. But I cannot do it. Confucius, the great Chinese philosopher and teacher, passed on this gem of metacognitive wisdom: it's good to know; its better to know when you do not know. There are books and articles, camps and schools that purport to know how creative potential is released. I feel none of that assurance. I don't know any sure-fire formulas for nurturing creativity because, by its nature, creativity cannot be formulaic. What I do offer are a few ideas that *might* contribute to a conversation about fostering the creative potential which, I believe, exists in all children. If the conversation pieces that follow and precede this section strike a resonant chord in your mind, perhaps you can build on them. But in the final analysis, you must depend on your own creative instincts to structure a classroom that will influence the creative potential your children possess.

Multiple Intelligences

The word *intelligence* in our society is closely identified with verbal literacy. We tend to think that those who speak, read, or write well are intelligent. Students who score well on tests, such as SAT and ACT, are presumed to be intelligent. Perhaps they are, but this definition of intelligence is too narrow; it is based primarily on verbal and mathematical knowledge. Are there students who do poorly on the SAT and ACT but have extraordinary intelligence of another sort? I believe so, for it is manifested in millions of individual achievements from artists to zoologists.

How should we understand and identify human intelligences? I know of a school for the gifted that uses the Wechsler Intelligence Scale for Children (WISC) to identify the gifted. High scorers get in, average scorers seldom qualify. Low scorers—well, let them eat cake. This school has confused creativity with traditional measures of intelligence. School officials would say they are objective, that they make decisions without bias or prejudice. But this sort of objectivity, typically identified with standardized testing, is merely subjective judgment dressed up in objective clothing. Every item on a traditional IQ test represents a subjective judgment of some sort made by someone. Traditional understanding of intelligence is largely based on verbal and mathematical reasoning, and it assumes a one-dimensional view for assessing individual potential. There is a broader view of human capability than traditional intelligence testing suggests.

Multiple faces of intellect: Gardner (1993) proposes a multifaceted view of human potential which he calls "multiple intelligences." I believe his approach to understanding human potential is promising. The multiple intelligences paradigm Gardner proposes formalizes what many parents and teachers have understood for decades: *there is more to human potential than traditional intelligence tests measure.* Gardner describes his theory of multiple intelligences in the following statement:

Multiple intelligences theory, on the other hand, pluralizes the traditional concept. An intelligence entails the ability to solve problems or fashion products that are of consequence in a particular cultural setting or community. The problem-solving skill allows one to approach a situation in which a goal is to be obtained and to locate the appropriate route to that goal. The creation of a *cultural* product is critical to such functions as capturing and transmitting knowledge or expressing one's views or feelings. The problems to be solved range from creating an end for a story to anticipating a mating move in chess to repairing a quilt. Products range from scientific theories to musical compositions to successful political campaigns. (p. 15)

Gardner and his colleagues have identified seven intelligences: musical, bodily-kinesthetic, logical-mathematical, linguistic, spatial, interpersonal, and intrapersonal. While Gardner identifies seven intelligences, he points out that other intelligences are likely to be identified as research continues. The seven intelligences he lists may be subdivided in various ways to account for specific examples of intelligence with which we are familiar. For example, Gardner does not list an "artistic" intelligence, but artistic talent may fit under what he labels *spatial intelligence.* In a general sense, Gardner's view is not new. Guilford's (1965) research on intelligence moved in a similar direction. John Dewey (1916) and Hughes Mearns (1929) laid out philosophies of education compatible with Gardner's theory.

While Gardner's theory is more complex than I have presented here, it represents a starting point in discussing a broader view of human potential. Gardner's theory defines human intelligence broadly and places human intelligence within a cultural context. His theory runs counter to the traditional view, which places great emphasis on verbal and mathematical intelligence. Consider, for example, expert Native American trackers of the eighteenth century. Expert trackers could track a man or animal across plains, forests, or bare rock and do it unerringly. An expert tracker could read subtle signs and disturbances in the terrain that would be indiscernible to a highly "intelligent" physicist or linguist of today. In a society where tracking is crucial, tracking might well represent the peak of intelligence—intelligence defined within the bounds of a culture that placed a high value on tracking.

Teachers routinely observe children expressing intelligence in ways an IQ test would never identify. In my first year of teaching I had such a student. No book or assignment could keep Bob's attention for more than a few minutes. In my state of ignorance, I thought he was dumb—he didn't match anything I had come to think of as intelligent behavior. I soon discovered that I was the real dummy in that classroom. One day, while running the movie projector, I discovered Bob's true intelligence. Bob asked if I would show him how to run the projector. I said "yes." In no time, he had taken over my job, and did it with admirable competence. When the machine broke down, Bob quickly fixed it. Within a few weeks, he was running the projector for the teacher next door. In thirty years of teaching, Ms. Avery had never learned to operate a projector, though everyone thought of her as highly intelligent. Ms. Avery taught the "smart" kids in that school, and Bob was not smart in the traditional sense. But because he ran the projector for Ms. Avery, the "smart" kids envied his privileged status.

At the age of ten, Bob was a mechanical virtuoso. His father ran a junkyard—old cars, tractors, and trucks that had died the death. Bob could salvage parts and make minor repairs on cars, trucks, and tractors. My accidental discovery of Bob's mechanical intelligence gave me an instructional lever. Privileges granted required reciprocal responsibilities. In exchange for granting Bob the status of chief mechanic of room 12, I expected and got a better effort, though not spectacular results, in reading, writing, and arithmetic. I do not know if Bob ever became a good reader or writer, I suspect not. He certainly didn't in my class. But I like to imagine he's out there somewhere making mechanical things run smoothly—a man with the creative intelligence needed to make things work.

Bob's special talent, perhaps we may call it an *intelligence,* is not unique. Bob is representative of millions of children who possess creative potential confined to a small fraction of the human terrain. Bob's creative potential would not show up on a traditional IQ test. More likely, an IQ test would place him somewhere below average. But Bob had creative potential, as do millions of other children. This leads me to propose the following hypothesis: *There is a much greater range of intellectual inventiveness and imagination among children than has been generally recognized; traditional IQ tests do not measure such traits.*

Perhaps this seems like a wobbly idea, since there is little objective evidence for the hypothesis I have proposed. It may sound hopelessly optimistic and idealistic because it is based on experience, on a philosophical premise, perhaps on faith. Some research, such as Gardner and Guilford's, supports this hypothesis, but I cannot claim strong research support. On the other hand, there is little evidence to suggest that current IQ tests are satisfactory measures of human potential. The hypothesis I have proposed may be impractical, it may even be wrong, but I do not believe it can possibly be harmful. If you'll let this hypothesis enter your mind, if you'll act on it in your work with children, you might begin to identify more potential, more imagination, more artistic and intellectual inventiveness among your children than you have previously believed possible. If a butterfly flapping its wings in Australia can influence the weather on the other side of the world, and some computer models suggest this may be so, then there is no reason why you cannot flap your wings and influence the course of events in your classroom and in the world.

Special needs children: Multiple intelligences is particularly pertinent when we consider children with special needs in reading and writing. These children are often neglected in the discussion of intelligences. It would be a terrible mistake with sad consequences if we should fail to recognize the talents of children who have, often inaccurately, been diagnosed as having a learning disability, dyslexia, Attention Deficit Disorder, or any of the myriad of possible diagnoses. Sometimes second language learners are also counted among the special needs children. Perhaps more than most, these children need our full attention.

Richard showed up on a Saturday wanting to know if he could come to the Reading-Writing clinic I direct at Oakland University. I asked, "Did your parents come with you?" "No." he said, "But I have my own money, and I need to read better if I'm going to graduate." He explained that he was in the eleventh grade, and while he could read, he thought he didn't read nearly well enough. Of course, we took him into the clinic on a scholarship. I assigned a fine teacher to work with Richard. He had difficulty with word recognition and reading comprehension, however, his vocabulary and hearing comprehension were well above average. Richard was reading at a sixth grade level. Later, I learned that he had been diagnosed as "learning disabled."

A few days later, I stopped to ask Richard how things were going. He explained that he was writing a poem. I asked if I could read it when he finished. "Sure," he replied, "Would you like to see my other poems?" Next day he brought in a portfolio of his poems. As I read Richard's poetry, I was reminded once again of how misleading labels can be. His poems were beautiful; his diction sound; his mechanics accurate. How, I wondered, does this "learning disabled" young man write such good poetry? So, I asked: "I work on my poems until I get them right. I ask for help when I need it. I spend a lot of time making them as *perfect* as I can make them." Read Richard's poem. I think you'll agree he has something special to offer the world.

As the sun rises on the horizon,
Seeming to come out of the vast sea,
The huge rocks in the shallow water
Cast their shadow on the shore.

The seagulls soar
    around the rocky cliffs
        above me,
Searching for food or
    flying just for fun.
As the tide begins to roll in,
The waves travel in harmony with the wind
And start their never ending task
    of cutting the rocks
        and moving the shore.

As I continue to walk along the beach,
The sand, warmed by the rays of the sun now high above,
    sifts between my toes.

Richard

I put little faith in the diagnostic categories and labels so often assigned to students like Richard: Learning Disabled, ADD, ADHD (Attention Deficit Hyperactive Disorder), Dyslexic. The diagnoses that precede these labels are fuzzy, often inaccurate, and nearly always misleading. These labels are more often excuses for the failure of schools to educate these children than they are descriptive of intractable deficiencies. I've worked with many children assigned these labels, yet I've never known one who did not make satisfactory to excellent progress given effective instruction. Many of these children are creative and possess one or more of the multiple intelligences that Gardner (1993) describes. Special needs children can learn to read and write when the instructional circumstances are right. Practices for helping special needs children are listed below.

SPECIAL NEEDS CHILDREN

1. Do not assume that the labels and diagnoses of special needs children are accurate. The examiners, instruments, and procedures used to identify disabilities are not rocket science. They are often wrong, but seldom in doubt.

2. Trust your professional judgment when you have reason to doubt the validity of a diagnosis. Remember, an outside examiner may observe a child for a few hours before arriving at a diagnosis. A classroom teacher may observe that same child for hundreds of hours.

3. Strive for small successes in the early stages of instruction; they build the confidence needed for larger successes as development proceeds.

4. Often the mechanics of writing hinder written expression. Good ideas may be silenced when children are fearful of making errors. Pay special attention to ideas. As children gain confidence in the worthiness of their ideas, the mechanics of writing can then be taught more effectively.

5. Don't assume that low or moderate achievement in reading precludes other talents. Children posses many gifts; identify each child's gift; use this gift as the passport to other successes.

6. Special needs children often require a slower instructional pace and more individual attention than normally progressing children, especially if they have fallen far behind.

7. Do not search for unique instructional strategies for special needs children. Strategies that work for other children work for special needs children. This is fortunate since there are no unique strategies that work only for special needs children.

8. Teach to the heart and you will reach the head. Children who have experienced learning difficulties need to know you care about them. Convince them you care. It's the first and most important step in overcoming learning difficulties.

Bilingual, bicultural children: America's history and destiny are tied to immigration. From its inception, America has been blessed with cultural and linguistic diversity. America is a cultural and linguistic paradise. Walk the streets of New York, Chicago, Detroit and you will hear that beautiful Tower of Babel—languages from around the world melding into the English language. What language, other than English, has been so enriched by tens of thousands of foreign words? What culture, other than American, has been so lavishly endowed with the traditions, cuisine, and entrepreneurship of its immigrants? No other nation on earth has been so blessed.

We live in a multicultural world. Unfortunately, too often we have regarded cultural and linguistic diversity as a handicap; too often bilingual learners have struggled because their educational needs went unmet; too often second language learners have felt unwanted in America's classrooms. Bilingual, bicultural children have special needs that must be recognized. At the same time, these children have special traits and capabilities that enrich our classrooms. Working with bilingual children may, indeed, require a significant expenditure of energy and present a challenge to our intellect, but if we succeed with bilingual children we present a gift not only to the children we teach but a gift to American culture. Suggestions for working with bilingual, bicultural learners are shown below.

BILINGUAL, BICULTURAL LEARNERS

1. Learn what you can of the culture and language of the children you teach. You cannot learn everything nor is it necessary. But there are important elements of knowledge that can help you identify with your students.

2. Honor the culture and language of your children. Show your appreciation of their language and culture. Respect given earns respect in return.

3. Be a language model. The manner in which you use English, and the examples you use to illustrate English language concepts will help your bilingual children develop their own English skills.

4. Appreciate and respect your own culture and language; this is the first step in appreciating the culture and language of others. The more you know of your own language and culture the more you can empathize with the language and culture of your students.

5. Make friends with folks of other cultures and languages. Come to know them as individuals, and you will find that you share many of the same human dreams, hopes, and aspirations.

The "Terrible Law" of Learning

Mearns (1929) calls it the "terrible law" of learning: *we shall have whatever we approve*. Of course, it's only "terrible" if you approve of the wrong things; if you approve of the right things it can be wonderful. Classroom activities can restrict or expand the opportunities for creative potential to emerge. For instance, if we strongly approve of correct factual answers to trivial questions, that is what we shall have. If we approve of divergent answers to challenging questions, that is what we shall have. Narrowly tailored instructional practices shut out potentially creative responses. Creative responses often come from children not identified as the best and the brightest. I have found that the seemingly indifferent or tuned-out students are often the very ones who respond imaginatively to questions that require interpretative, evaluative, or inferential responses.

Many students are capable of deeper thought and greater achievement than they are given credit for. Jamie Escalante demonstrated this with predominantly poor Hispanic students in his work at Garfield High School in East Los Angeles. Under his tutelage, students who had shown little aptitude for math learned challenging calculus concepts so well that they were accused of cheating. Subsequent retesting demonstrated otherwise. Over and over Mr. Escalante told his students, "Ganas is all you need"—guts and determination. This story is told in the movie, *Stand and Deliver*. The response Mr. Escalante got from his students demonstrates what Mearns meant by the "terrible law" of learning, i. e., we shall have whatever we approve. Mr. Escalante believed in his kids. He taught them to believe in themselves. He insisted on hard work. He approved of them as individuals, and he approved of the challenge they had taken up together. Mr. Escalante got from his students that of which he approved. It is the "terrible law" of learning.

Making Mistakes and Recovering

Teachers learn from cases, as all good practitioners do. Psychiatrists learn from the patients they heal as well as the ones they fail to heal. Cabinetmakers learn from the cabinets they build, and surely their first cabinets are not as good as their last. Teachers learn from the children they teach or fail to teach. My greatest failure as a first year teacher was my inability to teach Gary how to read. I tried, energetically and sincerely, all of the things that a good teacher of reading would surely have avoided: flash cards, endless repetition, and so-called "easy" words first (the, those, them, etc.). I confess, with shame, I even tried ridicule: "Gary, didn't I just tell you that word is *the*. How could you forget it so quickly?" I can also say that my greatest success as a first year teacher was to recognize my own abysmal ignorance. I did something about it, and quickly. I found somebody who knew how to teach reading, Professor Iver Moe, and got the help I needed. Do not wallow in guilt over mistakes you make in teaching. Do not allow your children to do so either. Many scientific advances, such as the discovery of penicillin, came about as a result of mistakes. Turn mistakes into stepping stones toward greater future achievements.

Restoring Wings

Mearns (1929) had in mind titling a chapter, "All God's Chilluns Got Wings." Then he remembered that not all God's "chilluns" are permitted to use them. Many children, he thought, have had their wings removed at a tender age. The rules for wing removal are simple. Keep your feet on the ground; no more undisciplined flying; no more soaring flights of fancy. Kids can't learn in a noisy, disorderly environment. Arrange the desks in a row. Assign seats. Don't wag your hand furiously when I ask questions. Raise your hand demurely. Answer politely. It's time to get down to the serious business of learning.

If you saw someone removing a bumble bee's wings, you'd put a stop to it. It's too cruel to endure. Yet, we routinely permit wing removal in our schools and classrooms. Of course, wing removal isn't done maliciously. No, it's always done in the name of discipline, orderliness, standards. Wings may not be removed or clipped deliberately, but the result is the same. Bumble bee can fly no more, at least not in this school.

Some things are impossible to do, others difficult but manageable. You cannot, for instance, rebuild a ship at sea. But in the safe harbor of a classroom led by a caring teacher, wings can be restored, difficult though this may be. Fortunately, there are many fine teachers who specialize in healing broken wings and grafting back missing wings. The elusive flight of the bumble bee, hovering on the cusp of a rose, is a beautiful sight to behold. More beautiful still, are the marvelous ways of a creative teacher who has restored wings to children who once soared, temporarily lost altitude, but are flying high again.

IDEAS FOR WRITING

1. Nature walk and poetry: Take a nature walk in the school yard. Fall and Spring are especially good times for a nature walk. Before going, make a list of the kinds of things you might find. For example, what kinds of animals, plants, or insects do you think you may see? Collect a few samples and write a cinquain, haiku, or free verse poem about one or more of the items you collected. Here is an example.

   The flowers bloom bright,
   With smiling faces in the sun,
   As they wait till dark.

   Stephania

2. A seedy story: Find ten different kinds of seeds. Return to class and draw and label each seed. Find the names of the plants from which the seeds came. Write a story about one seed telling what might happen to it as it seeks to find a place to grow.

3. Animal story: Write a story where an animal is the narrator—the one who tells the story. Decide on a setting for your story (red wood forest). Think of the main characters who will appear in your story (wolf, bear, owl). What goal will the characters try to achieve? (keep loggers from cutting down the trees) What problems or incidents will occur as the story proceeds? (bear gets hurt by a falling tree, wolf is caught in a trap, owl has an idea) How will your story end?

4. Questions leading to poetry: Ask questions like the ones below. Write a one-word answer to each question. Then write a free verse poem using each one-word answer in your poem.
   - If you were a tree, what tree would you be? Answer: oak
   - If you were an animal, what animal would you be? Answer: wolf
   - If you were a teacher, what kind of an teacher would you be? Answer: gentle
   - If you were a song, what song would you be? Answer: ballad
   - If you were a bird, what bird would you be? Answer: eagle

Example poem: *oak, wolf, gentle, ballad, eagle*
The old *oak* tree
sheltered a lone *wolf.*
A *gentle* breeze
Whispered a *ballad* while
Overhead an *eagle* circled lazily.

5. Walking in someone else's shoes: Sometimes parents are a pain. Maybe they tell you what to do and how to do it. Sounds like a good job, doesn't it. But suppose you were the parent telling your child what to do and how to do it. What information, advice, ideas, and values would you give? Put your ideas in a letter to your imaginary child.

6. Research: Most slaves who escaped slavery used the Underground Railway with the help of many brave "conductors." But a man named Box Brown was shipped from Delaware to Ohio in a packing crate to escape slavery. Check in your library for books and magazines that tell about escape from slavery. Then write a report on what you have learned.

7. Writing to music: Get a large piece of paper. Listen to two kinds of music: your favorite and a form of music you don't usually listen to. Write words and phrases that come to mind for each type of music. Use different colored pens for the different moods and ideas that occur to you as you listen. When you have finished listening and writing, organize your words and phrases into lines for a free verse poem. If you prefer, write paragraphs describing each type of music.

8. Hey, Rube: A Rube Goldberg device is a machine or idea for making a simple task difficult. For example, it takes about three seconds to tee up a golf ball. Recently some college students invented a machine that tees up a golf ball using 45 different mechanical actions. Draw a machine or think of an idea that does a simple task or idea in a complicated way. Here are some simple tasks that need a more complicated way of getting done: sharpening a pencil, opening a door, turning on a faucet, pushing an elevator button, giving directions for getting from your house to the house next door.

9. Go to jail: Do you remember the story of "Jack and the Giant Beanstalk"? If not, get a copy of this story and read it. Now Jack is usually considered a hero, but a friend of mine, a cop, claims that Jack ought to have been jailed for burglary. She thinks the Giant was the victim. What do you think? Suppose you are the Giant. As you see it, Jack has illegally broken into your house and stolen your goods. Rewrite the story as it might have occurred if the story were turned on its head: Giant as good guy, Jack as bad guy.

10. Solving problems: Sometimes writing can help you solve personal problems just by writing about them. Start a journal, if you haven't already done so. For three days in a row, write about something that is troubling you. You need not share your writing with anyone unless you want to. After three days, ask yourself if you are feeling better about whatever it was that troubled you.

11. Adventure: White rhinos are endangered species. It is possible that in a few decades there may not be any white rhinos left in the wild and only a few left in zoos. White rhinos have dwindled from 65,000 four decades ago to as few as 2,500 today. Recently two veterinarians and a group of other workers spent a year in Africa helping to move white rhinos from a location where they are killed illegally to a safer location. Have you ever imagined doing something similarly heroic? Write about it.

REFLECTION AND SUMMARY

Reflection

If a tree falls in the forest and no one hears it, does it make a sound? If a child fails in a classroom and no one cares, does it matter? I don't know the answer to the first question, but I know the answer to the second. Yes. Emphatically yes! It matters to the child. It matters to caring teachers. It matters in the larger world. Teaching is about caring. Caring about children. Caring about teaching. Caring about what happens to children while they are in school and after they leave. Some children who fail in school will succeed in life beyond school. Those who do will have made their success out of something they possessed when they were in school. Some children who failed in school will also fail in life after school. Many children who fail in school or endure without distinction possess unrecognized and unreached creative potential. They may have passed through classrooms whose environment offered little to arouse the great boulevards of their unchallenged minds. Well-managed classrooms, presided over by caring, competent teachers, can change all this. It is our privilege as well as our mission to do our best for every child who passes through our classooms.

Summary

This chapter has presented the following main ideas:

1. Teachers can create good environments for writing. Twelve instructional environments were discussed.
   - Physical environment: The organization and arrangement of the physical environment of a classroom facilitates learning.
   - Intellectual environment: Ideas must be valued, tolerance promoted, respect given.
   - Emotional-social environment: A cooperative, hopeful social-emotional environment makes for a secure and stable workplace.
   - Risk taking environment: Encourage experimentation with new ideas and activities, attach no stigma to failure.
   - Responsibility environment: Children and teachers are jointly responsible for crafting a pleasant, effective learning environment.
   - Cooperative environment: Promote cooperation between and among children and build cooperation into daily activities.
   - Self-assessment environment: Show children how to regulate and assess their writing performance and their use of time and resources.

- Workshop environment: Organize an informal, cooperative working atmosphere to promote writing and learning.
- Literate environment: Multiple forms and perspectives on reading and writing are the heart of a literate classroom.
- Predictable environment: Write on a consistent, predictable schedule.
- Integrated environment: Integrate reading and writing with content-accumulating experiences across the curriculum.
- The expectation environment: Performance is enhanced when teachers' expectations for children are high and vice-versa.

2. Children possess creative potential and it must be nurtured and cherished. While there are no reliable formulas for accomplishing this task, there are important issues that should be considered, such as the following:
   - Creativity is difficult to define, and in the end teachers must depend on their own instincts to structure a classroom that will influence the creative potential in children.
   - There are many more "intelligences" than IQ tests typically identify. Gardner identified seven such intelligences and others not yet identified are likely to emerge from subsequent research.
   - Mearns maintained that we shall have whatever we approve and called this the "terrible law" of learning. If we approve that which is good and right we shall have it; if we approve lesser things we shall have that as well.
   - Mistakes are a natural part of learning, and we must learn to recognize and value this law of learning.
   - Creative teachers can restore the "wings" of children whose creative potential may have been damaged through misguided educational practices.

QUESTIONS FOR REFLECTIVE THINKING

1. What distinction does the author make between cultivated and perpetrated environments?
2. What factors make for a good intellectual classroom environment?
3. The author claims that, "A safety net is essential if we wish to get kids to take academic risks." Do you agree or disagree? Explain.
4. Explain how competition and cooperation might exist within the same classroom framework?
5. Open-ended questions are useful for stimulating self-assessment. Add three or four open-ended questions to the list of six found in this chapter.
6. Can creativity be taught either directly or indirectly? If yes, how might you go about it? If no, explain why you think this is so.
7. Gardner argues that there is more to human intelligence than traditional intelligence tests measure. Do you agree or disagree? Make a case for your view.

8. Some teachers view mistakes in a highly negative light. Describe a more positive way to contemplate mistakes?

9. What is the "terrible law" of learning? What is so terrible about this "law"?

10. Mini case study: Maria is 11 years old and in the sixth grade. Highly artistic, she draws and paints beautifully, yet her writing is underdeveloped. What would you do to make use of her artistic talent that might enhance her writing development?

REFERENCES

Atwell, N. (1998). *In the middle: New understandings about writing, reading, and learning,* 2nd ed. Portsmouth, NH: Boynton/Cook Publishers Heinemann.

Dewey, J. (1916). *Democracy and education.* New York: Macmillan.

Gardner, H. (1993). *Multiple intelligences: The theory in practice.* New York: Basic Books.

Graves, D. (1983). *Writing: Teachers and children at work.* Exeter, NH: Heinemann.

Guilford, J. P. (1965). Intellectual factors in productive thinking. In *Productive thinking in education,* edited by Mary Jane Aschner and Charles E. Bish. Washington, D. C. National Education Association.

Mearns, H. (1929). *Creative power: The education of youth in the creative arts.* New York: Dover Publications, Inc.

The Dream Keepers, Volume I. (1999). Detroit, MI: InsideOut.

Vonnegut, K., Jr. (1999). Writers on writing: Teaching a craft many say can't be taught. In The Living Arts, *New York Times,* May 24, pp. B1 and B2.

Appendix A
Good Books on Writing

The following books have influenced my thinking about writing. It is a short list, consequently, many excellent books are not on it. Perhaps your favorite author is missing. Do not take offense. Your list *should* be different from mine. There is no foreordained reason why all of us should be influenced by the same authors. Check out a few of these books, and see if you find them as helpful to you as they have been to me.

Atwell, Nancie. (1998). *In the middle.* Portsmouth, NH: Heinemann. Ranks among the most influential books on writing. It is particularly appropriate for teachers in the middle and high school grades. This book sings with authenticity. Teachers often tell me that Atwell's book has influenced their teaching more than any other book.

Burrows, Alvina Treut, Doris Jackson, and Dorothy Saunders (1939). *They all want to write.* New York: Doubleday and Co., Inc. First published in 1939, this book went through at least four editions. The authors were pioneers in stressing integration of the language arts and had an early understanding of the importance of writing in a literacy program.

Calkins, Lucy McCormick. (1994). *The art of teaching writing,* Portsmouth, NH: Heinemann. An excellent book on teaching writing by one of the masters of the genre. First published in 1986, it richly deserved its classic status as an exceptionally well-written book that serves the practical needs of teachers everywhere.

Clay, M. (1975). *What did I write?* Auckland, New Zealand: Heinemann. A beautiful little book you can't do without if you want to understand how writing emerges.

Clegg, Alec B. (1972). *The excitement of writing.* New York: Shocken Books. First published as a report on writing in schools in West Riding of Yorkshire, England, Sir Clegg's book contains outstanding examples of children's writing along with astute commentary on writing instruction.

Cowley, Malcolm. (1957). *Writers at work: The Paris Review interviews.* A compilation of interviews with famous writers. This volume includes interviews with E. M. Forster, Truman Capote, and others. It contains one of the best accounts of Faulkner's writing philosophy. One of the best books I've read on writers' methods, philosophy, and idiosyncrasies.

Dyson, Anne Haas. (1989). *Multiple worlds of child writers: Friends learning to write.* New York: Teachers College, Columbia University. A fine book describing the social forces that energize writing growth among very young children. Filled with authentic dialogue and examples of young children's writing.

Gilbar, Steven. (1989). *The open door: When writers first learned to read.* Boston: David R. Gordine, Publishers, Inc. Thirty well-known writers tell how reading influenced them on their way to becoming writers. This book is a pleasure to read. It offers inspiring stories of how these writers came to be writers.

Graves, Donald. (1983). *Writing: Teachers and children at work.* Portsmouth, NH: Heinemann. Arguably the most influential book on the writing process ever written. Graves writes movingly about the importance of teaching writing and shares his insights into how teachers can create a writing world within their classrooms.

Graves, Donald. (1994). *A fresh look at writing.* Portsmouth, NH: Heinemann. A decade after having written the book that changed the face of writing instruction *(Writing: Teachers and children at work),* Graves takes a fresh look and modifies some of his earlier views.

Kennedy, X. J. (1986). *An introduction to poetry,* 6th ed. Glenview, IL: ScottForesman Co. An absolutely thorough book on just about anything one might wish to know about reading and writing poetry. Its completeness and its thoughtfulness are its major virtues.

Lewis, Richard. (1966). *Miracles: Poems by children of the English-speaking world.* New York: Simon and Schuster. A selection of poems illustrating the extraordinary creativity of children throughout the world. Every poem is a testimony to the power of children's language, thought, and feeling.

Mearns, Hughes. (1929). *Creative power: The education of youth in the creative arts.* This is a book for the heart as well as the head. My all-time favorite book on writing. Mearns understands children and knows what it takes to release the creative power children possess.

Murray, D. M. (1985). *A writer teaches writing: Second edition.* Houghton Mifflin: Boston. Murray is, in my view, the Godfather of the writing process movement since he had a profound influence on Graves, Calkins, Atwell, and others prominent in the movement.

O'Conner, Patricia T. *Who Is I.* New York: Grosset Putnam. A humorous and lively book on grammar. While grammar is not my favorite subject, I found this book an exception. Readable and filled with clear examples illustrating grammatical points.

Sternburg, Janet. (1980). *The writer on her work.* New York: W. W. Norton & Company. Edited volume. Well-known women writers talk about their work. Authors from Joan Didion to Alice Walker tell what it means to be a writer and a woman writer.

Temple, Charlie, Ruth Nathan, and Nancy Burris. (1982). *The beginnings of writing.* Boston: Allyn and Bacon, Inc. Contains one of the best treatments of early writing features and contains excellent chapters on poetic and transactional writing. Children's writing samples rank among the best of any book on writing.

Walter, Nina Willis. (1962). *Let them write poetry.* New York: Holt, Rinehart and Winston. A handbook on the development of the creative impulse in children. Contains insightful suggestions for awakening the creative impulse in children.

White, E. B. and William Strunk. (1979). *The elements of style.* New York: Macmillan Publishing Inc. The most popular book on writing style ever published. Covers everything worth knowing about the elements of style. If you could only buy one book on writing style, this would surely be it.

Appendix B
Bibliography of Multicultural Literature for Younger and Older Children Second Edition 1998

This bibliography was compiled by Toni Walters, Professor of Education, Oakland University; Paula Webster, Ph.D. candidate, Oakland University; and Amy Ronelle Cramer, who earned her Master's Degree in Reading and Language Arts at Oakland University. I am grateful for their willingness to share their work in this appendix. The original bibliography is a much longer and more thorough work. The entries here represent about 20 percent of the original work.

AFRICAN AMERICAN WRITERS

Adedjourna, D. (1996). *The palm of my heart: Poetry by African American children.* Maywood: The Peoples Publishing Group, Inc.

Angelou, Maya. (1994). *My painted house, my friendly chicken and me.* New York: Crown Publishing of Random House.

Angelou, Maya. (1994). *The complete collected poems of Maya Angelou.* New York: Random House.

Angelou, Maya. (1983). *I know why the caged bird sings.* New York: Bantam.

Angelou, Maya and Margaret C. Clarke. (1996). *Kofi and his magic.* Maywood: The Peoples Publishing Group, Inc.

Asante, Molefi K. (1995). *African American history: A journey of liberation.* Rochelle Park, NJ: The Peoples Publishing Group Inc.

Barboza, Steven. (1994). *Door of no return: The legend of Goree Island.* New York: Cobblestone Press.

Beales, Melba Paltillo. (1994). *Warriors don't cry.* New York: Pocket Books.

Belton, Sandra. (1993). *From Miss Ida's porch.* Illustrated by Floyd Cooper. New York: Macmillan.

Bennett, Jr., Lerone. (1993, 1975). *The shaping of Black America.* Chicago: Johnson Publishing.

Bontemps, Arna and Langston Hughes. (1993, first published in 1932). *Popo and Fifina.* New York: Oxford University Press.

Boyd, Candy D. (1984). *Circle of gold.* New York: Scholastic.

Brooks, Gwendolyn. (1992, 1945). *Blacks*. Chicago: Third World Press.

Browder, A. (1992). *Nile valley contributions to civilization*. Washington, DC: Institute of Karmic Guidance.

Bryan, Ashley. (1997). *ABC of African-American poetry*. New York: Atheneum Books.

Bryan, Ashley. (1993). *The story of lightning and thunder*. New York: Atheneum.

Caines, Jeanette. (1988). *I need a lunch box*. Illustrated by Pat Cummings. New York: Harper and Row.

Caines, Jeanette. (1982). *Just us women*. Illustrated by Pat Cummings. New York: Harper and Row.

Chocolate, Deborah. (1997). *On the day I was born*. Illustrated by Melodye Rosales. New York: Scholastic.

Chocolate, Deborah. (1996). *Kente colors*. Maywood: The Peoples Publishing Group, Inc.

Chocolate, Deborah. (1992). *My first Kwanzaa book*. Illustrated by Carl Massey. New York: Scholastic.

Clarke, John H. (1993). *African people in world history*. Maryland: Black Classic Press.

Clifton, Lucille. (1992). *Three wishes*. Illustrated by Michael Hays. New York: Doubleday.

Clifton, Lucille. (1977). *Everett Anderson's 1-2-3*. Illustrated by Ann Grifalconi. New York: Henry Holt.

Collier-Thomas, Bettye. (1997). *A treasury of African-American Christmas stories*. New York: Henry Holt and Company.

Cosby, Bill. (1998). *Little Bill: Money troubles*. Illustrated by Varnette P. Honeywood. New York: Cartwheel Books.

Crews, Donald. (1992). *Shortcut*. Illustrated by the author. New York: Greenwillow.

Crews, Donald. (1985). *Freight train*. New York: Viking Penguin/Puffin.

Cummings, Pat. (1991). *Clean your room Harvey Moon!* New York: Bradbury.

Curtis, Christopher. (1995). *The Watsons go to Birmingham, 1963*. New York: Delacorte Press.

Davis, Ossie. (1990, 1976). *Escape to freedom: A play about young Fredrick Douglass*. New York: Puffin Books.

Draper, Sharon M. (1999). *Romiette and Julio*. New York: Atheneum.

Draper, Sharon M. (1997). *Forged by fire*. New York: Atheneum.

Everett, Gwen. (1991). *Li'l sis and Uncle Willie*. Paintings by William Johnson. New York: Hyperion.

Feelings, Diane Johnson. (1996). *The best of the Brownie's books*. New York: Oxford.

Feelings, Tom. (1995). *Middle passage.* New York: Dial Books.

Feelings, Tom. (1993). *Soul looks back in wonder.* Illustrated by the author. New York: Dial.

Flournoy, Valerie. (1985). *The patchwork quilt.* Illustrated by Jerrry Pinkney. New York: Dial.

Flournoy, Valerie and Vanessa Flournoy. (1995). *Celie and the harvest fiddler.* Illustrated by James E. Ransome. New York: Tambourine.

Gilchrist, Jan Spivey. (1997). *Madelia.* New York: Dial Books for Young Readers.

Giovanni, Nikki. (1999). *Grand-fathers.* New York: Henry Holt and Co.

Greenfield, Eloise. (1991). *Daddy and I.* Illustrated by Jan Spivey Gilchrist. New York: Black Butterfly Children's Press.

Greenfield, Eloise. (1988). *Grandpa's face.* New York: Philomel.

Greenfield, Eloise. (1988). *Under the Sunday tree.* Illustrated by Amos Ferguson. New York: Harper and Row.

Greenfield, Eloise. (1977). *Africa dreams.* Illustrated by Carole Byard. New York: HarperCollins.

Grimes, Nikki. (1998). *Sazmin's notebook.* New York: Puffin Novel.

Grimes, Nikki. (1997). *Wild, wild, hair.* New York: Scholastic.

Grimes, Nikki. (1995). *Meet Donator Brown.* New York: Lothrop, Lee & Sheppard.

Grimes, Nikki and Pat Cummings. (1995). *C is for city.* New York: Lothrop, Lee & Sheppard.

Haley, Alex. (1980). *Roots.* New York: Doubleday.

Hamilton, Virginia. (1995). *Her stories: African American folk tales, fairy tales, and true stories.* Illustrated by Leo and Diane Dillon. New York: Blue Sky Press, an imprint of Scholastic Inc.

Hamilton, Virginia. (1993). *Many thousand gone: African Americans from slavery to freedom.* Illustrated by Leo and Diane Dillon. New York: Knopf.

Hamilton, Virginia. (1989). *The bells of Christmas.* Illustrated by Lambert Davis. San Diego: Harcourt Brace Jovanovich.

Hamilton, Virginia. (1988). *Anthony Burns: The defeat and triumph of a fugitive slave.* New York: Alfred A. Knopf.

Hansberry, Lorraine. (1989, 1970). *To be young, gifted and black.* New York: NAL/Dutton.

Hansen, Joyce. (1994). *The captive.* New York: Scholastic.

Haskins, Jim. (1998). *Separate but not equal: The dream and the struggle.* New York: Scholastic Press.

Haskins, Jim. (1997). *Get on board: The story of the Underground Railroad.* New York: Scholastic.

Haskins, Jim. (1997). *Spike Lee: By any means necessary.* New York: Walker.

Hoffman, Mary. (1997). *An angel just like me.* Pictures by Cornelis Van Wright and Yin-Hwa Hu. New York: Dial Books.

Hooks, Bell. (1999). *Happy to be nappy.* New York: Jump at the Sun/Hyperion.

Howard, Elizabeth Fitzgerald. (1991). *Aunt Flossie's hats (and crab cakes later).* Illustrated by James Ransome. New York: Clarion.

Hru, Dakari. (1996). *The magic moonberry jump ropes.* Illustrated by E. B. Lewis. New York: Dial Books.

Hru, Dakari. (1993). *Joshua's Masai mask.* Illustrated by Anna Rich. New York: Dial Books.

Hudson, Wade and Cheryl Willis. (1997). *In praise of our fathers and our mothers: A Black family treasury of outstanding authors and artists.* East Orange: Just Us Book, Inc.

Hudson, Wade (Ed.). (1993). *Pass it on: African American poetry for children.* Illustrated by Floyd Cooper. New York: Scholastic.

Hughes, Langston. (1969, 1958). *Langston Hughes reader.* New York: G. Braziller.

Igus, Toyomi. (African American/Japanese American). (1996). *Two Mrs. Gibsons.* Illustrated by Daryl Wells. San Francisco: Children's Books Press.

Igus, Toyomi. (1996). *Going back home: An artist returns to the South.* Maywood: The Peoples Publishing Group, Inc.

Johnson, Angela. (1999). *Maniac monkeys on Magnolia Street.* Illustrated by John Ward. New York: Alfred Knopf.

Johnson, Angela. (1997). *Daddy calls me man.* Illustrated by Rhonda Mitchell. New York: Orchard Books.

Johnson, Angela. (1993). *Toning the sweep.* New York: Scholastic.

Johnson, Angela. (1990). *Do like Kyla.* Illustrated by James E. Ransome. New York: Orchard Books.

Johnson, Angela. (1990). *When I am old with you.* Illustrated by David Soman. New York: Orchard Books.

Johnson, Dolores. (1994). *Papa's stories.* Illustrated by the author. New York: MacMillan.

Johnson, Dolores. (1994). *Seminole diary: Remembrances of a slave.* New York: MacMillan.

Johnson, Dolores. (1993). *Your dad was just like you.* Illustrated by the author. New York: MacMillan.

Johnson, Dolores. (1991). *What kind of baby-sitter is this?* Illustrated by the author. New York: MacMillan.

Johnson, Dolores. (1990). *What will mommy do when I'm at school?* Illustrated by the author. New York: MacMillan.

Johnson, Herschel. (1990). *A visit to the country.* Illustrated by Romare H. Bearden. New York: HarperCollins.

Johnson, James Weldon. (1994). *The creation.* Illustrated by James Ransome. New York: Holiday.

Johnson, James Weldon. (1993). *Lift every voice and sing.* Introduction by Jim Haskins. Illustrated by Elizabeth Catlett. New York: Walker.

Jordon, June. (1981). *Kimako's story.* Illustrated by Kay Burford. Boston: Houghton Mifflin.

Katz, William L. (1995). *Black women of the old west.* New York: Atheneum.

Katz, William L. (1986). *Black Indians: A hidden heritage.* New York: Atheneum.

Lawrence, Jacob. (1993). *The great migration: An American story.* With a poem in appreciation by Walter Dean Myers. Illustrated by the author. New York: HarperCollins.

Lester, Julius. (1994). *John Henry.* Illustrated by Jerry Pinkney. New York: Dial.

Lester, Julius and Rod Brown. (1998). *From slave ship to freedom road.* New York: Puffin.

Malcolm X (with Alex Haley). (1964). *The autobiography of Malcolm X.* New York: Ballantine.

McKissack, Patricia C. (1997). *A picture of freedom: The diary of Clotee, a slave girl.* New York: Scholastic.

McKissack, Patricia C. (1997). *Ma Dear's apron.* Illustrated by Floyd Cooper. New York: Simon & Schuster.

McKissack, Patricia C. (1988). *Mirandy and brother wind.* Illustrated by Jerry Pinkey. New York: Knopf.

McKissack, Patricia C. (1986). *Flossie the fox.* Illustrated by Rachel Isadora. New York: Dial.

McKissack, Patricia and L. Fredrick. (1994). *Christmas in the big house, Christmas in the quarters.* New York: Scholastic.

Medearis, Angela. (1997). *The ghost of Sifty Sifty Sam.* Illustrated by Jacqueline Roger. New York: Scholastic Press.

Medearis, Angela. (1991). *Dancing with the Indians.* Illustrated by Samuel Byrd. New York: Holiday House.

Mitchell, Margaree King. (1983). *Uncle Jed's barbershop.* Illustrated by James Ransome. New York: Simon & Schuster.

Mitchell, R. P. (1993). *Hue boy.* Illustrated by Caroline Binch. New York: Puffin Pied Piper Books.

Myers, Walter Dean. (1998). *Amistad: A long road to freedom.* New York: Dutton Children's Books.

Myers, Walter Dean. (1993). *Brown angels.* New York: HarperCollins.

Nolen, Jerdine. (1999). *In my momma's kitchen.* Illustrated by Colin Bootman. New York: Lothrop, Lee & Sheppard Books.

Nolen, Jerdine. (1998). *Raising dragons.* Illustrated by Elise Primarvera. San Diego: Silver Whistle/Harcourt Brace.

Parks, Rosa (with Jim Haskins). (1997). *I am Rosa Parks*/by Rosa Parks. Pictures by Will Clay. New York: Dial.

Parks, Rosa (with Gregory J. Reed). (1996). *Dear Mrs. Parks: A dialogue with today's youth.* New York: Lee and Low Books, Inc.

Petry, Ann. (1991 first published in 1955). *Harriet Tubman: Conductor on the Underground Railroad.* North Bellmore, New York: Marshall Cavendish.

Pinkney, Gloria Jean. (1994). *The Sunday outing.* Illustrated by Jerry Pinkney. New York: Dial.

Ringgold, Faith. (1993). *Dinner at Aunt Connie's house.* Illustrated by the author. New York: Hyperion.

Rosales, Melodye. (1996). *'Twas the night before Christmas: An African-American version.* Retold and illustrated by the author. New York: Scholastic.

Rosales, Melodye. (1991). *Double dutch and the voodoo shoes: A modern African-American urban tale.* Illustrated by Melodye Rosales. Chicago: Children's Press.

Smalls, Irene. (1999). *Kevin and his dad.* Illustrated by Michael Hays. Boston: Little, Brown & Company.

Smalls-Hector, Irene. (1992). *Jonathan and his mommy.* Illustrated by Michael Hays. Boston: Little, Brown.

Steptoe, Javaka. (1997). *In daddy's arms I am tall.* New York: Lee and Low.

Steptoe, John. (1987). *Mufaro's beautiful daughters.* New York: Lothrop, Lee & Sheppard.

Steptoe, John. (1969). *Stevie.* New York: Harper and Row.

Tarpley, Natasha A. (1998). *I love my hair!* Illustrated by E. B. Lewis. Toronto, Canada: Little, Brown & Company.

Taulbert, Clifton L. (1989). *Once upon a time when we were colored.* Tulsa, OK: Council Oak Books.

Taylor, Mildred. (1990). *Mississippi bridge.* Illustrated by Max Ginsburg. New York: Dial.

Taylor, Mildred. (1976). *Roll of thunder hear my cry.* Illustrated by Jerry Pinkney. New York: Dial.

Thomas, Joyce Carol. (1995). *Gingerbread days.* New York: HarperCollins.

Thomas, Joyce Carol. (1993). *Brown honey in broomwheat tea.* New York: HarperCollins.

Thomas, Velma Maia. (1997). *Lest we forget: The passage from Africa to slavery and emancipation.* New York: Crown Publishers, Inc.

Walker, Alice. (1991). *Finding the greenstone.* San Diego: Harcourt Brace Jovanovich Publishers.

Walker, Alice. (1988, original copyright 1967). *To hell with dying.* Illustrated by Catherine Deeter. New York: Harcourt Brace & Company.

Woodson, Carter G. (1933, 1990). *The mis-education of the Negro.* Nashville, TN: Winston Derek.

Woodson, Jacqueline. (1995). *From the notebooks of Melanin sun.* New York: Scholastic.

Woodson, Jacqueline. (1994). *I hadn't meant to tell you this.* New York: Delacorte Press.

Wright, Richard. (1989, originally published 1945). *Black boy.* New York: Harper and Row.

Wyeth, Sharon Dennis. (1998). *Once on this river.* New York: Alfred A. Knopf.

Wynn, Mychal. (1990). *Don't quit: Inspirational poetry.* Atlanta, GA: Rising Sun Publishing.

Yarbrough, Camille. (1989). *The shimmershime queens.* Illustrated by Carole Byard. New York: Bullseye Books.

Yarbrough, Camille. (1979). *Cornrows.* Illustrated by Carole Byard. New York: Coward-McCann.

CARIBBEAN WRITERS

Bennett, Louise. (Ed.). (1981). *Jamaica Maddah Goose.* Kingston: Jamaica School of Art.

Berry, James. (1996). *Poems by James Berry: Everywhere faces everywhere.* Illustrations by Reynold Ruffins. New York: Simon & Schuster.

Berry, James. (1989). *Spiderman Anancy.* Illustrated by Joseph Olubo. New York: Henry Holt & Company.

Bloom, Valerie. (1991). *Fruits: A Caribbean counting poem.* Illustrated by David Axtell. New York: Henry Holt & Company.

Gunning, Monica. (1998). *Under the breadfruit tree.* Illustrated by Fabricio Vanden Broeck. Honesdale, PA: Boyds Mills Press, Inc.

Hanson, Regina. (1997). *The face at the window.* Illustrated by Linda Saport. New York: Clarion Books.

Joseph, Lynn. (1994). *The mermaid's twin sister: More stories from Trinidad.* Illustrated by Donna Perrone. New York: Houghton.

Joseph, Lynn. (1992). *An island Christmas.* Illustrated by Catherine Stock. New York: Clarion Books.

Joseph, Lynn. (1990). *Coconut kind of day: Island Poems.* Illustrated by Sandra Speidel. New York: Lothrop, Lee & Sheppard.

Linden, Anne M. (1994). *Emerald blue.* Illustrated by Katherine Doyle. New York: MacMillan.

Linden, Anne M. (1992). *One smiling grandma: A Caribbean counting book.* Illustrated by Lynne Russell. New York: Dial.

Mitchell, Rita. (1993). *Hue boy.* Illustrated by Caroline Binch. New York: Dial.

Rahaman, Vashanti. (1997). *A little salmon for witness: A story from Trinidad.* Illustrated by Sandra Speidel. New York: Dutton.

Sisnett, Ana. (1997). *Grannie jus' come.* Illustrated by Karen Lusebrink. San Francisco, CA: Children's Press.

ASIAN AMERICAN WRITERS

Cao, L. (1997). *Monkey bridge.* New York: Viking.

Hamanaka, Sheila. (1995). *Be bop-a-do-walk!* New York: Simon & Schuster.

Hamanaka, Sheila (Coordinator). (1995). *On the wings of peace: Writers and illustrators speak out for peace in memory of Hiroshima and Nagasaki.* New York: Clarion.

Hamanaka, Sheila. (1995). *Peace crane.* New York: Morrow Junior Books.

Houston, Jeanne Wakatsuki and James Houston. (1973). *Farewell to Manzanar.* Boston, MA: Houghton Mifflin.

Igus, Toyomi. (1996). *The two Mrs. Gibsons.* Illustrated by Daryl Wells. San Francisco, CA: Children's Books Press.

Kadohata, Cynthia. (1997). *In the heart of the valley of love.* University of California Press.

Lee, Huy Voun. (1998). *In the park.* New York: Henry Holt.

Lord, Bette Bao. (1984). *In the year of the Boar and Jackie Robinson.* New York: Harper & Row.

Murayama, M. (1988). *All I asking for is my body.* Honolulu, HI: University of Hawaii Press.

Ng, Fae Myenne. (1993). *Bone.* New York: Hyperion.

Say, Allen. (1997). *Allison.* Boston: Houghton Mifflin.

Say, Allen. (1993). *Grandfather's journey.* Boston, MA: Houghton Mifflin.

See, Lisa. (1996). *On gold mountain. The one-hundred-year odyssey of my Chinese American family.* New York: Vintage Books.

Tan, Amy. (1989). *The joy luck club.* New York: Random House.

Watkins, Yoko Kawashima. (1994). *My brother, my sister, and I.* New York: Bradbury Press of Macmillan.

Watkins, Yoko Kawashima. (1986). *So far from the bamboo grove.* New York: Puffin Books.

Wong, Shawn. (1995). *American knees.* New York: Simon & Schuster.

Yep, Laurence. (1997). *The case of goblin pearls.* New York: HarperCollins.

Yep, Laurence. (1997). *The dragon prince: A Chinese beauty and the beast tale.* Pictures by Kam Mak. New York: HarperCollins.

Yep, Laurence. (1993). *Dragon's gate.* New York: HarperCollins.

Young, Ed. (1998). *Mouse Match: A Chinese folk tale.* San Diego, CA: Harcourt Brace.

LATINO WRITERS

Ada, Alma Flor. (1997). *Gathering the sun: An alphabet in Spanish and English.* English translation by Rosa Zubizarreta. Illustrated by Simon Silva. New York: Lothrop, Lee & Sheppard.

Ada, Alma Flor. (1995). *I love Saturdays and Domingos.* Illustrated by Michael Bryant. New York: Atheneum.

Ada, Alma Flor. (1993). *After the storm.* Spanish Edition. *Despues de la tormenta.* Translated from the Spanish by Rosa Zubizarreta. Illustrated by Vivi Escriva. Compton, CA: Santillana.

Ada, Alma Flor. (1993). *The rooster who went to his uncle's wedding: A Latin American folk tale.* Illustrated by Kathleen Kuchera. New York: Putnam.

Alarcon, Francisco X. (1997). *Laughing tomatoes and other spring poems/Jitomates risuenos y otros poemas de primavera.* Illustrated by Maya Christina Gonzalez. San Francisco, CA: Children's Books Press.

Alvarez, Julia. (1997). *Yo!* Chapel Hill, NC: Algonquin Books.

Anaya, Rudolfo. (1995). *Farolitos of Christmas.* Illustrated by Edward Gonzales. New York: Hyperion Books for Children.

Anzaldua, Gloria. (1996). *Prietita and the Ghost Woman.* Illustrated by Christina Gonzalez. San Francisco, CA: Children's Books Press.

Anzaldua, Gloria. (1993). *Friends from the other side / Amigos del otro lado.* Illustrated by Consuelo Mendez. San Francisco, CA: Children's Books Press.

Baca, Ana. (1999). *Benito's Bizcochitos / Los bizcochitos de Benito.* Houston, TX: Pinata Books.

Belpre, Pura. (1996). *Firely summer.* University of Houston, Houston, TX: Arte Publico Press.

Bertrand, Diane Gonzales. (1999). *Family, familia.* Illustrated by Pauline Rodriguez Howard, translations by Julia Mercedes Castilla. Houston, TX: Pinata Press.

Bertrand, Diane Gonzales. (1999). *Trino's choice.* Houston, TX: Pinata Press.

Blanco, Alberto. (1994). *Angel's kite / La estrella de Angel.* Illustrated by Rodolfo Morales. San Francisco: Children's Books Press.

Brusca, Maria C. (1995). *Pedro fools the gringo and other tales of a Latin American trickster.* Retold by Maria Cristina Brusca and Tona Wilson. New York: Henry Holt.

Brusca, Maria C. (1995). *Three friends / Tres amigos: A counting book / Un cuento para contar.* Written with Tona Wilson. New York: Henry Holt.

Brusca, Maria C. (1994). *My mama's little ranch on the pampas.* New York: Henry Holt.

Cisneros, Sandra. (1994). *Hairs / Pelitos.* Illustrated by Terry Ybanez. New York: Knopf.

Cisneros, Sandra. (1994). *The house on Mango Street.* University of Houston, Houston TX: Arte Publico Press.

Cisneros, Sandra. (1991). *Woman hollering creek and other stories.* New York: Random House.

Cofer, Judith Ortiz. (1995). *An island like you: Stories of the Barrio.* New York: Orchard Books.

de Anda, Diane. (1999). *The immortal rooster and other stories.* Houston, TX: Pinata Books.

Dorros, Arthur. (1991). *Abuela.* Illustrated by Elisa Kleven. New York: Puffin.

Fernandez, Roberta. (Ed). (1994). *In other words: literature by Latinos of the United States.* Houston, TX: Arte Publico Press.

Garza, Richard. (1987). *My Aunt Otilia's spirits / Los espiritus de mi tia.* San Francisco, CA: Children's Books Press.

Gonzalez, Ralfka and Ana Ruiz. (1997). *My first book of proverbs / Mi primer libro de dichos.* San Francisco, CA: Children's Books Press.

Jenkins, Lyll Becerra de. (1996). *So loud a silence.* New York: Lodestar Books.

Martin, Patricia P. (1992). *Songs my mother sang to me: An oral history of Mexican American women.* Tucson, AZ: University of Arizona Press.

Mohr, Nicholasa. (1996). *The magic shell.* Illustrated by Rudy Gutierrez. New York: Scholastic.

Mohr, Nicholasa. (1993). *All for the better: A story of El Barrio* (stories of American Series). Illustrated by Rudy Gutierrez. Austin, TX: Steck-Vaughn.

Mohr, Nicholasa. (1977). *In Nueva York.* New York: Dial Press.

Mora, Pat. (1998). *The house of houses.* Boston, MA: Beacon Press.

Mora, Pat. (1997). *Tomas and the library lady.* New York: Knopf.

Mora, Pat. (1995). *The gift of the poinsettia / El regalo de la flor de Nochebuena.* Written with Charles Ramirez Berg. Illustrated by Danie Lechon. University of Texas, Houston, TX: Arte Publico Press.

Rivera, Tomas. (1995). *. . . . . y no se lo trago la tierra / . . . . and the earth did not devour him.* Translated by Evangelina Vigil-Pinon. University of Houston, Houston, TX: Arte Publico Press.

Rivera, Tomas. (1991, 1992). *Tomas Rivera: The complete works.* University of Houston, Houston, TX: Arte Publico Press.

Soto, Gary. (1997). *Snapshots from the wedding*. Illustrated by Stephanie Garcia. New York: G. P. Putnam's Sons.

Soto, Gary. (1995). *The mustache*. New York: Putnam.

Soto, Gary. (1993). *Local news*. San Diego: Harcourt Brace Jovanovich.

Soto, Gary. (1993). *Too many tamales*. Illustrated by Ed Martinez. New York: Putnam.

Soto, Gary. (1990). *Baseball in April*. San Diego: Harcourt Brace Jovanovich.

Stevens, Jan Romero. (1993). *Carlos and the squash plant / Carlos y la planta de calabaza*. Illustrated by Jeanne Arnold. Flagstaff, CA: Northland Publishing.

Velasquez, Gloria. (1995). *Maya's divided world*. University of Houston, Houston, TX: Arte Publico Press.

Velasquez, Gloria. (1995). *Tommy stands alone*. University of Houston, Houston, TX: Arte Publico Press.

Viramontes, Helena Maria. (1995). *The moths and other stories*. University of Houston, Houston, TX: Arte Publico Press.

NATIVE AMERICANS

Alexie, Sherman. (1993). *The Lone Ranger and Tonto fist fight in heaven*. New York: HarperCollins.

Allen, Paula Gunn. (1994). *Voice of the turtle*. New York: Ballantine Books.

Ata, Te. (1989). Adapted by Lynn Moroney. *Baby rattlesnake*. Pictures by Mira Reisberg. San Francisco, CA: Children's Books Press.

Begay, Shonto. (1997). *Navajo visions and voices across the mesa*. Illustrated by the author. New York: Scholastic.

Brant, Beth (aka—Degonwadonti). (1991). *Food and spirits: Stories by Beth Brant*. Ithaca, NY: Firebrand Books.

Bruchac, Joseph. (1997). *Bowman's store: A journey to myself*. New York: Dial Books.

Bruchac, Joseph. (1997). *Children of the Longhouse*. New York: Dial Book for Young Readers.

Bruchac, Joseph. (1997). *Lasting echoes: An oral history of Native American People*. San Diego, CA: Harcourt Brace.

Bruchac, Joseph. (1996). *Circle of thanks*. Illustrated by Murv Jacobs. New York: Dial Book for Young Readers.

Dorris, Michael. (1997). *The window*. New York: Hyperion.

Doris, Michael. (1992). *Morning girl*. New York: Hyperion.

Harrell, Beatrice Orcutt. (1995). *How thunder and lighting came to be*. Illustrated by Susan L. Roth. New York: Dial Books for Young Readers.

Hirschfelder, Arlene and Beverly R. Singer. (1992). *Rising voices: Writings of young Native Americans.* New York: Ballantine.

Hogan, Linda. (1990). *Mean spirit.* New York: Atheneum.

Johnson, Basil H. (1994). *Tales of the Anishinaubee: Ojibway legends.* Toronto: University of Toronto Press.

Northrop, Jim. (1993). *Walking the Rez Road.* Stillwater, MN: Voyageur Press.

Ortiz, Simon. (1998 revised. Originally published in 1977). *The people shall continue.* San Francisco, CA: Children's Books Press.

Ross, Gayle and Joseph Bruchac. (1995). *The story of the Milky Way.* A Cherokee tale. Paintings by Virginia Stroud. New York: Dial Books for Young Readers.

Rose, Wendy. (1993). *Going to war with all my relations.* Flagstaff, AZ: Northland Publishing.

Shenandoah-Tekalihwa, Joanne and Douglas M. George-Kanentho. (1980). *Skywoman: Legends of the Iroquois.* Illustrated by John Kahionhes Fadden and David Kanietakeron Fadden. Santa Fe, NM: Clear Light Publishers.

Silko, Leslie Marmon. (1996). *Yellow woman and a beauty of the spirit: Essays on Native American life today.* New York: Simon & Schuster.

Talashoema, Hershel. (1994). *Coyote and little turtle.* Santa Fe, CA: Clear Light Publishing.

Taylor, C. J. (1994). *Bones in the basket: Native stories of the origins of people.* Illustrated by the author. New York: Tundra.

Taylor, C. J. (1993). *How we saw the world: Nine native stories of the way things began.* Illustrated by the author. New York: Tundra.

Taylor, C. J. (1991). *The ghost and the lone warrier: An Arapaho legend.* Illustrated by the author. New York: Tundra.

Vizenor, Gerald. (1994). *Shadow distance: A Gerald Vizenor reader.* Hanover, NH: Wesleyan University Press.

Vizenor, Gerald. (1991). *The heirs of Columbus.* Middletown, CN: Wesleyan University Press.

Yue, Charlott and David Yue. (1988). *The igloo.* Boston: Houghton Mifflin.

Walters, T., P. Webster, and A. Cramer. (1998). *A never ending . . . never done . . . bibliography of multicultural literature for younger & older children,* 2nd ed. Rochester, MI: Oakland University.

Appendix C

Spelling Placement Test
R. L. Cramer

Grade 1	Grade 2	Grade 3	Grade 4
1. at	1. ten	1. must	1. picture
2. run	2. has	2. winter	2. doctor
3. up	3. hold	3. fine	3. rockets
4. go	4. like	4. don't	4. followed
5. flag	5. keep	5. threw	5. easier
6. men	6. room	6. point	6. playful
7. pet	7. grow	7. first	7. reason
8. name	8. far	8. taking	8. mistake
9. gave	9. hiding	9. inside	9. turned
10. use	10. player	10. Friday	10. ground
11. stop	11. bell	11. uncle	11. village
12. big	12. last	12. ever	12. computer
13. keep	13. even	13. skate	13. marbles
14. slow	14. lake	14. aren't	14. singing
15. ship	15. mean	15. flew	15. meaner
16. top	16. bloom	16. boil	16. graceful
17. time	17. load	17. early	17. season
18. tree	18. bark	18. tasting	18. lemonade
19. bikes	19. dancing	19. airport	19. pressed
20. when	20. farmer	20. Thursday	20. country

Grade 5	Grade 6	Grade 7	Grade 8
1. danger	1. equal	1. mumble	1. cashier
2. prize	2. settle	2. hurried	2. skis
3. practice	3. already	3. engage	3. laying
4. huge	4. defense	4. received	4. grouchy
5. strawberry	5. compare	5. edition	5. approximate
6. destroy	6. horrible	6. college	6. difficult
7. careless	7. entrance	7. admiration	7. universe
8. nearly	8. thieves	8. imperfect	8. selective
9. unfair	9. logic	9. attractive	9. weapon
10. argue	10. student	10. disease	10. contractor
11. hurricane	11. angel	11. whimper	11. dividend
12. squeezed	12. pistol	12. where's	12. octopuses
13. camera	13. leisure	13. enable	13. betrays
14. balloons	14. decent	14. pliers	14. accountant
15. karate	15. committee	15. compression	15. revolutionary
16. appointed	15. lovable	16. agility	16. aggravate
17. colorful	17. enclose	17. complication	17. monotonous
18. surely	18. liberties	18. illiterate	18. appreciative
19. inaccurate	19. public	19. achievement	19. metropolitan
20. repair	20. ancient	20. beneath	20. technician

Number
Correct _____   _____   _____   _____

Equals
Score of _____   _____   _____   _____

Formula: Number Correct × 5 = Percentage Score: Example: 17 × 5 = 85 %

Appendix D

Most Commonly Misspelled Words Grades 1–8

Grade 1

because	what	end	school
when	our	pretty	dinosaurs
like	their	sometimes	is
they	nice	I'm	made
went	of	one	much
too	once	other	next
said	I	saw	night
there	some	thank	out
house	that	come	played
know	little	Easter	think
with	then	everybody	wanted
have	to	party	where
very	and	sister	witch
friend	part	but	your
my	for	came	babies
was	favorite	didn't	bird
would	get	girl	funny
are	Mom	good	got
want	birthday	will	teacher
friends	going	always	them
were	her	brother	a lot
people	outside	don't	after
about	the	home	again
Christmas	could	love	around
play	Dad	scared	before

Grade 2

because	that's	like	have
too	house	started	knew
they	Halloween	to	nice
when	with	some	one
there	very	it's	there's
went	baseball	took	watch
their	heard	special	always
Christmas	then	they're	aunt
people	what	through	brought
favorite	everybody	caught	children
friends	I	really	everything
were	and	other	getting
said	another	presents	happily
our	little	swimming	him
a lot	first	where	second
would	night	don't	something
upon	sometimes	family	wanted
know	thought	into	world
friend	want	them	believe
outside	two	tried	cheese
Easter	about	was	down
once	every	beautiful	great
again	whole	brother	haunted
didn't	before	different	hurt
scared	could	found	I'm

Grade 3

too	different	would	swimming
because	they're	brother	very
there	once	could	who
their	until	pretty	back
a lot	where	caught	first
Christmas	before	whole	into
were	presents	morning	school
said	we're	took	stopped
went	and	believe	animals
they	another	his	brought
favorite	sometimes	it's	family
when	didn't	started	let's
friend	heard	beautiful	Mom
know	little	two	about
that's	through	almost	around
upon	off	clothes	bought
with	outside	cousin	friend's
our	something	everything	happily
really	thought	getting	teacher
friends	Halloween	I'm	told
then	people	scared	coming
I	everybody	was	happened
always	want	what	tried
finally	house	everyone	are
again	one	found	girl

Grade 4

too	where	first	before
a lot	caught	watch	doesn't
because	chocolate	people	dollars
there	friend	always	every
their	into	took	found
favorite	everybody	everyone	maybe
that's	off	morning	once
our	through	school	other
when	friends	something	stopped
really	swimming	with	there's
they're	want	would	and
were	you're	are	bought
it's	another	enough	Easter
know	beautiful	except	getting
finally	I'm	friend's	going
again	let's	probably	little
they	then	upon	no
Christmas	believe	vacation	stuff
went	cousin	brought	together
until	especially	house	turned
outside	happened	might	usually
said	heard	myself	against
we're	I	basketball	birthday
sometimes	whole	hospital	break
different	didn't	opened	buy

Grade 5

a lot	probably	there's	excited
too	Christmas	thought	outside
their	to	upon	piece
there	when	usually	school
because	didn't	Dad	field
favorite	heard	knew	friend's
that's	then	sometimes	myself
finally	we're	want	since
our	everybody	which	family
they're	Mom	caught	grabbed
it's	everyone	let's	once
really	one	stopped	people
different	went	TV	right
where	decided	beautiful	should
again	especially	before	vacation
until	getting	buy	weird
friend	Halloween	Dad's	what's
they	off	doesn't	already
you're	always	everything	college
friends	whole	except	exciting
through	happened	tried	first
were	I'm	and	himself
believe	into	another	surprised
know	maybe	clothes	threw
something	said	don't	aren't

Grade 6

a lot	again	especially	Hawaii
too	clothes	field	he's
it's	didn't	Florida	heard
because	everybody	friend	house
that's	off	grabbed	I
their	TV	since	I've
there	myself	something	into
you're	basketball	swimming	license
favorite	let's	to	met
were	there's	getting	no
everything	which	guess	now
finally	themselves	I'm	planet
our	then	know	someone
probably	always	one	sometimes
they're	awhile	want	started
until	Christmas	went	stopped
different	doesn't	would	than
really	except	and	together
usually	outside	bored	upstairs
beautiful	when	can't	wear
college	whole	cousin's	what's
they	beginning	environment	wouldn't
through	business	exciting	anything
where	don't	friends	anyway
we're	elementary	happened	around

Grade 7

there	usually	no	happened
a lot	we're	restaurant	into
too	went	Saturday	knew
their	sometimes	someone	against
that's	through	there's	awhile
it's	which	beautiful	clothes
because	doesn't	can't	field
don't	favorite	Mom's	friend's
probably	heard	outside	going to
they're	different	thought	minutes
Easter	everything	whole	morning
they	again	without	people
you're	believe	and	remember
finally	except	another	right
our	something	basketball	supposed
Christmas	were	beginning	to
off	always	couldn't	tomorrow
where	anything	Friday	trying
Halloween	especially	grabbed	upstairs
didn't	everyone	relatives	what's
until	friends	vacation	backyard
buy	everywhere	wasn't	before
let's	around	college	caught
really	everybody	Dad's	coming
then	maybe	downstairs	cousin's

Grade 8

a lot	going to	maybe	again
too	through	now	anyway
it's	they	wear	awhile
you're	to	business	coming
their	which	since	except
that's	different	were	happened
there	everything	couldn't	heard
they're	believe	downstairs	knew
because	Christmas	families	one
probably	clothes	friend's	separated
don't	I'm	into	thought
we're	no one	lose	tried
finally	our	restaurant	whole
there's	than	what's	about
where	especially	whether	aren't
can't	let's	without	cannot
usually	then	your	Dad's
doesn't	weird	beautiful	decided
really	favorite	definitely	every day
allowed	friends	everyone	everywhere
didn't	know	friend	experience
off	outside	grabbed	Grandma's
TV	always	hear	having
until	beginning	no	myself
something	college	people	nowhere

Credits

1. "Youth" by Aline Wechsler. From *Creative Power: The Education of Youth in the Creative Arts* by Hughes Mearns. Copyright © 1929 by Hughes Mearns and 1958 by Dover Publications Inc. Reprinted by permission of Dover Publications Inc.

2. Several lists of frequently misspelled words appear in this publication. These lists were first published in *Spelling Research and Information: An Overview of Research and Information.* Ronald Cramer, James F. Cipielewski, Kathryn Marine, James Beers, W. Dorsey Hammond. Copyright © 1995 by Addison Wesley Educational Publications Inc. Reprinted by permission of Addison Wesley Educational Publications Inc.

3. Excerpt from *LET THEM WRITE POETRY* by Nina Walter. Copyright © 1962 by Holt, Rinehart and Winston and renewed 1990 by Nina Willis Walter. Reprinted by permission of the publisher.

4. I wish to acknowledge four teachers who gave permission to publish their poems.

Carmeneta Jones: "Education in Crisis 1."
George E. Coon: "Homophones."
Lisa E. Montpas: "The Ark."
Terry M. Blackhawk: "Shop Closed (due to the death of the shoemaker)."

5. The poems listed below were written by students in the Detroit Public Schools. These poems first appeared in publications sponsored by the InsideOut Writing Project and are reprinted by permission of Terry M. Blackhawk, executive director of the InsideOut Writing Project.

Markila Beeks: "Memory."
Jaquita Sanchez: "If You Knew."
Maisha Wells: "Daily."
Solomon Harewood: "Tears."
Sara Hillman: "One Face."
Myra Allen: "Song As Far As the Eye Can See."

Index